WHITBREAD
the INN behind the SIGNS

A history of the 250 Public Houses
included in the five series of Whitbread Inn Signs
issued between 1949 and 1955

AND

A HISTORY OF THE BREWERIES

Illustrated and also depicting beer labels

by
DAVID HARPER

Published by David Harper,
"Twin Mays",
Plumpudding Lane,
Dargate, Faversham, ME13 9EX.

First Published 2005.

Copyright © 2005 David Harper

1,000 copies only, ISBN 0 9549477 0 3

Printed by A.R.Adams & Sons (Printers) Limited, Dour Street, Dover, CT16 1EW.

CONTENTS

INTRODUCTION

How did my obsession about compiling this book begin? What possessed me to delve back fifty years, or as it ultimately proved, several centuries, into an era when people had little money, their pleasures were simple, and there was a tremendous community spirit?

The story starts back in 1949. In those not-so-far-off days the main hobbies of your average eleven-year old were collecting cigarette cards, milk bottle tops (the kind where you pressed out the circular ring in the centre), marbles, Dinky toys and reading the Dandy and Beano. Those and working during the school summer holidays, which in Kent encroached into September, so as to enable a large number of school children to help in the huge number of hop gardens that spread across the county.

This was pretty tame stuff so just imagine the frisson of excitement that swept Kent when in May 1949 Whitbread issued the first series of 50 inn sign miniatures printed on aluminium, (at the time there were paper shortages,) and in full colour. They were launched at a lunch held at the Savoy Hotel, London with each guest receiving a full set in a red leather wallet. The signs were produced by A.N. Holden & Co. Limited and delivered to the landlord in packets inscribed "100 – Aluminium Tablet Inn Signs". On the packet I saw was hand-written "The Lord Clyde, 20, Walmer". Living in Maidstone we fared well compared with those pubs situated in the Hastings and Rye area. Most were close to hand in the Weald and at that time Wateringbury alone had seven Whitbread houses, eight if you included the "Railway".

These little gems were the brainchild of a couple of Whitbread employees. One, Walter Daish, who died in 1963, was an acknowledged expert on Inn-Signia and was much in demand as a speaker at village halls where he would delight in sharing his knowledge. The other, John Marchant, commenced his career with Whitbread as a brewer at Chiswell Street prior to moving on to Frederick Leney's Phoenix Brewery at Wateringbury where he was ultimately to become managing director. I am told his background was ex-Guards and journalism. Prior to 1937, as old photographs will show, few of the Whitbread pubs in Kent had a hanging pictorial sign unless it was the work of a talented landlord who created his own or an itinerant artist who would paint a sign for an unlimited supply of free beer. All that hung was a simple board with the pub name printed upon it often in the Whitbread livery. Whitbread first began designing and building their distinctive signs in 1937 with this continuing during and after the war.

By 1937 Marchant had gathered together a team of artists and designers and it is their talents which we now see displayed in our inn sign miniatures. Amongst his other interests Marchant ran a play-reading group and it is reported that several of the artists were personal friends who met him via this mutual interest. In any event their work has stood the test of time as admirers of my collection frequently comment on how fresh and up to date some of these designs remain. In general three designs for each sign would be submitted and Marchant would indicate his preference with a blue cross on the reverse. I have seen rejected designs for the "Red Lion" at Offham and the "Startled Saint" at St. Leonard's Cross. I was fortunate to receive in 1999 from a later designer a collection of mainly rejected roughs designed for Wealden pubs with some bearing waspish comments from Marchant to the effect that they were "too much like Walt Disney creations". This design work was far ahead of its time but a few ultimately found favour and one hung at the "Hooden Horse" (formerly the "Swan") at Wickhambreaux until the pub closed. The signs were produced at the Phoenix Brewery, Wateringbury, with the following process usually followed. The roughs were about six inches square. After Marchant's final approval the design was drawn to quarter of full size in flat poster paint for the sign painters to "grid up" to full size, etch outlines and paint in enamel colours. Anyone could paint them and quite often employees who could no longer cope with some of the more manual tasks were moved to the paint room. Only individual colours were employed with no blending permitted. Once agreed the sign could not be amended in any way.

The first signs that we recognise were erected in 1937 (the "Chequers" and "Red Lion") with a few more trickling through until 1939, aptly the "British Volunteer" being one, then there was a lull during the war years followed by an explosion from 1946 onwards. As early as the 1950's signs were changing, in particular the "Chequers", with several distinctive designs quickly replacing the standard "Chequers" sign seen across the county. The one exception was at West Farleigh which retained the original until the name change to the "Tickled Trout". The Chequer appeared in the coat of arms of the local De Warrenne family, which in the reign of Henry III had the privilege of licensing ale houses. We find about fifty "Chequers" in Kent with a similar number in Norfolk and only another hundred so-named throughout the rest of the country. It was a delight in 1997 when passing the High Halden "Chequers" to see it had acquired a brand new sign showing two gentlemen of the time in the chequer parlour, and hanging on the wall a coat of arms, which incorporated the old Chequer sign. The initial "Royal Oak" sign as seen at Wrotham Heath was soon to spawn numerous new designs and the original disappeared quite quickly. There were several different signs for pubs with a similar name. The "Man of Kent" sign shown at the Ashford house also hung at one time at St. Michaels. It is interesting to note that although ale houses and pubs have been in existence for centuries it was not until 1751 that the law stated that every house must have an approved name.

Marchant realised the marketing potential of these distinctive signs springing up all over Kent, and in 1947 plans were put in place to exploit them culminating in the issue of the first series of inn signs in May 1949. They were an immediate success not only with small boys but with virtually everyone living in the county. In addition, soldiers, sailors and airmen, foreign visitors and travellers all played their part in distributing these miniatures throughout the world. Chiswell Street received many letters from all corners of the globe congratulating the company upon the quality of these productions. The initial supplies regarded as perfectly adequate to meet demand were soon exhausted and reprints had to be quickly produced to provide the landlord with sufficient stock to keep his drinkers happy. Today there are probably thousands of families who have at least a couple of signs in their possession. They became a world-wide phenomenon and, in my travels, I have found sets in both Australia and New Zealand reminding Men of Kent of their past links with the county. In Auckland I came across a book reproducing the signs of the "King's Head", Wye and the "Hop Pole" at East Peckham.

Prior to the issue of the First and Second series David Burley, who worked from a studio at Birchington, was commissioned to produce a metal map measuring 22 inches by 32 inches covering West Kent and East Sussex showing, in full colour, a miniature of the sign and the village or town in which the pub is situated. These maps were displayed in the pubs and in 1951 a second map was issued covering East Kent. Unfortunately most are now faded, damaged, or have just disappeared. A pristine copy is a sight to behold with its well-designed map of Kent and bright colours. They are now incredibly difficult to find and command a handsome price. Rumour has it that shortly before the closure of the Phoenix Brewery at Wateringbury surplus stocks were nailed to the roof to prevent water seeping through missing or broken tiles! The landlord at the "Dolphin" in Faversham used his to "draw up" the bar fire.

The first three series were printed on aluminium (I believe in Holland) but by 1951 costs were increasing but paper was no longer rationed. As a result, in August 1951 a special series of four signs was launched, printed on cardboard, to see how the public reacted. The new cards were favourably received so in 1952 the third series was re-issued on cardboard as were the final two series. However, in my view the card signs could never produce the crisp and bright appearance of the first miniatures.

Unfortunately, little is known about the majority of the designers of these fabulous signs. Whitbread retains no records and letters to the Kent Messenger group of newspapers produced no response whatsoever. The most prolific artist, Kathleen M. Claxton lived in Hanwell, London W7. and died in March 1997 in North London aged 91 at which time over 100 of her design roughs came to light. She was one of the first artists to see her signs hung. In her early days her family travelled extensively in India. She learnt her craft in an art studio, possibly in the Ealing area of London, established by a young aunt and, besides this talent, she also played the violin and piano. She studied for three years at the Royal College of Arts before becoming an Associate. Subsequently she became a teacher but found this not to her liking so jumped at the opportunity to work for Whitbread as an inn sign designer. She knew John Marchant very well and other lasting friendships were obviously made as another designer, Kathleen Doyle, aged 90 in 1998 and living in the Guildford area, received a small bequest in Kathleen Claxton's will. I am told she died in 2001 in South London. In 1953 Kathleen Claxton appeared on "In Town Tonight", a popular radio programme. Violet Rutter, another prolific designer, also reached a ripe old age being 90 when she passed away in 1987. Violet was another versatile lady being involved amongst other things in the design of the floating Mulberry Harbour. She studied Russian language and literature and possessed a deep knowledge of English literature as well as writing poetry, plays and exhibiting her paintings. She received an award for her design of the "Spyglass and Kettle". I am told that Mervyn C. Balston lived in Kent for about 10 years during the 1940's before moving to London then possibly to Huntingdon where he died in about 1993. He came from an artistic family and could turn his hand to most things. Of the others, not a jot. One is left to ponder why Erma York, the creator of the beautiful "Cypress", appears but once; perhaps she was a late-comer to the scene. Prudence Rae-Martin appeared to concentrate on Heraldic signs.

Since the war we have witnessed a reduction in what my generation would call the public house. Drinkers in these spit-and-sawdust establishments were usually local agricultural labourers and in the larger towns included the industrial workers. The pub was where they sought refuge from the scolding wife and numerous children. Some friendly houses remain – try the "Railway" at Nettlestead or the "Shepherd and Crook" on Romney Marsh. Change has always taken place but not on the scale that we now see. A glance at parish records of a hundred years ago will reveal numerous re-namings. Titles no longer seen or even remembered today – normally trade names – have been replaced, but at least the pub continued to serve the community. Not now – they are closing in their droves with East Kent at present particularly hard hit.

I will mention, in no particular order, just a few influences that have accelerated this trend since the turn of the century.

Slate, Thrift or Tontine Clubs

The pub and church are no longer the dominant features in most peoples' lives and in general the days of the pub Slate or Thrift club are long since past. This might well be a blessing so far as the Brewers are concerned, for it was not unknown for the Brewery to have to dispatch a senior official to an inn to make good a shortfall in funds on pay-out day or indeed account for the total sum! It makes quaint reading now to see that in December 1931 46 members of the "Camden Arms", Sissinghurst Slate club shared out £170 – a good sum in those days. For some reason this form of regular saving was called a Tontine club in the Medway towns area. They obviously were not true Tontine clubs, named after Lorenzo Tonti, an Italian banker, who first operated a club in France in 1653 where subscribers paid into a fund, the surviving subscribers of which received annuities increasing as they became fewer. The last survivor scooped the pot. The landlord was forbidden to act as treasurer but this did not prevent numerous defalcations. Thus we read headlines in the Chatham Standard in 1902 "Licensee and Wife on trial – Tontine Charge". In 1937 the Medway towns Tontine club payout was estimated at £50,000 – a huge sum in those days when a house could be purchased for about £500. Another feature, as far as I can ascertain peculiar to the Chatham area, was for pub regulars to come to the aid of the recently bereaved or others suffering some other misfortune by gathering together for a large meal held at the pub with all the profits from the evening passed to the unfortunate family. Also most pubs in this area had a children's room.

Rat and Sparrow Clubs

Of lesser importance is the total demise of the Rat and Sparrow clubs that abounded across the county and indeed probably the country in the first half of this century. The members normally met on a regular basis at the village inn to display their haul of vermin and maintain records so that at the year-end an overall winner could be declared whilst the members enjoyed a sumptuous feast prepared by mine host. Subscriptions were paid to cover the cash prizes for the winners. The modern conservationist would have apoplexy when reading what comprised vermin in those days. Besides the obvious rats and mice (and as the club name implies, sparrows) we also find larks, linnets, blackbirds, bullfinches, hawks, stoats, weasels and thrushes to name but a few. Indeed the lists seem to include anything that the farming community considered to be a pest or hindered the war effort to produce food. The inhabitants of Pluckley appear to have been particularly vigilant, for in 1913 they accounted for 27,000 pests which included a good number of song birds, whilst the more delicate burghers at Waltham enjoying their repast at the "Lord Nelson" could only muster 4,205 victims, with rats accounting for 3,035 of the total. Obviously the inhabitants of Waltham had a social conscience! The annual dinner was normally accompanied by excellent songs involving both the landlord's family and the villagers. The Chairman of many of these clubs was usually the local Lord or Squire.

Hop-Picking

It has been estimated that at the turn of the century in any one season up to 80,000 hoppers, mainly from South East London and the East End, would descend upon the county. This vast horde would be supplemented by local pickers. To cope with such an influx the farmers had to be highly organised to prevent this army of workers wandering around the county not knowing where work was available and without accommodation. In general, a month before picking commenced, farmers would write to last year's pickers confirming when picking would commence. Rail and bus companies would be contacted as would the medical services, local shopkeepers and publicans, church organisations and the local refuse collectors. The police knew they were in for a tough time. On the first day of picking the "Rules of the Farm" were read to the assembled pickers and the penalties for any infringements spelt out. This would normally be dismissal.

Picking spanned a six-week period from mid-August into September and had an enormous influence over events in the county. Pay was poor but the vast numbers brought prosperity not only to publicans but to the village shops, the itinerant traders and tinkers who would visit the farms, the pieman and ice-cream vendors and a whole host of other leeches who swarmed for this one great payout. The sensible matriarch would ensure that at least some of this hard-earned money, and it was hard-earned, returned with them on the journey back to London. The majority of men were oblivious to this requirement! All kinds of statistics were influenced by this visitation – births, marriages and deaths all shot up in the host village. At the turn of the century the small village of Wateringbury hosted five thousand East Enders requiring fifty-eight special trains steaming into Paddock Wood station. It was a common occurrence for the good ladies of this hospitable little town to meet the hordes descending from each train with trestle tables burdened with tea, freshly-cut sandwiches and cakes with lemonade for the children. The local farmers would then transport the hoppers to their holiday home for the next few weeks. The same families would arrive year after year quite often to occupy the same hut on the same farm. Around the "Bull" at Hunton were three farms all with at least one hundred hoppers' huts.

During the picking season two types of currency would be acceptable throughout the county. One would be the coins of the realm, the other special tokens issued by the wily farmer. The reason for the latter was that, particularly if the weather was bad or the harvest poor, if paid in tokens this transient workforce couldn't return home but more importantly the farmer could more easily sell farm produce, milk etc., to his captive market. Even so, after the evening meal the hoppers would descend upon the pubs in droves. The prudent wife would have secreted part of the earnings away but the pub or visiting tinkers and piemen would take the rest. Despite their spending power hoppers, with their coarse manners and even worse habits, were not welcome in many pubs. It is fair to say that numerous houses barred them from entering the actual bars. If the village had more than one pub, which was very likely, the individual landlords would mark their glasses in some way, quite often with coloured spots, and charge a shilling deposit for each glass which would be refunded if returned at the end of the picking season. More often than not a large and not particularly clean galvanised bath would be placed outside the pub, filled with beer, and sold to the East Enders who would mill around on the village green providing their own form of entertainment much of it quite unknown to the locals. Indeed with their use of rhyming slang much of their language was also unintelligible. The "Unicorn" and "John Jorrocks" used this method of serving the hoppers whilst other variations were sash windows or the like which could be lifted and the beer passed out in flagons. The "Railway" at Nettlestead did this as did the "Chestnut Tree" at Yalding. Indeed for quite a little while the "Chestnut Tree" was referred to by locals as the Hole in the Wall. Another pub where hoppers were never allowed into the villagers' bar was the "Phoenix" at Wateringbury, this had a little side bar with a brick floor which the hoppers had to use. The beer would be passed out to this small and dingy room – they really were regarded as the lowest of the low. Not surprisingly fighting with the locals became a common occurrence and in one particularly savage brawl outside the "Torrington Arms" at Mereworth a hop-picker was killed, his body laid out in the pub barn, and the inquest held at the pub! London and local churchmen were appalled at the conditions their parishioners had to tolerate on the farms although these were far better than in other areas of the country where hops were grown. These men of the cloth established their first headquarters close to the "Woolpack" at Winchet Hill. About the same time an inquisitive priest from Stepney followed his flock down to the hop gardens and he in turn was quite horrified by what he saw. Eventually, in 1910 he was able to acquire a defunct pub, the "Rose and Crown", at Five Oak Green, which he converted into a Hoppers Hospital. This worthy cause survived for nearly sixty years and the building remains to this day. The period between the wars produced the most rapid improvement in living conditions. For the duration of the last world war trenches were dug in the fields with the hop bines arranged to provide some cover and the pickers would jump into these during air raids. Sadly most of this community activity came to an end in the early 1960's with the advent of mechanisation, and with its passing the fate of many an isolated public house was sealed. Most of the villages had too many pubs anyway so it really came down to the ability of the landlord to cope with a shrinking number of hardened drinkers and cater for a more sophisticated clientele who were looking for rather more than the celebrated bag of Smiths crisps with the blue twirl of salt.

Another influence was the closure or relocation of a major employer in the area. Many pubs closed in Hythe when the military and small arms establishment left town.

Changing social habits and increased mobility

Until the 1950's the church and pub were the hub of village activities. By this time the revenue from smuggling had disappeared as had the posthouse income. Trades Unions, Friendly Societies, Craft Unions, Gardening Societies, even choral societies were in decline but the pub remained a popular venue for Cricket, Football and Dart teams. Many societies still hold their Christmas festivities at the inn.

After the war many ex-servicemen became landlords and very sociable and at times eccentric mine hosts did they make. I am told at the "Bull's Head" at Adisham a well-regarded former military man, "Topper" Brown, would don his regimental cap and, marching smartly up and down behind the bar, would call "last orders gentlemen!"

Many of the smaller ale houses were unable to produce a sufficient income to support a family and certainly until the 1960's it was quite common for the landlord to have a day-time occupation leaving the running of the business to his wife or adult children. Few pubs then provided other than the most basic snacks. During the 1950's two East Peckham landlords worked on the railway at Paddock Wood, one as a signalman the other as a shunter. Records indicate that in 1939 the landlord of the "Chequers" at Tudeley, Sidney West, was employed during the summer months and the hop-picking season at the Whitbread Beltring complex as a painter, assistant carpenter and hop measurer. He was paid 36/6 a week – a fair wage when compared to the horse lad's pay of 16/9. Until the last war many a publican would also be the village blacksmith – this was the case at the "Blacksmiths Arms", Harrietsham and "City of London", Dymchurch. The pub could also double as the village shop like the "Harrier" at Link Hill. Favoured second occupations were working on the railways, a coalman or haulier, and quite often the pub would act as the village posthouse. The favoured second income, however, came from a modest smallholding. Most rural pubs sat on a good-sized plot of land on which the landlord could grow his own fruit and vegetables or graze animals but gradually this became impracticable and in most instances the land was tarmaced over to become the pub car park. A versatile landlord could turn his hand to anything.

The pubs that remained open during the war years provided sustenance, entertainment, and generally raised the morale of servicemen and those working at home to fuel the war effort. The men in the armed services came from all over the British Empire but whilst all were greeted and entertained with warm hospitality it appears the Canadians and Poles were remembered as the great drinkers! It was normally the one place where people could let their hair down and enjoy a good knees-up. Most pubs had a piano. Quite often part of the building would be requisitioned by the services to act as an Officers' Mess (the "Bull's Head" at Adisham) or a planning room, with a fair number used to billet troops.

A seasoned drinker of some antiquity living at Paddock Wood told me that after the war the beer was not particularly strong and was regarded as "conversational" bitter. The average working man could retire to the pub at the day's end to enjoy a chat with his friends, play darts or cribbage, and generally relax away from the children. It was a place where one could barter one's occupational skills for food – fish and garden produce were particularly popular. The landlord would often provide the best Guy Fawkes party for the whole family – in those days drinking was almost exclusively a male occupation.

This unsophisticated, almost happy age, started to unravel towards the end of the 1950's. A good proportion of the population began to read newspapers and television was in its infancy. People realised there was another world out there. Employment opportunities and wages tended to improve so that youngsters in their 20's could afford such things as a Vespa or Lambretta scooter or even a cheap car, (my Austin 16 cost £50) and thus become mobile and able to seek more exciting forms of recreation such as the Snooker halls or Palais de Dance which were springing up. There was also a rapid improvement in affordable public transport. Pubs had to change or die. There is no doubt there were far too many houses after the war and only the best or most innovative would survive.

Looking back this became the age of vandalism so far as public house premises were concerned. Before the Second World War the standard Whitbread house would have brown glazed tiles at the base and rough-cast above. After the war the tiles were increasingly difficult to obtain so, when they needed replacing, the whole of the exterior would be rough-cast. Also at this time standard plate-glass windows were installed; the main contractor was James Clarke & Eaton of Canterbury. The established brewers realised they must modernise to appeal to a new generation and large capital expenditure budgets were created to achieve the desired effect. Out went the mahogany bars to be replaced with Formica, the grandfather clocks disappeared, and pewter gave way to stainless steel. If local councils were recalcitrant the necessary planning permission could normally be obtained by stating the house had to be redesigned to create internal toilets. Before the last war almost all toilets were a shed-like structure attached to the pub.

In 1960 Fremlins took over the entire estate of Frederick Leney & Sons Limited. Within the body of this book selling prices are quoted but this was purely a paper exercise and no money ever changed hands. The same comment applies to the Tenterden Brewery Company.

Following the Whitbread takeover of Fremlins, in 1968, rationalisation quickened with an annual target set for realisations. All properties, when the tenant gave notice, were assessed as to future potential ie: managed, tenanted or sale. At this time the managed house estate enlarged dramatically. In some instances it was decided to close the pub, de-licensed, or to sell it on as a freehouse. A few years later the Monopolies Commision report led to the disposal of a number of houses, in the main to Shepherd Neame.

There are frequent references in the following pages to the Net Monopoly Value being paid. As I understand it, this was a self-financing system imposed on the brewing industry. When a house was granted a Full On licence the brewery had to pay an agreed sum into a fund, and when a house was de-licensed and closed the brewers received compensation for the loss of licence from the same fund. It was the usual practice within the brewery trade for the brewer to take a deposit from the tenant as a guarantee for debts.

The drink/drive laws were the final straw for many a rural house and those that survived probably thought they were over the worst, but who could have foreseen the recent phenomenon of the booze cruise which has wrought havoc with many East Kent pubs. Ironically pubs were still able to provide sanctuary to the modern buccaneer and it was as late as May 1998 that the "York House", close to Dover harbour, lost its licence as it had become the favourite haunt for the practitioners of this latest form of bootlegging! Fortunately the inn has reopened under a new landlord but with a name change to the "Flagship". It is estimated that a million pints a day now come into the country from this source having previously been exported by our own brewers to Calais so it is little wonder that we continue to witness great upheaval within the trade.

Whitbread's strong presence in Kent arose mainly as the result of acquisition of competitor breweries. The chief concerns were the well-known Mackeson Brewery based at Hythe which was taken over in 1929 and ultimately closed in 1968. Mackesons controlled about 140 tied houses almost exclusively in East Kent and virtually every inn appearing in the inn sign series in that part of the county is a former Mackeson house. Frederick Leney & Sons Limited whose pubs were mainly in Mid Kent, the Medway towns and the Hastings area was equally important. Next came Jude Hanbury whose inns were spread across the county possibly because brewing capacity was moved in 1924 from Wateringbury to Canterbury. The Jude estate was ultimately split between Leney and Mackeson. There were other minor amalgamations such as Ash's East Kent Brewery but these were generally small, local breweries with far fewer tied houses. Indeed it would be fair to say that in the 1800's any place of moderate size would have its own brewery. This was important as small isolated ale houses would only receive three or four deliveries a year but the ale would contain all the necessary preservatives to remain fresh. During this period many a pub would brew its own beer and quite a few housewives would run a small business from home perhaps just supplying their neighbours. It was interesting to find that the freehold of some houses, on closure, were still vested in the name of say Frederick Leney & Sons Limited although the house had traded under the Whitbread name for many years. Also, certainly in the 1950's, many pubs were closed and sold off at very low prices but the sale contract included a restrictive covenant to the effect that the property could not reopen as a public house. This was to limit competition but had a drastic effect on some remote villages. The licence was often transferred to the nearest Whitbread house, for example the licence for the former "Man of Kent" at Crundale went to the "Lord Nelson" – itself another fairly recent casualty. One or two new houses were opened in the 1950's notably the "Bailiff's Sergeant" and "Shrew Beshrewed" – both Mackeson pubs. Despite Whitbread owning all of these Kent breweries the staff maintained a tremendous loyalty to their "own" brewery. Thus at the opening ceremony of a Mackeson house a representative from Wateringbury would always attend to ensure all went smoothly. Also the official photographs would show only the signs or the house but never both together as the house would have Mackeson hoardings whereas the sign would indicate Whitbread.

As we enter the twenty-first century change continues apace. One constant, however, is the steady decline in the number of public houses. So what fate befell the houses that comprised the first five series of Whitbread Inn Signs and the special series of four?

Series One issued in May 1949

(Aluminium)

1	G.I., Hastings	26	Torrington Arms, Mereworth
2	Wishing Tree, St. Leonards-on-Sea	27	Duke Without a Head, Wateringbury
3	Princes, Hasting	28	North Pole, Wateringbury
4	Fountain, Hastings	29	Queen's Head, Wateringbury
5	Old Golden Cross, Hastings	30	King's Head, Wateringbury
6	Warriors Gate, St. Leonards-on-Sea	31	Phoenix, Wateringbury
7	British Queen, St. Leonards-on-Sea	32	Harrow, Wateringbury
8	Dripping Spring, St. Leonards-on-Sea	33	Telegraph, Wateringbury
9	Marina Inn, St. Leonards-on-Sea	34	Railway Hotel, Nettlestead
10	Nag's Head, St. Leonards-on-Sea	35	Hop Pole, Nettlestead
11	William the Conqueror, Rye Harbour	36	Woolpack, Yalding
12	Queen Adelaide, Rye		
13	Ypres Castle, Rye	37/38	Two Brewers, Yalding
14	Ship Inn, Winchelsea Beach	39	Chestnut Tree, Yalding
15	Black Horse, Tenterden	40	Harp Inn, East Peckham
16	Harrier, Sandhurst	41	Merry Boys, East Peckham
17	Oak and Ivy, Hawkhurst	42	Chequers, Tudeley
18	King William IV, Benenden	43	John Brunt VC, Paddock Wood
19	This Ancient Boro', Tenterden	44	Bull, Hunton
20	Royal Oak, Wrotham Heath	45	Kent Arms, Fowl Hall
21	Startled Saint, West Malling	46	Prince of Wales, Collier Street
22	Cricketers, Maidstone	47	Duke of Wellington, Collier Street
23	Queen's Head, Maidstone	48	Fountain, East Peckham
24	Hare and Hounds, Maidstone	49	Unicorn, Marden
25	Black Lion, Mereworth	50	Red Lion, Offham

No 1. The G.I., Hastings

*(Re-named **New Central** in 1962 and **Town Crier** in August 1979) F. Leney, Fremlins, Whitbread*

The new town centre of Hastings was developed on the drained Priory marshes with this site chosen because it was close to the railway which reached the town in 1851. The present building was constructed in the early 1850's on land known as Priory Meadow and originally formed part of the development known as Queen's buildings. The inn now stands in Queens Road.

The pub is probably unique in all five series in as much as the name appeared for a while in the Guinness Book of Records as being the shortest pub name in the British Isles. Over the years there have been numerous name changes. In the 1860's it was called the "Oyster Luncheon Bar" and from 1876 until 1945 traded as the "Central Hotel". During this period the house boasted the largest and most up-to-date Saloon in the town together with three billiard tables. In the 1870's the house hosted a museum of Australian Curiosities and one is left to ponder if its fame spread around the world – for in the late 1960's the Aboriginal Australian cricket team visited the town. In 1890 Joseph Bean was the landlord and as was usual in those days other members of the Bean family owned several lodging houses nearby. Frederick Leney & Sons Limited purchased the freehold on 17th July 1939 at a cost of £22,500. On 27th November 1945, as a tribute to the many American Servicemen who had passed through the area, the hotel was renamed the "G.I.". A ceremony and luncheon was held attended by local dignitaries and several G.I.s. The sign was unveiled by Sergeant Hastings (US Army) of Hastings (USA) whose wife was a local girl born in Hastings. Unfortunately, in 1962 the pub was re-named the "New Central" – it was felt that this trendy title would appeal to younger drinkers who were just appearing on the scene. At the same time capital expenditure of £2,500 was sanctioned as well as £260 spent on improvements. Following further substantial refurbishment costing £25,000 in August 1979 the pub was renamed the "Town Crier".

For long periods the hotel remained in the hands of three local families – the Links, Reads and Woods, the latter being tenants for about 30 years. The comfortable premises attracted local businessmen and despite the elegant furnishings it could still undercut its competitors by charging 3½d a pint as opposed to 4d. Later many organizations including, in the 1950's, the Pheon group of local artists would meet at the G.I. They would exhibit for a month and many of the paintings would be sold to the locals.

It remains a busy town-centre pub with a strong bias towards the younger generation.

No 2. Wishing Tree, Hollington, near St. Leonards-on-Sea
F. Leney, Fremlins, Whitbread

The "Wishing Tree" is a large, not particularly attractive house, but it does have an interesting history. It is the third youngest pub to appear in the Inn Sign series occupying its present premises and taking its new name on 25th June 1946 on the special removal of the licence of the "Swan Hotel". However, its roots go far deeper.

Hastings, and its public houses, suffered greatly in the last war with many old taverns destroyed by enemy bombing. Amongst the pubs and hotels to suffer a direct hit was one of the town's oldest and much-loved hostelries, namely the "Royal Swan Commercial & Family Hotel" which, until 23rd May 1943, had stood in the High Street. Is there a curse on any pub occupying this site? Let us hope not for the sake of the "Wishing Tree" but consider this: When Hastings was no more than a fishing village it is said an enraged mother in Cromwell's day placed a curse on the "Swan's" ancestor, when an alleged traitor informed on her son there, and that either two or three successive inns were burned down.

Despite this the house was rebuilt and was to become, by the early 1800's, the "Swan Hotel". All went well until the arrival of the railway in 1851 when the fortunes of the hotel went into sad decline. Trade ultimately picked up but the premises again suffered badly from two subsequent fires. It was closed for a period, and then – almost unique in licensing – was reopened in place of two other houses. Prudently on 11th May 1923 the fire insurance was raised from £1,000 to £5,000 with fixtures valued at £500. There has been at least one suicide and one non-fatal accident. Matters went from bad to worse, however, when, in 1939, a very old servant was fatally injured by a barrel which slipped and fell upon him while delivering.

The end came when the house took a direct hit on 23rd May 1943 and all the occupants including the licensee and his family were killed. Thus, as a result of enemy action, the "Wishing Tree" was born. The local newspaper commented as follows:- "Remembering the "Swan's" history, nothing could be more apt than the sign of its successor".

The brewer's war damage claim was settled in 1949 at £4,172/5/5 with the site ultimately sold in 1953 to Hastings Corporation for £575.

The village of Hollington expanded rapidly during the period spanning the two world wars, including the building of a large council estate, which resulted in the renaming of an old country lane to Wishing Tree Road. A stranger to the area would never have realised that during this period large quantities of hops were grown locally. Shortly after the end of the war a redistribution of licensed premises took place with the licence for the "Swan" transferred on 29th June 1946 to a property dating back to at least 1843 called

Norton's Farm House. The brewers completed the purchase of these premises for £2,000 on 2nd September 1946. The pub almost certainly took its name from the recently named road but rumours do state that there is a connection with the local and ancient Scrag Oak. The modern pub quickly became established and was the focal point for the growing population. It was the meeting place for the Wishing Tree Social Club, an organisation independent of the pub, which was formed to provide for the social needs of the community. It also became the driving force for the area's leisure activities which included torch-light processions and a huge bonfire on Guy Fawkes night. In 1950 the Central Land Board settled the company's claim for loss of development value amounting to £1,200. Improvements costing £400 were completed in 1963.

A not uncommon occurrence is for public houses to possess a resident ghostly apparition but the "Wishing Tree" can go one better with both a phantom Victorian lady pushing a pram, perhaps the late farmer's wife, and a poltergeist!

The pub still plays an important part in community life but it was unfortunate that the original sign was replaced in 2000.

No 3. The Princes, Hastings
(Closed in 1993 and re-opened as an Italian Restaurant) Jude Hanbury, F. Leney,
Fremlins, Whitbread, Shepherd Neame

Like the "G.I." the "Princes" is built on land that formerly comprised the old Priory Marshes which were drained in 1836. Constructed in the early 1860's as a modest hotel, it stands at one end of South Terrace, conveniently close to the recently-established railway station and the stage coach terminal, which was already in rapid decline.

The hotel opened in 1865 at about the same time as the central cricket and recreation ground. Its fortunes were closely linked to this sporting activity with many of the lesser-known names in the game regularly frequenting and lodging at the house. Their more famous counterparts would stop at the more opulent "Castle Hotel". Sadly the popularity of the game waned as did the fortunes of the "Princes" as a hotel. Its death knell was sounded when the town was downgraded as a cricketing venue with the loss of the ever-popular Festival Week. It struggled on for a while as a public house before closing in 1993. Following conversion work the premises reverted to a most successful Italian restaurant.

Shepherd Neame leased the premises on 6th May 1992 but they surrendered the lease on 1st October 1993.

Much work was carried out in the early 1900's including creating urinals and installing gas and in 1936 building works costing £800 were completed.

On 27th April 1931 Jude Hanbury sold most of their pubs in this area, seven in all, to Leney for £20,055. The sale price was arrived at by using a multiplier of £15 per barrel resulting in this house being sold for £2,872. T.W. Dunn became the licensee on 21st August 1939 and on being called up for war service his wife Mrs. H.L. Dunn took over on 3rd September 1940. At that time the rent was £50 p.a. with the inventory valued at £245. A full licence was held. In the early 1950's Mr. and Mrs. Percy Bevan were incumbent. They were famous locally for the size of their giant geraniums (some reached seven feet high).

These were exhibited in the bar and became a talking point with both regulars and visitors alike.

An impressive, three-storey, wedge-shaped building, it provided 17 letting bedrooms and, following conversion to Pissarro's, the bar and restaurant area had 78 covers. The former hotel was readily identifiable in 1995 as it still advertised Whitbread ales and carried Whitbread facia boards. This was always one of my favourite signs commemorating the two young nephews of Richard III – Edward V and Richard Duke of York – murdered in the Tower in 1483. Quite what the connection with Hastings is I do not know.

No 4. The Fountain, Hastings
Jude Hanbury, F. Leney, Fremlins, Whitbread, Shepherd Neame

Leaving the town centre a brisk walk away from the G.I. will quickly bring you to the "Fountain". This large, square, three-storey building, stands on a road junction in a mainly artisan area where the shops merge with the residential part of town. Built in 1851 Jude Hanbury purchased the freehold from W. Edwards in 1885 paying the sum of £2,770. The first landlord I could trace was a Mr. Benjamin in 1890. Almost anonymous, little is known about its past history but it must have served the local community well as it is a survivor.

Money was spent on the property during the early 1900's including fixing a pair of "Hayward's" flaps costing £21/8/- and installing a bath in 1918 at a cost of £30/7-. A fire broke out in 1909 resulting in renovation work amounting to £21/16/-. In 1902 the business was valued at £2,800. The house and adjoining shop were purchased in September 1917 for £2,500 and the following year the shop was incorporated to expand the premises. In 1930 the total ingoings were £985/7/10 plus expenses. This was one of the seven local Jude Hanbury houses sold to Leney on 27th April 1931, selling for £2,745.

During the war years the pub was closed from the 15th October 1940 until the 10th June 1943.

What a pity that the beautiful sign was replaced in 1995 whilst renovation work was carried out. There is nothing now to differentiate this sign from any of the other countless "Fountains".

Leased from Whitbread on the 6th May 1992 the freehold was purchased by Shepherd Neame on 13th September 1993.

No 5. The Old Golden Cross, Hastings
(Re-named **Heroes** in 2003) Mackeson, F. Leney, Fremlins, Whitbread, Free House

Back in the town centre you will find this substantial house standing close to Hastings railway station and the sea front. It could justifiably be described as a hotel with a horseshoe-shaped, split-level bar, a function room with a dance area on the first floor, nine double bedrooms on the upper floor and a basement. Indeed, in 1890 it was named the "Golden Cross Hotel" with the landlord a Mr. Richard Pincham. It was numbered 57 Havelock Road, number 56 was owned by his wife Mrs. Annie Pincham. The latter was described as a boarding house. It is quite likely that at some later date the two properties were amalgamated.

In April 1912 Mackeson agreed to purchase the freehold and trade fixtures for £2,250, plus legal expenses of £104. Completion took place on Wednesday 18th September 1912. The purchase was financed by a mortgage of £2,000 over three existing properties one of which was the "Hope" at Lydden. Mackeson then leased the premises for a 28-year term at an annual rent of £95 plus £15 for the fixtures and fittings to Tom and Kitty Branson who, by all accounts, managed a thriving brandy-shipping business. For some time the brewers paid the sum of 1/- p.a. to the estate of W.N. Oldham deceased in respect of a rain-water pipe. On 8th October 1934 Mackeson sold the house to Leneys for £6,500.

On 2nd May 1955, to reduce the size of the pub the shop adjoining was leased to Mr. Albert Tulip for 21 years at an annual rent of £160. Fremlins acquired these premises in 1960 when they took over the Leney estate. A building of some character it was erected in about 1860 and contained much historical architecture. The brewers vandalized the place in the 1950's ripping out the mahogany panels, counters, the terrazzo flooring, embossed mirrors and similar plate-glass windows. They did have the good grace to store these items at Wateringbury and they were subsequently used in a pub conversion in London.

This was another Hastings house to close during the war years – from 2nd October 1940 until 4th May 1945.

The series five sign was erected in 1954 and the only subsequent change was the new red background. That is until the pub was re-named Heroes in 2003.

In 1998 the freehold was offered for sale at £250,000.

"If you rightly bear your cross, it will bear you." Kempis

No 6. Warriors Gate, St Leonards-on-Sea
Truman, Hanbury, Buxton & Co Ltd, Mackeson, F. Leney, Fremlins, Whitbread

This is one of the oldest pubs in town. The first records I traced date back to 30th January 1832, one being a deed of covenant by the Reverend Sir J. Godfrey Thomas and the other an appointment by the reverend gentleman to George Hyland. Stephen Pilcher was in residence in 1846 in what was a good old spit and sawdust place catering for the residents of the new village of St. Leonards. The house was conveyed from John Phillips to George Cuthbert on 2nd December 1854 at a consideration of £850 and on 18th June 1862 George conveyed it to Henry Lamb, who was renting the house, at an increased price of £1,000. By this time there was a 100% mortgage in favour of Miss E. Durrant. In 1893 the Lamb family still owned the house but borrowing provided by Truman, Hanbury, Buxton & Co. Limited had risen to £3,700. In 1906 the property passed to Charles E. Beeching and on 6th May 1907 Trumans surrendered their leasehold interest.

Mackeson came into the picture on 22nd December 1913 when they purchased the freehold plus premises adjoining from Walter Cheesman and others for £5,300 (over twice the sum paid for the "Old Golden Cross") plus commission on purchase of £30, legal fees of £116/12/6 and additions to the inventory totalling £220. It was agreed with the vendors that £3,533 was to remain on mortgage at 5%, reduced to 4 1/2 % if the interest was paid promptly. Stamps and costs of £74/5/- were incurred. During 1917 the brewers spent £250 on converting part of the hotel into shop premises.

On 9th June 1932 the company was asked if it would dispose of the hotel, the licence not being required by the buyer. The intended purchaser was informed that the company owned the whole block of 14, 16 and 18 London Road and they could not consider the sale of the "Warriors Gate" in isolation, but they would consider selling the whole for £15,000. On 24th August an offer of £8,500 was made for the hotel. This sum was quite out of the question but the purchaser was told the company would be willing to sell at a reasonable price. On 8th October 1934 Mackeson sold the freehold to Leneys for the following sums :-

> *The hotel £5,930.*
> *14 London Road – unlicensed. £ 800.*
> *16 and 16A London Road – unlicensed. £1,130.*
> *18 and 18A London Road – unlicensed. £ 980.*
> *Less the outstanding mortgage. £3,533.*

This old building survived until the war when it was destroyed, along with the "Swan", by enemy bombing on 23rd May 1943. A photograph exists showing the sign, surrounded by rubble, swinging defiantly in the breeze. Previously, in common with many Hastings houses, it had closed on 22nd November 1940.

The pub was rebuilt and re-opened on 18th July 1945 occupying only part of the former site. In 1951 a War Damage claim was settled at £4,650/5/5 and the following year the remainder of the plot, 12 and 14 London Road, was sold to the Post Office for £5,500. In 1960 Fremlins acquired the Leney estate which included the flat which was let to Mrs. E.J. Norman at a rent of £52 p.a.

The sign was one of the last survivors of the miniature days being replaced in 1995 by a scene from the Bayeaux Tapestry.

No 7. British Queen, St. Leonards-on-Sea

*(Re-named **The Fox** in 1992) Hewetts of St. Leonards, Burfield's, Smiths of Lamberhurst, Jude Hanbury, F. Leney, Fremlins, Whitbread*

In 1828 James Burton purchased part of the Gensing Farm Estate and employed local labourers to construct the "new town". This area grew quite rapidly and it was in about 1860 that the "British Queen" was built. It was certainly selling beer in 1862. It was always a popular pub with a very low turnover in landlords. The first "mine host" was George Linton who survived until 1896 with his wife keeping up the family tradition until 1909. The Lintons sold their home-bottled whisky in specially-etched bottles and certainly into the late 1980's an example could be seen in the pub. Later the Galloway family was in residence for over thirty years. Another interesting point is that at least three of the landlords served their apprenticeship in the fish bar that used to exist in North Street.

In September 1921 Alan Simpson, the managing director of Smiths of Lamberhurst, retired and the assets of the company were sold off with the "British Queen" fetching £3,800 in March 1922. Whether to purchase or not was discussed at some length by the board of Jude Hanbury. It was decided to leave negotiations in the hands of Major Hanbury. To finance this, plus other purchases, the brewers, in 1922, mortgaged the pub in the sum of £2,000. On 27th April 1931 Jude Hanbury sold this house plus six other local pubs to Leney for £20,055 with the "British Queen" accounting for £3,375 of this sum. A problem arose in September 1933 with a change of tenancy when Leney, the new owners, agreed that Jude Hanbury would contribute, ex-gratia, the sum of £125 towards the amount payable to the outgoing tenant, with

Leney's taking over the fireplace etc. leaving only the customary fixtures and fittings to be sold to the ingoing tenant by valuation. The landlord in 1939 was J.R. Peacock paying a rent of £45 p.a. with his inventory valued at £189/18/-. That same year repairs totalled £1,384/18/3, a considerable sum in those days.

There really were too many public houses in this artisan area and inevitably some fell on hard times, including the "British Queen". The pub closed in about 1990 and remained empty for eighteen months. Despite falling into disrepair a brave soul purchased the premises and carried out some refurbishment; at which time the distinctive red terracotta tiles were lost. The pub re-opened in 1992 as the "Fox". Again, what a pity the distinctive name disappeared together with the brilliant sign – in my view one of the best miniatures in all five series.

A pleasant place – this is a squat, flat roofed, sandy-coloured building standing within easy walking distance of the "Warriors Gate" and the "Nag's Head".

No 8. Dripping Spring, St. Leonards-on-Sea
H.T. Wickham & Co, Jude Hanbury, F. Leney, Fremlins, Whitbread, Free House

Dating back to 1840 this is probably the oldest pub in the St. Leonards area. In those days it stood on the northern outskirts of the town and from here to the hamlet of Hollington were cornfields. One can still walk down Cornfields Terrace. The present pub was probably originally built as two small cottages with the right-hand side becoming an ale house with just one modest bar.

In 1921 Jude Hanbury acquired the pub via H.T. Wickham & Co. and at the same time wrote off a bad debt of £174/1/5. At the time a book value of £1,332/10/- was attributed to the property. A mortgage was then raised with Charles Hook over numbers 34 and 35 Tower Road for £400 plus interest. This was one of seven East Sussex houses parcelled up by Jude Hanbury and sold to Leney on 27th April 1931 on the basis of £15 per barrel sold which amounted to £3,105. In 1935 a Mr. A.E. Comins made an offer of £375 for 34 Tower

Road but this was declined and it was ultimately incorporated into the pub in 1951. At the same time a single-storey toilet was added. Prior to this 34 Tower Road had served as a bakers (the remnants of the ovens can still be seen), a cobblers, a greengrocers and finally a hairdressers.

There is much conjecture as to how the house acquired its unique name. I prefer the simple explanation that the pub stands on the junction of Tower Road and Spring Street. The spring rises in nearby Alexander Park and flows in a culvert under the pub which has a very large cellar. The house stands on a modest incline but at one time the pavement was terraced so that one dropped down every so often by descending two or three steps. The rain water would run along the pavement then drip down the steps. It is felt that the pub may have been called the Spring with Dripping added at some later date.

Always a friendly pub it has had some good landlords including Mr. and Mrs. C.G. Martin who took over on 14th June 1921 remaining until 1952. Their initial rent was £20 p.a. and the inventory was agreed at £350. In October 1926 some repairs and painting accounted for £119/0/5 and during 1940 further repairs cost £500/5/6. On 28th October 1949 the brewers paid £650 to the Central Land Board for development charges etc.

In 1992 the pub was re-named the "New George and Dragon". The new owner lived in Yorkshire and the pub was managed by George with the Dragon, his wife, the sister of the owner. This appears to have been a bleak era for the fortunes of the pub and when I visited in mid-1994 it was a soulless place. Fortunately, in February 1995 new owners took over and by June had re-established it as a house worth a visit, and restored the old name and the magnificent sign. It is now a good old-fashioned back-street pub and is the second-largest outlet for real ale in Sussex. It was placed second in the CAMRA national pub of the year competition.

It was granted a beer and wine licence in April 1938 and a full licence on 30th March 1950 with the monopoly value settled at £850.

It is too small to have a restaurant, pool table or live music and in any event these intrusions would not be welcomed by the clientele.

No 9. The Marina, St. Leonards-on-Sea
(Closed and delicensed on the 25th November 1996) Tenterden Brewery Co, Smiths of Lamberhurst, Jude Hanbury, F. Leney, Fremlins, Whitbread, Shepherd Neame

This was a sad little pub sited in a dilapidated part of town.

Not much is known about its past history but it probably dates back to the1840's. It stood at the end of Caves Road hard up against the cliff face, an area originally developed to provide accommodation for agricultural workers. Unfortunately cliff face falls were a regular feature with a particularly bad one in the 1970's. The rubble was allowed to lie on the road to act as a barrier against further falls and prevent cars using the road. It was three months before the rubble was removed and this feature coupled with poor parking facilities did little to assist trade. The landlord at the time, Mr. Derek Standen, still considered the area a potential risk to pedestrians.

Back in 1852 it was trading as an ale house with the Tenterden Brewery leasing the premises from Smiths of Lamberhurst at a rent of £25 p.a. In April 1922 the brewers agreed to make a loan

of £150 at 6% interest to Mr. T.S. Frazer against the security of his lease and the trade of his house. The pub did appear to provide a reasonable living as, when J.C. Davis took over on 20th October 1926, the ingoings amounted to £941/6/6 (the corresponding figure for the "Nag's Head" was £352/1/6). Mr. Davis' initial rent was £80 p.a. and he remained until 24th June 1940. In September 1926 the house was offered to Jude Hanbury at a price of £5,000 which they thought excessive. Agreement was subsequently reached at a purchase price of £4,245/10/- including costs. However, when Jude Hanbury sold their interest to Leney on the basis of £15 per barrel of trade on 27th April 1931 they only received £2 963. During 1927 a swing sign was erected at a cost of £25 and further alterations costing £50 were carried out. Capital expenditure totalling £600 together with improvements costing £300 were completed in 1964. After passing through Whitbread's hands the pub was acquired by Shepherd Neame on 8th February 1977.

In common with many Hastings houses this one closed during the war from 17th October 1940 until 30th May 1945.

When I called in 1995 the house was run down and the sign had fallen and was propped up against the wall. The only redeeming feature was that the sign remained very similar to the miniature. This area of the town is referred to as Marina, hence the pub name. The new owners spent a lot on renovating the property but trade remained insufficient to warrant opening and the final straw came when it proved impossible to obtain Insurance cover due to frequent landslides.

It has now been converted to a private house.

No 10. The Nag's Head, St Leonards-on-Sea
Eldridge and Young, Breeds, Jude Hanbury, F. Leney, Fremlins, Whitbread, Free House

The development of Gensing Road began in 1832 with some of the building materials coming from the old America ground whilst the sandstone used in the construction was quarried from what is now the site of Christchurch. The "Nag's Head" was the first of several small public houses to be built outside the St. Leonards boundary and it actually backed on to the town wall. The current pub is the result of amalgamation with an adjacent cottage a long while ago. Jude Hanbury purchased the "Nag's Head" from a Mr. Rogers in 1920 paying £2,250. A deposit of £225 was paid in August 1920 with completion taking place on 15th September. To raise capital, in 1921 the brewers mortgaged this property plus the dwelling house adjoining for £1,000 with Mrs. Friend Chapman. In 1931 Jude Hanbury sold their seven East Sussex houses to Leney on the basis of £15 per barrel. The total sale proceeds amounted to £20,055 with this house accounting for £2,310 of this sum.

In 1840 Jesse Hack supplemented his income from his road-building activities by becoming the landlord of this popular house in a now thriving part of town. During this era the ale was either brought up from Hastings or brewed on the premises. By the 1850's Eldridge and Young were brewing at the local Crown Brewery and became the house suppliers.

During the years leading up to the First World War the pub had established itself as the social centre for the ordinary working man. Affairs of state were discussed and from time to time an Irish housepainter called Robert Noonan would call in to preach the Socialist cause. Under the name of Robert Tressell he wrote the satirical tome "The Ragged Trousered Philanthropist". Many of his observations are apposite today, in particular his comment about politicians "they vote for what they get and by God they get what they vote for".

A. Platt was the landlord during the war years paying a rent of £40 p.a. with his inventory valued at £245/11/6. There is no mention of the house closing during this period.

Due to lack of trade the pub closed in 1989 and became virtually derelict but, fortunately, a great deal of money was spent on the place and it re-opened in 1991 as a freehouse. It now presents a breezy and welcoming appearance. The groaning of the swinging sign used to keep the landlord's children awake so it is now screwed to the wall. This politically incorrect sign has been copied in various ways including representation on drinking mugs.

"It is better to dwell in the wilderness than with a contentious and an angry woman." Proverbs.

No 11. William the Conqueror, Rye Harbour
Obadiah Edwards (Tenterden Brewery), Jude Hanbury, F. Leney, Fremlins, Whitbread, Shepherd Neame

Although the sea has now retreated a good half mile one can find this popular pub down at Rye Harbour, a village about a couple of miles from the town. The area has atmosphere and is particularly busy during the summer months.

Dating back to the early 1800's it probably started life as a fisherman's cottage. It was one of the houses that formed the estate of the "Tenterden Brewery" which, at one time, was owned by Obadiah Edwards. In 1891 Edwards purchased the property from William Watson and converted it to a public house in 1892. It was offered for sale at auction on 31st January 1921 at Elwick Auction Rooms, Ashford, as lot No. 6. It was described as "Occupying a unique position, about two miles from Rye railway station and directly opposite the Harbour. It is the only fully licensed house in this district. The house is brick built and slated and contains :- Billiard Room, Bar, Smoking Room, Private Entrance, large Kitchen with excellent kitchener, Private Sitting Room, Dining Room, Large Sitting Room on the 1st Floor with a separate staircase, 5 Bedrooms, 2 Attics, Bath Room (h & c), Lavatory Basin, Pedestal Water Closet, Landing with hot air cupboard, Cellar, Scullery, outside W.C. In the rear is a timber built Coach House and Stable. Water laid on, Modern Sanitation. Frontage 23 feet with a depth of 80 feet. The house is in the occupation of Mr. R.D. Watson who has resided here for about 57 years paying a rent of £24 p.a.".

Clearly this was a substantial property. It probably remained unsold as Jude Hanbury purchased the pub in March 1922 from Obadiah Edwards, paying £1,200. Sadly for Mr. Watson one of the first acts of the new owners, on 7th April 1922, was to instruct the company secretary to write to him requesting settlement of his account without delay. A change of tenant took place six months later. In 1924 it was mortgaged to Mrs. G. Luck and another. In 1926 the brewers increased the value of this house in their books from £1,210 to £2,196.

On 2nd June 1937 Frederick Caister moved in and, on volunteering for war service, his wife Annie ran the pub from 29th November 1939 until 15th August 1940 when it was requisitioned by the War Office and closed down. It re-opened on 1st August 1945 happily with Fred again behind the bar.

At one time there were two bars called the Poop and Mess deck as befits a fisherman's pub. Although now extended to both front and rear and completely re-modernised the old windows etched with Whitbread and Co. still remain. During the 1950's a novel home-made clock face showed a scaled-down version of the inn sign. Inside one will find a memorial to a local man killed in the first Gulf War in 1991. Much smuggling went on in this area and during the Leney days the house was regularly raided by the Revenue men, but due to its isolated position, the local inhabitants had ample time to warn the landlord and nothing was ever discovered!

Shepherd Neame leased the pub from Whitbread on 6th May 1992 and purchased the freehold on 27th September 1996. The house is popular with holidaymakers particularly during the summer months.

The old sign disappeared years ago but at least the pub has been spared the indignity of being re-named "Conkers" as happened to the inn of a similar name at nearby Iden which is now a bed and breakfast establishment.

No 12. Queen Adelaide, Rye
Alfred Leney of Dover, Ash & Co, Jude Hanbury, F. Leney, Fremlins, Whitbread, Free House

Queen Adelaide, consort of William IV from 1843 to 1846, inspired the naming of only a few public houses throughout the country.

The pub stands close to the railway station and is a half-tiled eighteenth century building. The first records I have traced date from the 1840's showing P. Pankhurst as the landlord in 1846. For a while the pub was in the ownership of Alfred Leney the Dover brewer who possibly sold it to a Mr. Tapsell who in turn sold it to Thomas Ash. His two sons were entitled to a sixth share in their father's estate and in 1870 a conveyance of a moiety (half share) over this house plus yard, washhouse and back-yard buildings was granted to Thomas Ash Junior by George Ash. Thomas Ash died on 12th March 1875 with this house forming part of his estate. On Thomas' death the landlord, W.G. Warren, was paying an annual rent of £12. A tenancy agreement dated 9th August 1933 shows A. Jamieson taking over the house at a rental of £25 p.a. plus improvements of £12 p.a. The inventory was valued at £70/10/-. A full licence was held.

The present house is the result of the combination of three old cottages which has left the bars on different levels. One, the games room, is the lowest and is approached via steps down from the bar. At one time there were two entrances and three bars but these have been knocked into one. The original pub probably occupied the middle cottage.

The pub stood close by the old fish market and one could purchase from Jack Simmonds, a local fisherman, skinned sole plus a bottle of Guinness for half a crown. Prior to meetings in Maidstone the local Whitbread area manager would pop in to buy a box of flats to share with his colleagues. The local bookie's runner was also a regular drinker, who at the same time collected the bets. The police normally apprehended him once a year. Several colourful characters managed the house with one, Bill Beusden, in situ for over 20 years, remembered with particular affection.

The pub was closed by Whitbread in the mid-1960's but was sold with licence.

When I visited in 1994 it was in a very dilapidated state with one of the signs leaning against the house next door. It has recently been spruced up and repainted and remains one of the very few pubs still retaining the original inn sign.

No 13. Ypres Castle, Rye

Eagle Brewery (poss.), Alfred Leney of Dover, Jude Hanbury, F. Leney, Fremlins, Whitbread, Free House

This 17th Century weather-boarded inn stands in the shadows of the 700-year old Ypres Tower built by Henry III as a mini fortress. It has also served as the town prison and for the first half of the last century it was also a mortuary. It is now a museum. I digress, but have no doubt that whatever function the tower served, it brought custom to this charming inn. Back in the 1860's Rye boasted another tavern called the Ypres Globe Inn.

The pub can only be approached by climbing or descending Gun Garden Steps. Needless to say, perched on a hill with splendid views over the marshlands and frequented by the fishing fraternity, it just had to be involved in the smuggling trade. The local fishermen, besides being skilled at that trade, were also canny wildfowlers. Earlier last century Rye Bay teemed with duck and other fowl.

The first records go back to 1838 when on 24th May the Mayor, Aldermen and Burgesses of Rye rented the premises for £2/2/- to George French for a period of 75 years. A new lease in favour of Alfred Leney & Co. was created on 29th September 1913 for a 50-year term at an annual rental of £23. They must have assigned their interest to Jude Hanbury in about 1920 as, in 1923, Jude paid £23/2/6 to have electric lighting installed. The following year a mortgage was raised over the leasehold interest plus Alexandra Cottage in the sum of £500 from Henry James Bracher, paying an interest rate of 4%. This was subsequently redeemed by Leney & Sons in October 1956 as, on 27th May 1953, they had purchased the freehold together with the site of the former Alexandra cottage for £3,600.

Always popular with holidaymakers, nowadays it is frequented by the younger generation. It has an excellent range of real ales drawn from six hand pumps, good home cooking, particularly fish, and all can be enjoyed in a pleasant garden with splendid views.

Again we are fortunate to see the original sign still swinging in the breeze.

"A noble relic of times long gone by, casting its halo o'er the past of Rye" Holloway

No 14. Ship Inn, Winchelsea Beach.
Mackeson, F. Leney, Fremlins, Whitbread, Shepherd Neame

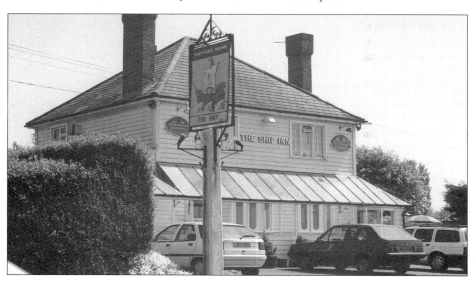

The original "Ship Inn" stood in splendid isolation but just a little too close to the fickle sea for comfort. It was timber-framed, remote, and at times during the winter months could only be reached on horseback unless one was prepared to get wet feet. In 1931, during one particularly violent storm, the sea lashed the beach with a vengeance, undermined the foundations and swept the pub away. I am told Colonel Whitbread flew over his stricken house to witness it drifting away on the tide. A particularly good photograph exists depicting this tragedy.

Events unfolded as follows. On 26th January 1906 – yes, the saga commences that far back – an application was made for the removal of the licence of the old "Ship Inn" at Pett by the tenant of that house at the annual licensing meeting at Hastings in February. In the event of the new licence being granted the company would erect a new house on the land over which they had an option from the War Office. In November 1907 Mackeson purchased from the War Office a plot of freehold land at Cliff End, Pett for £125 for the purpose of moving the licence of the "Ship Inn" at Pett to this spot. On 18th April 1912 the brewers decided that the various restrictions placed upon the licence probably made the removal uneconomic. By October 1925 the "Ship" was in a dangerous position owing to the inroads of the sea, but no definite action was decided upon by the local authority. However, in November 1925 the local authority proposed to extend certain sea defence work which would result in protecting the "Ship", provided Mackeson covered one seventh of the cost up to a maximum of £200. On 26th March 1928 the brewers considered an enquiry from Mr. Swinburn-Bailey as to whether the company would sell or lease the land at Cliff End in the event of the "Ship Inn" Pett becoming untenable. The company agreed to sell for £100 with completion taking place on 7th January 1929. Work went ahead on strengthening the sea defences, but in mid-December 1931 the partially-erected defences and the pub were destroyed by the sea. Again consideration was given to the removal of the licence to another site and premises. On 11th January 1932 Mr. Marchant reported that he had taken an option to purchase a piece of ground in the neighbourhood of this house for £75, which would be suitable for a small building costing about £1,000, to which the licence might be transferred. With a small additional expenditure an adjacent piece of land could be acquired, the two pieces providing an ample site for permanent premises. On 18th February 1932 the company seal was affixed to the tenancy agreement for the first landlord at the new "Ship Inn", a Mr. William Hickman. On 23rd February 1932 the two plots of land at Icklesham (Winchelsea Beach) were purchased, paying Mr. Downton £130 and Mr. Walter £75. On 4th March 1932 a report was received that a special order for the removal of the licence to premises erected on land at Icklesham was obtained. On 11th April 1932 Leneys advised that total expenditure in connection with the removal of this licence from Pett to Winchelsea Beach amounted to £1,162/11/6. This sum included £873/7/- for cost of building, £7/10/- for special insurance against storm and tempest, and a bonus of £5 to the building foreman. It was agreed that the old "Ship Inn" would be left in the hands of Leneys to dispose of if possible. Indeed, on 8th October 1934 Leneys purchased the new "Ship Inn" from Mackeson, paying £1,168 plus £10 for the site of the old "Ship Inn". It was not until 1950 that the brewers disposed of the former site for £60 to Rother and Jury's Gut Catchment Board.

The new building, constructed of wood, was to act as a temporary measure, but owing to the advent of war, a new structure was never built. In 1954 the brewers dedicated approximately 68 square yards of land to East Sussex County Council for road widening with the Council paying legal costs, erecting a boundary fence, and creating a car park at the pub.

Much modernisation took place in 1962 when £2,000 of capital expenditure and £1,150 of improvements were carried out. The new house has proved as popular as its predecessor. There is an enterprising menu and you can also buy take-away fish and chips. Still close to the shore this inn remains very popular with holidaymakers.

The pub was leased to Shepherd Neame on 6th May 1992 with the freehold purchased on 29th September 1995. The original inn sign is still in place.

"Guarded with ships, and all our sea our own." Waller.

No 15. Black Horse, Tenterden

*(Re-named **William Caxton** in 1951) Obadiah Edwards (Tenterden Brewery Co.),*
Jude Hanbury, F. Leney, Fremlins, Whitbread, Shepherd Neame

This typical Wealden inn, dating back to the first half of the 16th Century, stands on the T-junction with the Smallhythe road. It was probably a hall house with the chimney inserted 100 years later. In the early 1800's the greater part of the house was demolished, apart from the original western end, to be replaced by the new eastern end. It is this remodelled building which became the "Black Horse". It traded under this name for generations but changed to the "William Caxton" as part of the town's Festival of Britain celebrations. These festivities were a quite splendid affair, held from 22nd July to 14th August 1951. The opening ceremony was carried out by Dame Edith Evans, D.B.E. The re-naming ceremony took place on 19th July 1951 with the new sign unveiled by the town mayor, Mr. A.J. Wright. At an informal luncheon afterwards Mr. W.F. Deedes, (now Lord Deedes), even now a regular contributor to The Daily Telegraph, thanked the brewers for honouring the town's most famous son. As a souvenir of the occasion a special colour miniature of the sign had been printed for visitors to the festival. The theme of the Festival of Britain celebrations revolved around Caxton, and although it is generally believed that he was born in the town in 1422, it has to be said that the link is somewhat tenuous.

A great attraction during 1953 was "Georgie", an albino squirrel. He was found in the woods nearby by a relative of the licensee, Mr. A.G. Chandler, and was brought to the pub as a curiosity. He was tamed and became a favourite of the landlord's daughter, Jennifer. He became so famous that an article was written about him in the London "Evening News" describing how he even answered to his name.

Ideally situated to pick up passing trade the inn has a small restaurant and a fine collection of old prints. It was common in this area not to welcome hop-pickers into the more prestigious establishments and this probably applied here all the more as the town "watch", forerunners of the modern police, used to meet here. Standing at the head of the marshes this old pub was a regular stopping-off place for smugglers.

On 18th December 1924 the Tenterden brewery arranged a mortgage of £2,000 over these premises with Mrs. Emily Hughes – this was redeemed in 1935. The group properties were revalued in July 1926 and the book value of this pub was increased from £3,090 to £3,348. It was noted that during 1925 the pub sold 186 barrels of ale. In 1960 Fremlins acquired Cherry Tree Cottage adjoining the pub when they took over the Leney estate. At that time the tenant, Mrs. G. Clarke, was paying a rent of 35/- per week.

The house was leased to Shepherd Neame on 6th May 1992 and they purchased the freehold on 29th September 1995.

"There is no good horse of a bad colour." Izaak Walton.

No 16. The Harrier, Link Hill, Sandhurst
*(Re-named **The Missing Link** (1991), and reverted back to **The Harrier** in 1997. Closed March 2001)*
Sharpe & Winch, F. Leney, Fremlins, Whitbread, Free House

Sadly another recent casualty. The "Harrier" of the 1950's was rebuilt in 1938 to the rear of a 200-year old weather-boarded inn affectionately referred to as the "Shant" – Australian slang for a shack. Its service was restricted and it was not particularly comfortable, nevertheless it was missed by the locals living in this rural area. Despite the nick-name it was a place of some importance. When, in 1900, Miss Dengate sold the property at an auction held at the Swan Hotel, Sandhurst it was described thus :- "Freehold Beerhouse, Grocers and Drapers also including Warehouse, Stable, Coachhouse, and Outbuildings. Two thirds of the purchase can remain on mortgage at 4%". At the time the rent was £35 p.a. Almost certainly the purchaser was the Cranbrook-based brewery Sharpe and Winch, as this was one of the houses acquired by Leney when they were taken over in 1928. In May 1936 Leney sold the cottage adjoining the "Shant" for £150. On demolition in September 1938 the brewers purchased the tenant's inventory for £63/16/-.

The new house was designed by Basil H. Jackson, ARIBA whose fees amounted to £163/3/7 and was built by a High Halden contractor. New furniture was purchased costing £126/8/- with £100/19/6 charged to the tenant. A gratuity of £5 was paid to the foreman who oversaw the building work. The monopoly value was set at £900. To a degree the modern pub appears out of place in the quiet tranquillity of this area. The premises are typical of the pre-war era, but a certain rustic ambience is achieved by the russet facing of hand-made tiles. Character is added by the addition of a barrel window. The window served a double purpose as, for many years, the inn was also the village general stores – an unusual combination in Kent. This dual purpose ended in 1961. The "Shant" only had a six days' licence and was a beer house, but the new pub provided a complete service. A cask dating back to 1954 showed NMA – New Mild Ale.

The inn took its name as a result of its connections with either the Rother Valley Harriers (the River Rother is opposite the pub), or the Link Hill Harrier pack – probably the latter. The sign was designed by Kathleen M. Claxton and depicted a hound from the Link Hill pack named "Faithful". The hounds were kennelled over the road.

Despite its rural setting the pub is on a busy coast road and picked up much passing trade. It was a favourite with hop-pickers – indeed during that era the takings from the pickers had to subsidize the rest of the year. It was both roomy and comfortable and on my visits the bar was well patronized. During the war years it was a regular for soldiers billeted in the area.

It is rumoured that a ghost haunts the gents' toilet, of all places. Perhaps he is the last connection with the old "Shant".

No 17. Oak and Ivy, Hawkhurst
Sharpe & Winch, F. Leney, Fremlins, Whitbread, Shepherd Neame

This comfortable panelled inn with its Tudor interior is rumoured to date back to the early 1400's. A local assured me that the exact date is 1426. It is almost certainly an old hall house – not dissimilar to the "Old House at Home" at Edenbridge – with its massive oak beams, huge chimney with hooks for smoking bacon, and "Queen Pin" holding together the spectacular roof. The property stands well back from the road and is fronted by a large car park and pretty gardens. When I passed by early one morning the only car parked was a pristine Ford V8 Pilot which admirably complemented the house. There is one large bar which includes the restaurant area with the previous small bar providing an extra dining room and children's area. There are several interesting prints and detailed plans on view. These include the proposed plan of the boundary line and the amended layout of the cellars of the "Stag's Head", Ramsgate, drawn up in August 1938 for Mackeson, together with further plans dated July 1954 for proposed alterations for Frederick Leney & Sons Limited at the "Two Brewers", Yalding, concerning the two bars and parlour. The main objective was to improve facilities by doing away with the outside toilets.

The first licence was granted in 1645. During the mid-1700's it became the haunt of the notorious "Hawkhurst" gang of cut-throats who were finally brought to book at Chichester. On the trading tracks from the marsh to the inland market towns smuggling thrived and rumour has it, besides wine and spirits, the odd Jacobite was slipped to the continent via this route. It is said if oak leaves could be seen in the window it was safe to enter – if ivy keep well away. Once in a while a "free trader" fell under a customs officer's fire, and inscribed on the tombstone of one George Walker, buried on the marsh, is the sad little couplet:-

> *"Let it be known that I am clay,*
> *A base man took my life away."*

From 1788 to 1804 the property acted as the village poor house before reverting back to licensed premises. Sheep would regularly be driven through Hawkhurst on their way to market with the animals penned in the adjacent field whilst the drovers slaked their thirst in the bar. Until 1914 a sign hung stating "Sheep taken in – good beds".

On 18th July 1928 the assets of the Cranbrook-based brewers Sharpe & Winch were sold at auction with Frederick Leney & Sons Limited purchasing for £20,000 the 13 pubs which included the "Oak and Ivy". It was described thus: "All that messuage or tenement called "Pipsden" and now used as a beer house commonly known as the "Oak and Ivy" Beerhouse together with the Granary (formerly an Oast House) stable garden orchard and piece of land".

Joseph Goldsmith acquired the tenancy of the "Oak and Ivy" on 19th September 1928 together with the buildings, yard, and meadow adjacent at an annual rental of £40. Electricity was installed in 1934 for which he paid an additional £1/10/- and he had to supply all the lamps and fittings. It remained a beerhouse until granted a full licence on 8th April 1948 when the net monopoly value of £750 was paid. In 1951 Leney accepted the sum of £450 in respect of loss of development value of land and buildings on the site.

The inn has seen many good landlords over the years with the Taylors being particularly popular. The first Taylor, father of Doris, arrived in the village to manage the pub in 1926. There followed various other tenants including Frederick Cronk, formerly the poet at the "North Pole", and he was succeeded on 7th May 1951 by Frank Taylor and on his death in 1973 his widow Doris managed the pub until she passed away in 1980. During the 1950's the Taylor children established a speed track for cycle races complete with a Union Jack hoisted in the centre. This proved very popular – a photograph shows hundreds of spectators and those classic Maidstone and District coaches pulled up in the car park. Prior to this funfairs and circuses used the field.

The garden is dominated by an ancient oak and this coupled with the ivy which clad the old brick walls is how the pub acquired its name.

Shepherd Neame leased the premises from 6th May 1992 but only held it for a short while surrendering it on 11th November 1993. The pub and restaurant continue to thrive. It was described in sale particulars in 1999 as a Grade II listed building still retaining five acres of land.

No 18. King William IV, Benenden
H.T. Wickham & Co., Jude Hanbury, F. Leney, Fremlins, Whitbread, Shepherd Neame

A popular sign to commemorate a popular monarch. At the tender age of 23 the young man absconded from his naval post to seek his fortune elsewhere. For his pains he was subsequently created the Duke of Clarence and granted an annual pension of £12,000. He came to the throne in 1830 and often appeared in naval uniform. His wife was Queen Adelaide.

This venerable old inn started life in the 16th century as a chapel and subsequently became a rest home for pilgrims. It was licensed in the 18th century and became a stopping-off point for pilgrims wending their way to Canterbury.

In 1921 the Yalding brewers H.T. Wickham & Co. were acquired by Jude Hanbury and Frederick Leney. They split the Wickham houses between them with this one going to Jude Hanbury. It was granted a full licence on 28th April 1950 when the net monopoly value of £800 was paid. Said to be built of ships' timbers it appears to have occupied this site close to the village green for all time. Low ceilings, simple furnishings, half tile-hung, a massive central chimney-piece and a small garden all complement the excellent food offered to the traveller. At one time it was tile-hung down to the pavement but the lower seven feet have at some time been removed. Smuggling and the "Hawkhurst" gang are entwined in its history.

The landlord during the war years was A.E.G. Chandler who later moved to the "William Caxton". At that time it was a simple beer house with the rent set at £40 and the deposit £50. The inventory was valued at £112.

The property was purchased by Shepherd Neame on 24th February 1977.

No 19. This Ancient Boro, Tenterden
*(Formerly the **New Inn**. Closed in 1968. Now Honeymoon Chinese Restaurant)*
Obadiah Edwards (when trading as the New Inn) Jude Hanbury, F. Leney, Fremlins, Whitbread

This small pub never had much of a trade and suffered from lack of car parking facilities. A few townspeople can still remember it but not much has come to light as to its past history. This is a pity as it occupied charming premises. Just after the last war, however, it did boast a great darts team. They won three local cups and in the winter of 1946 nearly 100 players, members and supporters of the competing teams gathered at the "Boro" to witness the mayor, Councillor F.G. Bourne, present the trophies. The

meeting was presided over by Mr. Jack Weaver the donor of the Jack Weaver Cup. I wonder if this is still played for. The darts team captain was a Mr. Hart and the landlord was Mr. T.D. Devereux who arrived on 28th May 1936. This was a modest house – his rent was £25 p.a. and the inventory £85/4/6.

A history of Tenterden indicates the "New Inn" occupied No. 3 of a row of 15th – 17th century buildings known as Nos. 1-5 East Cross. No. 3 was the odd one out. This was the service end of a large 15th century Wealden hall house, still with its original steep sloping roof, with the upper end chamber jetted to the front and side; the dragon beam supporting the jetty hoists is still intact. About half the original open hall remains, no longer open, but floored very extensively in the 17th century. At a later date the house was sub-divided with the western end demolished to make way for a separate cottage. The jetties at the eastern end may have been built under by the 18th century,

and sash windows inserted, but the present ground floor bay windows were not added until the 19th century, when No. 3 became a beer house known as the "New Inn". The pub changed its name in 1948.

In March 1922 Jude Hanbury acquired the house paying Obadiah Edwards the sum of £1,200. Shortly afterwards it was mortgaged along with the "Bull" at Rolvenden and "Castleton's Oak", in the sum of £4,500 with Miss K.N. Champion paying an interest rate of 4%. By 1934 the house had been acquired by Leney and was valued in their books at £1,300. The original mortgage was redeemed in 1956, and in 1960 alterations were carried out at a cost of £1,217.

No 20. The Royal Oak, Wrotham Heath
Jude Hanbury, F. Leney, Fremlins, Whitbread, Beefeater

Courtesy of the Kent Messenger Collection

The original "Royal Oak" was a fine hostelry dating back to 1760 when it was a licensed ale house. In its early days it catered for retainers of medieval Archbishops, was a noted coaching inn, then a small house of call for mostly local wayfarers. The pub possibly took its name from the famous warship, although close by stood the massive Royal Oak Tree – unhappily long since gone – which was reputed to be the dead centre of Kent. It is said that an unfailing test of sobriety was the ability to drive a trap at full speed "between the Inn and the Oak" without so much as a scratch on either. However, the tree was a sycamore!

The first traceable landlord was Samuel Sheafs in 1787. A seven-year lease between Sir William Richard Powlett Geary, Bart., and Charles Andrew and Thomas Becket was entered into on 13th October 1843 with the rent fixed at £80 p.a. By 1846 Robert Fowler was running the "Royal Oak" inn and posting house. In 1903 the pub was sold for £360 to Mr. Findlay. On 13th January 1913 the long and eventful reign of John Samuel Swift commenced. When he first took over the rent was £60 p.a. and he inherited from Mr. Findlay a menu which ran as follows:-

> *Breakfast: plain 9d; with eggs or meat 1/3.*
> *Lunch or supper: cold meat, pickles, salad and cheese 1/6.*
> *Tea: plain 9d, with eggs or meat 1/3.*
> *Late dinner by arrangement.*
> *Single bedrooms 1/6 – double 3/-.*
> *Accommodation for carriages, motors and cycles.*

So clearly this was a house of some size – it also catered for the local hunt.

During these early days it was a Jude Hanbury house, the brewers having acquired the freehold for £3,000 in January 1910. In January 1920 they had plans drawn up by E.G. Wildin for a proposed motor works to be erected at Wrotham Heath. His fee was to be 5% of the cost of works. The original plans had been prepared by A.L. Dartnell but these had been rejected. The garage was let to Rootes Limited and in April 1926 they offered to purchase the premises for £3,000, but did not proceed. However, it was ultimately sold to them in 1945. In 1921 the villagers of nearby Platt had raised a considerable sum of money to erect some form of memorial to local men who had perished in the First World War and, after much debate, it was agreed to erect a village hall. The site was donated by Jude Hanbury. In September 1923 the Southern Railway offered a piece of land adjoining the pub to the brewery for £50. Jude stated that they would inspect and purchase if considered advisable. No conclusion appears to have been reached. The old inn served the community until 1932 when the construction of the great London to Folkestone road demanded the presence of a modern road house to cater for the vast increase in passing traffic.

The new premises were opened on 19th March 1932 and were specially designed to appeal to all tastes. Business thrived, but during the Second World War tragedy struck. On the dull dark evening of Tuesday 15th October 1940 at 9.30pm a German bomber dropped a stick of 16 bombs, the first of which scored a direct hit on the "Royal Oak". The clock in the bar faithfully recorded the exact time as it stopped at that hour. It was left lying there for some while after the raid as a silent tribute to the devastation. The pub was full with a darts match in progress. In all four people were killed and seven injured. John Swift, the landlord, survived and although shaken had the presence of mind to switch off both the gas and electricity. One person had a very lucky escape – the local golf professional. Bombs regularly peppered the area and on the afternoon of 15th October a stricken Polish airman landed his plane on the golf course. Armed men were sent to guard the plane and the pilot was taken to the clubhouse for refreshments. As he spoke no English it was late in the evening before final particulars were taken – thus the golfer was too late for his nightly tipple at the "Royal Oak". The house was rebuilt in September 1941.

A Captain Thomas lived on the opposite side of the road at Wrotham Heath House. He was a pugnacious man who enjoyed boxing and it was his practice to invite customers at the pub over to box on his lawn. Unfortunately these premises also took a direct hit resulting in further damage and injuries. Close by stand Daisy Cottages named after the daughter of Thomas Styles who was the innkeeper in 1882.

John Swift's long tenure came to an end on 15th December 1942 when he was succeeded by Frederick Harrison. The pub flourished during the 1950's and 1960's as Londoners travelled by coach down to the Kentish seaside resorts, but the coming of the M20 has affected passing trade.

"You truly fortified Britain with wooden walls." Address to Pepys, 1702.

No 21. Startled Saint, St. Leonard's Cross, West Malling
(Closed in 1993) F. Leney, Fremlins, Whitbread

"Thousands of bomb craters in the white chalk… This was known as the jettison area where a windy Hun would pull the plug, and leg it for home… That first night we stood by, but the weather was bad, and Group released the squadron about nine. Down to the "Startled Saint" we went to sample the beer; it was good and everyone was happy." Thus wrote the war legend Guy Gibson, VC, in his book "Enemy Coast Ahead". The pub never regained the popularity it enjoyed during the war years when the RAF and later the American Air Force were around. It is said that Max Bygraves learnt his trade here during this period.

The pub took its name from St. Leonard who having slain a dragon in Horsham Wood was granted a wish by God to recognize his boldness. His request was for the total silence of the nightingale as its song distracted him from his prayers. Violet Rutter, the artist, depicted his likely request in 1940. It was close to this spot that the Crusader St. Leonard is said to have rested during his flight from a Saracen prison to prevent his wife's second marriage. Whilst he succeeded in his objective he expired the next day from a chill!

The premises were built between the months of January and September 1940 as was its sister pub at Wateringbury the "Duke Without a Head". Designed by the same architect, these two houses, initially, were the same in every respect. The naming ceremony took place on 16th December 1940 with the pub opening a few months before the "Duke". At the time the pub was valued at £4,250. Close by stood the much older "Five Bells" but when this new house opened the "Five Bells" was de-licensed and let. In 1960 it was leased to Mrs. A.A. Baker (see below) at a rent of 8/- per week before the freehold was sold on 25th July 1962 for £1,223/5/-. The house came back on the market in April 2004 but this time the asking price was £385,000! Some timbers in the "Startled Saint", however, are marked "Five Bells" and Kathleen Claxton's jester sign which ultimately hung at the "Merry Boys" was designed for the "Five Bells". Unfortunately the pub only survived until 1993 when Whitbread sold the premises which were then converted into a private residence. Sadly the "Duke" suffered a similar fate and has been demolished!

Collecting Inn Signs became a world-wide hobby and generated much correspondence in overseas papers. A columnist in the Melbourne Sun took up the theme that "Too many Australian pubs are called "Railway" or "Commercial" with Melbourne having numerous houses with repetitive names. Why couldn't they be like the English with their rich variety of names?" He then went on to describe the one that particularly appealed to him – the "Startled Saint". One little oddity here is that I have seen a photograph of a proposed sign for the "Startled Saint" showing in the bottom right-hand corner a hooded and truly startled saint facing a Spitfire diving down towards him from the top left-hand corner. I have never met anyone who can recall this sign hanging so can only assume it was a further design that was rejected by John Marchant.

The former RAF station closed many years ago and has been developed into a prestigious housing and industrial area styled "Kings Hill Park". In late 2001 Shepherd Neame, at a cost of £1.5 million, built a brand new house which now employs 20 people. It was opened by former wartime ace Air Chief Marshall Sir Christopher Foxley-Norris and as part of the celebrations a Spitfire flew over the premises. As this is the only pub to serve this area, a competition was held to decide a suitable name. I suggested resurrecting the "Startled Saint" because of its connections with the old airfield and also the original sign is still available. However, I gather towards the end of its days the pub had acquired a poor reputation and it was felt this memory could linger on and handicap the new venture. The new house has been named the "Spitfire" which I suppose is a pretty good alternative.

Sadly during the war the landlord, Mr. Baker, was killed in action and his wife, Alice, took over the tenancy and carried on for many years. During her time RAF Police dog handlers were frequent visitors and if a dog was retired he was first offered to Alice as a pet. As this is still quite a remote spot a steady stream of ex-police dogs would be quite a comfort.

No 22. The Cricketers, Maidstone
Jude Hanbury, F. Leney, Fremlins, Whitbread

This pub stands on a T-junction close to idyllic Mote Park, one of the homes of Kent County Cricket Club, hence the name. A variety of signs have hung here. Up until 1941 we see a batsman scrambling for the crease, the inn sign miniature then hung until about 1980, and there is now a W.G. Grace character smiting the ball to the boundary.

The property was bought by William Jude, Godfrey Burrel and Ernest Osgood Hanbury of Watering-bury, Brewers, in about 1875 as it appears in a deed of 1877 as:- "The "Cricketers" Beerhouse and house adjoining situate at Mote Road, Maid-stone." The adjoining house was incorporated into the pub in 1929 at a cost of £1,387/0/7. In the Jude Hanbury registers from 1903 - 1922 it is referred to as the "Three Cricketers". A beer and wine licence was acquired in April 1938 and a full licence on 8th March 1949 when the net monopoly value of £1,250 was paid.

In 1900 water was laid on at a cost of £4/16/11 and six years later £13 was spent on new drains. 1910 saw the building of the bottled beer store costing £16/1/- and the following year £1/10/8 was spent on fixing a gas service in the bottle store. In 1871 the landlord was Thomas George Punnett who also carried on the trade of a painter. John W. Calthorpe moved in on 14th September 1938 paying a rent of £40 p.a. with his inventory valued at £135/9/-. The house remained within the Calthorpe family until 8th May 1956. It became a Whitbread-managed house on 16th June 1981 and was sold by Whitbread in 1997. This is a successful two-bar house which in the late 1990's was decorated in the Victorian style. It was one of the last pubs to carry Fremlins Hogshead Mild.

No 23. The Queen's Head, Maidstone
(Closed Circa 1986. Now a Pizza Hut) F. Leney, Fremlins, Whitbread

This comfortable old coaching inn, built in the 16th century, has been reduced to the status of a Pizza Hut and to add insult to injury the great sheep of Maidstone – all four tons of it – at one time was parked outside the former hotel during the summer months!

The premises occupy a prominent position in the High Street and all through the 19th century it was an important coaching inn. Tickets could be purchased at the General Coach Office, housed on the premises, for the oddly named "Balloon" coach to Oxford Street which left the premises daily (except Sundays). Inside 10/-, outside 6/-. Other through-coaches to seaside towns such as Folkestone also stopped at the hotel. As late as 1925 horses were stabled with the carts parked in the middle of the lower High Street.

In June 1929 Jude Hanbury expressed an interest in purchasing the house from Leney's at a price of £9,000 – it was valued in the Leney books at £8,500 the ultimate purchase price. It would appear that Leney were then in the process of purchasing the freehold as they had issued a cheque for £850 representing a 10% deposit on 15th August 1929. Completion took place on 30th September 1929 when the balance monies, £7,650, were paid over. The vendor's agent's costs amounted to £185 and the solicitors' fees came to £83/ 6/ 8. In 1935 the brewers purchased a proportion of the inventory for £320.

In 1848 John Freeman moved here from the "King's Head", Wateringbury and died at the pub. His widow, Mary, then ran the house until about 1855. The splendidly named Blades Pallister was the next landlord, whilst also acting as excise officer, with Henry Martin managing the "Queens Head Commercial Hotel" in 1871. He also owned the "Bell Commercial Hotel", 26 Week Street – long since closed. Henry S. J. Martin moved in on 29th October 1935 and on departing for war service his wife Mrs. R. C. Martin took over on 21st January 1941. As befits a house of this importance the rent was £150 p.a. with the inventory valued at £1,200. The hotel was subject to a war damage claim in 1941.

Functions were held here on a regular basis. One particularly important occasion was the retirement of Mr. M. Relf who had served the brewers for more than forty-five years. He joined the Wateringbury brewery as a clerk in 1909 and both his father and uncle had worked there for many years. On retirement in January 1956, he was Leney's Chief Representative. He was presented with a set of bowls woods from tenants, as well as an inscribed silver coffee set from a large circle of friends. The presentation was made by Mr. G. R. Breeze of the "South Eastern Hotel", Tonbridge.

Despite its importance and High Street position, not a great deal else has come to light. On 24th June 1958 63A High Street was leased to Bennitts for a period of 7 years at an annual rental of £275 with this subsequently increased to 14 years from 1st January 1960 with a rent of £300 for the first seven years and £350 for the remainder of the lease. The other side of the building, 62 High Street, was leased to H. J. Pocock for seven years from 24th June 1958 at £325 p.a. The freehold to both of these shops passed to Fremlins in 1960.

Improvements to the hotel facilities in 1964 cost £3,900. On a change of landlords it would take so long to check the inventory that the area manager would drop a dozen bottles of Mackeson in to encourage the outgoing tenant to provide a good meal. One landlord was married to the ex-wife of Joseph Chamberlain, the radical Birmingham MP.

In its later days the hotel boasted a fine restaurant and was a popular rendezvous for local sportsmen, cricketers in particular. At one time the walls of the four bars were adorned with photographs of cricketing personalities past and present.

It is generally felt that when the pub closed in 1986 we lost a truly regal inn sign designed by Harvey James.

No 24. Hare and Hounds, Maidstone
Jude Hanbury, F. Leney, Fremlins, Whitbread

As the name indicates this old inn once stood in the countryside but even though it has now been swallowed up by the expanding town it is still only a stone's throw from the North Downs.

The house, situated close to Invicta Park Barracks where the Royal Engineers were stationed, hit the national headlines on 25th September 1975 when a soldier noticed a suspicious package near a car parked outside. The police were alerted, the area cleared, but unfortunately two officers were injured in the subsequent explosion, dead on the stroke of 10pm, which could be heard as far away as Bearstead. Very extensive damage was caused to the pub with the interior wrecked. The body of the vehicle was blown over the prison wall opposite but amazingly, as with many pubs destroyed by enemy action, the hanging sign remained unscathed. As to be expected the house was busy, with army personnel the main drinkers. Due to this it was widely assumed that the explosion was the work of the I. R. A., although no formal admission was ever made. The landlord at the time was Mr Wooster who possibly went on to become a prison warder. Roy Cheval, an ex-policeman, took over the rebuilt pub. A previous tenant, Bill Robinson, had taken a photograph of two lags shinning down a rope to make their escape from the prison. When asked what he would have done if they had called in he said "bought them a drink!"

The whole area around Lower Boxley Road has been extensively redeveloped leaving the pub somewhat isolated. However it is a lively place and besides serving good ale, holds barbecues on the back patio and hosts the occasional gig.

Formerly a simple beerhouse, it acquired a beer and wine licence in April 1939 and was granted a full licence on 28th March 1950 when the net monopoly value of £1,000 was paid.

Some repairs were as follows:-

> 1899. Laying on water up to W.C. £ 7/2/6.
>
> 1901. New W.C.'s. £70.
>
> 1911. Paint and grain and write signboards. £5/5/-.

In 1936 the interior was rearranged and the exterior modernised.

No 25. The Black Lion, Mereworth
(Closed and de-licensed 21st January 1957. Now a private house) John B. Jude, Jude Hanbury, F. Leney

This modest little hostelry was one of my favourite haunts. It was erected in about 1750, roughly the same time as the "new" village church was built, and a very fine church it is too. A beer house, it did not acquire a wine licence until 1947. The land tax was redeemed in 1950.

The pub was always immaculate and in the 1950's the mahogany counter gleamed following a good polish using the landlord's own concoction. He was reduced to tears when his handiwork was ripped out to make way for formica furnishings. The "Black Lion" stands very close to the neighbouring property and permission had to be sought from the owners to chisel out of the walls of both properties sufficient brickwork to enable barrels to be brought to the rear of the premises. A schoolgirl drew a lovely picture of the inn sign which the present owners used as a design to create an almost full-sized tapestry of the sign which is used as a fireguard until such time as the fire is lit.

Opposite the house is Black Lion field and it was here that the drovers of old penned the sheep for the night before proceeding on to Maidstone market. They would then retire to either the "Black Lion" or "Torrington Arms" just up the road to slake their thirst and bed down for the night. This house had five bedrooms. Carved into the side brickwork in immaculate lettering is the name "R. Allman – 27th June 1939". Who was he? – a passing drover perhaps or more likely a drayman on one of his regular visits? The present house retains many of the original features. A little replica plaque by the front door tells the visitor that this is Black Lion house and inside one of the doors is numbered 2 and "The Bar" remains engraved in one of the windows. The sign lives on but not at Mereworth. The landlord of the "Red Lion" at Appledore on being shown the inn sign miniature was so impressed with the design that he had it copied to hang at his house.

This was another pub that relied for its survival on hop-pickers with the main street awash with revellers during the season. When this source of income fell away, coupled with the retirement of the tenant, a long hard look was taken at the viability of the inn, particularly if there were more than one in the locality. In this instance it was decreed that the "Black Lion" should close leaving the "Torrington Arms" to serve the village. Messrs E.J. Parker & Sons auctioned the property on behalf of Frederick Leney & Sons Limited at the Royal Star Hotel, Maidstone on Thursday 14th March 1957 at 3p.m. The purchaser was Mr. D. McConnell who paid the princely sum of £1,900. Following closure the village Post Office operated for a while from the premises. The last landlord was Cyril Weekes.

The first records hinting at the premises operating as a beer house date from 1857 when the property was purchased by John Beal Jude. It formed part of his estate at the time of his death on 2th September 1871. The vendor was Thomas Andrews and others and it was described as "All that messuage or tenement with the Wash House and Bakehouse Stable Yard and garden in the occupation of Martha Long Stanford". Martha could well have been the first tenant.

In 1885 G. Burrell, (who was also part owner of the "Cricketers") died and W. Jude and E.O. Hanbury purchased his interest in the "Black Lion Beer House" with carpenters shop, stabling and garden.

Repairs were carried out on a regular basis and included in 1900 a new barrel pump costing £4/14/9 and two years later enlarging the urinal for £6/14/-. In 1905 there were various works including installation of the 20 foot 6 inch super mahogany counter at a cost of £8/7/11. This became the pride and joy of all future tenants. The largest sum spent on repairs was £306/9/3 during 1939.

In September 1924 Jude Hanbury proposed to Messrs. Bushell, Watkins and Smith, brewers at Westerham, that they exchange six of their houses in the Tunbridge Wells area for a similar six in East Kent. Included in the batch selected was the "Black Lion" but the transfer never proceeded. A long-serving landlord was Horace J. Smith who became the licensee on 6th October 1937 paying a rent of just £30 p.a. The inventory amounted to £100/1/-.

No 26. The Torrington Arms, Mereworth
(Closed and de-licensed 1999. Now a private house) F. Leney, Fremlins, Whitbread, The Famous Pub Co.

This house continued to serve Mereworth for a further 42 years before it suffered the same fate as the "Black Lion" – falling trade and high capital expenditure. With large grounds and outbuildings available to be converted the end was inevitable.

The building dates back to the early 1700's and like so many properties in the village was originally owned by the Torrington family who lived at Yotes Court. They leased the premises to the Leney brothers on 26th February 1886 for a 21-year period at a rental of £70 p.a. payable to Viscount Torrington. Following renewal of the lease the brewers entered into negotiations to purchase the freehold and although their first offer was declined, an increased offer of £1,500 was accepted. Standing on a large plot in 1951 loss of development value was paid in the sum of £365 in respect of land to the east side of the pub. On 1st September 1955 a small plot of land adjoining the pub was sold for £168/11/5 to the Kent Police Authority for the purpose of building a police house. Far more land was sold in 1962 for £2,773/0/7. In 1960 Fremlins acquired from Leney some land here which was tenanted by Mr. Veale of Snodland who paid a rent of 10/- per annum.

This was another rustic village local which relied for its income on local agricultural workers and the annual invasion of hop-pickers although it always had a reputation, particularly in the 1960's, for good food. During the hop-picking-era fights amongst both the pickers and locals were frequent and on one occasion one poor fellow was killed. His body was laid out in the pub barn with the inquest subsequently held at the pub. The barn normally provided stabling. In common with most pubs in the area the pickers were served drinks via a bath on the green but the "Torrington Arms" took this one stage further by also selling off the kitchen waste cheaply to the hoppers.

From about 1848 until 1882 the pub was in the capable hands of the Sharman family. The only other landlord of note was C. Fry who took over on 17th January 1927 and was still there in 1945. In 1939 he was paying a rent of £30 for the pub, £10 for the land and £1 for gas. In 1941 substantial repairs were carried out costing £254/3/4.

"Torrington House", a substantial five-bedroomed property but now with little land, was offered for sale in April 2004 at an asking price of £540,000.

No 27. Duke Without A Head, Wateringbury
(Became Mulligans fish bar. This failed and the building was demolished in August 1995 to make way for four "executive" houses) F. Leney, Fremlins, Whitbread

Not so much the Duke Without a Head – more the Duke Without a Pub! This unique name came about when, in 1940, the brewers wished to transfer the licence from an old village pub called the "Dukes Head" to this new, purpose-built, tavern standing some way out of Wateringbury on the Tonbridge Road. The magistrate's order to transfer the licence stated "Permission is given to remove the Duke's Head" – so there we have it.

The re-naming ceremony took place on 16th December 1940. One cannot be too sure how the sign was accepted by strangers – one hop-picker wrote home to say he had drunk at the "Iron Duke with Two Heads". Another suggested explanation is that Buckingham Palace refused a request to allow the Duke of Windsor's likeness to be reproduced on the sign so the artist painted a Duke's head, complete with coronet and his collar, but minus the facial details. Personally I prefer the first explanation.

The modern pub has little history but the former "Dukes Head", which still stands to the rear of the new house in Old Road at Pizien Well, had a rich pedigree. It was an ancient inn which I can trace back to 1803. A long-standing landlord, David Boorman, was behind the bar from 1848 to 1880 and earlier we saw Robert Durrant from 1803 till at least 1816. The old pub together with the former carpenter's shop was acquired by Fremlins in 1960 when they took over all the Leney premises. The carpenter's shop was let to E.J. Gibbs who paid a rent of £5 p.a. In 1933 it had been owned by the Tenterden Brewery Co.

This was the sister pub to the nearby "Startled Saint" but both proved to have a very short trading life although the "Saint" did escape demolition. Both inn signs were designed in 1940 by Violet Rutter. Although popular with hop-pickers and pilots from nearby RAF West Malling the pub was isolated and business poor so it came as no surprise when Whitbread decided to convert the inn to one of their "Mulligans" fish and sea-food chain in about 1990. I am told the fish and chips were excellent but trade was insufficient and, occupying a large site, the temptation to close and demolish was too great. The casual passer-by would have no idea at all that this house had ever existed.

No 28. The North Pole, Wateringbury
Jude Hanbury, F. Leney, Fremlins, Whitbread

This rural inn sitting atop Red Hill overlooking Wateringbury has continued to provide excellent service and food to both locals and visitors alike since it was built in 1826 by Richard Gibbon on land belonging to Matthias Prime Lucas of Wateringbury Place. He erected a modern public house complete with the necessary stabling and coach-houses to attract the traveller. Richard bought the freehold of the land on 4th November 1828. To finance the project he borrowed money but trade failed to match expectations and in 1835 the house was offered for sale "by order of the mortgagees". It was finally sold, in January 1836, to John Beal Jude and later came into the possession of Jude Hanbury & Co.

Many years ago the old "Greyhound Hotel", situated at Hadlow, was demolished and after the stucco facing was removed several old placards were revealed including a poster advertising the sale by auction of the "North Pole Inn".

In 1899 £16/7/11 was spent on rebuilding a wall and in 1903 water was laid on at a cost of £4/3/8. Repairs to part of the stable roof were carried out in 1908 and the following year emptying the cesspool cost 16/-.

In 1951 loss of development monies amounting to £80 were paid in respect of the conversion of the store into two flats. When Fremlins acquired the Leney premises in 1960 the lower flat was let to P.J. Willsher at 7/6 per week and the upper flat was vacant.

The pub was renovated in 1995 and unfortunately lost the much loved "Polar Bear" sign. This was replaced by a hop garden scene containing a "North Pole" – every hop field has one. There are many fine photographs in the bar taken during the Jude Hanbury days, one showing a charabanc full of drinkers setting off to the sea-side. The house has now been divided with the drinking area to the left and restaurant to the right.

In 1846 Thomas Lester, who was also a plumber and later in 1855 a farmer, was the tenant. Fred Cronk, who was inn-keeper from March 1914 until the early 1920's fancied himself as a poet and penned a six-verse poem styled the "North Pole", the first verse of which reads:-

> *"If your wanting a quiet little public*
> *For a rest when you're out for a stroll*
> *At Fred Cronk's there is always a welcome*
> *His place is the famous North Pole."*

I wonder if this is the same Frederick Cronk who was landlord at the "Oak and Ivy" in 1950?

In the 1940's and probably later the West Kent Hunt met here – one of the hunt followers was Mrs. Marchant.

Why was the pub so named? One theory is that it is situated in an area known locally as the "North Pole" and another that opposite the pub stands the gatehouse to a former toll road and the name is a corruption of "North Toll". Neither appears that convincing. The 1871 Kelly Directory states the pub is situated in an area called the Heath.

I was told some little while ago that the Polar Bear was to be re-instated but to date he hasn't put in an appearance.

No 29. The Queen's Head, Wateringbury
(Closed and de-licensed 5th November 1976. Now a private house)
Jude Hanbury, F. Leney, Fremlins, Whitbread

This small friendly inn with its one large bar, a smaller bar and jug and bottle stood little chance of providing a reasonable living with so much local competition. The brewery was based in Wateringbury and there were seven Whitbread pubs in this small village. Due to a succession of good landlords it struggled on until 1976.

Traceable history begins in about 1710 on the death of James Codd who left no children. In accordance with Kentish custom of "Gavelkind" his estate was divided in equal shares between his nephews and nieces who decided to split the estate by dividing it into four and then drawing lots for their own portion. Thomas Kerby, a descendant of James' sister Ann, inherited "All that one messuage or tenement with the barn stables close garden orchard and the piece or parcel of land with the appurtenances ... five acres … in Wateringbury". Eventually the property passed to Thomas Laurence, a shoemaker, in 1849 and within 12 months a new house was built on the site. This is what John Beale Jude bought in 1865 and converted into a pub which he called the "Queen's Head". It remained so until 1976 when it closed and stood empty until sold unlicensed on 10th January 1978. The house remains much as it always was although the outbuildings have been pulled down to make way for a small housing development. In May 1996 an article appeared in The Daily Telegraph which included a photograph of the old pub stating it was for sale at about £150,000.

In March 1921 the butcher's shop was extended and cold storage was built at a cost of £168 and in June 1924 two shops were sold for £240 to Mr Smith. A reference in 1935 refers to two lock-up shops but it is not possible to ascertain if these were now in the possession of Mr. Smith. There was an outbuilding at the rear of the pub which was later converted to a first-floor flat over the garage. This was used as a clubroom and during the Second World War from 1943 – 1945 was requisitioned by the War Department. A further building to the side was demolished in the 1940's and this had housed a barber's shop. A funeral director and taxi business also operated from the office at some time. A well at the rear of the premises supplied water to the Jude Hanbury brewery.

> Repairs carried out give some idea of the versatility of the premises:-
> 30th December 1900. Repair to roof and urinal. £1/5/3.
> 29th September 1906. Repair floor of butcher's shop. £2/2/-.
> 30th June 1907 Matchboarding hairdresser's shop. £4/10/-.
> September 1909 Unstopping drains and clear out well. £3/0/3.

The first recorded landlord is W.W. Barton in 1873. On 18th October 1937 Frederick Bills moved in and he was the longest serving landlord retiring on 4th July 1952. In 1939 his rent was £35 p.a. with the inventory valued at £157. The pub was granted a beer and wine licence in April 1941.

A former Whitbread employee who lived nearby clearly recalls, in very wet weather, the pub cellars flooding resulting in the beer barrels floating up and out of the window and on to the main A26. The "Queen's Head" always had a good darts team. During the Battle of Britain the hop-pickers were reluctant to go into the fields so at times the hops were pulled and taken down to the land surrounding the pub to enable them to be picked in relative safety.

It is now called Nightingale House.

No 30. King's Head, Wateringbury
(Became the Wateringbury Hotel in the late 1970's) F. Leney, Fremlins,
Whitbread who sold it as a going concern in the mid-1990's

Both the old and new "King's Head" were the flagship pub/hotel in the village. The old "King's Head" stood on the village crossroads and was a most interesting building. It dated back to the 18th century and was originally a farm house owned by Thomas Luck. William Croson was the inn keeper in 1754 and William Luck, surely the son of Thomas, in 1803. In a conveyance dated 1823 it is described as the "King's Head" together with certain buildings adjoining used as a schoolroom together with the yards and gardens. From about 1820 the tenant was an old and kindly man affectionately referred to as "Uncle Freeman" by the village children and by 1846 his son John had taken over. He is also described as a saddler and harness maker. In 1848 Robert Harris, who was also the village butcher, succeeded John who moved on to the "Queen's Head" in Maidstone.

Frederick, Charles Frederick and Augustus Leney acquired the property for £3,100 on 27th December 1876 from W. and I. Day who at the same time also sold them the "Harrow". Twenty years later Augustus sold this house plus stables, coach-house and garden to the limited company for £2,750. It had been valued at £2,800 in 1881 and £3,100 in 1890. A book of old photographs shows the "King's Head" under the caption "famous posting house in the days of the Stagecoaches. Every morning the Reliance called at 8.45a.m. and the Tally Ho at 9.30a.m." The pub's most famous customer arrived by coach. Queen Victoria was travelling from London to the coast and decided to stop at Wateringbury to enjoy a meal. Naturally, being the finest hostelry in the village, the "King's Head" was the choice. In the 1930's, under the stewardship of W.E. Bennett, a large advertisement offered luncheons, dinners and teas. Road widening swept away the old posting house which closed on 17th February 1938. On 8th March 1938 the doomed pub and frontage to Harris meadow was sold to Kent County Council for £2,500 and the following month the plot of land adjoining was sold to the Council for £50. Most of the outbuildings were left, one being used as a rifle range for a number of years. Leney's owned land to the east of the site fronting the Tonbridge Road and the new hotel opened on 18th February 1938. The architects were Seymer, Orman & Adie whose fees amounted to £136/15/1.

The new building retained the same name but in the 1970's a hotel annex was built and it was then re-named the "Wateringbury Hotel". It remained with Whitbread until the mid-1990's when it was sold as a going concern to another hotel chain.

Bernard H.J. Covington moved up the hill from the "Railway" in 1951 remaining until 1963. He smoked like a trooper and there were anything between 10 and 15 ashtrays spread along the bar all containing a smouldering cigarette-end. A man with forthright views he would always emphasize a point with the comment "Never with a naked finger". He is still remembered with affection by the older residents.

Numerous brewery and village functions were held here including a dinner in 1923 to celebrate Richard Tapply's fifty years service with Frederick Leney. He joined the firm in 1873 and rose to become joint managing director. It is believed that one of the Leney daughters had married his father. John Marchant retired in October 1958 and a presentation dinner was held here in his honour. Having achieved such a great deal during his tenure at Leney's he would now have time to pursue his other interests namely field sports and amateur dramatics.

"Princes are like to heavenly bodies which have much veneration, but no rest." Bacon.

No 31. The Phoenix, Wateringbury
(Closed and de-licensed 21st January 1957. Now a private house) F. Leney

Another of my favourites but again, situated half way up Red Hill, totally unable to provide a sufficient income for a landlord. This was one of the first casualties. A Tonbridge exile, Geoff Hayman, who now corresponds from Lytham St. Annes, remembers the "Phoenix" with affection. He was a member of a local cycling club who rested here on the return journey to Tonbridge and to their delight found the first round of drinks was on the house as it was the last day of business.

This fine old weather-boarded building dates back to the late 1600's. It was never more than a beer house for most of its life and had no bar as such, the beer being served from barrels in the kitchen. However, in 1947 a wine licence was granted. Those few weeks when the hop-pickers arrived were its hey day although they were not allowed into the "bar", as the locals refused to drink with them, but were served in a separate area which had a brick floor. At the turn of the century one landlord eked out his living from the pub by operating a carter's business.

The inn obviously takes its name from the nearby Phoenix Brewery which operated at Wateringbury from 1843 until brewing ceased in 1982. Shortly afterwards the brewery building was demolished. The pub was affectionately referred to as the tap room for the brewery.

On 10th May 1886 Augustus Leney purchased these premises plus six cottages for £2,000 from I.S. Vickers. In the late 1800's this was a substantial property with reference made to:- "The "Phoenix" beerhouse and six cottages, stables, oast house and land comprising 2acres, 1rod, 7perch in parishes of Teston and Wateringbury". The whole had been valued in 1881 at £2,037/19/6. About this time the brewers were renting the property and land from James Freeman at a rent of £90 p.a. payable half-yearly in March and September. The houses and land adjoined Pelican and Orpines farm.

In 1939 the landlord, George Hodges, was paying an annual rent of £20 for the beer house, £8 for the land and £1 for electric light. He must have known every nook and cranny in the house and every blade of grass in the fields as he arrived at the "Phoenix" on 19th August 1912 and remained until at least 1945.

I am told the last tenant moved on to the "Queen's Head" and then the "Duke Without a Head" both of which ultimately closed. He must have been jinxed! When de-licensed and sold the property fetched £1,200 and at the same time two acres of orchard land adjoining were sold for £400.

No 32. The Harrow, Wateringbury

(Closed and de-licensed in 1968. Now a private house) Brenchley & Co., F. Leney, Fremlins

Until the "new A26" road from Wateringbury to Tonbridge was built this rustic inn stood on the former main road. This is now a quiet backwater but the "Harrow", closed 36 years ago, is still easily identifiable.

The property was built in the late 1600's with the roof space still basically a tangle of old wooden struts. It was never much more than an ale house although it was granted a wine licence in 1947 and eleven years later a full licence. Its main source of trade, apart from a few travellers, were the local agricultural workers. Opposite the pub, where a house now stands, was an earth bank where farm labourers used to sit in the sun and enjoy a pint. When the area was excavated numerous old clay pipes were found – a reminder of those carefree days. Very popular with hop-pickers, a local resident can recall them falling out of the pub late at night and then singing at the tops of their voices as they wended their way through the surrounding orchards on their return to the camps as they were afraid of the dark! On either side are some old cottages

with the present property little changed from 50 years ago except that the bar entrance that abutted the road has been filled in.

In 1870 the "Harrow" was leased for 21 years to Brenchley & Co. of Maidstone, brewers, but on 30th December 1876 the Leney brothers bought the freehold for £1,150 from W. and I. Day and others. It was described as "A Beerhouse called the "Harrow" with a fishmonger's shop and three cottages adjoining…". Augustus Leney, on 25th March 1896, sold the inn and three cottages to the limited company for £1,580. From 1881 until 1908 the value of the house and cottages was quoted at £1,150 and a nominal rent was paid weekly.

H. Baker moved in at a cost of £146/15/9 on 20th June 1938 paying a rent of £25 and the following year repairs costing £96/0/8 were carried out. A fine photograph exists, taken in 1954, showing the tenants Mr. and Mrs. Martin calling "time". A letter had been published in the Daily Mirror asking why publicans throw a towel over the beerpumps when time is called. Mrs. Martin was able to explain that "it is a survival" of the general custom of "putting the bar up" at closing time. This was done in the old days by dropping a brass or iron bar into sockets on each side of the pumps, the bar being padlocked into place on the serving side. The pumps could then no longer be pulled. This is now done by suggestion – by placing a towel over the pumps. Older readers will know what I am talking about.

Following closure the freehold was sold on 16th January 1969 for £1,961. The property is still called the "Harrow". When the "Chestnut Tree" at nearby Congelow closed on 25th November 1957 the licence was transferred here.

No 33. The Telegraph, Wateringbury
(Closed and de-licensed circa 1975. The pub was demolished about 1989 and old peoples' homes built on the site) Jude Hanbury, F. Leney, Fremlins, Whitbread

This handsome inn stood virtually opposite the old Leney Phoenix brewery and just a few hundred yards further down the hill one will find the "Railway". The "Telegraph" became the "Tap Room" to the brewery and every Thursday, Bert Pickett, the Leney cashier, would do the wages then go straight over to the "Telegraph" for a pint.

The pub probably opened in 1870 and by 1900 is described as the "Telegraph", two cottages and a coal wharf. In October 1903 Jude Hanbury built a new bar on the south side of the house and added the ornate concrete structure at a cost of £350. Also the attached grocer's shop was re-roofed at a cost of £38/13/9 and extra work on ventilators in the parlour and draining the old well cost £7/6/7. In 1913 the exterior of the pub, cottages, coal pen and forge were painted for £73/10/-. The two cottages and coal pen were sold in July 1924 to Mr. Honey for £475. From 28th May 1951 until closure the brewers paid W.A. Green 3/- a week to rent a garage.

For many years the pub was in the capable hands of the Adams family. T.J. Adams signed a tenancy agreement on 7th February 1927 to be succeeded by W.A. Adams on 1st February 1937. He retired on 16th August 1947. On taking over his inventory amounted to £102/3/- plus rent of £40 p.a. The house was granted a beer and wine licence in April 1940. Gus Adams is still remembered in the village as a very affable landlord and capable saddler. At one time there was a coach-house with stables at the rear but these were ultimately converted into garages for cars. An entry in the brewer's books for 1916 states "Horse purchased £19/3/-". Following the departure of Gus there was a succession of landlords but in an over-pubbed area a living could not be made and the house closed in about 1975. It stood empty for a long while, was vandalized, and became a danger to the public. The premises were finally demolished at the end of the 1980s to provide access to a modern old peoples' home. During the war a bomb dropped close to the pub causing some damage which ironically was repaired by Italian prisoners of war.

No 34. The Railway Hotel, Nettlestead
(Originally *The Kent Arms* until circa 1875) Brenchley, F. Leney, Fremlins, Whitbread

This thriving pub was purpose-built for John and Alexander Coare Brenchley, forerunners of the firm Isherwood, Foster and Stacey. They purchased the land in 1847 and by 1851 the public house had been erected. It was then sold together with hop and fruit land to the three Leney brothers. At the time there was an outstanding mortage of £1,000 with Martha George of Bishops Stortford which was redeemed on 4th February 1859. It is thought that the name was changed to the "Railway" in about 1875 as the Tonbridge to Maidstone railway line ran close by. However, the first passenger train stopped at Wateringbury on 25th September 1844 and to celebrate, the paying customers were accompanied to Maidstone by the band of the Lancers. The house still contains, besides some very interesting characters, a fine array of railway memorabilia. It continues to attract coach parties, cater for village functions, and on 9th June 1951 Wateringbury Brewery Sports Club held their second annual dinner here. The rear of the premises was used for these functions and at one time also acted as the village morgue. During 1932 the clubroom was requisitioned by the military. Popular with hop-pickers, the pub had a flap window through which the hoppers could pass their jugs.

The house is low-lying and with a culvert running to the side was prone to flooding, the latest two occasions being in 1968 and 1974. As a precaution there is a non-return valve in the cellar and, during the last flood in 1974, a workman carrying out some alterations volunteered to dive in the depths of the cellar when it was nearly submerged to ensure that the valve was switched on to make the property safe. Ultimately the cellar was rebuilt upstairs.

This is a sizeable house and in 1951 a loss of development value claim was settled at £35 in respect of the conversion of stables and a cottage. Land adjoining the pub was sold in 1960 for £799/10/-.

In 2003 the leasehold interest was offered for sale at a price of £55,000 "all at" plus stock at valuation. The rent was £25,000 p.a.

No 35. *The Hop Pole, Nettlestead*
F. Leney, Fremlins, Whitbread, Free House

The original quite small building dates back to the 18th century and at one time was occupied by the churchwardens and overseers of the poor. At the time it was converted to a pub the property was owned by R.F. Spicer who died in 1873. The premises were then sold for £950 to the Leney brothers on 28th May 1874 by L. Sheperd being described as "… All that cottage or tenement then converted into a public house and called the "Hop Pole" … occupation … afterwards of Mr. Noble then of Jane Pointer and then of Richard Sears and then of F., C.F. and A. Leney…". On transfer to the limited company in 1896 the pub also comprised a stable, out-houses and two rods of land. In December 1916 the brewers agreed to pay the landlord the sum of £20 as their contribution in respect of the pub's shrinkage in trade, probably due to the war.

The original building has been extended, the property is in good order, and one invariably sees most attractive flower boxes. The menu is interesting and the food well cooked. There is a good display of prints, brass, and copper. As the name implies at one time it was surrounded by hop gardens but these have given way to orchards. One can find the pub a mile or so down the road from the "Railway".

During the 1950's there was constant trouble with blocked drains which were shared with another property on the other side of the road. This pleasant inn has come close to closure several times. One narrow escape was in the early 1960's when there was a problem with landlords and it was decided to close the place. To create as bad an impression as possible brewery employees did their best to vandalize the premises but the arrival of a new enterprising landlord persuaded the brewery that the pub was viable and it was reprieved. The damage done had to be repaired! The last landlord to serve under the Whitbread colours was also a milkman. The house had two small bars and as part of the re-organization after the amalgamation of Fremlins with Whitbread the pub was closed on 28th January 1975 and sold with licence on 21st April 1975.

To the rear of the premises stands a memorial to one of our brave RAF war-time pilots. On 25th June 1944 flying RM 617 an Australian pilot, Warrant Officer Blumer, accompanied by Lieutenant H.F. de Bordar (Free French) left West Malling at 22.30. At 23. 05 the Lieutenant destroyed an enemy plane near Tenterden and turned for home. With fuel running low they re-fuelled at Advanced Landing Ground at Staplehurst. They then took off for the short trip home but for some inexplicable reason the plane plunged into the ground just behind the "Hop Pole" killing Warrant Officer Blumer. In 1992 keen aviation archaeologists discovered the plane buried in the clay and were able to recover most of the aircraft together with the pilot's personal belongings. Fifty years later to the day a memorial in the form of a cross was erected at the exact spot of the accident.

In 2001 the pub changed hands for £450,000. In 2002 a new twenty-year lease was advertised at a nil premium but a rent of £50,000 per annum.

No 36. The Woolpack, Benover, Yalding
Jude Hanbury, F. Leney, Fremlins, Whitbread, Shepherd Neame

This delightful house was the subject of a very fine painting by Stanhope Forbes R.A. who, in 1937, selected it as a typical English Inn to paint in oils. He did, however, omit the petrol pump on the pub car park which was removed at the outbreak of the Second World War. The picture was exhibited at the Royal Academy in 1938. The pub's reputation thus spread far and wide. The appearance of the house has changed not a jot since except the road and forecourt are now tarmacadamed. The property was modernized in the early 1980's but the tile-hung exterior remains timeless. A portion of a film titled "Dartmoor" was shot within the panelled and beamed bar and the cast of "extras" appearing in the film were local people, one of whom also featured in Stanhope Forbes' painting.

The house dates back to the mid-1600's and was originally a timber-framed property with the interior heavily beamed, probably of old ships' timbers. Situated on one of the routes up from the marsh, stories of smuggling abound. Up until the 1850's a wool fair was held on the green outside the pub with this type of event attracting numerous undesirables. The local wool staplers of the Weald would have brought their fare up to the pub by pack-horse where it would be stored in the premises with dealings transacted in the bar. In 1887 the splendidly-named Caleb Unicume was the landlord and by 1895 his widow, Kate, had taken over. They had at least two children including Harry and Fred. A note in the school register dated 12th August 1895 stated that the school discovered that Harry was stealing money from his mother's till and this was shared out with his brother Fred and two school chums. The schoolmaster recognized the position and informed the mother and as punishment it was decided to "put all four boys into Coventry". Despite this youthful indiscretion his mother was to have good reason to be proud of Harry, as during the Great War he made the ultimate sacrifice. If one makes a brief detour to the village church one will find inscribed on the war memorial therein the name Rifleman H.C. Unicume.

Some repairs carried out included:-

> *1899. Repairing pump down well. £ 3/19/0.*
> *1902. Four chimney pots and repairs to roof. £18/18/3.*
> *1902. Water supply public house and cottage. £ 8/10/8.*

Somewhat isolated the pub, together with its near neighbour the "Chestnut Tree", would, in the season, attract countless hoppers who would sing and dance the night away. This pub used a galvanized bath from which to serve the beer. The local hunt also set off from here. Built on the notorious Yalding flood plain, calamities happened on a fairly regular basis. During the dreadful autumn of 2001 trade was 60% down but one intrepid drinker arrived in his wet suit. He was not recognized – it was assumed he was working nearby!

As to be expected there are many "Woolpack" inns in Kent. The name relates to the Wool Staple, one of the first forms of commodity taxation. A woolpack is a large bail of wool weighing 240lb and is the badge of the Worshipful Company of Woolmen. To encourage the development of the woollen industry Parliament passed an act in 1666 ordering "Buryings shall in future be only in woollen".

Nos 37. and 38. The Two Brewers, Yalding
(Closed in 1997) H.T. Wickham & Co., F. Leney, Fremlins, Whitbread, Free House

The property dates back to the mid-1800's and over time the small cottage next door was incorporated into the pub premises. In days gone by this was a hive of activity, as besides the pub, owned by H.T. Wickham & Co., their brewery was located to the rear of the premises. This edifice has now virtually disappeared. The "Two Brewers" passed to Leney when they and Jude Hanbury acquired the Yalding brewery in 1921. In May 1924 Jude made a tentative enquiry about buying out Leney's share of

the brewery and also taking over the "Two Brewers" but this proposition was never pursued. On 8th June 1930 the brewers purchased the manorial rights for £9/18/9. Leney paid £46 in April 1938 as a part purchase of the inventory.

If one buys a drink in the "Oak and Ivy" one will find the framed plans, drawn up in July 1954, for proposed alterations for Frederick Leney & Sons Limited to the two bars and parlour here. The main objective was to improve facilities by doing away with the outside toilets. Just as well as this pub was, and still is, regularly flooded.

The Two Brewers represented on the inn sign miniatures are Samuel Whitbread Senior and his son – replicating portraits painted by Reynolds and Opie. This could be so, but in 1921 the Wickham Brewery was purchased jointly by Jude Hanbury and Frederick Leney & Sons Limited – could these companies not be the "Two Brewers"? More likely, but the strongest possibility is the two Wickham brothers. There is also an obscure reference to "two brewers named Twiffin". On 29th January 1641 Mrs. Julian Kenwood together with Thomas and John Twiffin, brewers of Kingston, Surrey, gave a small tenement lying in Yalding to the parish. The annual rent was £10, and £5 of this sum was to be spent educating five poor boys to read and write at the school in Benover whilst the other £5 was to be distributed to the poor. The Twiffins appear to have the best claim.

In 1846 the landlord was William Tubb, and in 1871 we find John Baker behind the bar. He supplemented his takings by his hair-cutting activities. John Baldwin took over in 1874 and he operated as a coal merchant and a cooper. However the most famous occupant is David Sadler. His father, Bert, was a popular landlord and traded here for many years. During this period the place would be heaving with hoppers during the season. They used the public bar, the regulars the saloon. One riotous night, a regular, returning from the gents, dashed into the bar to tell Bert that the pub piano was being loaded onto a lorry to be transported to the hop gardens! David had a meteoric climb to fame. A talented footballer, his career blossomed as follows:- Yalding, Maidstone United (in 1961 whilst still attending Maidstone Technical School), England Amateurs, Manchester United and then England. He was also a talented cricketer – a demon fast bowler. He used to serve in the bar in his spare time.

At times this could be a rowdy house that attracted travellers who, on occasion, could cause trouble. On 30th September 1989 a vicious fight took place involving thirty people. One witness described seeing seven or eight men take it in turns to beat up a young man who had slighted them. The pub was closed down after this riot, re-opening on 16th February 1990.

The house closed for good in 1997 and has been converted into a private residence.

No 39. The Chestnut Tree, Congelow, Yalding
(Closed and de-licensed 25th November 1957. Now a private house) H.T. Wickham & Co., F. Leney

This quaint little inn was small, very small. Sandwiched between the numerous pubs in Yalding and the much larger "Woolpack" at Benover it relied totally for its trade on the local agricultural workers and the hop-picking season.

The building is listed and at least part of it dates back 400 years. From the old portion that remains it is thought likely that originally it was quite a large property that fronted the road. Not much is known about its initial history but it probably became an alehouse in the late 1800's. Drinkers would go straight through the front door into the only bar. No stock of wines and spirits is included in change statements, although in 1948 it did acquire a wine licence. On 1st July 1925 Leney's completed the purchase of the ground rent and reversion for £950. In November of the following year S. and H. Tully purchased the forge adjoining for £15, and in June 1927 the two cottages adjoining the pub were sold to E.T. Edwards for £100.

During the hop-picking season the house was also known as "The Hole in the Wall" – a name that stuck. The pickers were not allowed in – it couldn't have accommodated many anyway – but the hatch in the wall acted as a servery for the thirsty workers.

The old tree that stood in the front has long gone. But what specimen was it? Rumour has it that the "Chestnut Tree" and the "Walnut Tree," another Yalding pub, had their trees planted at the same time. Unfortunately, however, the trees got muddled up and the "Chestnut Tree" ended up with the Walnut Tree and the "Walnut Tree" the Chestnut Tree!

Members of the Caselton family were landlords here for a long while. Tom moved in on 29th July 1935 and paid a rent of just £16 p.a. – his inventory was valued at £35/1/-. Jack took over on 28th July 1947 and he handed over, in August 1953, to Henry Pearce, the last landlord. The pub closed on 25th November 1957 and was sold on 11th April 1958, for £970, to K.A. Westgate. The licence was transferred to the "Harrow". When I called in 1994 the house was empty and the garden over-grown. However, the new owners have expended much love and care in creating a quite splendid home – fortunately named "Chestnut Tree".

No 40. The Harp, Hale Street, East Peckham
Jude Hanbury, F. Leney, Fremlins, Whitbread, London Inns

Up until at least 1938 this was no more than a beer house.

Dating back to 1817, the first reference that I have come across was in 1875. In its early days it was quite a place, as, in 1896, there was also a coach-house, stabling, assembly rooms and premises.

Low ceilings, a fine array of old china, mugs, cups and records adorn the bars and the first series of Inn Signs were attached to the bar woodwork. An attractive garden and good quality food made this a popular pub with both locals and visitors. It was a two-bar house providing the usual games of darts, cribbage and dominoes. At one time there were two cottages to the side but these

have been demolished to make way for a car park. Prior to this parking on the busy road was dangerous and the local police would move customers on.

The following maintenance was carried out:-

1899. New drainage and general inside repairs. £19/4/ -.

1910. Open and clean out well. £ 13/1/-.

1919. 42inch Larbert range with boiler and open and close fire and fixing. £11/4/ 9.

Bertram Forster was the landlord in 1935 and he stayed until 1942 paying a rent of £20 with his inventory valued at £57/6/-. These figures give one a good idea of how little trade there was even in those days. There was then a rapid turnover in landlords and on 11th July 1960 John Waghorn came to the "Harp". Both he and his wife Kate were extremely popular. By day he worked as a shunter with British Rail based at Paddock Wood with Kate running the pub during his absence. Job-sharing was very common as few village pubs produced an income sufficient to feed and clothe a family. During the 1950's Charlie Brooks was in residence combining this occupation with that of bailiff on the nearby hop farm.

If legend is to be believed this must be the most haunted pub in the land. Kate Waghorn died in the bar and it is said that she still pays her much-loved house the occasional visit. A young girl of about twelve playing with a doll's house is also a visitor. A lady wearing a black riding habit appears annually standing at the top of the stairs. One may also see a fellow who arrives and sits at a table by the front door – this chap is thought to be an ex-landlord. In order to see any of these apparitions it is advisable to get along sharply as unfortunately, like so many wayside inns, trade has dwindled and I feel the pub's days are numbered. It did close for a short period from 1988 to 1990.

In 2001 there was a proposal to convert the inn to a private house but it was acquired by London Inns who shortly afterwards offered a new twenty-year lease at an annual rent of £27,000. Let us hope it is successful.

"'Tis believed that this harp which I now wake for thee,
Was a siren of old who sang under the sea." Moore.

No 41. The Merry Boys, East Peckham
*(Formerly the **Mitre**) Jude Hanbury as the Mitre, F. Leney, Fremlins, Whitbread, Free House*

The present building dates back to 1850 and originally traded as the "Mitre". The original "Three Merry Boys / Merry Boys" was situated at nearby Snoll Hatch. This was an old pub with Elizabeth Willard the landlady in 1754. By 1867 the "Three" had disappeared and we were left with the "Merry Boys". In 1871 William Hayes was the landlord and he is also described as a coal and coke merchant. The inn offered "good beds and accommodation" with "stall stabling". The first sign was either three cricketers with their arms linked or a soldier, sailor, and cricketer standing in a similar fashion. The pub closed on 21st April 1934 with the licence transferred to the "Spotted Cow" at Larkfield. However the villagers liked the old name and on 1st January 1936 the "Mitre" was re-named. The old building is still called Merry Boys cottage.

Whilst trading as the "Mitre" new water closets and sanitary work costing £93/3/9 were installed in 1905 and ten years later there were various repairs to the coach-house and stables. There must have been bad weather in 1916 as repairs to the roof damaged by wind amounted to 9/6 in March and 9/10 in April.

The present building is solid with foundations built of Kentish Ragstone but, during the great gale of November 6-7th 1952, this did not prevent a large chimney stack from toppling and crashing through the roof into the bedroom below. The sleeping occupant was fortunate as the stout iron frame of his bedstead saved him from serious injury. There is an interesting and good-sized cellar. It is possible that the inn was originally built as a coaching house or that it was the residence adjacent to such a property. Certainly the building to the rear has a horse-tethering ring. One has to climb a flight of five steps to enter the one large bar. Fortunately there is a handrail, fitted in 1899 at a cost of 16/10. At one time the pound, a fenced enclosure where stray animals were held until such time as the owner paid for their release, was opposite.

As with so many pubs in this area it was extremely popular with hop-pickers. I was waylaid for a good thirty minutes in the "South Eastern" at Tonbridge by a happy old crone reminiscing about her experiences here during this period. It certainly sounded exciting and was definitely not politically correct!

A nice little story relating to the pub refers to one "Dusty" Miller – a regular for many years he was an ex-merchant seaman living in a hut on a farm nearby. He fell ill and finished up in a sanatorium at Robertsbridge. One day, whilst watching a cricket match, a fellow patient made a crayon portrait of the old man who was so pleased with it that he sent it to his friends at the "Merry Boys" "so that he might be with 'em although he couldn't be there".

The old sign showing the jester, with a few embellishments, hung until 1995 but the landlord never liked it so it was replaced with a perfectly ordinary sign with the name in letters. A pity. The jester sign was designed by Kathleen Claxton and was originally intended for the former "Five Bells" at West Malling.

It became a freehouse in about 1991. Towards the end of 2001 a planning application was submitted to convert the pub into apartments but this was not pursued.

No 42. The Chequers, Five Oak Green *(rather than Tudeley as on the miniature)*
(Closed in 1965) F. Leney, Fremlins, Whitbread

It is only with difficulty that I managed to trace this house as the inn closed years ago and for about five years the property remained empty. A lively place in its time it has almost faded from most peoples' memories.

Esther Hilder was the landlady in 1754. She was succeeded in 1760 by John Catt who remained until 1803. A member of the Catt family was still in residence in 1867. This is an unusual surname and very localized, as a glance at the telephone directory will reveal several Catts still living in the village of East Peckham. Also a family named Catt lived for many years close to a bend in the road just outside Tudeley – this is now called Catts Corner.

In 1916 the tenant applied for a reduction in his rent but unlike the generous treatment given to the landlord at the "Hop Pole", Nettlestead, he was called in to discuss his request. By 1920 the innkeeper was a Mr. Nelson who also worked as a policeman – an unusual combination! Electric light was installed on 5th February 1929 and this plus other maintainance cost £263/1/6. After the war, circa 1948, the landlady was a Mrs. Dimmock who then handed over to her husband, a military man, R.S.M. Dimmock. The R.S.M. was of quite small stature whilst his wife was a formidable lady with plenty of talent. They had a piano in the pub and later screwed to it, rather like a 1950's mincer, an organ keyboard. Mrs Dimmock would play the bass notes on the piano with the remainder of the melody played on the organ. I am told that the patrons enjoyed many a jolly evening. Other landlords had naval connections.

The obvious question for such an isolated pub is where did the customers come from? A succession of first-class landlords created a warm and welcoming atmosphere. A favoured walk for East Peckham courting couples was to stroll along the banks of the Medway or the quiet country lanes for a romantic drink here. Also the river, which was navigable up to East Peckham, was another source of income with bargemen mooring up outside. During the war years it was very popular with servicemen based in the area particularly the Americans billeted at Paddock Wood and men of the Queen Victoria Rifles who were actually based on the Whitbread hop farm. Sadly few of these brave men returned from France.

This pub was one of the closest to the Whitbread hop gardens so one can just imagine the scenes during those heady early autumn days. The pickers would arrive from the East End, Millwall and the Isle of Dogs, and those rather more upmarket pickers from the Farnborough and Orpington areas would arrive by horse and cart. Unusually the hoppers were allowed into the public bar, but because of the crowds and the difficulty in serving them, an old tin bath would be lugged out onto the green by two heavies and filled with beer. One would collect the money whilst the other filled the glasses. The customary one shilling deposit per glass would also be taken. During this period, and this period only, the locals could use the saloon bar at no extra cost but if they used it at the end of the season the price of a pint rose by 2d. To add to the general confusion, gypsies and tinkers would park their caravans on the small green opposite the pub, take their fill, trade horses, go fruit picking, remove any items they thought had been abandoned, and generally added to the mayhem. As if this weren't enough the entrepreneurial locals would also use the green to set up stalls from which to trade lace and other knick-knacks. A local can vividly remember this going on whilst he was selling El Dorado ice cream (remember it in blue cartons?). A regular at the pub can recall thirty years later, whilst visiting the nearby Whitbread Museum, finding, tucked away in a corner, a photograph of his father and other local men digging a very large trench in which the hoppers would take shelter from Hitler's bombers. The bines were arranged to block the pilot's view. Whilst all this activity was going on the landlord, Sydney West, was employed, during the summer and hop-picking season only, on the Whitbread hop farm. His duties were to act as a painter, assistant carpenter and hop measurer for the then princely sum of 36/6 a week. At the outbreak of war he volunteered his services and went off to fight. His wife Mrs. Q.E.P. West took over on 5th December 1939 paying a rent of £35 p.a. This caused a certain amount of upheaval for Sydney's father, who lived in Tonbridge, as he had to make arrangements to stay every night at the "Chequers" as, during the war years, a landlady could not be left alone at night. He would return home in the morning. Fortunately Sydney survived the war and returned to the village to manage his pub.

The original pub, dating back to the 1700's, was a fine weather-boarded high-pitch roofed house with an Oast to the side. These buildings were demolished in the late 1800's to be replaced by a very substantial property that included a coach-house and stables. On the left-hand side was a small extension, now demolished, which was the hamlet sweet shop. The property was surrounded by cherry orchards. In 1896 when Augustus Leney transferred his estate to the limited company the property was described as the "Chequers" plus ten acres of hop, fruit and meadow and small ash plantation. C. Leney had purchased the inn on 12th July 1873 from Thomas Selby and others, paying £1,855. The house had a public and saloon bar. The public bar was L-shaped and for private functions, such as a wedding, the long part of the L could be closed off using a sliding door, but it still contained a bar. The River Medway was something of a mixed blessing as, before the war, it would frequently flood during the winter months with the waters rising to engulf the second of the three steps one had to climb to enter the pub. If local lads were caught misbehaving a favourite punishment was to pump out the flooded cellars.

The "Chequer's" popularity spread far and wide and coach parties would leave towns such as Dover for a tour of the Kent countryside stopping here for liquid refreshment. Out of season it was supported by locals and agricultural workers. However, by the mid-1960's, trade was on the wane. Although Whitbread had modernized the place and given it a new sign, later landlords were no match for their predecessors. To boost trade they encouraged all kinds of undesirables to drink here, which upset the locals. Towards the end patrons would be so drunk that they would flop out on the grass in front of the pub. There was one spin-off from this as years later a fellow with a metal detector found numerous coins including old silver three-penny bits which had spilled out of the revellers' pockets. Following repeated troubles the brewers decided to close this fine old inn in 1965.

The place remained empty for a while before being purchased for £19,000 by Alf Roberts. He in turn sold it, plus three acres, in March 1975 to the present owners for £33,000. Whilst they were carrying out renovation work on one of the chimneys they found it stuffed with old Players Weights cigarette packets. John, the owner, could recall when he was a lad Weights stood for "When England invaded Germany Hitler's troops surrendered". It now trades as the "Chequers" bed and breakfast establishment.

No 43. John Brunt VC, Paddock Wood

*(Formerly the **Kent Arms** until 1947. Re-named the **Hopping Hooden Horse** in 1997)*
Jude Hanbury, F. Leney, Fremlins, Whitbread, Hooden Horse Inns

This was one of a large number of pubs sold by Augustus Leney on 25th March 1896 to the limited company. The sale price, £3,250, included coach-house, stabling and hop and fruit land.

This late nineteenth-century inn which stands close by the town railway station was renamed the John Brunt VC on 9th December 1947 to celebrate and honour the name of one of the town's heroes. John's mother and father Tommy, manager of the local Smedleys canning factory, attended the renaming ceremony.

John Henry Courd Brunt was born in Shropshire on 6th December 1922 but spent most of his teenage years at Paddock Wood. A brilliant athlete, he shone at rugby winning his colours at Ellesmere College, and he was also good at swimming, football, cricket and boxing. He was at college until 1941 when he had already volunteered for the Army. In October 1941 he was called up and trained with the Queens Own Royal West Kent Regiment. Commissioned to the Sherwood Foresters on 1st January 1943, he was posted to Tunisia as part of the 1st Army and whilst serving there was wounded three times. He moved on to Italy where he won the MC for his exploits when leading patrols in the vicinity of the River Peccia. The river became known as Brunt's Brook because of the number of times that he crossed it in pursuit of the enemy. He was then attached to the Lincolnshire Regiment and at the tender age of twenty-two went on to win his VC. He was serving as a Captain at Faenza in Italy on 9th December 1944 when he repelled an attack by German Panzers killing sixteen enemy soldiers with a Bren gun. When he ran out of ammunition he fired at the enemy with a rocket launcher and a two-inch mortar. He thus successfully held up the enemy attack and allowed his platoon to retake their position and rescue injured comrades. The very next day Private Chapman, who was wireless operator for Captain Brunt during the whole action, said that during a lull in the fighting they had a few hours sleep and he was cooking breakfast for them – this was the first food they would have had for 48 hours. A shell came over; the only one fired that day, and killed Captain Brunt who Private Chapman described as the best officer, civilian and gentleman in the battalion. His father revealed that he had 87 notches on the butt of his tommy gun. A memorial was erected in Faenza War Cemetery and at the soldiers' chapel of St. George in Lincoln Cathedral. Whitbread and the local population felt it right to honour his memory by the renaming of the old "Kent Arms".

Right from the start this inn played an active part in town life. A large building housed the bars with the rear rooms available to hold local events. The goings-on were endless. The pub acted as the headquarters for the local football, cricket and bowls clubs and was also the meeting place for the Ancient

Order of Foresters. The local amateur dramatic society was also based here. In the 1880's the landlord could also obtain the use of the cricket field opposite the house and behind the pub was the town bowling-green. Bean feasts were catered for and even in those far-off days it boasted excellent catering facilities. Horses and carriages could be hired or let and good stabling was available. The pub also acted as a posting house. All in all quite a busy place, but I just wonder why the locals referred to it as the "Rats Castle"!

Back in 1884 the best Strong Ale XXXS was provided for family functions at 68/- per barrel 31/6 per Kilderkin 15/9 per Firkin and 1/9 per gallon!

From the 1870's to the turn of the century and probably for a while after that, the house was in the hands of the Bowles family. Henry was here from at least 1874 to be followed in 1899 by S.J. Bowles. In July 1923 Jude Hanbury raised a mortgage of £2,000 over the property with Tom and Charlie Blest; this was transferred to G.V. Miskin in January 1925 and was subsequently redeemed by Leney in October 1956.

During 1904 the signpost was painted at a cost of 12/6 and in 1907 the drainage throughout the property was reconstructed costing £94/15/6. In 1936 £23/10/- was spent installing beer-piping, a bath and a geyser with this sum subsequently recovered from the tenant. The brewers purchased the outside inventory in 1938 for £160.

The function rooms fell into disrepair and were ultimately demolished. In 1950 the brewers sold to Tonbridge Rural District Council 3.7 acres of land adjoining the pub for £475.

One can only imagine the uproar locally when the pub was re-named the "Hopping Hooden Horse" in 1997. Articles appeared in the national press with a very emotive story in The Sunday Telegraph. Apparently Whitbread felt the house was attracting the wrong kind of clientele so they sold the pub to the Hooden Horse Inns chain – hence the new name. Despite the fact that the new owners took some heed of local feeling by incorporating JB VC into the new sign and erecting in the bar a granite plaque bearing witness to John's valiant deeds, many former locals vowed never to set foot in the place again. The new owners have spent a large sum of money on sprucing the place up and improving the kitchen facilities that now provide Mexican dishes.

Every story has a happy ending – in 2003 the name reverted back to John Brunt VC.

No 44. The Bull, Hunton

(Closed 21st October 1975 and de-licensed 30th October 1975. Now a private residence)
Jude & Co, Jude Hanbury, F. Leney, Fremlins, Whitbread

The house dates back to 1635 and is to be found a little out of the village down a twisting narrow lane. It was possibly built to house labourers working at Stonewall farm. It is marked as a vicarage on an old tithe map and would have been used by "assistant" clergy in the 17th and 18th centuries. It then became a very popular public house.

Jude Hanbury was renting the premises at the end of the 19th century and on 9th October 1899 a premium of £250 was paid for a five-year lease. This was renewed for ten-year periods from October 1904 and October 1914 with a premium of £500 paid on each occasion. In November 1920 consideration was given to purchasing the freehold and it was decided, via the Managing Director of Jude Hanbury, that an offer of £2,500 be made. The purchase proceeded but at the much higher figure of £5,250 – completion took place on 26th January 1921. The house was mortgaged in 1926 in the sum of £1,500 with interest charged at 5 1/2 %. Although the pub had a full licence for all of its known life the tithe was not redeemed until 1948 and the land tax in 1950.

Nicholas Brigdon was the landlord in 1758 and by 1867 J. Gilbert was the tenant and is probably the John Gilbert who, on 12th April 1905, handed over to his son Harry E. Gilbert who remained until 6th July 1942. Both paid a rent of £20 p.a. On retiring, Harry and the incoming tenant were unable to agree the value of the inventory resulting in an umpire, whose decision was final, adjudicating and settling on a valuation of £216/12/-.

The stables were repaired in 1900 costing £89/15/- and in 1903 £2 was spent on cleaning and repairing the drains and building a catchpit. A small fire occurred in June 1916 with renovation work costing £3/15/-.

During the 1800's landlords supplemented their income by various farming activities. The son of the last Gilbert to tenant the "Bull" told me that the house relied heavily for its trade throughout the year on the local agricultural workers with tobacco regularly sold on the premises. However, during the hop-picking season, when East Enders descended on the region in their thousands, the area really came alive. There were three large farms in the immediate vicinity of the "Bull" and each contained at least one hundred hop-picker huts. Like so many pubs in the Weald the landlord and locals would not let the pickers into the pub and beer was passed out via a hatch.

Another period of high activity was the war years. Those pubs that remained open during this fraught period all did very well. Hunton Court Park was home, for a short period, to numerous fighting men including a fair-sized contingent from Canada who were fondly remembered as particularly heavy imbibers! The front room was the tap bar and what was called the parlour occupied the big room.

If you wished to make your fortune this was the place to be. In 1953 the tenant, Mr. F. Guess, won £2,500 on the football pools. His house had just won the Kentish League (Marden and District) darts cup for the third time and whilst making the presentation, Mr. Lywood, of Frederick Leney & Sons Limited, presented Mrs. Guess with a facsimile of the cheque. Shortly afterwards the family left for a new home they had built. His successor, Mr. Bright, was only here for a few months before he also won several thousand pounds on the pools!

A pub named the "Bull" normally had religious connotations, possibly named after the Papal Bulla or seal of the Pope, so it may have taken its name as a result of the religious connections in the 17th century. However the sign is somewhat unusual as it shows a Spanish fighting bull rather than our domestic animal.

A combination of its isolation, the mechanization of the hop gardens, and the introduction of the drink/drive laws all gradually throttled trade. The pub struggled on until 21st October 1975 when it closed its doors for good. It now makes a fine family residence with the structure of the building barely changed. The pub is almost forgotten and it took me a long while to find a resident who could identify it.

"By time even the savage bull is made submissive to the plough." Ovid.

No 45. The Kent Arms, Fowle Hall

*(Formerly the **New Inn**. Closed in January 1996) Benjamin Baker, F. Leney,
Fremlins, Whitbread, Free House*

Another isolated house where, however many times I visited, I always had to ask directions. Initially I stumbled across it by accident when I took the wrong road from Brenchley to Maidstone.

The "Kent Arms" is truly situated in the Garden of England and even today is surrounded by fruit farms although the hop gardens, which at one time encircled it, have almost disappeared. At the time the pub joined the Leney estate in 1896 it came with stabling, a coach-house and premises. The nearby dwellings are called New Inn cottages. On 9th December 1947 when Whitbread re-named the "Kent Arms" just down the road at Paddock Wood to the "John Brunt VC." they transferred the name here. They appear to have had a phobia about any tavern called the "New Inn" as about the same time three more "New Inns" were all re-named to "This Ancient Boro'", "Wyf of Bathe" and the "John Jorrocks".

Little has come to light about its past history but I do know the house was built in 1797 and ceased to trade in January 1996. What a pity it could not quite stretch to an unbroken two hundred years.

This is one of the inns formerly owned by the Tonbridge brewer Benjamin Baker Senior. When sold by his executors on 16th November 1905 it was subject to two life annuities in favour of his daughters Miss Baker and Mrs. Peach. The latter was bought out in 1946. When Mr. Harry Frost took over on 2nd May 1921 he paid £92/3/6 for the inventory and stock. At that time the house was valued at £1,705. Landlords came and went on a regular basis and in 1890 we see the amazingly-named Arrow Smeed behind the bar. In 1937 the brewers purchased the inventory for £64/6/- and at the same time made a "special" allowance of £10 to the tenant on leaving and also paid part of the rates amounting to £1/5/11. In 1939 Percy W.G. Bishop from the "New Inn" was also employed on the Whitbread hop farm as a general labourer and oast-hand on a wage of 34/- plus piece work. The pub had a large garden and many landlords were self-sufficient in vegetables. In the spring of 1954 Percy was amazed that one of his Savoy cabbages grew to giant proportions weighing 24lb and measuring four feet across. To make way for his other vegetables it had to be cut down, although many of the drinkers complained it was cut off in its prime. Percy paid a rent of £15, his deposit was £30 and the inventory was valued at £64/6/-. The last landlord to trade in the Whitbread colours was Peter Ward. He took over on 21st January 1975 with the pub being sold with licence on 1st December 1975. It then became a freehouse. As late as 1950 the house did not have gas or electricity.

During the 1950's trade consisted almost entirely of local land workers and, during the season, hop-pickers. Villagers always regarded the "Kent Arms" as a community pub with its private and smaller saloon bar plus a jug and bottle. Ultimately the place was converted into a one-bar house. There was also a flat-roofed extension which became the games room. The place also served modest, but good, food that attracted a few lunch-time patrons from Paddock Wood and I.C.I. employees from the former works at Yalding. Tucked away from the prying eyes of the law, after-hours drinking was a regular occurrence – the pub closed when the last customer departed. During the great storm of 1987 the chimney at the far end of the house crashed down through the bedroom into the bar but fortunately nobody was injured. In an effort to drum up business the last landlord introduced live music but the regulars were not impressed, trade dwindled, and the house closed.

The original sign remained to the end although the background colour had changed from sandy yellow to blue. It is now a private house called "Greenviews".

No 46. Prince of Wales, Collier Street (although closer to Haviker Street)
(Closed and de-licensed 13th May 1968) H.T. Wickham & Co, Jude Hanbury, F. Leney, Fremlins

At one time confusion reigned, as there was another house called the "Prince of Wales" close by on the outskirts of Hunton. Sadly both are now closed.

The property probably dates back to the early 1800's and although now a private residence it is little changed from its Jude Hanbury days. Early on the house and some land were given to the church. Yalding was a poor village and the church could feed six undernourished children from the income produced. The house still retains a large area of land but the majority was sold off in 1938.

It took me some time to trace the building as few locals can remember it. Following closure the house was sold de-licensed on 8th July 1968 for £7,500 less costs of £263/5/-. Much renovation, which included the incorporation of all the fine timberwork, then took place. The present lounge served as the public bar. One can easily identify where the dartboard hung by the countless pockmarks left by many a wayward dart. Perhaps this was a throw-back to its busy hop-picking days when the place was heaving. A photograph taken in 1937 shows a Leney lorry fully loaded with crates and barrels from just one weekend's drinking during the hopping season. The pub had no cellar, the beer being stored in a back room. The rear extension was added about a hundred years ago.

It commenced life as a simple beer house. In 1874 Daniel Savage was in residence and he remained until at least 1890. He is described as a beer retailer at Collier Street but, by 1878, the property is called the "Prince of Wales". Daniel was succeeded in 1897 by William Kemp Savage. A member of the same family appears to have been the landlord of the nearby "Duke of Wellington" with Frederick Savage behind the bar there in 1887. In 1921 Jude Hanbury acquired the premises when they, in conjuction with Frederick

Leney, took over the Yalding-based brewery of H.T. Wickham & Co. and split the houses between them. They attributed a book value of £2,207/10/- to this pub. Shortly afterwards Charles Easton signed a tenancy agreement on 15th December 1921 and he stayed until 1945. In 1939 he paid an annual rent of £25 and his inventory was valued at £210/10/6. A beer and wine licence was granted on 17th April 1939 and a full licence in 1955. As late as 1950 the house had no gas or electricity supply.

In 1921 the brewers mortgaged the property in the sum of £500 to Henry James Bracher paying an interest rate of 4%. This was subsequently redeemed by Leney's on 1st October 1956. In 1934 the house was valued at £2,700 in the Leney accounts. Land was sold in 1938 for £300.

The last landlord was Alfred H.W. Grant who moved in on 25th July 1966.

No 47. Duke of Wellington, Collier Street
(Closed in 1996. Now trades as the Wellington Garden Centre)
H.T. Wickham & Co., F. Leney, Fremlins, Whitbread

A sturdy property built as a farmhouse in the 15th century. It is grade two listed with an abundance of exposed internal beams, studwork, and an inglenook fireplace besides a massive central chimney.

It was converted to a public house in about 1840 and ultimately came under the control of the small local brewery H.T. Wickham & Co. Initially it relied for its trade on local agricultural workers swelled by the annual hop-picking invasion. At one time the Royal Victoria Union Society met here. Over the years it developed a very fine restaurant with the dining tables in individual booths. This must have been some achievement as the catering, and indeed all services, was very primitive indeed. The pub also boasted a skilled darts team. In 1947 they won the "B" division of the Marden and District league with Mr. Relf of the Wateringbury brewery making the presentation. As usual in such a thinly-populated area trade declined and the pub closed in 1996. On closure it was discovered that the person operating from the premises was acting in an unofficial capacity with the consent of the landlord and this did result in delays in marketing the property. Much renovation has been carried out and the site now trades as the Wellington Garden Centre.

For a long while the pub was simply called the "Duke Inn". In addition to his farming activities John Bird was the landlord in 1841 and after him we find the Savage family who were also at the "Prince of Wales". George Moore became the licensee on 24th June 1921 at about the same time as the Wickham brewery was taken over – this time Leney took on the house. In 1939 George, who remained until 1945, was paying a rent of £40 plus a £50 deposit. It was about this time that the change of name to the "Duke of Wellington" took place. I wonder how the Duke would view present times for, after his first Cabinet meeting as Prime Minister, he wrote to a relative "Today I had my first Cabinet meeting as Prime Minister, an extraordinary affair. I gave them their orders and they wanted to stay and discuss them".

In 1951 a loss of development value in respect of the land was settled for £35. During the early 1960's the landlady employed a coachman as she never used a car. He lived in the flat above the coach-house and was still driving in his 90th year. Towards the end landlords came and went but none could restore the pub to its former glory.

No 48. The Fountain, East Peckham
(Closed 11th September 1973 and sold unlicensed) Jude Hanbury, F. Leney, Fremlins, Whitbread

You would have to search for this inn at the far end of the village in an area known as the Bush. The "Fountain" stood close by the better-known and uniquely-named inn called the "Bush, Blackbird and Thrush" which still trades.

The "Fountain" was another old and popular house that over the years played a full part in village life. It was probably erected in the 15th century as a farmhouse, but in 1793 it became the parish workhouse. For the villagers consigned to these premises life was grim indeed. However, on 29th March 1837, the property was conveyed by the Guardians of the Malling Union to Mr. W. Walter and one part subsequently became Ireland's shop and bakery and ultimately the post office which closed in 1978. The other part became the "Fountain Inn" and this was acquired by Jude Hanbury on 29th January 1925 from the executors of J.F. Wheeler. The pub also had a large oven in the kitchen and from time to time during busy periods this was used by the baker.

Early maintenance costs included:-

> *1899. Repairs to shutters, cesspool and bar floor. £6/12/-.*
> *1907. Clear away piggeries and rebuild end boundary wall. £5/16/11.*
> *1910. Open, clean and carry out maintenance to well. £2/ 6/9.*
> *1912. Remove old range and supply and fix 30inch "Belle" range (oven only)*
> *with smoke pipe. £3/ 7/6.*

C.W. Cook took over the tenancy on 9th November 1933 paying an annual rent of £25. He was succeeded by Sidney G. Holmes on 19th July 1937 paying a similar rent with his inventory valued at £145/9/-. He was also a skilled carpenter and crafted the oast cowlings at the nearby Whitbread hop farm.

By the late 1950's Harry Tomlin was the landlord and he supplemented his income by working on the railway at Paddock Wood as a signalman. His son stood in for him during the day. An enterprising gent, he ran a Morris 1000 Traveller in which he transported the family pig which lived in the back garden until its appointed hour. He also acted in a modest way as the local coal merchant. A resident told me of the day Harry was cycling home from work after completing the early turn shift when he stumbled across a sack of fertilizer lying by the side of the road. Never one to waste anything he hoisted it onto his bike but on arriving at the "Fountain" noticed that via a small hole in the sack a trail of white dust indicated the fertilizer's ultimate home. His solution was to tie a broom to the back of his bike and retrace his route.

Both the pub and landlords are remembered with affection. At the turn of the century the Hadlow Harriers Hunt used to meet here and patrons would cycle from the outlying villages to listen to a good story and enjoy a first-class pint. During the hopping season one could barely move in the narrow streets. On a Sunday the hoppers would drop the Sunday lunch off to be heated up and collected later and then the roads around the "Fountain" would be chock-a-block with swaying bodies enjoying this short break from the fields. Every available seat was occupied inducing some to sit on the bonnets of cars parked in the vicinity. The bonnets must have been considerably stronger in those days!

Competition in the area was fierce and the "Fountain" found it impossible to survive. It closed its doors on 11th September 1973 and was sold unlicensed when both parts of the building again reverted to a private house. After closure, the first owner ran a small antiques business from the premises but without planning permission. The inn sign remains in the form of a little plaque by the front door and when I called in 1995 the owner still had a few of the old miniatures in his possession.

No 49. The Unicorn, Marden
Jude Hanbury, F. Leney, Fremlins, Whitbread

The Unicorn as we now know it developed over the centuries. The oldest part dating back to the 1600's is the middle portion and this was extended in the 18th century to the right and in the 1800's the left-hand side was added to provide accommodation for the landlord. This later part became the pub restaurant. In February 1929 an agreement was entered into with the Mid Kent Water Co. to supply metered water. In May 1934 it was decided to purchase from the Tenterden Brewery Company, through Jude Hanbury & Co., the house and shops adjoining the pub for £145. Fremlins acquired all the Leney properties in 1960 and included was the shop adjoining the "Unicorn" which was let to A.R.M. Town at a rent of £175 p.a. In March 1938 some land was purchased for £25.

Drainage was installed in 1901 at a cost of £70 and in 1905 £1/8/6 was paid for "carting stone for the yard". Five years later the cesspit was rebuilt together with a new gully to the urinal for £2/10/9 and in 1911 fitting a bath and new hot water cistern cost £11/7/-.

Originally it was a handsome stone building but latterly this has been masked by pebble dashing. The property was large enough to act as a hotel and also a posting house and to the rear of the premises was the stabling – at one time the site of the village market. A nice old print shows the place in its Jude Hanbury days advertising Courage & Co. Porter and Stout. The Whitbread engraved windows were still in place in 1998.

The "Unicorn" was another pub heavily involved with the hoppers, but again they were not allowed into the premises. During this era the house had sash windows enabling the beer to be served through these or from a bath which was placed outside in the street. Each local landlord would identify their glasses via a coloured dot and charge a customary 1/- deposit.

The goings-on during this era pale into insignificance when compared to a "disgraceful occurrence" reported in the "Maidstone Journal" in June 1847. The paper tells us "On Wednesday last, the following iniquitous scene was witnessed in Maidstone Market. A man (formerly of Marden) named William Payne, sold his wife and two children to a person named James Laddams, of Marden, for ten shillings. The woman was led in to the market with a halter round her neck, and thus exposed for sale, and after the purchase had been completed, the man and woman returned to an adjacent inn and indulged themselves with a hearty dinner. Immediately after this nefarious transfer had been concluded, the wife coolly addressed her husband, "Well, George, (was this his middle name?) after this, I hope you will not molest me any more, nor attempt to come near me"; to which her husband replied "No, not as long as I live". On returning to Marden, by which time all parties were inebriated, an argument developed over the husband's furniture, which his successor claimed was included in the bargain. A fight ensued, which ended in Payne being stabbed in the face with a knife, though not seriously.

Five weeks later the "Maidstone Journal" reported on the sequel to this event.

"It will be remembered, a few weeks back a disgraceful scene took place at the Maidstone market, a person from Marden bringing his wife thither with a halter for sale. Last Sunday morning, this man was met about four o'clock on his road home. Soon after his arrival, the neighbours were alarmed, and when they came to his assistance, found he had bled to death. On Tuesday last, an inquest was held on the body, at the "Unicorn" Inn, Marden, before W.T. Neve, Esquire. Aneurism of the aorta, it appeared, caused his death. Verdict, "Died by visitation of God"."

The "Unicorn" remains a fine old village pub still serving good food to villager and traveller alike.

No 50. The Red Lion, Offham
(Closed in July 1997. Now a private house) Jude Hanbury, F. Leney, Fremlins, Whitbread, Free House

Forget the M20 and the A20, this was an old coaching inn situated on the edge of the village on what was in those far-off days the former Dover Road. Memories have not dimmed, however, and in the 1930's, during the summer season, scores of coach parties turned off the London – Folkestone road to call in at the "Red Lion" to rejoin the main A20 a little further on.

The house was built in two stages with the rear erected circa 1650 and the front in the 1700's. The rear of the house is about two feet lower than the front. Opinions differ as to its history with some saying it was built as a coaching inn and others that it converted to licensed premises circa 1870. In June 1925 Isherwood, Foster & Stacey, the Maidstone brewers, suggested to Judes that they exchange the "Maidstone Arms" in Ramsgate for the "Red Lion". The proposal was investigated but did not proceed.

To the front of the building is an old stepping-stone for the use of the coach driver and this is now the subject of a preservation order. It was too small for passenger use. The stabling was to the rear. Long after this trade had disappeared these cobbled buildings were used as stabling for the pony of the daughter of a former landlord. This area has now been incorporated into the house. Originally a two-bar pub with a jug and bottle to the rear, subsequent renovation work left it as a large single-bar house. At one time there was a well outside the dining room but it is rumoured that following the suicide of a former landlord, this was blocked up.

We saw the usual story with hop-pickers. No admittance; tin bath with a scoop to serve the beer; and the standard deposit. However the hop garden "stilt walkers" were always welcome and were a regular sight in the village having a tipple at their favourite local almost at roof level. These were the workers responsible for "stringing" from pole to pole.

Jane Smith is recorded as being the landlord at the "Lyon" in 1754 and then Rod Parks for a long while in the early 1800's. During the late 1800's the brewers rented the property from James Phillips for an annual rental of £25. For much of the 1800's the house was in the hands of the Stickings family. John was the landlord in 1846 and William by 1871.

The following improvements were carried out:-

1900. Take down ceiling and replace with matchboard in large room. £ 9/10/-.
1901. Repair club room roof. £13/10/-.
1911. New lead to well. £8/6/-.
1919. Laying on water £16/10/-.
and new drainage. £52/12/-.

Even after its former glories had faded the pub still provided a reasonable living, possessing a particularly good restaurant that drew trade from quite a large area. However the quality of the landlords deteriorated with the last traditional landlord retiring in 1993. This was always a village pub appealing to the locals but after 1993 a quick succession of landlords with modern ideas failed to make a go of the place and it closed, despite the villagers' protests, in July 1997.

A few years ago an original design for the pub inn sign by Violet Rutter, dated 1940, was discovered on hardboard backing and hidden by a picture. However, this shows a Lion statant, similar to the "Black Lion" at Mereworth.

In May 2004 the freehold was offered for sale at a price on £725,000.

"The Lion (sure) is not so fierce or stout,
As foolish men do paint or set him out". Roland Watkyns.

Second Series issued in 1950

(Aluminium)

1	Angel, Strood	26	Chequers, West Farleigh
2	Belisha Beacon, Rainham Mark, Gillingham	27	Clothworker's Arms, Sutton Valence
3	Bridge House, Gillingham	28	Duke of Wellington, Ryarsh
4	Canopus, Borstal, near Rochester	29	Fleur-de-Lis, Burham
5	General-At-Sea, Chatham	30	Good Intent, West Farleigh
6	Hook and Hatchet, Walderslade, Chatham	31	King's Arms, Headcorn
7	Mr. Samuel Pepys, Gillingham	32	Red Rover, East Malling
8	Rose and Crown, Chatham	33	South Eastern, Staplehurst
9	Sportsman, Strood	34	Spotted Cow, Larkfield
10	Spy-Glass and Kettle, Wigmore, Gillingham	35	Vigo Inn, Fairseat, Wrotham
11	Two Sawyers, Old Brompton, Gillingham	36	Windmill, Hollingbourne
12	World's End, Chatham	37	Chalk Tavern, Sittingbourne
13	Bell, Southborough	38	Forester's Arms, Sittingbourne
14	Camden Hotel, Pembury	39	Wyf of Bathe, Sittingbourne
15	Cardinal's Error, Tonbridge	40	Bull, Sissinghurst
16	Half Moon, Hildenborough	41	Crown Inn, Cranbrook
17	Grove Tavern, Tunbridge Wells	42	Swan, Wittersham
18	Hop Pole, East Peckham	43	Woolpack, Winchet Hill, near Goudhurst
19	Oak, Rusthall, near Tunbridge Wells	44	Coach and Horses, Sedlescombe
20	Cypress, Tunbridge Wells	45	Hope Inn, Guestling Green
21	Papermaker's Arms, Plaxtol	46	Peace and Plenty, Playden, near Rye
22	Star and Garter, Tonbridge	47/48	Robert de Mortain, The Ridge, Hastings
23	Walnut Tree, Brenchley		
24	We Three Loggerheads, Tonbridge	49	Plough Inn, Eynsford
25	Blacksmith's Arms, Harrietsham	50	Royal Oak, Shoreham

No 1. The Angel, Strood
*(Re-named **Pitchers** in 1994) F. Leney, Fremlins, Whitbread*

An inn called the "Angel", with the Strood tollgate adjoining, dominated this spot for over 300 years. During this period we saw demolitions but a new "Angel" always rose from the ashes – until February 1961. The attractive building then standing was demolished and replaced, a few hundred yards away, by a 1960's two-storey flat-roofed house. When I called in 1994 it was in a sorry state but renovation subsequently took place with a re-naming to "Pitchers". This certainly improved the appearance of the building.

In 1793 the "Angel" was listed in the "Universal British Directory" with the landlord named as William Birch. In the middle 1800's the "Angel" was an impressive building but it is likely its predecessor was a former inn called the "Salutation", which then became the "Angelus" and after the Reformation the "Angel". The Strood Burial Society, founded in 1843, held their meetings here for many years and by 1893 had paid away £2,741 in benefit. The balance in hand stood at £78/7/6 with arrears owed by members amounting to £1/4/-. Stabling was available. The pub played an important part in town life and towards the end of the 19th century the inquest into the death of pretty Mary Abbott was held here.

In 1872 landlord Rodnell made application to remain open until 12p.m. during the Strood fair but his request was not granted. The following year Mr. Mitchell applied for permission to keep the house open on the occasion of the Parochial dinner but again this was turned down. The police obviously kept an eye on the place as, on 4th July 1892, Edmund Boynton, a non-voter, was alleged to have paid 10/- in cash to a person unknown at the "Angel" at about 12.30p.m. This was highlighted at the Rochester Election Enquiry but the case was dismissed. In 1893 landlord H. Fiske proved more persuasive as his application for an extension of an extra hour on the occasion of a benefit smoking concert was granted. Such concerts were usually held to assist someone in financial trouble due to, say, bereavement.

The Breeze family was long associated with the "South Eastern" at Tonbridge but George Henry Breeze made the short journey to Strood to take up employment at the local South Eastern Goods Station. It was not long before he took over the licence here where he successfully conducted the establishment until July 1908. He then moved on to the "Glass House", Sheerness, before returning home to the "South Eastern" in 1919 until his death in April 1925.

Events moved on and in 1896 the house featured prominently in a photograph showing the closing down of the Tollgate. The old pub was demolished in 1899 to be replaced by an even more splendid building. This incorporated livery and bait stables, a miniature billiard table together with a large clubroom for smoking concerts. Carriers for Hoo, Stoke and Isle of Grain commenced their journey from here three times a week. A problem arose in 1927 when a proposed road-widening scheme would have resulted in the property being "set back". Any compensation claim would have been in the region of £10,000 but the project was not progressed.

The "Angel" was purchased by the three Leney brothers from Richard Heath for £2,268 on 17th January 1878 and was valued in 1881 at £2,200. Title passed to the limited company in 1896.

It is surprising that such a prominent house did not acquire a full licence until 1953. In February 1961 as part of the redevelopment of the area the old "Angel" was pulled down with the licence transferred to the new house built just a little way down the road.

No 2. Belisha Beacon, Rainham Mark
*(Re-named the **Hop and Vine** in 1982) F. Leney, Fremlins, Whitbread*

This is a modern house built in 1938, but it has an interesting past history stretching back a long way. In May 1938 Leney purchased a lease and premises at Rainham Mark for £375 and in June the freehold and extra land for £1,900 together with an option on additional freehold land for £50. Prior to opening they spent £143/2/8 on furniture plus an electric kettle for £1/5/3. These sums were subsequently recovered from the tenant.

But first we have to return to Old Brompton, the corner of Wood Street, where, for over a hundred years, there had been a comfortable hostelry called the "Crown". This had been purchased by C. and A. Leney from H. Wickenden on 6th November 1876. The "Crown" had entertained, besides locals, servicemen home from the wars or on their way to new ones. Immediately adjoining the barracks, the Army had long coveted the site and following several attempts to acquire it, it finally fell to the wiles of Mr. Leslie Hore-Belisha, then at the War Office. The legal costs incurred in the removal of the licence to the "Belisha Beacon" amounted to £42/10/2. In October 1938 the premises were sold de-licensed for £1,200 with a loss suffered on the inventory of £142.

Leney's thought it apt to name their new house, built a few miles away, the "Belisha Beacon" for two obvious reasons. One, to commemorate the War Minister's tenacity in acquiring the "Crown" and the second, it was he who introduced and gave his name to this type of pedestrian crossing. By coincidence the new pub stands to the side of a pedestrian crossing. The inn sign was designed by Kathleen Claxton, but did she make an error? The pub opened to considerable publicity in the national press, which introduced it to millions of people both home and abroad. This led to correspondence that Kathleen had designed the sign with the beacons on the wrong side of the crossing. Whilst acceptable abroad where they drive on the right hand side of the road, here we drive on the left and thus the beacon should stand on the right. Oh well – it was a great sign anyway.

On the day the alterations were completed and the house opened Mr Hore-Belisha sent a telegram of greetings to the "citizens gathered at the sign of the "Belisha Beacon". During May 1947 the former War Minister visited the house and the honoured guest shook hands with the landlord Mr. Percy Wells, chatted to the locals in the public and saloon bars, and posed for a photograph beneath the sign. Needless to say drinks were on the house. In the 1954 New Year Honours List it was noted that a barony had been conferred on their patron and the locals toasted and sent formal greetings to Lord Hore-Belisha. He responded by telegram to state "Delighted to have greetings from the Belisha – Beacon – Watchers and only wish I was there with them to beg a bottle and share a glass, I look forward to my next visit". Percy Wells was still in situ. When the pub opened he paid a rent of £40 p.a. and a deposit of £50 was held; this was subsequently raised to a £100 on 21st August 1940.

The inn appeared to lead a fairly uneventful life, but in June 1945 William George Gorman, a 25-year-old naval rating, admitted to stealing £28/3/4 from the pub. In 1947 a radio programme called "Up and Doing" held a discussion on the origins of pubs with curious names including this one.

The pub acquired a full licence on 8th April 1948 with the monopoly value set at £1,600. In 1952 the brewers purchased, for £100, a plot of land adjoining the house.

For some quite inexplicable reason, following considerable refurbishment, this unique name was changed to the "Hop and Vine" on 6th January 1982. In 1938 there was a beer garden to the rear and the house had extensive views across the Estuary to Southend, but this is not so now. Standing on the busy A2 with redevelopment going on all around, a less rural scene is hard to imagine. However, the pedestrian crossing remains.

No 3. Bridge House, Gillingham
(Closed about 1992. Now a vicarage) George E. Osborne, F. Leney, Fremlins, Whitbread

This fine pub, the first outside the great dockyard gates, has been a favourite rendezvous of numerous ships' companies. In 1949 when HMS London returned to Chatham after her dramatic action in the Far East, the sailors immediately organized a celebration at their "own" pub the "Bridge House". Mr. L. Woolcott, the landlord, and his wife were entertained aboard the ship and afterwards at the Lord Mayor's luncheon in the City. The badge of HMS London, together with the crests of many other ships of the Royal Navy, was proudly displayed in the bar. Another connection with the Navy related to the brand new vessel, H.M. Survey Ship Owen, which, after trials at Chatham, set sail for distant lands carrying the Whitbread Inn-signia map.

The property was probably built in 1871 for George E. Osborne of Gillingham Road, Gillingham. The house was to sell by retail, beer and cider to be consumed on the premises. Osborne rented the premises to A. Leney who paid an annual rent of £30 p.a. by quarterly instalments of £7/10/-. The lease was due to expire on 25th December 1898, but Augustus Leney acquired the freehold on 17th December 1891 from G.E. Osborne and mortgagee paying the sum of £715. On 8th April 1870 the beerhouse certificate, previously held by Henry Joseph Bennett of the "Bridge House", High Street, Gillingham, was transferred to George William Marshall, he being the person not disqualified to hold such a certificate. About this time the pub was known as the "Bridge Tavern". In June 1893 William Kemsley, landlord of the "Bridge House Tavern" back in Medway Street, was summoned for unlawfully keeping his licensed house open for the sale of intoxicating liquors during prohibited hours. He blamed the barmaid. A policeman reported that he saw a lady approach the pub at 11.20p.m. with a jug. On knocking at the door she was told she was too late and the door was closed, but a few seconds later she knocked again and this time was admitted. The policeman called a minute later and caught her red-handed with a jug of beer. The bench imposed a fine of 10/- with 9/- costs. A long-standing landlord was C.A. Roots who moved in on 31st May 1927 staying until 1942. In 1939 his rent was £32 p.a. plus £1 for the bath in addition to a deposit of £100. He acquired a beer and wine licence in April 1938. In 1943 William John Alfred Dolling moved down the road from the "Army and Navy" to take up residence.

The house and garden adjoining the pub were purchased for £500 in September 1928. Some land at the rear of the premises, 217 square yards in all, was sold in 1957 for £115 to Gillingham Corporation for housing purposes.

Alas, like so many things, the dockyard closed, the fortunes of the pub waned, and in about 1992 it closed. At the time more land was sold for housing. The property stood empty for a while and in December 1997 was bought by the Church – a photograph in the local paper showing the vicar pulling a pint! When I called in 2001 the vicar was kind enough to show me around. The interior is still recognizable as a pub and the cellars contained much of the old piping, several beer barrels, and the former windows with Whitbread engraved in them. I also acquired three mildew-encrusted books on the delights of running a public house. I am told that the impressive sign is in the hands of a local collector.

The house acquired a full licence on 7th April 1949 with the monopoly value set at £1,400.

No 4. The Canopus, Borstal
F. Leney, Fremlins, Whitbread

The old "Belle Vue Inn", a house familiar to Dickens, stood at the junction of Cookham Hill and Hill Road. It probably took its name during the Napoleonic period when French prisoners were accommodated in hulks on the nearby River Medway. By all accounts it sounded a rough and tumble place. A court case in December 1920 described a fracas that arose over the charms of the landlord's daughter. Apparently the remark "Some people take things very funny of a morning" led to the plaintiff being invited outside where he received severe facial injuries. His Mum told the court that as a result he could only eat bread and milk for several days. In 1890 the house was valued at £800 with the rent set at £25 p.a. The "Belle Vue" adjoined the "Canopus" and was demolished following the opening of this new house.

What better name for a public house perched on a hill overlooking the reaches of the Medway from where Short Bros. Empire flying-boats took off on their trials? Truly a monument to those history-making aircraft and the local craftsmen by whom they were built. In all a fleet of twenty-eight Empire flying-boats was constructed by Short Bros. Limited for Imperial Airways.

The inn opened on 21st September 1938 and the first landlord was Mr. H.H. Green. His rent was £70 p.a. with the inventory valued at £300. The house was designed by Mr. R.G. Muir, FRIBA, and the builders were Messrs. Corben and Sons Limited of Maidstone. The same gentleman also designed the nearby "Ordinary Fellow". The architect's fees amounted to £365 and the building foreman received a gratuity of £5. The building looks rather like a substantial country house and inside it is elegantly panelled with the furnishings costing £199/8/9.

The note under the framed reproduction of the sign in the inn parlour states "To the honour of those local craftsmen whose industry was responsible for the pioneer and most famous flying boat of our Empire air route" by permission of Imperial Airways and Messrs. Short Bros. Limited. In granting this formal permission, Sir John Reith (later Lord Reith), the then head of Imperial Airways wrote:-

"We welcome your suggestion to name your inn after our flying boat Canopus. In England the names and signs of inns have usually been indicative of contemporary and local interest, and in the realm of transport they have frequently been named after wooden ships, the stage coach and, since the advent of steam, after locomotives and steam ships.

Your inn is probably the first named to commemorate the newest form of transport – that of the air – and it is therefore appropriate that you should have chosen the name of the first great Imperial flying boats which were built close by at the works of Messrs. Short Bros. Limited. We wish every success to the old inn under its new sign".

In fact there was another inn named after a flying machine – the "Comet" at Hatfield. When the Canopus was withdrawn from service in 1947 the steering column was presented by Short Bros. Limited to the pub. However, the name lived on, and when the Queen and Duke of Edinburgh departed for an overseas trip in November 1953 they travelled in the BOAC aircraft Canopus. The regulars at the pub assembled to drink a loyal toast with their good wishes reciprocated by the Prime Minister and Foreign Secretary a week later.

In the spring of 1951 the same Mr. Green decided to introduce the game of bat and trap to the area. It was already very popular in East Kent and it didn't take long to establish a pitch with the grand opening of the game in the Medway towns taking place on 1st June 1951.

In July 1989 the pub was able to add to its seaplane links when Mr. Ted Willougby, a regular customer and former fitter at the works, presented the house with his framed print of the seaplane Canopus.

Short Bros. closed in Rochester just after the war but the "Canopus" continues to thrive.

"For you, the Pathway of the Sky." Contes.

No 5. General-at-Sea, Chatham
F. Leney, Fremlins, Whitbread, Shepherd Neame

Who was the General-at-Sea? Such appointments were made from the sixteenth century to the early eighteenth century and in this instance the recipient was Admiral Robert Blake (1599-1657) appointed by Oliver Cromwell in 1648. Born in Somerset this was a worthy honour as his record will show. He was Commander of the Parliamentary forces and captured Taunton in 1644. By 1649 he was Admiral of the Commonwealth Fleets defeating the Dutch fleet commanded by Prince Rupert at the Nore.

As befits an inn bearing such a name we find a long and interesting naval story that goes back much further than the opening of this pub in December 1947. On the return of the British fleet from its triumph at Trafalgar the only Englishwoman present at the battle took up residence in a little cottage – 52 John Street, Chatham. She had served in the lookout frigate Euryalus but was always associated with Nelson's

flagship "Victory". As a result the modest little inn just around the corner came to be called the "Victory" in honour of Chatham's woman sailor. Nearly 140 years later the house was demolished in the blitz that razed the whole street to the ground (see also the "Trafalgar Maid").

Although the old "Victory" had disappeared its licence (beer and wine) was removed to a property belonging to Leney in Balfour Road, some distance away. Already operating as a retail off-licence it only required a few alterations to create the house we now know. It was fitting therefore to honour one of Britain's greatest seamen of rank.

The pub's close association with the sea continues and in January 1988 the enterprising landlord, Bing Neil, was able to enthuse his regulars to raise the grand sum of £1,278 in under two months to donate to the Royal National Lifeboat Institution. Previously his wife June had raised a considerable sum for Cancer Research by taking part in a sponsored parachute jump.

The house was granted a full licence at the Brewster Sessions held on 7th April 1949 when the monopoly value was fixed at £1,400. In the spring of 1962 improvements totalling £150 were carried out. In 1998 Shepherd Neame acquired the property.

No 6. Hook and Hatchet, Walderslade
*(Re-named the **Poacher's Pocket** in 1973) Phillips of West Malling, F. Leney, Fremlins, Whitbread*

So we know the identity of the "General-at-Sea" but what lies behind the name of this old pub? Again it is a naval connection, being the badge of a Chief Petty Officer Shipwright. The pub is so named because of its age-old connections with Chatham dockyard, with much of the timber used in the dockyard coming from the forests in this area. The woodcutters would slake their thirst here.

The history can be traced back to 1670. Between then and 1885 there are at least fourteen transactions involving the site but one cannot ascertain what trade was being carried on in those early days. Some of the names that appear, for example, Rigden in 1739, Winch in 1885 and Phillips in 1893, could indicate that the property operated as some kind of licensed premises. In 1893 the owner was Thomas Phillips of West Malling and by 1923 Leney's were the freeholders.

In 1872 the premises were licensed to sell by retail excisable liquors to be consumed on the premises. On 16th April 1887 an inquest was held here on the body of an unknown infant found on 2nd April in a disused chalk hole between Chatham and the pub. Later in 1893 Elizabeth Rebecca Baker, the landlady, sued James Kent, a bus cab proprietor, for £7/2/- for breach of contract in respect of the sale of a horse. In February 1927 Leney's agreed to the building of a urinal at the pub in return for the sum of £1 p.a. from the local corporation in respect of this "convenience". Five months later the sum of £16/14/3 was paid to the Ministry of Agriculture to redeem the tithe. A landlord in the 1930's also operated a spile and fencing business.

In 1951 the brewers accepted the sum of £1,470 in respect of loss of development value relating to land surrounding the pub. Approximately 4^{1}/2 acres of land were sold to Chatham Corporation in 1954 for £1,109/14/2 to be used as a public open space.

The premises were rebuilt in 1908 after being gutted by fire and the house was "remodelled" in 1958. It closed in 1973 for a couple of months for further refurbishment, which included amalgamating the three bars into one plush unit and the installation of central heating. It re-opened in June 1973 as the "Poacher's Pocket" with the guests of honour a poacher, a gamekeeper and local police dignitaries. The former name can be traced back to the 1800's. At one time there was a bowling alley but this gave way to the pub restaurant.

Situated within a high-density housing estate this has always been a busy place. Back in 1955 the landlord, Mr. L. Woolcott formerly of the "Bridge House", was one of the first to install a battery of optics on his shelf – to hold the bottles of spirits required for his many customers.

No 7. Mr. Samuel Pepys, Gillingham
*(Formerly the **New Inn**. Closed 24th June 1979 See below) F. Leney, Fremlins, Whitbread*

We have all heard of Mr. Samuel Pepys the be-wigged and famous diarist born in 1633, the son of a London tailor who lived off Fleet Street. His diaries spanned a nine-year period from 1660 to 1669. A talented but vain man he also held the post of Secretary of the Navy and as a result was a frequent visitor to the town. The inn sign was copied from a then unpublished portrait in possession of Dr. Arthur Bryant, an authority on Pepys. So we have yet another naval connection.

This substantial property was built in about 1860 and was variously described as being situated in Railway Street and High Street, New Brompton. In the old letting, a hall, mainly used as a meeting room for local clubs, was included as a separate let for £12 p.a. It obtained in 1872 a licence to sell by retail, beer and cider to be consumed on the premises. At this time the owner was Mary Ann Pogue who had succeeded her husband, William, and she remained until 26th August 1873 when ownership passed to William Smith. Frederick Leney & Sons Limited acquired the premises on 25th March 1876 from William and Phillis Smith for the sum of £550. Fanny Sturla was the landlady from 1878 until 7th August 1891 and much later, in 1935, the licensee is Jessie Ward who was granted a wine licence in April 1935. The legal fees amounted to £22/12/8. In about 1886 the place was from time to time referred to as the "New Inn and York Tavern". The house did not acquire a full on-licence until 1952.

A newspaper report of 1893 describes a pleasant gathering that took place at the "New Inn" to make a presentation to Mr. H. Wallace who had retired after 27 years' service in the painters' department at the nearby dockyard. In 1896 an inquest was held here on the body of the male child of Rosina Booth, wife of a stoker. The verdict was accidental death through having been overlaid by its mother while in bed.

The name change occurred on 8th February 1943. This area contained far too many public houses and the decision was taken to close this one on 24th June 1979 when the premises were sold. Various enterprises have subsequently traded from here including the Nationwide Building Society and a mobile phone shop, but none has lasted for very long. The last time I saw the premises they were, again, empty.

Building works totalling £150 were carried out in 1936 with further substantial development costing £1,878 in 1960 – this included the supply of six tables, six armchairs and three gas radiators. The old inn sign is in the hands of a Rainham collector.

No 8. Rose and Crown, Chatham
(Closed about 1990) F. Leney, Fremlins, Whitbread, Free House

This quaint former inn looks sadly out of place in modern Chatham High Street.

On 7th December 1877 the Local Board of Health for the District of Chatham sold a plot of land fronting the High Street to Frederick, Charles Frederick and Augustus Leney and within the next 12 months they erected a beerhouse which was named the "Rose and Crown". The following year on 15th April George Moss sold some land in Gundulph Road to the Leney brothers. The pub was let to a Mr. Shelton. It is possible that a much older pub called the "Royal Oak", owned by Mary Ann Bassett who lived at Aylesford, had originally traded from the site, as the first identified landlord is Thomas Dawson in 1812.

In 1881 the pub was valued at £1,820 and the quarterly rent was £10. By 1908 the house had appreciated in value to £1,890. In 1896, when Augustus Leney sold his estate to Frederick Leney & Sons Limited, this house was described as the "Rose and Crown" beerhouse and land plus land adjoining in Gundulph Road. The sale price was £2,250, a figure in excess of the 1908 valuation. A wine licence was granted in April 1933 and a full on-licence on 28th April 1950 at which time the net monopoly value was set at £750. On 21st September 1923 the company entered into a tenancy agreement with Emily Ann Lloyd at a rent of £35 p.a., but by 1944 this had reduced to £31/ 4/-. In the early days the bar housed a large collection of natural history objects which earned the pub the nickname the Museum.

In 1945 a 39-year-old fitter stole two cigarette lighters from the landlord, but we are not told what fine was levied. On 3rd May 1957 the landlord was found drunk in the saloon bar. It was stated in court that he had consumed 24 bottles of stout and two bottles of rum in a single day. Apparently a fracas had been going

on all morning and he had been trying to eject the culprits! He was fined the maximum sum of 10/-. In the 1960's the pub had established a good reputation for the quality of the food and was one of the first houses to serve coffee. At that time the landlord was Don Grant-Smith who remained until 1984. By 1989 most of the patrons were from the gay community, which caused some friction with a local paper reporting on 1st March 1989 that there had been death threats at the gay pub with CCTV cameras installed and five guard dogs lived on the premises. Possibly as a result of this publicity the pub closed circa 1990. The property, although sporting an attractive sign, remained empty for a very long time before being converted into flats.

No 9. The Sportsman, Strood
F. Leney, Fremlins, Whitbread, Free House

This is a comfortable back-street pub that has served the local community well for many years. It was built circa 1860 in a mainly artisan part of the town close to the shopping centre. Thomas Ames sold the house for £1,540 to the Leney brothers on 26th June 1883.

The Medway towns suffered greatly during the last war and when a bomb dropped on nearby Cross Street the residents were evacuated to the "Sportsman". As befits a house that gets on with it without making a fuss, little past history has come to light. However on 23rd September 1954 a careless deliveryman left the cellar flap doors open and unguarded. About noon a customer left the public bar and promptly fell into the cellar only to crash into the deliveryman who was coming up the steps! Although this arrested his fall he still broke his nose and required hospital treatment. The delivery-man was fined £1 for negligence.

The pub was in the very capable hands

of the Quinnell family for very many years. O. Quinnell took over the licence on 2nd September 1908, handing over to A.T. Quinnell on 9th March 1937. It was on this change-over that much needed renovation work was carried out. This gentleman's rent in 1939 was £70 and a deposit of £200 was held. During 1940 there were further repairs costing £226/6/4. The house was valued at £1,560 in the 1921 company books.

When I visited in 1994 the pub was in decline with the sign missing. Fortunately refurbishment was carried out in 1997 and a new enterprising landlord restored the pub's fortunes. It boasts one large bar and has a good-sized garden area, making it a popular venue for families. The regulars support high-flying pool and darts teams and were considering trying their hand at petanque. To add to the enjoyment it is also a television-free zone.

To this day I cannot imagine how I was persuaded to give a lad called Oscar Burrows nine of my swaps for one copy of the "Sportsman" – being so close to Maidstone the inn sign would have been easy to collect.

No 10. Spyglass and Kettle, Wigmore
F. Leney, Fremlins, Whitbread

The "Steam Engine" was an old house that stood at 22 Arden Street and was first licensed in 1872. The owner was William Tollast, The Bell, Frinsbury, who was to sell, by retail, beer and cider to be consumed on the premises. Its history appears to include fairly frequent breaches of the licensing laws, particularly by landlord William Charlton. On 31st August 1886 Augustus Leney purchased the premises from W. Bliss and S. Wells. Following closure the pub was sold de-licensed in January 1937 for £500.

Over at 47 Upper Wood Street, Old Brompton we find the "Lord Nelson". This had been purchased on 15th January 1879 by the three Leney brothers from George Burleigh. Again, this house closed and was sold de-licensed in January 1937 for £825.

The fate of both of these houses had been sealed in 1935 when Leney's wished to be represented in the rapidly-expanding area of Wigmore. Land had already been acquired and in March 1935 the balance of the purchase price, £525, was paid. In July a deposit of £24 was paid on a further plot of land, and in September a building stage-payment of £1,211 was made. As building work progressed five further payments totalling £5,000 were paid to the builder G.E. Wallis and Sons Limited. A further payment of £4,640/11/7 was made in September 1936 and £55 was spent on laying out the garden. Architect R.G.

Muir, FRIBA, drew up the design for this new house, which opened its doors on 6th April 1936. Sir Sydney Neville presided at the opening ceremony when sundry expenses amounted to £31/6/- and a Miss Ansell received a present costing £9/19/6. On that same evening both of the former pubs served their last pint. A provisional ordinary removal grant dated 4th February 1935 stated that the new pub was to be known as the "Lord Nelson", with the name altered on the day of opening. Leneys held a competition amongst their employees to find a suitable name for the new house, and one enterprising soul came up with the "Spyglass and Kettle" – a play on both of the former pubs' names. In 1936 £31/2/7 was spent on the signpost, sign and fittings and the inventory was sold for £229/11/-.

To celebrate the pub's 21st birthday in April 1957 a party was held attended by, amongst other dignitaries, John Marchant and G.C. Swain who had been Chairman of the Bench at the time of the original opening. Aptly the toast was to Horatio Nelson and James Watt and the "Spyglass and Kettle".

During 1987/8 a battle royal took place with Gillingham Borough Council. The brewers had erected, without planning permission, a childrens' playground in the very large pub car park. This enterprise found no favour with local residents who claimed that their peace was shattered by noisy children clambering on the big frames. The council insisted that planning permission was required and, when Whitbread appealed, the council health officers slapped in an order restricting noise coming from the playground. At this point the brewers conceded and the equipment was dismantled. The local residents had raised a petition containing over 700 names. Further disappointment followed in 1994 when plans were put forward to create a two-lane bowling alley. The brewers wished to build an extension to the side of the house to accommodate the enterprise, but again Gillingham councillors took a dim view and the application was rejected.

Despite these setbacks the pub continues to thrive and retains the original inn sign.

*"The glory of great men should be measured
by the means which they have used to acquire it."* La Rochefoucauld.

No 11. Two Sawyers, Old Brompton
*(Closed about Christmas 1997) Isaac Wildash (Brewer), John Baird, F. Leney,
Fremlins, Whitbread, Free House*

This fine old coaching inn was one of the dominant features of Old Brompton High Street and played a full part in town life. From 1832 onwards the Industry coach set off for Canterbury from the "Two Sawyers" every morning (Sunday excepted) at half past nine.

Landlords can be traced back to Robert Simmons in 1759 with Joe Green behind the bar in 1803. By 1846 the long tenure of John Baird began and he was to remain until 1888. It was in 1872 that he acquired a licence to sell, by retail, excisable liquors to be consumed on the premises.

In 1786 there is reference to an indenture between Isaac Wildash of Chatham, a brewer, and a grant of premises at Larkhill, St. Margarets, Rochester, for 1,000 years, by Richard Lee, gentleman of Great Delce. On 17th May 1888 Frederick Leney & Sons Limited leased the property from John Baird for a period of 21 years at an annual rent of £150. In April 1892 an inquest was held here on William Deighton, a potman in the employ of Mr. A. Wisdom, who committed suicide by hanging himself. A verdict of suicide during temporary insanity was returned. In May 1893 the sudden death of Mr. John Wisdom is recorded. He had been the landlord for some years past and had greatly improved the premises. That same year, a large gathering took place in honour of C.S.M. W. Flatman, 7th Field Company, of the Royal Engineers, who was leaving the corps. Somewhat surprisingly, in 1901 when Henry Gaunt was landlord, the police opposed the licence of the house as the pub was within 50 yards of other licensed premises. The proposal was not accepted. Perhaps the police application was as a result of Henry, on the 5th March that year, being fined £2 with 10/- costs at Chatham Police Court for selling adulterated whisky to the prejudice of the purchaser, and also £1 and 10/- costs for doctoring his brandy.

In 1901 W.E.R. Randall offered for sale this valuable fully-licensed freehold public house by way of auction held on Tuesday 16th April 1901 at seven o'clock precisely. The agents' particulars read as follows:- "Occupying a very prominent and bold position in the centre of the High Street, Old Brompton, together with two substantially built cottages, Stabling and Coach Houses in the rear, with a right of way into Manor Street. Held on lease by Augustus Leney Esq. of Wateringbury, for a term of which 8 years will be unexpired on 24th June next at the apportioned rent of £115 p.a. The licence for the house is insured for £3,000". Almost certainly the premises were purchased by Augustus Leney, as the limited company owned the house by 1904.

1902 also proved an eventful year. In February the licensee and his wife, Victor and Margaret Long, went on trial charged with being concerned together in fraudulently converting to their own use £418, the property of Ernest Wassell, secretary of the Tontine Club. Later this year, in July, a disastrous fire destroyed the original wooden building with it taking over an hour for water to arrive! The premises were subsequently rebuilt. A convenience was installed in July 1913.

Over the years trade dwindled, and when I visited in 1995 a sign in the window stated one could enjoy "Strippers and D.J. on Wednesday nights". Despite these endeavours the house closed in late 1997 and a couple of "To Let" notices appeared in the bar windows.

A Sawyer was always regarded as the least skilled tradesman and invariably one will find a jokey sign depicting this.

No 12. World's End, Chatham

*(Became the **Trafalgar Maid**, Series 5, Number 42) William Henry Austin, F. Leney, Fremlins, Whitbread, Free House*

"TO THE SURVEYOR OF THE CHATHAM LOCAL BOARD.

Dear Sir,

I hereby give notice that I intend to erect a new Beer house viz. the "World's End" on site shown on plan and a cottage adjoining same, subject to the approval of accompanying plan and description given below.

The buildings are to be of brick. The roof to be covered with slates. There are to be three W.C. – two in beerhouse and one in cottage.

The soil will be run in cesspools as shown 20 feet deep and 4 feet 6 inches diameter the waste water in two others of same dimensions. The soil drains to be laid with 6 inch stoneware socket pipes well jointed in cement. The waste water drains to be laid with 4 inch similar pipes similarly laid. Disconnecting pits and ventilating pipe to be put as shown on plan.

Yours faithfully, W. Austin.

P.S. The plans have passed the Licensing Committee".

Thus was the "World's End" born. Unfortunately the document is undated but a record dated 1867 shows Mr. Austin as a clay-pipe maker and beer seller. He was still here in 1872 when he obtained a licence to sell, by retail, beer and cider to be consumed on the premises. His address at the time was Jenkins Dale, Chatham. In March 1898 Frederick Leney & Sons Limited agreed to purchase the premises, but the Austin family was still involved with the pub. The name is variously spelt Austin and Austen. For its day this was a substantial property and in 1894 the brewers placed a value of £8,000 upon it.

In August 1876 Mr. Austin obtained an extension of time for an extra hour on Monday night on the occasion of an annual gathering when a party went upon an excursion by road in the morning, and returned at night to finish up with a pleasant evening at home. In June 1887 an inquest was held here into the death of a man, name unknown, who was found burnt to death in a lime kiln close by sometime on Saturday night. Verdict: accidental death. On a Wednesday evening in early January 1892 friends of Mr. W. Austin assembled to celebrate the 60th birthday of their genial host. In 1904 George Shirley Austin was granted a full licence. In January 1911 an inquest was held at the pub, now described as being in Skinner Street, touching on the death of Albert Edward Hollies, the infant son of a dock labourer. The doctor stated death was due to asphyxia caused by overlaying. A verdict of death by misadventure was returned. On 9th August 1912 the brewers entered into a tenancy agreement with John W. Taylor who was to pay a rent of £50 p.a.

The house acquired a beer and wine licence in April 1934. In 1939 Albert Edwin Poole was paying a rent of £100, his deposit was £230, and the inventory was stated as £295/9/-. He stayed until September 1946 when Chatham magistrates sanctioned the full transfer of the licence to Harold George Phelps. He proved to be a very popular landlord with a great love of children – he had six daughters. On New Year's Day 1947 he entertained over a hundred children of customers and soldiers who lost their lives during the war. Unfortunately his tenure was short-lived as he died in 1949.

Death appears to feature regularly at this house and one of the daughters of Mr. Phelps, Mrs. Kathleen Russell, offers the following explanation for the name change which took place on 31st December 1952:- Prior to Mr. Poole, Mr. Reader was landlord – he died, then Mr. Poole took over the "York" and died a few months later. Mr. Phelps died here in 1949 to be followed by Mr. Chadwick but we don't know his fate. Mrs. Reader told Mrs. Russell's mother that the land on which the pub was built had belonged to a gypsy and when they built the "World's End" he placed a curse on all future landlords. This fact, coupled with the unfortunate name, caused the locals to press for a change of name!

For the remainder of the story turn to the "Trafalgar Maid".

No 13. The Bell, Southborough
(Closed Easter 1997) J.B. Jude, B. Baker, F. Leney, Fremlins, Whitbread, Shepherd Neame

The pub commemorated by the Inn Sign was erected circa 1840 and stood on the site of, or was very close to, a much older house called the "Bell", records of which can be traced back to 1803. On 12th September 1855 an application was made by Edmund Latter to the Petty Sessions at Tonbridge for a spirit licence for a beer house known as the "Bell". This application was refused, but a year later on 10th September 1856 a similar application was granted. From 1860 the pub was owned by J.B. Jude who died in 1871. The property was not listed by his executors in a sale in 1873 so the house must have been sold prior to his death, possibly to the Tonbridge brewer Benjamin Baker. In 1892 Baker leased the premises to Frederick Leney & Sons Limited at an annual rental of £70 and they purchased the freehold on 16th November 1905.

The house acquired a reputation as a widow-maker and on at least four occasions the licensee died in harness with his widow taking over. The two longest-serving landlords are William J. Douch from 1885 to 1911 (in 1897 he was fined 5/- for selling adulterated gin) and Henry D. Lawrence from 19th June 1928 until 1958. When Henry moved in his rent was £100 p.a. and the inventory was valued at £590.

In July 1870 it is recorded that E.J. Tanner had left refusing to give up his licence, but Tonbridge Petty Sessions agreed to transfer the licence to William Davis. Walter Dunk, the landlord in 1874, placed an advert in the local newspaper stating that the inn was "newly-built" and could offer increased accommodation but, almost certainly, he should have stated re-built. Frederick Tanner came to the "Bell" in 1913 and was an immediate success, due in part to his interest in local football and the development of youth teams. Despite these attributes he did have his weaknesses, being fined, on 11th May 1920, £5 with £1/1/- costs for selling gin and rum at excessive prices. Perhaps excessive prices went with excessive men for, during the first word war, a regular at the "Bell" was Sergeant Horton of the Royal West Kent Regiment. He was a man of huge girth, both double doors had to be held open so as to allow him access. Unfortunately Mr. Tanner was to suffer an early death in January 1924, aged only 49, and this event robbed the town of a very popular figure. A local resident, Mrs. Wickens, tells me that, certainly up to the time of the last war, photographs hung in the pub of all the Southborough footballers.

In 1902 agreement to the erection of a distributing standard of the National Telephone Co. was given, i.e. a telegraph pole could be erected. In October 1928 some land to the rear of the premises was sold for £140. What used to be the hayloft was converted into public conveniences some while ago.

The premises were large and included clubrooms and as a result capital expenditure was high. This, coupled with a mainly artisan clientele, resulted in a high beer trade but little spirit sales. The area is well served by public houses and the "Bell" found it difficult to compete, and as a result in its later days the place became run down, and at Easter 1997 the inn was vacated and abandoned. On 2nd February 1998 the premises were partially destroyed by fire.

Shepherd Neame leased the pub on 6th May 1992 and purchased the freehold on 27th September 1996. Following closure the site was sold to Sainsburys on 27th August 1999.

No 14. Camden Hotel, Pembury
F. Leney, Fremlins, Whitbread, Beefeater

This small Grade 2 listed coaching house with its coffee room and stables was built in about 1820. Alas, the coffee room is no more and the stables were demolished to make way for a bus station, which later became the car park. The name relates to the local Pratt family who lived nearby at Bayham Abbey. The property once formed part of the Marquis of Camden's estate.

Charles F. Leney acquired the hotel at auction in March 1883 paying £3,150 for the inn, stables, outbuildings and yard. The house, less some land to the west which was sold, passed on 29th July 1886 to Augustus Leney for £2,800 and it was included within a large number of houses that he sold to Frederick Leney & Sons Limited on 25th March 1896. At that time it also included 1 acre 2 rods and 22 perch of land. During the 1880's the hotel was run by Miss Gage who, on marriage to William Urquart, moved on to form a most successful partnership at the "Castle Hotel", Tunbridge Wells until her death in 1893. In 1881 the house was valued at £2,830/10/- which sum had increased to £3,300 in 1908. The rent then was £112 p.a.

On the main road from the Kentish coast to London, this hotel was popular with both locals and coach parties. In the autumn of 1949 the recording unit of the European Service of the BBC visited the premises. They were accompanying two coach loads of visiting tourists of various nationalities from Scandinavia and Eastern Europe to record their reactions to the British way of travelling by coach for a sea-side trip, and subsequently to broadcast sound-pictures in their own language to the folks back home. Naturally they formed a good impression of the trip and the hotel. In 1954 motorcyclists from all over the Home Counties took part in the first annual Camden Cup Trial arranged by the Kent and Sussex Motor Cycle Club. A gruelling course, starting at the hotel, with eighteen observed points of especial difficulty was planned but the Arctic weather and bad road conditions cut down the proposed route from 35 to 20 miles. Only one competitor failed to last the course, retiring with bent spokes. The Marquis of Camden was actively involved by assisting riders in trouble and thoroughly enjoyed the event, which was won by D. Farrant of the Tenterden club on a 348 c.c. A.J.S.

Over the years numerous improvements have been carried out, including work on the toilets. The architect concerned can remember being told to ensure that all wash basins were re-inforced as the hotel was frequently host to coach parties of East End ladies and, if the toilets were all occupied, if desperate, they would use any convenience to hand.

Some of the land adjoining the premises was sold in 1966 for £3,500.

No 15. Cardinal's Error, Tonbridge
B. Baker when the White Hart, F. Leney, Fremlins, Whitbread

Once upon a time there was a comfortable little pub called the "White Hart" situated in the Upper High Street, Tonbridge. It was a popular watering hole possibly due to the fact that landlords remained for quite a while. G. Brotherhood was behind the bar from 1886 until 1903, followed by Hammon Cole until 1924 when he was succeeded by his wife. The brewers were Benjamin Baker of Tonbridge who leased it to Frederick Leney & Sons Limited in 1892 at an annual rent of £60. The freehold was purchased on 16th November 1905.

The town of Tonbridge was notorious for its traffic problems, and in 1946 Kent County Council decided a solution would be to widen the High Street, and to this end acquired, amongst other properties, the "White Hart". In September 1947 the council paid the brewers £4,000 for the pub, but the road-widening scheme was never progressed, and with the aid of the Tonbridge Civic Society, this historic building was saved. Meanwhile Leney had purchased Lodge Oak Cottage for £4,000 early in 1946 and on 13th August 1946 the special removal of the licence from the "White Hart" to Lodge Oak Cottage was confirmed. Thus the "Cardinal's Error" came into being. The house was granted a full licence on 7th April 1949 with the monopoly value set at £725. The new pub is on the outskirts of Tonbridge in a rapidly expanding part of town, which previously had no local to cater for its needs. Locals recall that in days of yore the cottages acted as a half-way house for smugglers on the road from Romney Marsh to the lucrative London markets – so it just has to be haunted. Fortunately one story has the ghostly inhabitant as a "friendly spirit" even if prone to throwing items around, whilst another source tells us the pub is haunted by a collie dog slumbering beneath an old walnut tree in the garden on summer evenings. Real live dogs are said to be aware of its presence and slink past with their tails between their legs.

In 1951 the sum of £1,000 was accepted by the brewers in respect of loss of development value on land surrounding the pub, and in January 1962 part of the land was sold for £1,550. The house was extended in 1988 to cater for the ever-increasing business.

So what was the "Cardinal's Error"? It can best be described in the words of Mr. Miskin, Leney's solicitor, when applying at Tonbridge Police Court for transfer of the licence from the "White Hart". At that time Whitbread were developing an heraldic theme for their new outlets and the proposed name fell within this category. In the time of Henry VIII, Cardinal Wolsey suppressed the famous Priory at Tonbridge, but at the same time he promised the good townsfolk that he would provide them with a "great new grammar school" in its place. Shortly afterwards the Cardinal was to fall from grace and he lost his Cardinal's hat and Tonbridge lost both its Priory and the promised grammar school, although ultimately the town was to acquire its famous school.

Converted from a pair of 16th century cottages and with attractive gardens, this is a welcoming hostelry affectionately referred to by locals as the "Error". The name is unique and as such was mentioned on the "Up and Doing" radio programme on 9th August 1947 during a discussion on the origins of curious pub names.

In April 2004 the leasehold interest in the pub plus contents was offered for sale at £70,000, subsequently reduced to £52,000 in June.

No 16. Half Moon, Hildenborough
B. Baker, F. Leney, Fremlins, Whitbread

From the present-day exterior one would never imagine that parts of this inn date back almost 500 years. The front was extended in the early 1700's when the landlord was William Peckham. Another very early landlady was Rose Johnstone who managed the house in 1732.

In its early days it was called the "Old Half Moon Inn", with Matthew Eason running the pub in the 1860's. During the stage coach era the mail coach would pull in here to enable the horses to be changed. It is also rumoured that Dick Turpin paid a visit from time to time. In 1892 the freeholder was Benjamin

Baker who leased the house and stables to Frederick Leney & Sons Limited at an annual rent of £100. Leney in return received a rent of £50 p.a. from their tenant. They purchased the freehold on 16th November 1905. In 1896 it is described as the "Half Moon" with coach-house, stabling, assembly rooms and premises. The Queen Anne's Bounty tithe amounting to £13/4/- was redeemed on 2nd May 1930.

This sign is generally associated with the Crusades, but it is worth mentioning that the "Half Moon" is the name of the ship that Henry Hudson sailed to the Barents Sea seeking a North East passage to the Orient. It was a small vessel weighing just 73 metric tons, but despite this it reached the New World and sailed into New York Bay and explored the Hudson River. It was manned by a mixed English and Dutch crew who ultimately mutinied.

The pub has always been popular with the sporting fraternity, in particular cricketers, with one landlord a player of some repute. Following the 39th Servants' Annual Cricket Match held on 7th September 1904 there was a supper in a marquee behind the pub provided by Mr. Austen and the landlord Mr. F. Oaten. The team captains were G. Robinson, coachman to Mrs. Hills of Bourne Place, and E. Jelley, bailiff to Charles Stewart of The Hurst, Coldharbour Lane. In a close-fought match Mr. Robinson's team won by 29 runs. Over the years the house has been a regular haunt of Kent County Cricket team players who used to coach local youngsters.

A sad event occurred on 27th October 1940 at 8.30a.m. when a Spitfire piloted by Pilot Officer John Romney Mather of 66 Squadron based at Gravesend, crashed in the grounds. The pilot was killed and was buried at Ifield near Crawley. Subsequently, in 1972, Malcolm Pettit, a local enthusiast, located and recovered the engine from waste ground behind the "Half Moon".

This house had several long-serving landlords. Charles T. Thorne took over on 13th February 1912 to be succeeded by W.R. Crowdy on 17th August 1943 and he remained until November 1960. In 1939 Thorne paid a rent of £52/10/- plus £1/10/- for electric light. This was on the high side but could be the result of the property having been extended to the front in 1935. In 1960 land adjoining the pub was sold for £450.

The modern sign does not bear comparison with the 1950's miniature, but fortunately the original now hangs at the house bearing the same name at nearby Lye Common.

No 17. Grove Tavern, Tunbridge Wells
F. Leney, Fremlins, Whitbread

This house holds two records. Almost certainly it is the oldest pub still trading in the town and it had the longest-serving landlord of all the inn sign pubs. It started life as one of the first houses built upon Mount Sion. The Poor Rate records can be traced back to May 1689 when Jo Jordan was the occupier. It was a simple ale house and a subsequent landlord named Mathews called his pub "Mount Sion" as it was built on the hill. This hilly part of town overlooking the Walks was the heart of the little town that grew up around the springs and the Pantiles.

David Richard Hoper was licensee from 1874 to 1876 and when he left he opened a small greengrocery shop just below the tavern and was the last surviving tradesman of his era when he died in December 1927 aged 89. On 28th February 1894 Augustus Leney purchased the property from M.E.I. Marley for £800.

I wonder how many inn sign collectors popped into the "Grove Tavern" during the 1950's to obtain this miniature. If you did it would have been handed to you by Henry Okell Dadswell. This kindly gent retired in 1963, but amazingly he took up residence on 23rd October 1911. In 1939 his rent was £42 p.a., he had paid a deposit of £50, and his inventory was valued at £150. He acquired a beer and wine licence in April 1938. He was a dab hand at bowls and represented the County on many occasions and in 1936 he was appointed captain of the Grove Bowls Club for whom he had played for 15 years. In 1949 the Licensed Victuallers of Tunbridge Wells presented him with a clock for his mantelpiece to acknowledge his long service to the community. Shortly after he retired Pat Burke arrived in 1964. He also proved to be a most popular landlord and the locals therefore were mystified when at the beginning of June 1985 he called "last orders" closed the pub and promptly disappeared! The brewers, Whitbread Fremlin, declined to comment but did say the pub would re-open – which it did. Where did he go?

Times move on and it is now a large lively house in need of a few roof slates. The youngsters enjoy the music on offer but this is not to some locals' tastes.

Reconstructed inside, and added to in the past century, the pub ultimately incorporated the "Bugler's Arms" which traded next door from about 1850 to 1914. The freehold premises adjoining the "Grove Tavern" were purchased in July 1922 for £400. A rental of 1/- p.a. was paid to the Corporation of Tunbridge Wells for an inspection chamber that took the drainage from the rear of the premises. This sum was still being paid in 1959. In 1960 Fremlins acquired from Leney 32 Little Mount Sion, a vacant property, adjacent to the "Grove Tavern", which was subject to a demolition order. It was insured for £962.

A house of this antiquity just has to have a ghost – and so it does – a slightly disreputable one at that. Beneath the pub is a network of tunnels besides the cellar. The apparition is old Joshua a former drayman who, it is said, died in a tunnel. Totally confused by modern traffic and the absence of his dray horses he now roams the tunnels searching for his wench who was employed in the brothel. A lady saw him only three months ago.

In 2002 the leasehold interest plus contents was offered for sale at a price of £35,000 plus stock at valuation.

No 18. Hop Pole, East Peckham

(Closed in 1970. Now a private house)B. Baker, F. Leney, Fremlins, Whitbread

Not a great deal has come to light about this pub that was never much more than a beer house. It was, however, valued by the company in 1922 at £1,800 with the landlord paying a rent of £20. A wine licence was granted in 1947.

The surrounding area is now built up, but prior to 1927 the property was enclosed by hop fields – hence the name. There had been a chronic shortage of workers' homes in the village going back many years, and in 1927 a Mr. Martin sold some land next to the "Hop Pole", on which eight houses were built. No doubt this improved the trade enjoyed by the longstanding landlord Mr. William J. Cockrell. This gentleman had taken over the beer house on 7th April 1924 and remained until 29th October 1940, to be succeeded by Henry Alfred Venus. Just before his retirement in 1939, Mr. Cockrell was paying an annual rent of £15, his deposit was £25, with the inventory valued at £88/15/-, which figures give some indication of the amount of trade. Indeed in 1916 the brewers agreed to pay the landlord £13 as their contribution to the shrinkage in his trade due to the war. There was a beer room but no cellar. However, the pub did have its moments. The new housing probably gave rise to the complaint made to the council that "men were committing a nuisance opposite the "Hop Pole Inn" at closing time without taking any precautions respecting the public". It was agreed that "drastic measures should be taken to have a stop put to the nuisance and that the Superintendent of the Kent County Constabulary at Malling be written to". At the next council meeting it was reported that "evidently it had leaked out that

the place was to be watched as on two occasions when the police were watching the men came out and used the urinal belonging to the house"!

Another long-serving landlord was Donald E. Taylor who took over on 20th July 1950. He started life as a charcoal burner, with the charcoal used to start the fires in the local oast houses.

The property dates back to the early 1900's. Following closure it traded for ten years as an antique shop and then housed an architect's practice. It retains much of its original charm, with the original bar doors still in place. In 1999 the freehold was offered for sale at a price of £295,000 with this figure increasing to £499,950 in September 2004.

No 19. The Oak, Rusthall
B. Baker, F. Leney, Fremlins, Whitbread, Beards of Herstmonceux

Another Baker of Tonbridge house leased to Leneys in 1892 at an annual rental of £100 with the freehold purchased on 16th November 1905. The landlord's rent in 1922 was £50 p.a. The agreement read "A messuage tenement and premises known as the "Oak Inn" together with coach-house and stabling situate at Rusthall in the occupation of Frederick Waters for £100 a year".

The first landlord traced was John Goldsmith circa 1858 until 1865. He also traded as a baker. Mr. and Mrs. Waters were landlords from 1892 to 1905. They were a kindly couple, and in January 1895 provided a magnificent tea to about 120 children. The party was held in a recently-built room that was decorated with banners, chains, and evergreens. In the centre was a large banner proclaiming "Welcome to All". There was a decorated Christmas tree that was burdened with a present for each of the children, whose ages ranged from 2 to 13. A Mrs. Scott played the piano and eight young women helped with the food. Contained within the vote of thanks was the sentiment that it was hoped that Mr. and Mrs. Waters would enjoy a long life with health and happiness. The tea became an annual event. Another landlord who remained a long while was Alan William Lyon who took over on 14th August 1922 paying a rent of £70 p.a. In 1934 a further £2 a year became due for the new garage. He remained until March 1941.

The "Oak" is a one-bar, lively house.

No 20. The Cypress, Tunbridge Wells
(AN OFF-LICENCE. Closed in 1975) F. Leney, Fremlins, Whitbread

This modest little establishment is unique amongst all the houses making up the five inn sign series. For a start it was an off-licence and, as such, is the only miniature not to appear on the David Burley metal map of West Kent. The delightful sign was designed by Erma York – her only offering in all five series. Did she also design the equally impressive sign for the "Elm Tree" not far from Paddock Wood?

Why did the name change in 1948? Prior to then it traded as the "Cyprus Stores". It is a semi-detached property with the whole house called Cyprus Villa. Did John Marchant ask Erma to design a sign for the "Cyprus" and she thought of the tree rather than the island?

The place held a great affection with the local community. The Kent and Sussex Courier, under its Warwick's notebook banner, kindly published a request from me for information about local Whitbread houses. This provoked a good response – far more than normal – and almost without exception the "Cypress" is mentioned. Besides providing a first-class service within its catchment area I feel the many long-serving tenants also played their part.

I am told the property was built and operated as a pub in 1878. Augustus Leney was leasing the premises until 25th March 1901 from J.W. Dodd at an annual rent of £50 but on 14th May 1884 the Leney brothers purchased the freehold from E.B. Dodd and mortgagee for £1,000. It was described as a shop for sale of beer. In 1896, when Augustus transferred his estate into the company name, the property is described as the "Cyprus Stores" with stables and yard. In October 1929 the company had the opportunity to acquire the lease rent, which was then £40 p.a., and the reversion in 1936. Leney were prepared to negotiate within a price range of £600 to £800 but the agents acting requested £1,800. Negotiations were dropped. I believe the company subsequently purchased the freehold for £510 subject to a life annuity. The pub traded until 1914 at which time new licensing laws resulted in it converting to an off-licence and it traded as such until it closed its doors in 1975. It then became a bric-a-brac shop before conversion to a private house. The very large garage was once a stable with hay loft. In about 1930 a kitchen and extra bedroom were added – the kitchen used to be in the cellar. It is still readily recognizable as a pub and still boasts the brown terracotta tiles standard to many Whitbread houses. Older residents believe that round about the turn of the century the publican also ran a coal merchants business.

Whilst trading as a public house the first landlord I can trace was Edwin Scragg in 1886 and the last was F. Moon who was here from 1900 to 1915. Albert Humphrey took over on 13th May 1918 paying a rent of £48 and he remained until 15th April 1940. The highly respected Mr. and Mrs. Norman then moved in paying a reduced rental of £26. On 12th January 1942 a deposit of £100 is recorded. Mr. and Mrs. Norman stayed on until 1953 when George Weekes arrived. Unfortunately this gentleman died in July 1955. He had served in the Royal Navy for 24 years from October 1895 until 1919. A freeman of the city of London he had spent most of his life there. In 1922 he took over his first public house, the "Claremont" in Bermondsey. In 1936 he moved on to the "Plough" at Stockwell and in 1940 arrived at the "We Three Loggerheads", finally finishing his career here. Within the trade, whilst under the tutelage of Mr. and Mrs. Norman, it was felt that problems were always dealt with straight away as the couple had "connections" at Wateringbury. Perhaps it was just the way they managed the business. Certainly, in 1940 repairs totalling £841/18/2 were carried out. Until April 1949 the off-licence held a beer and wine licence only, but during the Normans' stay they were granted a full off-licence. In July 1968 Leney sold the "Cypress" for £4,000, although I believe it continued to trade until 1975.

A local resident recalls the place had three hand-pulled "Engines" pumps, one for cooking bitter (ordinary bitter), one for best and one for mild. As the beer could not be consumed on the premises it was carried away in jugs. Sunday lunchtimes were a particularly busy period. Another can remember the kindly Normans who kept the garden immaculate and the shop spotless. They always proffered the coveted inn sign to each lad after dispensing a glass of lemonade.

The David Burley metal map hung on the wall – omitting the "Cypress".

No 21. Papermakers Arms, Plaxtol
F. Leney, Fremlins, Whitbread, Free House, Enterprise Inns

This house takes its name from the nearby paper mills in the valley of the Bourne at Basted (now a bookstore for Odhams) and Rough Way. The paper was custom supplied to the Bank of England. Locally it was said you could always recognise a man employed in the papermills, as due to the nature of the work their hands would tremble. The original beer house was in Poste Cottage just up the hill. This was held under a lease dated 31st December 1885 for a term of 14 years at an annual rent of £25. S. Whitwick owned the property. On 8th November 1898 Miss A. Markis and others sold these premises plus the block

adjoining to Frederick Leney & Sons Limited.

The present house was built in 1902 and in 1921 a value of £2,000 was placed upon it. On 13th April 1928 the brewers extinguished the manorial incidents relating to the "Papermakers Arms" plus two other pubs at a cost of £32/19/4.

In the 1930's this was a simple beer house which also doubled up as a grocery and general store. It acquired a beer and wine licence on 8th April 1940. On 1st September 1924 Bob Twort took over. He was a popular tenant, but unfortunately, in 1934, whilst pruning his rose bushes he pricked his finger on a thorn and subsequently died of lockjaw. His successor Charles T. Rabbitt (Bunny) also proved a most able landlord. In 1939 he paid a rent of £25 p.a. plus £1 for electricity. The inventory was valued at £86/14/-. Customers, in the main, were papermakers, agricultural labourers, hoppers, and the village bobby. Although they did not meet at the "Papermakers" the members of the local Rat and Sparrow club used to hold their annual dinner in the smoking room. Bunny could produce a mean rabbit pie and his cheeses and onions were a popular dish. The rabbits were often supplied by a local lad, Tom Gunner. Darts, daddlums, skittles, dominoes and crib were all played here. During the war Mr. Rabbitt acted as one of the village air-raid wardens, using his son as his runner. Both were awarded medals but the lad's was taken away as he was considered too young to do the job. About this time the pub sign stood in the front garden. This was a raised earth bank in which the landlord would grow his vegetables and keep chickens. Trade suffered due to the lack of car parking facilities but during Mr. Rabbitt's tenure Whitbread refused to tarmac over the garden to create a car park. As soon as he left, in 1952, these improvements were carried out.

On several occasions the future of the pub has been in doubt, but, following the demise of amongst others the "Rorty Crankle" it is now the only house trading in the village.

No 22. Star and Garter, Tonbridge
(Closed in 1994) B. Baker, F. Leney, Fremlins, Whitbread

In 1892 Bakers leased this house to Frederick Leney & Sons Limited for £55 p.a. and they purchased the freehold on 16th November 1905. The landlord's rent in 1922 amounted to £24 p.a.

For some reason this house always had a slightly unsavoury reputation and it finally lost its licence in 1994 – possibly due to the misuse of drugs. However, its history can be traced back to the 1700's. In 1742 Thomas Harvey, gentleman, of Tonbridge bought about 10 acres of land on the outskirts of the town which remained in the ownership of the family for 87 years, until it was sold off in 17 lots in 1829. John Carnell bought lot 5 for £150 and in 1865 this plot came into the possession of John Taylor Baker, brewer, of Tonbridge. Shortly afterwards the "Star and Garter" was built. It was subsequently leased to Frederick Leney & Sons Limited who went on to purchase the freehold in the early 1900's. In 1896, besides the pub, there was a coach-house, stabling and premises. In 1960 Fremlins took over the Leney estate, which

included two cottages adjoining the pub. One was let to Mrs. Lomas, who paid a rent of 12/8 per week; the other was vacant.

L. Hewitt was the landlord in 1874. By 1886 G. Whitehead was behind the bar and he remained until 1909. In 1896 he was fined 10/- with 10/- costs for selling adulterated whiskey. A very popular landlord, George Terry, took over in 1916. Previously he had been the landlord at the "Bridge Hotel" Uckfield. A keen football supporter he never missed a Tonbridge game, which he used to attend with his dog. He died on 4th November 1932 – for a short while his widow, Edith, continued to run the pub. Another landlord, Henry Waters, was up before the beak in 1948 for selling adulterated gin. He was fined £40 with costs of £2/2/ -. In 1931 the brewers were recompensed £6/6/- for damage to the sign.

This was a traditional pub, but trade was affected by the lack of car-parking facilities. The local bus stop, however, was called "Star and Garter" and it was felt this somewhat offset the disadvantage of having nowhere to park. For a long while there was a water fountain to the front of the building and it did have a pleasant garden. Various signs hung outside, some quite garish. Although I never saw it, I am told that the most popular was a copy of a famous photo of Marilyn Monroe! In the early 1990's a local competitor told me that this was "not a good pub", having acquired a bad name in the late 1980's. It ceased to trade in 1994. Following closure it was re-named the "Star" and converted into a non-alcoholic venue for youngsters. Later it became known as "Switches", whilst remaining a coffee shop and information centre for young people. Now very dilapidated it is still readily recognizable as a former public house with the brown terracotta tiles still in place.

The building's days are probably numbered as this is a busy road junction and for years the property has been under the threat of demolition for much-needed road improvements.

No 23. Walnut Tree, Brenchley
(Closed for the second time in 1996) Jude Hanbury, F. Leney, Fremlins, Whitbread, Free House

This wayside inn stood on the Brenchley – Matfield road in an area variously described as Walnut Tree hamlet or Markets Heath.

An abstract of title commences with a deed dated 23rd February 1838 under the hands and seals of the parish officers of Brenchley and others. Previously there existed an Act of Parliament under King William

IV entitled "An Act to facilitate the conversion of Workhouses and other properties of the parishes and of the incorporation or union of parishes in England and Wales". As a result of this Act the cottages, of which the "Walnut Tree" formed part, were once owned by the parish of Brenchley and used as homes for the poor. When sold the occupants were transferred to the Pembury Institution – now Pembury Hospital.

On 9th February 1863 the beerhouse and six cottages were offered for sale described thus:- "Recently erected brick and slated premises consisting of six tenements. One built expressly for and used as a beerhouse. Has underground cellars, front and back parlours separated by moveable partitions and forming if necessary one room 24ft. by 12ft. Tap room, sitting room, wash house and four good bedrooms. Five cottages adjoining in the occupation of James Browne, Thomas Hanbury, and others. Detached bakehouses and a well in the back yard".

The purchaser was John Beale Jude. It was not until the census of 1871 that we pick up Henry Moseley, aged 46, trading as a beerhouse keeper. His wife Frances was aged 37. The 1881 census reveals that James Neale had taken over. He was aged 31 and was also a watchmaker. His wife, Amelia, aged 27, had three children and was an apprentice watchmaker. They were still here in 1886, but it is reputed that James shot himself in the pub and since then the house was said to be haunted.

About a hundred years ago the following improvements were carried out:-

1904. Writing in front of house in gold and shaded. £ 4.

1910. Remove brick floor of washhouse and lay concrete floor
6 inches deep and repair roof of washhouse and house £ 6/19/-.

1929. Providing and fixing electric light by S. Terry. £29/ 2/6.

Always a modest little inn, the inventory in 1939 amounted to £90/17/-. The place acquired a beer and wine licence on 8th April 1940 and a full licence in 1951 when the net monopoly value was settled at £450. Its heydays were the war years and the hop-picking season. Very popular with servicemen, who enjoyed a good sing-song around the piano, it could get quite rowdy. The pub was sited on a nasty bend and had only modest parking to the rear, so it was quite difficult to stop at the "Walnut Tree". One inn sign collector recalls being warned by the landlord that his barley wine was quite strong. He tells me it was only with considerable difficulty that he found his way back home to Paddock Wood. The landlord was probably Kenneth Whymark who became licensee on 18th February 1947 and stayed for about twenty years. His wife ran the Walnut Tree Stores. The cottages appear to have passed through several hands. In the 1930's Walnut Tree Cottage was owned by the Tenterden Brewery Company and was let at 2/9 per week. On 15th June 1934 it was sold for £60 to Leney via Jude Hanbury. In 1960, when the tenant was L. Rofe who paid a rent of 11/10 per week, the cottage was acquired by Fremlins together with the shop and store, which was by then vacant.

The pub closed in 1973 but was sold on 15th July 1974 with licence. It subsequently re-opened with modest restaurant facilities, a feature of which was an old cast-iron range in the recessed fireplace, but trade remained minimal and it closed for good in 1996. The original witty inn sign hung until the end.

In 1997 the property was sold for about £145,000 with planning permission to convert to a private dwelling.

"A woman, a dog and a walnut tree. The more you beat 'em the better they be." Old Proverb.

No 24. We Three Loggerheads, Tonbridge

(Closed as a recognizable pub in 1993) W & G Bartram's Brewery,
B. Baker, F. Leney, Fremlins, Whitbread

This pub must hold two records:- (1) the house that traded under the most names; and (2) moved premises most frequently.

The very first pub was in the High Street, but this was demolished in 1908 when the High Street was re-aligned. The town post office was ultimately built on the site, but in due course this was moved to more modern premises and the building reverted back to a Weatherspoon pub called the "Humphrey Bean". Weatherspoons give a great deal of thought to the naming of their houses and although the name probably means nothing to most local residents, Humphrey was the landlord at the old pub from 1886 to 1892. In those days the house was frequented by bargees, as the Medway Navigation Company's wharves were just across the road. Originally in the late 1700's the workforce had used the company's own pub, the weather-boarded "Castle Inn", formerly the "Six Bells". When the great bridge was rebuilt in 1888 the "Castle Inn" was demolished and the men found its replacement, the refined "Castle Hotel", not at all to their liking and hence frequented the rough and ready "Loggerheads". In those days a quart of beer was part of the day's pay and an apprentice would be sent along to the pub with mugs ranged on long poles to collect the beer. The original sign, much as the inn sign miniature, shows two simple-minded bargemen looking at the third – you! In those days the house was called "We Three Loggerheads Be" or simply "Loggerheads". Following demolition the local bench did not renew its licence when it came up for its annual renewal.

From where did the idea for this name and the original sign come? Quite probably thus. If one takes a trip to the Loggerheads Country Park situated between Mold and Ruthin one can quench one's thirst at the "Loggerheads". In that hostelry a copy of a painting produced in the second half of the eighteenth century can be found. The artist was Richard Wilson (1714 – 1782) who lived locally and the painting depicts the two men that we recognize and is titled "We Three Loggerheads".

In 1905 Benjamin Baker sold the "Station Bridge Hotel" to Frederick Leney & Sons Limited. It was situated on the corner of Waterloo Road opposite the railway station. It was decided to redevelop the site and plans were drawn up by F.W. Reeve of Leneys to rebuild the property and re-open it under the name of "We Three Loggerheads". The new house would include a public, saloon, private and ladies' bar together with a childrens' room and servery. The renovated house, under its new name, opened in July 1939. To the rear of this pub was another Leney house – the "Good Intent" which was also demolished. During the war years this was quite a rowdy and busy venue. G. Weeks took over on 4th December 1940 when the inventory amounted to £607/2/6. His rent was £150 and the deposit was £200. Repairs totalling £2,239/3/3 had recently been carried out. These were quite large sums in those days. His last pub had probably been the "Dun Cow" in the Old Kent Road. In 1960 Fremlins took over the Leney estate, which included a shop which formed part of this pub. It was leased to Stanford & Co, (Tonbridge) Limited at an annual rental of £375. Sadly the premises were demolished in the early 1970's to make way for a Safeway supermarket. The name and sign then moved to new modern premises a few hundred yards away in Quarry Hill Road. This building resembles a modern office block or a bowling alley rather than a public house. It wasn't long before the pub converted to a nightclub trading under the name of "Flatfoot Sam's", then "Hotshots" and finally "Watchdog". At times it has also traded as "Three Loggerheads" and "Loggers".

"Did you never see the picture of we three?" Shakespeare – Twelfth Night.

No 25. Blacksmith's Arms, Harrietsham
(Closed 23rd May 1975)
Jude Hanbury, F. Leney, Fremlins, Whitbread

Although the smallest beer house in the village, this was a homely welcoming inn. At one time it was quite a sizable establishment. The property was built in 1779 and the outbuildings, over the years, served as a wheelwright's shop, forge, village mortuary, dance hall and coal yard. The wheelwright's shop was purchased from Arthur Tong for £95 in August 1899 and the blacksmith's shop in June 1914 for £150.

Initially the property acted as the poor house for the parishes of Harrietsham and Hollingbourne. In about 1840 it was sold to James Tong, a bricklayer, who subsequently

became a beer retailer. He borrowed money secured against the property but fell in to arrears and the mortgagees foreclosed. Almost certainly the mortgagees were Jude Hanbury or a member of the Hanbury family. It was named the "Blacksmith's Arms" at about the turn of the century.

Regular maintenance and additions are seen:-

1899. New roof to stables. £94/12/-.

1900. Sanitary work. £29/ 7/-.

1901. Two oak posts and sill and hanging door between cottages and public house. £ 3/17/9.

1902. Deepening well. £ 5/11/3.

1905. Laying down water supply. £11/17/4.

In 1925 the adjoining forge, two cottages and the wheelwright's shop were sold off. The initial asking price was £500, but an offer of £425 was accepted. It is possible that the buyer was the Tenterden Brewery Company, as in May 1934 Leney purchased via Jude Hanbury the wheelwright's shop from the Tenterden Brewery for £90. All dealings in the unlicensed properties were a paper exercise and money never changed hands. Beer piping was installed in 1937 and a "special allowance" of £1/7/5 granted. In 1960 Fremlins took over, from Leney, the workshop abutting the pub, and this was let to Mr. H.R.S. Couchman who paid a rent of 15/- per week.

Before the A20 was re-routed to the south of the village, the pub stood on the old Dover road and benefited from coastal-bound traffic. Even then it knew its place in the pecking order. The coach and horses would pull into the plush "Roebuck" where the better class of traveller would be housed and the horses turned out into the fields to the rear. Lesser mortals would retire to the "Blacksmith's Arms". Any horse that required re-shoeing would be taken to the forge. A similar pattern was established when coach parties of Londoners would leave for a day at the sea-side. They would park at the "Roebuck" and the overflow would drift down to the smaller house. This type of trade fell away in the 1970's when cheap continental holidays were pioneered. Life for the landlord's family was primitive. Bucket toilets were in use until the early 1950's. There were gas mantles and an old black kitchen range.

In 1941 the landlord was J.W. Keall who paid a rent of £20; his inventory was valued at £102/1/-. He was followed by the very popular Hope family – Les and Coo remained until Mr. Hope retired in 1970. They then moved to the Licensed Victuallers National homes in Buckinghamshire, but sadly Mr. Hope died nine months later. Beer was in their blood as grandfather Hope had run the "Camden Arms", Sissinghurst, a brother, Bernard, was at the "Elm Tree" near Paddock Wood, another brother, Stanley, was at the "We Three Loggerheads" and an aunt, Lily Heath, was behind the bar at the "Robin Hood", Upper Halling. In 1941 it was a simple beer house – it was not until the late 1960's that it was granted a full licence. To supplement the family income Mr. Hope worked as a signalman at the village railway station. The place was very popular during the war years with American G.I.'s travelling up from Headcorn, and Welsh soldiers billeted on the Pilgrims Way. A doodlebug was shot down and crashed into the local trout farm and a bomb blew out the back windows and brought the ceiling down. However, the family cat proved invaluable with its sixth sense warning the Hopes of impending danger. It had just had kittens and whenever it felt the kittens' lives were threatened it would carry them down to the cellars. It was rarely wrong. During the war years four land girls stayed at the "Blacksmith's" and Mrs. Hope and her daughter slept in the cellars.

The house required total refurbishment by the time it closed and was sold off for £14,500. Although I knew it very well I didn't recognize the newly-renovated property which was operating as a bed-and-breakfast establishment; the front bar had been converted into a letting room. The pub had a good sign that hung until the pub closed, and was the only one in all five series designed by L.B.H. Cremer.

In July 2003 the house was placed on the market at an asking price of £395,000.

No 26. The Chequers, West Farleigh
*(Now **The Tickled Trout**) F. Leney, Fremlins, Whitbread*

This old timber-framed building was erected in 1541, probably as a hall house. Subsequent renovation took place in the mid-1700's when it was converted into an ale house. For a long while in the 1800's the Leney brothers were tenants of William Fitzherbert paying an annual rent of £96. The lease dated 7th December

1878 also included a meadow and woodland comprising 21 acres 3rods and 21perch. Frederick Leney & Sons Limited purchased the freehold on 21st September 1921 for £2,750; the house was valued at this figure in the company books the following year. By 1925 the valuation had dropped to £2,350 – this was probably accounted for by the fact that, in 1924, Leney had sold, for £350, woodland, 2 1/2 acres of land plus grass to Mr. A. Margetts. This same gentleman, in February 1930, purchased further land for £325 and the valuation dropped to £2,025. In 1962 improvements were carried out at a cost of £570.

During 1916 a tenant was experiencing financial difficulties and the brewers considered a reduction in his rent. The outcome of the negotiations is not known.

Any inn sign collector who called in the 1950's could not fail to be impressed by the massive chestnut tree standing on the pub forecourt, but sadly this has long gone. It is, however, still a very pleasant experience to call here as the house backs on to the River Medway and a path winds down to the river. Unfortunately the pub was re-named the "Tickled Trout" in about 1990, possibly to reflect the good fishing to be had nearby. The original inn sign remained, until the name change, whilst all the other "Chequers" had new designs. This is one of the oldest names for a public house and depicts the Romans' enjoyment of tavern games and their practice of changing money there and calculating on a ten-square chequer board.

The house boasts a popular restaurant, its speciality being sea food. It also houses a fine collection of match-box tops.

"And life? 'Tis all a chequer-board of nights and days, Where destiny with men for pieces plays."

No 27. Clothworker's Arms, Sutton Valence
Jude Hanbury, F. Leney, Fremlins, Whitbread, Shepherd Neame

The "Clothworker's" is a popular and busy village local with magnificent views over the Weald. In its early days it was called the "Drovers Rest" and was nothing more than an old shack in, what is now, the back garden of the present pub. The drovers would have driven their flock up from the marsh and penned the sheep in the field to the rear. The pub was called the "Drovers Rest" when Jude Hanbury purchased it together with three cottages for £500 in 1897. The house was then rebuilt – £550 was spent that year and the balance of rebuilding costs, £496/18/3, was paid the following year. Architect's fees amounted to £75/14/-.

It was about this time that the pub took its present name commemorating the achievements of one of the village's most famous sons – William Lambe. He was born in 1495 during the reign of King Henry VII at a time when trade and exploration were encouraged in order to boost the King's coffers. He made his

fortune in London and become Master of the Guild of Cloth-makers. The inn sign depicts two shearing knives and a teazle used for combing wool. In 1576, towards the end of his life, he founded the famous school at Sutton Valence.

During 1899 painting and papering was carried out at a cost of £27 and in 1905 fruit trees were purchased for £2/5/-. J. Botley became the licensee on 22nd January 1940 and remained for several years. He paid a rent of £20 p.a. and a deposit of £25. At this time the "Clothworker's" was no more than a beer house, but it did acquire a beer and wine licence in April 1941. Always popular with sportsmen, the pub runs darts, bar billiards and pool teams. There is a fine display cabinet exhibiting their numerous trophies. In the 1950's agricultural workers were the main source of income and during the season the pub was popular with hop-pickers, but the house now relies on local trade.

In 1960 Fremlins acquired, from Leney, Clothworker's Cottage – the tenant was C. Holloway, who was paying a rent of 20/3 per week. The pub still has the original windows etched Whitbread, but Shepherd Neame purchased the freehold in 1972.

No 28. Duke of Wellington, Ryarsh
*(Formerly the **Cock and Coney**) Jude Hanbury, F. Leney, Fremlins, Whitbread*

The "Duke of Wellington" is everything a village pub should be; it serves excellent food and has a pleasant beer garden. Its history goes back a long long way.

The present house was built in the reign of Henry VIII but the original, an old chapel, dated back to the days of William the Conqueror. The land was farmed by Benedictine monks, who baked their own bread and brewed ales. It also acted as a pilgrims' rest for those on their travels to Canterbury. Unfortunately the chapel was destroyed by fire in the late 1400's.

The first owner of the new building was Septimus Quylle, a farmer, hop grower and brewer. The original licence, granted in 1516, was for the sale of ales and ciders only, with the building registered as a Kentish Ale House. His wife, Elanor, managed the public house, and on the death of Septimus in 1545 the licence was transferred into her name. In 1610 the house was extensively modernized with the wattle and daub generally giving way to bricks and tiles, although the visitor can still see a little wattle. Daniel Deeds was the new landlord and was licensed to sell distilled gin and liquors.

The beer house was originally named the "Cock and Coney", then between 1815 and 1818 the "Wellington" to honour the Duke's victory at Waterloo, and thereafter the present name.

In October 1900 the brewers spent £3/4/9 on having the well water analysed and two years later a sanitary system was installed and this plus other works cost £105/15/6. During the war years the landlord was A.E. Waters who paid a rent of £40 for the pub, shop and three cottages. At one time there were five cottages, as in May 1934 Leney acquired these from the Tenterden Brewery Company, via Jude Hanbury. In 1960 Fremlins acquired the Leney premises. These included Wellesley Cottage, where the Misses V.E. Bowden and G. Reynolds were paying a rent of 12/- per week.

Although close to the M20 and A20, Ryarsh remains a pleasant backwater famous for its brickworks. Over the last few years a lot of money has been spent on renovating the pub and the original sign hung until 1994.

No 29. Fleur-De-Lis, Burham
Staceys of Maidstone, F. Leney, Fremlins, Whitbread, Marr Taverns

This is a nice old-fashioned village pub which still retains its long bench seats.

It was built in the sixteenth century and it is felt that it could have been the wine house frequented by the household of J.H. Rosney, the French Ambassador to the English court from 1597 until 1604 during the reign of Elizabeth I. Over a period of seven years from 1795 to 1802 William Dunning acquired the house that was described as the "Flower de Luce". The conveyance included a slaughterhouse amongst the outbuildings and two acres of fruit orchard. In 1804 he leased the pub to Stephen Page Seager of Maidstone, a brewer, for a term of fourteen years at a rental of £25 p.a. This business later came under the control of Staceys of Maidstone which became part of Fremlins in 1929 when trading as Isherwood, Foster & Stacey. The property was part of the marriage settlement for his daughter Ann Elizabeth and remained in the family until 18th August 1885 when it was sold by Mrs. C.E.M. Hughes to Augustus Leney for £1,500. The family never appear to have run the pub themselves as in 1843 it was leased by Mrs. Ann Fowle for a term of 14 years at a rent of £30 to John and Michael Lock; in 1859 by Lewis Fowle and others to Robert Hanbury, and in 1866 William King leased the house for a term of 7 years at a rent of £40 to Edward North Buxton of Brick Lane, London, renewing the lease for two further terms of 7 years in 1873 and 1880. All of the lessors were brewers. In 1896, when Augustus Leney transferred his pub portfolio into the company name, besides the pub there was also a cottage and land. In 1898 part of the property to the north was sold off for housing.

The "Fleur-De-Lis" is a fairly common name. The emblem was adopted by the Kings of England for their Royal Standard as part of their claim to the throne of France. This claim lasted from the reign of Edward II until the eighteenth century.

Edward Wingfield and NicholasWilkins were landlords during the 1700's, with John Wilkins the innkeeper in 1795. In 1881 the property was valued at £1,426/6/-; this was increased to £1,500 in 1890, when a rent of £40 p.a. was levied. A long-serving landlord was Fred J. Sleeth who arrived on 5th May 1924 and retired on 18th April 1943. Initially his rent was £28 p.a. for the pub and bungalow plus £1 for electric light. The inventory amounted to £162/11/6. During 1939 repairs costing £270/9/6 were carried out. In 1960 Fremlins acquired the vacant Fleur de Lis cottage.

No 30. Good Intent, West Farleigh
F. Leney, Fremlins, Whitbread

In its early days this was a modest little ale house but it has now blossomed into a thriving business. It has, however, had its ups and downs.

It was built in 1740 as a farm dwelling and was owned by Robert Gregory. There have been many subsequent additions. A wheelwright operated from the premises and in 1801 Stephen Shadgett applied for and was granted a licence to sell ales. The house had no name being referred to as the Ale House. Stephen was a seed crusher and corn merchant.

The house was registered as the "Good Intent" in 1838 by Thomas Larkin, a beer retailer from Maidstone. A brief history in the bar states that it took the name of a gun vessel of H.M. Fleet that was built at Sheerness in 1790. By 1796, following an engagement, the ship was badly damaged and decommissioned. It was repaired and limped along until 1801 when it returned to this country and was broken up. Hardly a pedigree to inspire the naming of a pub. I far prefer the explanation that the "Good Intent" was a smuggling vessel that, at various times, operated out of Dover and Rye. It had been carefully designed for its nefarious activities and it is said it could carry a vast number of kegs of good French brandy. It was eventually captured in 1837 by the Revenue Cruiser Sylvia. This date ties in with the naming of the house.

From 1866 until 1878 the landlord operated a saddlery business from the house. This could have been a lucrative business as throughout its history the inn has been a popular venue for travellers who used the large area of grassland surrounding the inn to park their caravans and graze their horses. These people did cause problems from time to time and were never popular with locals.

F. and C.F. Leney purchased a moiety of the premises for £380 from Nicholas Passmore on 7th July 1871 when it was stated that the pub was situated at Farleigh Green. It was a modest business in those days. In 1881 it was valued in the brewers' books at £350 and had only crept up to £380 by 1908, when the rent was £23 p.a. As late as 1939 the inventory was valued at only £96/16/-. In 1930 a strip of land was purchased for £20. It was granted a beer and wine licence on 8th April 1940 and didn't acquire a "full" licence until 1949.

In its later years it has provided a good living and in 1995, as a gift to the village, the retiring landlord resurfaced the lane leading up to the pub. The inn sign miniature hung until 1994 when it was damaged in a gale. A new, more trendy, depiction then appeared but the vessel seemed quite unsuitable for smuggling.

No 31. King's Arms, Headcorn
William Foster, Jude Hanbury, F. Leney, Fremlins, Whitbread

Housed in a gracious Grade II listed building, possibly dating back to the late 1600's with 19th century alterations, this is an excellent village local. A former coaching inn, it provides accommodation, a good restaurant and live music – jazz evenings are a feature. Certainly used by smugglers, a favoured haunt of the notorious Hawkhurst gang, it is also stated it was the secret rendezvous of local Jacobites in the days of the White Cockade. However, locals will tell you this is pure speculation – musings of a former vicar a long while ago. Certainly, in Headcorn, until recent times, on bonfire nights, an effigy of the Pope was burned.

The "King's Arms" was bought by James Waghorne of Headcorn, a butcher, in 1793 and he left it, together with other property, equally to his six children. In 1846 the pub and other properties were auctioned at the "King's Arms". A William Foster, of Rochester, a victualler, bought the pub for £700 and two years later he sold his 5/6 share to John Beale Jude who bought the other 1/6 share in 1862 for £100.

The first landlord that I can trace is John Jude in 1753. Chas Waghorne (surely a relative of James) was here in 1855 and is also described as a butcher and farmer. During his tenure £125 was spent on repairing the property. In 1884 it was occupied by Thomas Jones who had previously been goods foreman at Headcorn station. The "Coffee Shop Keeper" composed the following lines:-

> "Tom Jones, he was a porter. And used to tend the rail
> But, not quite liking that employ, He now attends the ale!
> He's a very decent fellow - I wish him all success
> If he goes on as he's begun, He will not do amiss".

During his tenure the pub was a hive of activity. The Gardeners' Society and Cricket Club regularly met at the "King's Arms" and Mr. Jones always got an off-licence when there was a cricket match or flower show, and ran a bar in the cricket field, which was then in Moat Road. At that time matches lasted all day, and Tom would provide a lunch, always the same – cold shoulder of mutton salad and fruit pie for 2/6 – one paid extra for drinks. In 1887 he placed an advertisement in the local press that ran as follows:- "The annual sparrow shoot will take place at the "King's Arms", Headcorn, on December 26th – A good supply of birds".

In November 1908 the juvenile members of the Bonfire Society sat down to a substantial tea provided for them by Mr. Jones' successor A. Atkins. The ladies who kindly collected on the "fifth" were also present. Games and songs were indulged in and a very pleasant evening was spent. From these small beginnings Headcorn Bonfire night developed into the best display in the area, attracting a huge crowd each November 5th from as far away as Maidstone and Lenham.

Considerable excitement occurred in the village in March 1912 when, early on a Monday morning, a life-size figure, fully attired, was found suspended on a gibbet in Wheeler Street, close to the gipsy encampment, with a large inscription – Len's Last Drop". It was deemed necessary that an inquest be held and the figure was removed to the "Kings Arms" and laid out on an improvised bier. Mr. F.E. Foreman undertook the duties of Coroner. About one hundred people attended and, after due deliberation, the jury found as follows – "Found hanging in Wheeler Street probably due to remorse and suffering for all past offences against the village". The remains were then enclosed in a coffin and, on Wednesday night, a torchlight procession accompanied the same through the village. The remains were duly cremated in the main street opposite the "Black Horse".

Quite a lot of work was carried out here at the turn of the last century. In 1899 painting, papering and repairs cost £99/10/- and in 1906 the bay window in the public bar was replaced at a price of £34/15/4. Four years later there was reference to expenditure on the butcher's shop and the new slaughterhouse. On 4th March 1936 Leney purchased the adjoining shop for £165 and Fremlins acquired the freehold in 1960. At that time it was leased to A.R. Cox who paid a rent of £72 p.a.

By 1923 Richard Toussaint Maynard had taken over, and in July 1923 he applied for an "occasional licence", at Bearsted police court, to sell intoxicants at the Annual Flower Show on 6th August from 10a.m. until 10p.m. The application was granted. In 1925 the Headcorn Conservative and Unionist Association held a smoking concert here, which was attended by about thirty people, with Mr. T.H. Batty from the central Conservative Association giving a stirring address, devoting most of his speech to agricultural matters. This was followed by a capital music programme. In 1930 Mr. Maynard provided an excellent repast to members participating in the local shove ha'penny league. Mr. Evans was the winner, securing the first game by two chalks, the second by one. Richard T. Maynard retired and subsequently died in 1944 at the age of 70. He was succeeded on 14th March 1938 by his son, Richard Harley Maynard, whose wife, Mrs. R.M. Maynard, took over on 9th June 1941 whilst her husband was on war service. In 1938 the rent was £50 and a deposit of £75 was taken. Sadly Richard died in 1946 at the young age of 42 and was succeeded by his widow. Graham J.C. Moore was another long-serving landlord from 1971 until about 1995.

There was obviously something amiss with the inn sign as in September 1948 John Marchant wrote to Kathleen Claxton stating – "Up to the time of going to press we have heard no more about the contretemps regarding the famous "Kings Arms", Headcorn – but it will come in due course".

No 32. Red Rover, East Malling
(Closed in either 1966 or 1968) F. Leney, Fremlins

The "Red Rover" was another early casualty, but fond memories linger on. These small ale houses serving a local, mainly rural community generated great warmth and were obviously the hub of most activities. This house was situated at Springetts Hill on the outskirts of East Malling and was not easy to find – the area is now known as Broadwater Road.

The pub dates back to at least 1872 and was originally built as five cottages, probably for agricultural workers. It is tempting to think that one of the women living here started brewing beer to quench the thirst of the workers who lived in the nearby 14 cottages and six houses, and the owner of Broadwater farm. There was also a shop in the area, but it was demolished many years ago. The pub came to occupy the two cottages on the left, the second was purchased in 1954 to provide the tenant with separate modern living quarters. In 1960 Fremlins took over the Leney estate including the two remaining cottages, one of which was let to Mrs. A. Pick and the other to A. Morgan – both paid a rent of 16/7 per week. The pub never had inside toilets, but electricity was laid on in 1936. In 1957 the third cottage was purchased and the three were converted into one large house with the tap room in the front extension. At this time the landlord was Thomas Card who stayed for 20 years. It was during his tenure that the house acquired a wine licence in 1947, followed shortly afterwards by a spirits licence. The pub had no cellar and the beer was stored out the back two to three feet below ground level to keep it cool. As a result the floor was ultimately levelled and the kitchen has a sloping roof.

Augustus Leney leased the pub from John Pierce in 1879 for a term of 21 years paying an annual rent of £40. On 4th May 1888 he purchased the premises and three cottages for £900. However, a copy agreement exists, dated 1896, which relates to the sale of the "Red Rover" plus three cottages for £1,280. In 1890 the pub was valued in the brewers' books at £900; this sum had increased to £1,025 by 1908 but the same figure was quoted in 1921.

The task of one man who remembers the pub well was to clean out the barrel-shaped cesspit which served all five cottages. It was 30 feet deep and towards the end of this back-breaking work he had to climb down into the pit to shovel out the dregs. On completion he would retire to the shed at the back of the garden, have a strip wash, don the old clothes that his wife had left and then go into the pub for a bath. He reckoned there were about ten lorry-loads of manure.

It was never much more than an ale house and for 68 years was managed by the Costin family; initially the parents, then the maiden sisters. Miss Elizabeth S. Costin was in situ from 6th March 1922 until May 1944. In 1939 she was paying a rent of £20 for the pub, £20 for the cottages, plus £2 for electricity. During her tenure, and long after, the pub was frequented by Londoners who came down to pick hops. In the war years trenches were dug in a nearby cherry orchard to enable the pickers to take cover during air raids. The pub was also popular with the RAF, as the little lane provided a back access to nearby West Malling. On the night of 16th April 1943, a most unusual event occurred. A squadron of 30 Focke-Wulfs set off from Germany to bomb London. The mission was not a success and the squadron broke up. Four pilots became completely disorientated, assumed they had crossed the Channel, and thinking they were over France proceeded to attempt to land at RAF West Malling! One of the aircraft ditched at Springetts Hill Farm and the pilot, Oberfeldwebel Otto Schulz, escaped with concussion. The ambulance men found him having a drink with a local who had witnessed the crash. Such chivalry was typical of the many characters who were regular imbibers at the "Rover". Each had his own particular song or verse to recite around the piano. Before the war Boxing Day was the highlight of the year. This was Aunt Tot's birthday and a party was always held here as she was one of the Costin sisters. A licence extension was granted and the party was thrown open to all the people on the hill as well as their relations and the village children. There was a turkey, a big boiled ham for sandwiches and a fine array of pastries. The usual melodies would be banged out on the piano and every one did a turn when it was sing, say, or pay a forfeit. There was also plenty of dancing. What would modern youth make of these simple pleasures?

When the pub closed the house and cottages were sold for £7,500 to Joe Wolfe and the pub was converted to a week-end cottage. In 2002 the house was offered for sale at a price of £299,500. The resourceful can still find the old haunt as the post and frame for the sign have never been removed. A nice touch is that the house has been named "Rovers End". A former landlord's daughter saw the original inn sign at Hastings antique market for sale at £7/10/- and to this day regrets her decision not to buy it.

"The fox has many tricks, and the hedgehog only one, but that is the best of all." Erasmus.

No 33. South Eastern, Staplehurst
(Closed in 1994) Sharpe & Winch, F. Leney, Fremlins, Whitbread, Shepherd Neame

The railway reached Staplehurst in 1842. It is quite likely that it would have passed through this area, but a station was built in the village, primarily to service the requirements of Henry Hoare, of banking fame, whose family lived locally at Iden Park Estate. In 1843 there were complaints that the village was not fully utilizing the benefits of this new mode of transport and in particular that there was no inn nearby. As a result the "South Eastern Hotel" was built in 1846 on Iden Estate land. It was a grand affair being a quite large hotel on a four-acre plot. There was a large kitchen garden to yield fresh vegetables and attempts were made to establish a market.

In 1846, with Mr. Bennet as tenant, the hotel was offered for sale at the London Auction Mart. The sale particulars mention a coffee room, a large assembly room used for local functions, stabling for 27 horses and a large and productive kitchen garden. An early landlord from 1855 to about 1870 was the splendidly named Zachariah Terrington. Formerly he had been the butler at Bedgebury House. The hotel was the focal point of the village with many organizations meeting here. In 1849 the hop growers would congregate and in 1852 a pigeon match took place between Mr. Kenyon of Hastings and a local man, Mr. Young. The prize was £50 – a good sum in those days – but there is no mention of a winner. In 1853 the ill-fated corn market was established.

Tragedy struck on 9th June 1865 when Staplehurst was the scene of one of the first fatal railway accidents in the country involving a passenger train. The train was the Tidal Boat Train en-route from Paris to London. Workmen repairing a bridge over the River Beult mistakenly believed that they had time to replace two rails before the arrival of the train. Time ran out and the train was de-railed. Aboard, travelling first-class, were Charles Dickens, his friend Mr. Balfour, the Prime Minister, and their travelling companions, Mrs. Ternan and her daughter Ellen, an actress. Ellen was later to become Charles' mistress. In all 10 people were killed and 49 injured. The initial inquests were held at the hotel with the subsequent official enquiry, held in September, also conducted there. There exists a postcard depicting the scene at the crash taken by Mr. Watson, a local photographer, although it was not until the 1970's that the glass photograph plates came to light. These were re-photographed and a copy was given to the Dickens museum at Broadstairs. Messrs. Dickens and Balfour were so grateful to the almighty for their party's narrow escape that they both covenanted a sum of money to the village school to provide two prizes a year to the scholars. The prizes were normally bibles, and the school still retains two bibles, donated by former prize-winning pupils, that were presented at about the time of the First World War. Due to the ravages of inflation the sum involved is now rather small so it is rolled up with other modest donations to form a larger sum that is administered by the church authorities. Whilst mentioning the school, it is worth noting that Henry Hoare was on the Board of Governors and the family presented the school with a bell, in 1898, which is still in use.

In 1842 Maidstone had no railway connections and until about 1871 Staplehurst was the bridgehead for the horse-drawn mail for a large area of Kent and East Sussex that stretched from Gravesend to Hastings. The mail was delivered by rail and then dispersed by horse-drawn coach – hence the substantial stable block. In 1871 the tenant, Thomas Miles, was also described as a postmaster, and in 1884 William Allingham was also a farmer and the hotel doubled as a posting house. A contemporary advertisement reads "Sharp's coach makes a night mail stop at this station and letters can be posted until 10.15p.m.".

For a long period the hotel was the centre of village activities. In March 1911 a dinner in connection with the Staplehurst and Frittenden Cottage Gardeners' Society was held here. Eighty people sat down to an excellent spread catered for by the landlord Mr. E. Moseley. The society was formed in 1880 and at that time had 21 members, but this number had grown to 74 in 1911. In 1880 the gate money was £1/12/9 and in 1911 it had grown to £16/12/9 – the society had a bank balance of £14/7/1. During the evening a resounding toast was proposed to the landlord and some excellent songs were sung. In February 1914 a pleasing and interesting function was held when a number of the principal tradesmen and agriculturists met together to do honour to their late stationmaster, who had been appointed to West Wickham. The man in question, Mr. Jeffreys, had served the village for 13 years and was held in the highest respect and esteem by the village folk. Amongst other gifts he was presented with a "purse of gold and a handsome album bound in red morocco stating the thanks and good wishes of the populace." Again Mr. and Mrs. Moseley were thanked for a most splendid spread and some excellent songs were sung. In October 1923 Mr. Moseley was again at hand to provide another fabulous meal, this time for both the thirty-fifth annual ploughing match and a show of fruit, hops and roots by the Marden, Staplehurst and Collier Street Agricultural Association. Colonel F.S.W. Cornwallis, CBE presided with a host of other dignitaries present.

In July 1928 the Cranbrook brewery Sharpe & Winch was advertised for sale by way of public auction, and the purchasers were Frederick Leney & Sons Limited who paid the sum of £20,000 for the 13 houses.

So life went on in sleepy Staplehurst until disaster struck on the night of 1st January 1932. Shortly after midnight on the Sunday a fire broke out in the adjoining tobacco and sweet shop that belonged to Mr. George Barnett and was used by Mrs. Smith. It was a wooden building and whilst Mrs. Smith was away with friends celebrating the new year, it is believed an oil lamp that had been left hanging on the wall caused the inferno. The fire was discovered by Mr. William Woods of Church Hill Cottages. He raised the alarm and a band of willing helpers did their best to contain the flames pending the arrival of fire engines from both Staplehurst and Maidstone. The weather was gusty and the flames quickly spread to the "South Eastern". The hotel had recently been renovated and redecorated at a cost of many hundreds of pounds and was reduced to a mass of ruins. The material damage to property and furniture was estimated to be in the region of £5,000. This could have been worse had it not been for the sterling efforts of Police Sergeant Belsey and PC Albon with the assistance of others in helping the occupants of the hotel to safety and removing furniture and effects. The fire brigade was of the opinion that if they had been able to obtain a plentiful water supply then the hotel could have been saved. Mr. Moseley was still the tenant, having served 27 years, but by now he was in poor health. Fortunately, friends rallied round to provide the family with temporary accommodation. He retired in the spring but unfortunately his successor, Mr. E.P. Ashley, died in March 1934 and his funeral took place at Camberwell Green Old Cemetery. The subsequent insurance claim amounted to £3,000 with rebuilding costs swallowing £1,500 of this sum. At the same time repairs amounting to £307/3/3 were carried out with £265/19/3 recovered from the tenant.

Not all landlords welcomed the army of small lads collecting inn sign miniatures and the incumbent at the "South Eastern" was one of their number. A young collector from Tonbridge tells me that the landlord had a habit of bending them as he picked them up to hand to any customer who had the temerity to ask for one. The miniature sign hung until the end but with colour variations.

Some land was sold for £2,000 in 1964 but the house still sat on a good-sized plot. The pub was far too large to survive in a village with stiff competition. Amongst others the "Railway Tavern" was close by. The pub closed and planning permission was sought in 1997 to convert the premises into six apartments appropriately called Dickens Court. One was offered for sale in 2002 at an asking price of £59,500. On the car park to the rear – formerly the kitchen garden – there are four units with one or two bedrooms.

Shepherd Neame leased the premises on 6th May 1992 but surrendered it on 29th September 1994, after which the pub closed.

No 34. Spotted Cow, Larkfield
H.T. Wickham, Jude Hanbury, F. Leney, Fremlins, Truman

An old cottage-style pub tied to Wickham's Yalding brewery occupied part of this site for a long while. Wickham's was acquired by Jude Hanbury and Frederick Leney in 1921 and the pubs were split between them. This house went to Jude Hanbury, who paid £350 for the leasehold interest in May 1921. In October of the following year Jude paid a further £1,100 to Mr. J.W French to acquire the freehold. At the time Larkfield was a quiet rural community with cows grazing in the fields. However, this idyllic scene was soon to change as the pub was on the busy road from London to the Kentish sea-side resorts. It soon became obvious that a more impressive house was needed to cope with the increased trade. In December 1925 land was purchased for £200 and a character property was built in 1926 at a cost of £2,321. The redundant pub was sold off in March 1927 for £1,000. F. Pierce was paid £2/10/8 for painting out and re-writing the sign.

In July 1928 Jude mortgaged the new house together with the "Fountain" at East Peckham and "Prince of Wales" at Collier Street in the sum of £5,000. In April 1960 part of the pub forecourt was sold for £100 to the Ministry of Transport for a road-widening scheme.

On 21st April 1934 the "Merry Boys" at Snoll Hatch, East Peckham closed its doors and the licence was transferred here. An entry of £1,000 was made, which represented the value of the full licence transferred. The first landlord at this new house was Mr. Mills. In 1934 the property was valued in the brewer's books at £5,000 – quite a high figure for those days. H. Aslett became the tenant on 6th December 1938, paying a rent of £75 and a deposit of £150. His inventory was valued at £237/9/6.

A resident of Tudeley told me that, in 1985, when she had to sit on jury service at Maidstone Crown Court, the defendants were a gang of local gypsies, who would tarmac drives, repair roofs etc. for old ladies and then march them down to the bank to draw out a hefty sum to pay for the services rendered. They met at the "Spotted Cow" to plan their activities – they were found guilty. The last "true" landlord was a Welsh rugby fanatic called "Fiery" Phillips who had previously served as a test pilot in the Royal Air Force. Although he retired in the late 1970's he is still remembered for his famous Scotch rump steaks.

The pub was refurbished in 1995 and remains a very busy and popular inn. The house has since been run by a succession of managers.

No 35. The Vigo Inn, Fairseat
F. Leney, Fremlins, Whitbread, Free House

This is an ancient and interesting inn that has remained within the same family, the Ashwells, for over seventy years.

The "Vigo" was originally called the "Upper Drovers Inn": there was also a "Lower Drovers" at the bottom of the hill. The pub was situated opposite a toll road. The change of name is thought to have occurred in 1732 when a former sailor, who fought at the battle of Vigo Bay, bought the pub. It has been stated that the money used to purchase the inn was provided by Admiral Sir George Rooke, commanding officer of the fleet, as the sailor in question had saved his life during the battle when he was blown overboard. The said mariner was also exempt from being pressganged. The great battle at Vigo Bay took place in October 1702 when a Spanish treasure fleet, returning from Havana and supported by the French fleet, was trapped in Vigo Bay. The combined fleets were routed with great booty captured and brought home to England. To celebrate, knighthoods were given out and medals minted from the captured silver. Vigo village thus obtained its name many years after the Battle of Vigo.

The Admiral was born near Canterbury and has a monument in Canterbury Cathedral. His third wife, Catherine, daughter of Sir Thomas Knatchbull, lived at Mersham Hatch, and it was there that Rooke died.

However, the history of the "Vigo" goes back much further. This isolated house, surrounded by woodland, dates back to about 1470, although some say 1432. The left-hand side is the oldest part. Quite when it became a coaching inn is not known. The pub was surrounded by five acres of land, thus providing ample room to park the coach. The horses grazed in the fields and the tack was dried in the large kitchen area. Richard Luxford was the tenant in 1759 and Thomas Jeale in 1781. By 1816 Jeremiah Jeale had taken over and he was still tenant in 1867 – another long-standing family connection.

During the late 1800's Leney paid a rent of £40 p.a. to the Coopers' trustees. The lease expired on 24th June 1900 and was renewed by W. Cooper to run for a further ten years at a similar rent. In May 1922 an extension of 14 years was signed and sealed on the Hisling lease with this becoming a regular feature, but by 1951 the rent had risen to £45. On 2nd June 1930 the long reign of the Ashwell family commenced when V.S. Ashwell acquired the tenancy. By 1939 his rent was £30, a deposit of £75 was taken, and the inventory was valued at £202. The "Vigo" remained open during the war years and was a popular venue for the Officer Cadet Training Unit and English and Canadian troops billeted just down the road at Vigo village. Leney and Whitbread were only ever tenants here and in 1965, when the house came up for auction, the Ashwell family succeeded in purchasing the freehold from the Church Commissioners.

A nice little ceremony took place in the spring of 1950 when HMS Vigo arrived in Kent waters and the ship's company soon discovered the amenities that this welcoming inn had to offer. To celebrate the occasion a copy of the crest of the Vigo (a rook in a laurel leaf) was presented to the inn, and in return the brewery company presented to the ship a copy of the inn sign. The latter ceremony took place on board HMS Vigo with Lieutenant Shaw receiving the sign on behalf of the ship's company. Also present were Mr. John Marchant and Mr. V.S. Ashwell. It is interesting to note that the badge of the Vigo is from the arms of the Admiral and not merely a play upon his name.

Trade has dwindled but this remains a popular house. It is one of only a few still selling real mild ale all year round and is a frequent haunt of local CAMRA members. Also it still retains that old Kentish game – Dadloms. The miniature inn sign still hangs and when I called in 1995 to take a photograph Mr Ashwell invited me in and presented me with his visiting card and an inn sign miniature, 45 years after they were originally issued! The telephone number on the visiting card is Fairseat 47.

No 36. The Windmill, Hollingbourne
Isherwood, Foster & Stacey, Jude Hanbury, F. Leney, Fremlins, Whitbread

This fine old pub is situated in Eyhorne Street at the foot of the Downs. It was built in the sixteenth century with a many-levelled timber interior containing splendid oak beams and an inglenook fireplace.

The licence was held by George Harrison in the late 1600's and he also ran, from the premises, a shop that stocked a tantalizing array of goods for those times. One could purchase stockings, lace, and thread as well as groceries such as cheese and oaten cakes. By this time the inn was fully established and included a hall and kitchen in which was stored 125 pounds of pewter. There was also a brew house with two furnaces where the house beer was brewed and pork, beer and milk were kept in two butteries. There were two acres of land attached to the pub that acted as a smallholding. George also kept a horse and on his death his estate was valued at £200. During the 1700's the pub was owned and operated by Anthony and Mary Norrington. Their daughter Hannah and her husband Thomas Swan, a bricklayer, inherited the property and took up residence in 1753.

Like most historic old pubs the "Windmill" can boast a ghost. If one is observant William Wood may be spotted gliding through one of the timbered walls. Sadly, in 1784, he was involved in a drunken brawl that developed into a general mêlée and all participants collapsed on to the floor. William failed to get up and was pronounced dead. To pursue this morbid line, in June 1860, Thomas Simmonds, 72, a master bricklayer, hanged himself in the village and the subsequent inquest was held at the "Windmill". The unanimous finding was that he was suffering from temporary insanity.

In October 1835 the first meeting of the Guardians of Hollingboure Union (the workhouse) was held here. The pub was also a meeting place for United Men of Kent Benefit Society and the tenth anniversary meeting was held here on 30th May 1842. It was a great event and the pub was bedecked with flags and bunting. A large marquee was erected in the field beside the "Windmill" and a good dinner was enjoyed by all. The society was founded in 1832 by Richard Thomas and, when the anniversary dinner was held, had over 130 members. In 1960 Fremlins acquired the strip of land at the "Windmill", which was let to Lady Grace Bazley White at a rent of 1/- p.a.

The "Windmill" was where the agent for the Earl of Jersey collected the annual tithe dues.

In 1878 the premises were leased for 14 years at £50 p.a. to Isherwood, Foster & Stacey. Jude Hanbury purchased the freehold in 1888, paying £2,200. At the turn of the last century the following sums were spent:-

30.9.1904. Varnishing sign and board. £3/2/6.
26.4.1906. Pull down and rebuild kitchen chimney. £5/8/5.
22.9.1909. Emptying and cleaning cesspool. £1/5/-.

The property is split-level and now has a central bar and a large dining area. It shares the local trade with the "Sugar Loaves" and its fine restaurant attracts customers from a wide area. Over the years it has expanded into a most handsome inn.

For such a fine hostelry, it is surprising to find tenants did not stay for very long – one or two for less than a year.

No 37. Chalk Tavern, Sittingbourne

(Closed in January 1998) Milton Brewery, F. Leney, Fremlins, Whitbread, Marr Taverns, Inn Business

With the exception of the "Shakespeare" all of the inn sign pubs in Sittingbourne and Milton Regis have disappeared – some quite literally. This house has an unusual name commemorating the workers in the nearby chalk quarries.

The tavern is situated in an artisan area of town where considerable development occurred either side of the Second World War. Land was dedicated to the council for further development and subsequent building at the rear required the erection of new fencing. In 1951 an explosion occurred whilst rubber tiles were being laid – the favoured means of floor covering in Whitbread houses just after the war. The following year permission was given to affix a hydrant plate to the pub. During April 1963 improvements costing £300 were carried out, and until closure the property retained its brown terracotta tiles.

The pub was built around 1870. When Leney acquired the Milton Brewery in 1899 the "Chalk Tavern" was one of the tied houses. In 1884 Mrs. Weston was the landlady.

Mr. Mudge was the tenant in 1908 and when he moved on to the "Forester's Arms" on 17th June 1912 Walter H.S. Vandepeer took over and remained until he retired in October 1935. Ernest Joseph Grant served during the war years and paid a rent of £70 and a deposit of £100. His inventory was valued at £145.

In 1920 a Mr. Roberkins offered Leney 29 Bassett Road (adjoining the "Chalk Tavern") at a price of £130. The brewers decided to offer £110 and, in the end, they split the difference and paid £120. The house was subsequently extended and in 1923 was valued at £2,570 in the Leney books. A wine licence was obtained on 23rd April 1934 and a full licence in 1948 when the net monopoly value was set at £900. The land tax was redeemed in 1950.

The "Chalk Tavern" was a two-bar house with a beer garden to the side. Last orders were called in January 1998 when the brewers decided the pub was not profitable. As a result the landlady, Mrs. Cilla Harvey, and her husband Malcolm threw a party to bid a fond farewell to all their regulars. The house was advertised for sale at a price of £99,995. This area is likely to be redeveloped so it is possible that the place may be demolished, although in 2003 it was operating as the Sittingbourne Educational Library – the property, however, appeared empty.

No 38. Forester's Arms, Sittingbourne
(Closed in November 1962) Milton Brewery, F. Leney, Fremlins

This is a fairly common sign quite often relating to the Ancient Order of Foresters, a charitable organization that normally held its meetings at a pub bearing this name.

The "Forester's Arms" was situated at 49 Berry Street, at the top end, close to the railway station. The house was closed and sold to the local authority by compulsory purchase order in April 1963 for the sum of £9,750. This part of town was redeveloped and a new relief road (St. Michaels Road) was built in the late 1960's. The pub, although close to the High Street, catered in the main for the local brick workers and papermakers. A Faversham resident who went to school in Sittingbourne can remember her parents forbidding her to take a route home that would involve passing the "Forester's". She tells me that she can remember, to this day, the clouds of cigarette smoke billowing out of the doors and windows together with some of the customers.

In 1894 Leney rented the pub from Mr. Hartridge on a 45-year lease at an annual rent of £4/11/-. This landlord would, in fact, have been the Milton Brewery, owned by Mr. E. Hartridge, that Leney purchased for £27,000 on 31st July 1899. On 15th May 1913 the former brewery was sold to the Guardians of the Poor of the Milton Beacon. In July 1919, when the freehold ground rent came up for sale by auction, Leney decided to bid up to about £100, but had to increase this figure to £350. The purchase was confirmed on 1st August 1919.

This was just another modest beer house, about which little is known. In 1908 the landlord was Jesse Allen and he was succeeded on 2nd July 1910 by William Mudge, late of the "Chalk Tavern", who remained until 8th March 1937. On 2nd October 1939 John Clayton Ernest Oxford (formerly of the "Victory" at Gads Hill) took over, paying a rent of £45 and a deposit of £50. His inventory amounted to £128/2/6. When he volunteered for war service on 13th July 1942 his wife Eileen Nellie Oxford held the licence. John returned to the pub on 7th December 1942 – was he invalided out? He remained until 28th June 1948 and was succeeded by Charles H. Thompson, who proved to be the last tenant, remaining until November 1962 when the house closed. Mr. Thompson moved on to the "Three Kings" in the town. The house was granted a wine licence in April 1939 with a full licence confirmed on 18th April 1951when the net monopoly value of £700 was paid.

At one time there were three pubs called the "Forester's Arms" in the town – a fine example survives in Charlotte Street.

No 39. Wyf of Bathe, Sittingbourne

*(Formerly the **New Inn**. Closed in August 1972) Milton Brewery, F. Leney, Fremlins, Whitbread*

This property dates back to 1870 and was another house owned by the Milton Brewery. In 1894 it was leased for a period of 45 years to Leney at an annual rent of £4/15/-. Leney purchased the Milton Brewery in 1899. In July 1919 the freehold ground rent also came up for sale by auction and the brewers decided to bid up to about £100 – they subsequently paid £350 – a similar tale to that related above, concerning the "Forester's Arms". The purchase was confirmed on 1st August 1919. The name change occurred on 19th April 1948.

In common with the "Forester's Arms" this is another modest beer house and little history has come to light. An early landlord was William Thomas Bolton and he was succeeded on 19th March 1923 by Samuel John Edwards who served behind the bar until 5th July 1943. In 1939 his rent was £30 with no mention made of a deposit or inventory. The licensee in 1951, Albert Victor Harkup, was a proficient life saver and, competing against seven others, including his two sons, won the "Harris Shield", recognising his prowess in this discipline. This competition, held under the auspices of the Royal Lifesaving Society, dates back to 1903. Mr. Harkup was 55 years old at the time, had been a keen swimmer and, at one time, a voluntary lifeguard at Sheerness.

Readers of Chaucer will know that the bawdy, much-married, Wyf of Bathe would have passed this way all those years ago. The point of her story is that what women love most is to control their husbands completely.

This was another artisan house close to the town centre and near the entrance to Bowaters' paper mill and the brickfields. It acquired quite a tough reputation. In 1994, on parking my car and asking the car park attendant if the pub still survived, I was told that it disappeared years ago. It was a real spit and sawdust place with fighting a frequent occurrence. In the 1950's it did have a half-decent darts team that reached the final of a local competition. Unfortunately the team lost 4-0 to the "White Horse" – the event took place in a dance hall and the players shared the stage with the band!

The pub was a victim of the redevelopment of the area around the railway station, where a trading estate was established and improved access was required. The pub closed in August 1972 and was compulsory purchased and demolished in 1973. The site is now a roundabout.

No 40. The Bull, Sissinghurst
Sharpe & Winch, F. Leney, Fremlins, Whitbread

To locals this village is referred to as Milkhouse Street.

The "Bull" is an imposing, former coaching inn of great antiquity. Built mainly in the seventeenth century, with later additions, the oldest part is said to date back to 1360. If this is correct the "Bull" must be one of the oldest pubs in the county. The original building is masked by a Victorian exterior. As one enters the inn one is confronted by massive old timbers and a finely carved Tudor stone fireplace.

The pub is first mentioned by name in 1754, but it was an inn of some importance at least as early as the beginning of the 17th century. The "Bull" was owned by Sir John Baker, and formed part of the Sissinghurst Castle property, and continued in this ownership until the sale of the Cornwallis Estates. It was also, until fairly recently, a thriving farm. In 1900 Underwoods conducted a sale on the premises on behalf of Mrs. S.F.W. Cornwallis.

At some time the "Bull" was acquired by the Cranbrook-based brewers Sharpe and Winch, which, in turn, was purchased by Frederick Leney & Sons Limited in 1928. This pub was one of the 13 houses within the estate. Shortly afterwards, on 2nd May 1930, the Queen Anne's Bounty tithe, amounting to £3/6/-, was redeemed.

In 1766 Mrs. Isabella Linford was fined 10/- for "suffering and permitting tippling in her house during the time of divine service". The "tipplers" were also fined 3/4d for the offence. Usually these fines were distributed by the churchwardens of Cranbrook among the poor of the parish, so perhaps the "imbibers" felt they were providing a social service. For a long while the house was managed by the Moore family with Mark handing over to Walter in 1876. Walter is also described as a farmer.

Close to the marsh, on one of the tracks leading towards London, the "Bull", with its deep cellars and escape hatch, was a natural haunt of smugglers. To assist these gentlemen of the night, there are said to be tunnels stretching all the way to Hawkhurst. As befits such a property there is a ghost – a little girl who was murdered – with several past landlords able to confirm this. In common with many public houses, the tenant maintained a thrift club that paid out at Christmas with the hope that a good proportion of the savings would be spent in the pub. In the December 1931 payout 36 members shared £73/10/-. In more modern times the Ashford Valley Hunt met here and the pub also made an appearance in Jeffrey Farnol's story "The Broad Highway". In August 1956 13 acres of land to the rear of the pub were sold for £1,000.

In 1995 the house boasted a first-class Italian Restaurant, specializing in pizzas and the like. Accommodation is provided, and as the pub is one of the closest to Sissinghurst Castle, there is probably a good demand.

No 41. Crown Inn, Cranbrook
Obadiah Edwards & Sons, (The Tenterden Brewery), Jude Hanbury, F. Leney, Fremlins, Whitbread

The history of the "Crown" is intertwined with that of the "Bell". The "Bell" still survives, but under the name of the "Crown" – the name changed in 1818. However, the "Bell" occupied another site on the opposite side of the road. Harman Sheafe owned the property in 1603 for which he paid a quit rent of 5d. By 1700 it was in the ownership of John Scott and was described as "house sometime called "Ye Bell"". A beer-brewer who died in 1656, Edward Steed, also occupied it at one time. It was not until 1754 that the name appears again when Duodecimus Knolden (I just had to mention this gentleman) enters into the customary bond for the good conduct of his inn. In 1764 the Swattenden trustees held some of their meetings here. Richard Beecher was the last landlord at the "Bell".

In 1818 the licence was transferred over the road to another fine old building housing the "Crown". When the share capital of the Tenterden brewery was offered for sale, Leney considered making an offer for the "Crown Commercial Hotel" in isolation. However, Jude Hanbury purchased the house on 25th March 1922, paying the Tenterden Brewery £2,000 for the pub and £400 for the cottage. In February 1922 the local licensing magistrates passed plans for rebuilding the property. In 1924 the brewers mortgaged this house to Harry Waters in the sum of £1,200, paying an interest rate of 4% p.a. The mortgage was redeemed by Leney in June 1956 to the estate of R.C. Roberts. The pub was valued in the brewer's books at £2,000 in 1925 and they increased this figure to £2,088 the following year. The value of the adjoining cottage remained at £400. The tithe of £1/9/4 was redeemed on 27th November 1930.

A very long-serving landlord was George Bignell who took over the house on 22nd March 1922 remaining until 1944. In 1939 he paid a rent of £20 for the pub, £5 for the bath and £1 for electricity. His deposit was £25. A local resident recalls the tenancy, during the late 1950's early 1960's, of Stonewall Jackson. In his words he was as deaf as a post and would shout and holler. The inn held a full licence. On 16th November 1949 Crown Cottage was sold at auction for £900 and, in 1960, George Cottage passed from Leney to Fremlins. The tenant was Mrs. O. Honess who paid a rent of 13/6 per week.

This is a homely, welcoming inn and is well worth a visit. The inn sign miniature changed years ago and quite often the new design has been a double-sider.

No 42. The Swan, Wittersham
Sharpe & Winch, F. Leney, Fremlins, Whitbread, Free House

The first mention of the "Swan" was in 1802 at which time John Wenham owned land called Great and Little Hop Garden Fields, which, at one time, formed part of Malthouse Farm. Shortly after 1802, on part of the waste land that was incorporated within these fields, Thomas Masters, a carpenter, built a house, and in 1807 he purchased the land. John Wenham died in 1808 with most of the land remaining in his heirs' ownership until 1876 when it was sold to William Barling Sharpe of Cranbrook, a brewer.

The land bought by Masters passed through the hands of a number of different owners until, in September 1842, it was bought by W.B. Sharpe. This was after a proposed sale to Thomas and Tilden Christmas, brewers from Robertsbridge, had fallen through. In 1890, after at least 46 years as a brewer, W.B. Sharpe sold the "Swan", as it was now called, to William Francis Winch, also of Cranbrook, an auctioneer. This and other properties remained in the firm's ownership until the business was sold to Frederick Leney & Sons Limited in 1928.

Most of Hop Garden Field, which had since become known as "Dog Kennel Field", was subsequently sold for local housing. In December 1928 a piece of land, approximately half an acre, adjacent to the pub was offered to Tenterden Rural District Council at £50, for the erection of cottages. In January 1931 further land was sold for £150.

During the 1870's the landlord was William Carpenter and in 1884 James Merricks held the licence. By this time the "Swan" was a collecting point for Sharpe's Mail coach. For a long while the licence was held by the Woodley family. Clement Augustus moved in on 27th September 1928 and, possibly on his death, was succeeded on 20th June 1940 by Mrs. E.S. Woodley. She remained for just over four years and paid a rent of £25 p.a. plus £1/5/- for the land. The deposit was £50 and the inventory was estimated at £75. Hop gardens abounded in this area and the pickers provided a valuable source of income.

I was told that a pub had been on this site for 400 years, but I have found no evidence to support this. It became a freehouse in 1992 and a full-size replica of the inn sign miniature, painted by a local artist, can be seen in the bar. The new landlord, who bought the premises in 1998, had been a regular customer for 30 years, so should know the pub. At the same time a restaurant was opened.

No 43. The Woolpack, Winchet Hill
(Closed in 1969) Sharpe & Winch, F. Leney, Fremlins, Whitbread

The form of construction – timber-framed, roof crown post, shuttered windows etc. would indicate that the building was erected in the late 16th or early 17th century. It housed a quite splendid pub and now makes a most appealing private residence. Just over the road one will find Woolpack Cottage. At one time there were toll gates at Winchet Hill.

The house sat in splendid isolation a few miles out of Goudhurst, hidden away in the woods. In front of the inn was a carefully manicured lawn with delightful flower borders. It was on this lawn that the annual wool fair was held – hence the pub's name. In the early 1800's the house was approached by a bridle path – now a road – that meandered through the trees. The wool fair aroused considerable local interest and the fleeces were actively bargained for and this together with other stalls and entertainments made the event an interesting family day out. However, as dusk fell, the "free traders" would appear through the trees on their way down to the marsh ports to trade their finest Kentish wool for brandy from across the channel. The later inn sign indicates such a scene with a loaded pack-pony.

Trade consisted of local agricultural workers and the annual influx of hop-pickers. Apart from the smugglers there was little passing trade. It is said that the Chandler family held the licence for about 300 years – certainly J. Chandler was the landlord from 1866 until 1908. He died at Holly Cottages, aged 83, in 1911. The Chandler family had an eye for business as a Mrs. Honess relates – "My grandmother, who had a shop, was sent there for her tea once, and she was charged more than she was accustomed to pay. When the messenger asked – isn't that rather dear? Mrs. Chandler replied – Mrs. Honess only sends down to me for tea when she runs out, so you can either take the tea or leave it!"

In May 1913 an open handicap walking contest took place, starting from the "Woolpack" to Marden village pump and back – a distance of nearly six miles. There were twelve entrants and the winner was T. Excell of Marden who had a 500 yard start. The first three walkers finished within two minutes of each other.

This pub, plus 12 others situated in the Weald, was acquired by Frederick Leney & Sons Limited when they paid £20,000, in 1928, to acquire the Cranbrook-based brewery Sharpe and Winch.

In September 1933 the pub suffered fire damage, but fortunately the fire was quickly brought under control. This event, however, led to a spat amongst the various parties who extinguished the flames, and led to letter-writing including the following "… you stated that the Maidstone brigade arrived in twenty minutes at the fire, but made no mention of the Goudhurst brigade. This has caused quite a stir in this village so I would be very pleased if you would insert a modified apology this week… The Goudhurst men were hampered by muddy water which reduced their effectiveness…". However, the fire damage was limited to one corner of the building.

A more recent landlord, in the 1930's, was Frank Bond, whose young daughter, Maisie, tragically died after eating wasp poison put down in an upper room. It is said that Maisie has since haunted the house – especially when children are in residence. There is a photograph of the little girl sitting in her pram. In 1934 a further blaze broke out resulting in repairs totalling £282/15/-. During the 1940's, and probably for a good while earlier, the brewers were paying 10/- p.a. to the Trustees of Goudhurst Grammar School.

With the demise of hop-picking, a good proportion of the pub's trade disappeared, it became uneconomic, and sadly closed. Locals still remember the jollity and sing-songs of 50 years ago. The exterior of the property has not changed at all, so one can easily recognize the old pub.

Hindsight is a wonderful thing – the brewers sold the property in January1970 for a net £9,677/17/6, and in 2003 the house, called Woolpack, was offered for sale at an asking price of £875,000!

No 44. Coach and Horses, Sedlescombe
(Closed about 1991) B. Baker, F. Leney, Fremlins, Whitbread

As one enters Sedlescombe from the direction of Maidstone, the pub on the top of the hill is referred to as the top house, and on descending the hill through this charming village one arrives at the bottom house – the "Coach and Horses". Unfortunately the top house survives – not so the bottom house.

This pub, the furthest outpost of the Baker empire, was rented by Leney at a rental of £105 p.a. under a lease due to expire on 31st July 1922. However the company purchased the freehold on 16th November 1905. In 1896, when Augustus Leney sold his portfolio of public houses to Frederick Leney & Sons Limited, the description was – the leasehold house called the "Coach and Horses" plus coach-house stabling and premises. It was therefore a coaching house, and for a good while afterwards is referred to as an hotel. Mains drainage was laid on during February 1915. On 30th June 1922 Leney received a letter of enquiry from Mr. Philp regarding the possible sale of the property at a price of £2,500. The matter was left in abeyance and did not proceed, as, on 17th October 1923 a tenancy agreement was entered into with Mr. H.L. Pope who remained until 3rd January 1927. A fire occurred during the 1920's and the plans for rebuilding the hotel were drawn up by Arthur L. Dartnell, architect and surveyor, of Wateringbury. Ebenezer Pollard became the licensee on 25th June 1934 and, on being called up for war service in 1940, his wife, Gertrude Pauline, took over. Ebenezer returned in October 1945 and remained until 19th January 1949. In 1939 the rent was £30 p.a. with a deposit of £100. The inventory was estimated at £200.

Following closure the pub was converted into flats.

No 45. The Hope Inn, Guestling Green
(Closed about 1996) Breeds & Co., Mackeson, F. Leney, Fremlins, Whitbread, Free House

The inn dates back to the late 1700's when the original much smaller house was built. It occupies a corner plot on the main Hastings to Rye road. In the 1950's an extension, which encompassed the well, was built to the rear and became the public bar. During the 1960's the next door cottage was used as bed and

breakfast accommodation. At this time the house had outside toilets and chickens were kept in the open yard at the rear. A modest wayside pub in a small village, this was always a very marginal business; however, it did survive in a somewhat eccentric fashion until 1996.

The land on which the pub is built belonged to the Ashburnham Estate. Mackeson purchased the property in 1920 paying £825 plus legal fees of £23/13/6. Their initial outlay was £400. In 1932 they carried out an overhaul and this, plus general repairs, amounted to £150/18/3. However, on 8th October 1934 they sold this house to Leneys for the sum of £1,275.

At one time the house boasted public, saloon and private bars, the latter being used by local farmers. A long-serving licensee was Mr. H.A. Brown, who moved in on 30th December 1936 and remained until 1966. Besides being a popular landlord, his particular sporting prowess was at bar billiards. In 1956 the team from the "Hope" won the Hastings and Bexhill Bar Billiards League, and the following year Mr. Brown won the individual championship cup. The pub's win was particularly satisfying as they could only muster seven players from which to make up the team of five. The "Hope" also boasted a very good darts team. In 1939 Mr. Brown was paying the modest rent of £20 with a £25 deposit. The inventory was valued at the paltry sum of £38/15/-. It traded as a beerhouse, but did acquire a beer and wine licence in May 1939 and a full licence in May 1949, when the monopoly value was set at £750. At the same time there was a development charge of £550 and alterations costing £500 were carried out. The house was valued in the brewer's books in 1935 at £1,275. In 1950 the Central Land Board settled the brewer's claim for loss of development value amounting to £550. This related to the difference between the site's restricted value and the un-restricted value. In 1948 the brewers dedicated nine square yards of land to the Ministry of Transport for a road-widening scheme.

Locals tell me that in the "old days" the fishermen from Hastings would walk the eight-mile round journey to the "Hope", arriving before opening time, to slake their thirst in their favourite pub. The enjoyment was probably heightened as the floor on the landlord's side of the bar was much lower and one always had the impression that, when serving, he was looking at one's knees. A Mackeson employee told me that due to the marginal trade, financial problems were experienced from time to time. In the 1960's a landlord kept un-caged birds in his bedroom and, when he vacated the premises, the brewery had to arrange to take out the bedroom window frame to enable the soiled furniture to be thrown into the street. Another tenant, Gus Stone, was very deaf and used a large hearing aid. When he bored of the conversation he would tone down the receiver when he had "nothing further to say".

Whitbread installed a manager in November 1976 and the house was sold, with licence, on 13th July

1977. It continued to trade for quite some while and, for the last twenty-five years, the landlord was Robert Kitson, an ex-Wellington bomber pilot. This was to be his retirement house, having moved over from the "Swan" at Appledore. Robert ran the house along military lines and had no time for "foreigners", which could include people living only five miles away. It became an exclusive little pub, serving only six or seven selected friends. Whisky was only served un-diluted. The house had an air of seedy elegance and gentle decay. Certainly when I called at eight o'clock one evening I was unable to gain admittance. Unfortunately the poor man's health deteriorated and the pub closed. In the end he relied on meals on wheels and his kindly neighbours for support. He refused to give up and remained, even though the fabric of the house was rapidly deteriorating. The property was finally placed on the market in 2002 at an asking price of £215,000. It was said to be in need of modernization and refurbishment. The inn sign miniature was still hanging to the very end.

No 46. Peace and Plenty, Playden
Alfred Leney of Dover, Jude Hanbury, F. Leney, Fremlins, Whitbread, Free House

The original inn was an old weather-boarded beer house, with the cottage adjoining used as the turnpike gate house. It dates back to the time of the Napoleonic wars. Part of the original inn was demolished in 1903 and a new front, which included a bar area was built in 1905. A charming photograph dated 1875, exists showing these premises, the toll-gate and what is reputed to be the last horse and cart to pay a toll. Indentures date back to 2nd December 1799, with many later documents in evidence.

The freehold passed from Alfred Leney to Jude Hanbury, who in April 1924 raised a mortgage in the sum of £2,000 over this house plus the "Crown" at Stone. Leney redeemed this in February 1956. Prior to the 1930's this was a simple beer house acquiring a beer and wine licence in 1933. Its clientele in the early days were agricultural workers and, during the season, hop-pickers. In 1954 the brewers dedicated to East Sussex County Council approximately half an acre of land for road widening purposes and, in return, the council paid the legal costs, erected a boundary fence and laid a paved car park for use by the patrons. In 1960 Fremlins took control of the Leney estate, including Peace and Plenty Cottage the tenant of which was Miss E.A. Saunders who paid a rent of 17/5 per week.

We now see a very smart house – more a restaurant than a pub. A small craft shop operates from the premises, and the restaurant is open all day. The original inn sign still hangs, but the background is now black.

An ironic little footnote to this history is that Playden was home to the Reverend Thomas Baker of the Wesleyan Methodist Church. The year 1867 found him in Fiji preaching the message of peace to the local natives. Unfortunately he succeeded in annoying a local chieftain and this led to him being the only European to have been killed, cooked and eaten on the island. Those with a morbid curiosity may see, in Ipswich Museum, a fork that was used during the feast.

Nos 47. and 48. Robert De Mortain, The Ridge, Hastings
Jude Hanbury, F. Leney, Fremlins, Whitbread, Free House

During a particularly vicious air raid on Hastings in October 1940, the much-loved and prestigious "Bedford Hotel", standing in Queens Road, was destroyed. The war damage claim was settled in 1948 in the sum of £3,966/16/7 and, in 1952, the site was sold for £2,000 to Carlick Estates Limited. The "Bedford" had been owned by Jude Hanbury and on 27th April 1931 was one of seven houses sold by them to Leney on the basis of £15 per barrel, valuing the house at £2,685.

On 2nd September 1946 Leney purchased, for £3,750, the freehold of Ripon Lodge at the Ridge. The

licence of the former hotel was transferred here and, following refurbishment and a change of name to the "Robert De Mortain", this modern and substantial house opened for business on 14th December 1946. Robert, brother of William the Conqueror, is credited with building Hastings castle. In 1960 Fremlins acquired, from Leney, Robert De Mortain Cottage where the tenant, T.W. Hatton was paying a weekly rent of 15/-.

The inn sign is no longer a double-sider, but miniature number 47 still hangs.

No 49. Plough Inn, Eynsford
H&V Nicholl's Brewery Co., F. Leney, Fremlins, Whitbread, Beefeater

In 1891 Whitbread acquired the Lewisham brewer H&V Nicholl's which held the lease of the "Plough" from the Hart-Dykes family of Lullingstone. Whitbread probably acquired the freehold when the Lullingstone Estate was broken up in 1934. They leased the inn to Frederick Leney & Sons Limited on 1st

April 1958 – a new lease was created for 22 years at an annual rent of £100.

The house was erected circa 1800 and was a typical ale house. It is now a smart, half-timbered, property but in its early days it was thatched. Then it was a good old-fashioned pub down by the river and on hot days one could paddle whilst supping ale. As trade grew the house was extended by incorporating the landlord's living accommodation. Customers were mainly agricultural workers who enjoyed a sing-song around the piano. It was the meeting place for the local hunt and a ceremony of "blessing the plough" for a good harvest was held here. Eynsford is an attractive village and with its river-side setting the house became ever more popular, and in 1981 it was altered for use as a Beefeater. It has a good-sized car park that stands on the site of a row of cottages which was destroyed during the war by a delayed-action bomb.

The licensee in 1804 was William Morgan who handed over to Thomas Morgan in 1816. Whilst Thomas was here an auction sale of property took place at the "Plough" on Monday 5th October 1818. During 1936 building works costing £200 were carried out and, the following year piping etc. was laid on at a cost of £27. That same year a "special allowance" of £9/7/6 was made to the tenant on his leaving the premises and, at the same time, £7/18/9 was written off in respect of an overpayment for cask beer. On 25th December 1952 a lease was granted at a nominal rent of £1 p.a. for 21 years to Dartford District Council over a plot of land adjacent to the "Plough" for use as a public car park. On 27th November 1958 Rushforth James Bew became the licensee and he was succeeded by his son-in-law John H.R. Cook on 2nd July 1964. On 8th October 1976 the pub became a Whitbread-managed house and finally a Beefeater on 1st September 1981. The "Plough" boasts a fine restaurant and remains a busy country pub.

No 50. Royal Oak, Shoreham
(Closed in August 2000) F. Leney, Fremlins, Whitbread, Free House

Situated in the centre of the much-favoured village of Shoreham, this house was built in 1840 with brick elevations and sash windows under a tiled roof. It was originally built as a boarding-house to house the navvies building the nearby railway and tunnels. The interior could best be described as "cosy" and since 1948 all the living accommodation has been incorporated within the house.

The pub was purchased for £750 on 15th July 1867 by F. and C.F. Leney from Thomas and Carey Izzard and, on 26th May 1905, A. Wood sold, to the limited company, a strip of land adjoining the house. For most of the pub's life it was nothing more than a beer house. In 1896, when Augustus Leney sold his estate to the limited company, the inn was valued at £500, although in 1881 Augustus had valued it at £550 and, by 1890, had increased this figure to £750 with the annual rent set at £20. In 1934 Leney decided to authorize the purchase from the Tenterden Brewery Co., through Jude Hanbury & Co., of the cottage, forge and garden of the "Royal Oak" at a cost of £170. The house acquired a beer and wine licence in 1935 with the legal fees costing £23/0/8. A full licence was granted in April 1950 with the net monopoly value set at £550.

The pub was in the hands of the Taylor family for over 70 years. The licence was transferred to T. Taylor on 18th January 1924 and he carried on until just before the war. In 1939 the rent was £20 p.a. plus £1 for electricity. On 5th March 1951 Whitbread tenants in the West Kent and East Sussex Area were entertained to lunch at the "Royal Star" hotel, Maidstone. The toast to the "House of Whitbread" was proposed by Mr. Percy Taylor when it was acknowledged that the Taylor family was one of the oldest tenants in Whitbread's Kent trade. The pub did a roaring trade during the hop-picking season and was also very popular with soldiers stationed in the area during the war years. The older lads of the village still recall the days when they would nip about collecting the empty glasses to reclaim the 2d deposit. The pub had a jug and bottle, plenty of sporting activities, and was a real family house – the parents would drink at the bar while their children supped lemonade in the landlord's lounge. Unusually for this type of modest pub there is no record of the tenant having a second occupation.

When I called, the place was busy with locals and numerous walkers who tramp this delightful part of Kent. The only reference that I could find that this was a former Whitbread house was the carpet fronting the dartboard, which had been cut up and guides one to the gents' toilet. The place was welcoming with nuts and cheese on the bar. At one time the inn sign miniature for the Iden Green pub of the same name hung here. Sadly, in August 2000 the landlord decided to sell up and placed the house on the market at an asking price of £379,500. This was a pity as the "Royal Oak" appeared to be a successful pub.

Third Series issued in June 1951

(Aluminium)
and Re-issued in 1952 (Card)

1	Anchor, Stowting, near Ashford	26	Plough Inn, New Romney
2	Artillery Arms, Ramsgate	27	Prince of Wales, Woodnesborough
3	Basketmakers, Littlebourne	28	Queen's Hotel, Herne Bay
4	Bouverie Arms, Folkestone	29	Rose in Bloom, Seasalter
5	Brewer's Delight, Canterbury	30	Royal Oak, Margate
6	British Lion, Folkestone	31	Shepherd and Crook, Burmarsh
7	British Volunteer, Ashford	32	Ship Inn, Ash
8	Bull's Head, Adisham	33	Stag's Head, Ramsgate
9	Botolph's Bridge, West Hythe	34	Star Inn, Newington
10	Castle Hotel, Saltwood	35	Sun Inn, St. Nicholas-at-Wade
11	City of London, Dymchurch	36	Swan Hotel, Appledore
12	Dolphin, Faversham	37	Three Bells, Swingfield
13	Duke's Head, Hythe	38	Three Mariners, Hythe
14	Eight Bells, Canterbury	39	Three Kings, Sandwich
15	Gate Inn, Rhodes Minnis	40	Waterloo Tavern, Canterbury
16	Guildhall, Folkestone	41	Welcome Stranger, Court-at-Street, Lympne
17	Hope Inn, Hythe	42	White Horse, Bridge
18	King's Head, Wye	43	White Hart, Canterbury
19	Long Reach, Whitstable	44	White Horse, Finglesham, near Deal
20	Lord Clyde, Walmer	45	Woodman, Barham
21	Lord Nelson, Waltham	46	Woolpack, Smeeth
22	Man of Kent, Ashford	47	York House, Dover
23	Martello, Folkestone	48	White Lion, Dover
24	Old City, Canterbury	49	Red Lion, Hythe
25	Pearsons Arms, Whitstable	50	Swan Inn, Great Chart

No 1. The Anchor, Stowting

*(Re-named **The Tiger** about 1985) Isaac Kennett, Mackeson, Whitbread, Free House*

This ancient inn has probably witnessed more changes of name than most. Originally referred to as a simple ale house, it was subsequently called the "Chequer" in 1749, by 1778 it was referred to as the "Four Bells" (the number of bells that hang in Stowting Church), then the "Anchor" in 1802, which co-incided with the house being acquired by the Mackeson brothers. About 1985 it was re-named the "Tiger". I am told that the villagers had tired of the old name, so the pub regulars decided they would all put their suggestion for a new name in a bucket and the pub would be called by which ever name was drawn!

In a village such as Stowting, difficult to locate and straddling quite a large area of the North Downs, most places are ancient – probably as old as the inn. The first reference to the pub that I came across was on 17th June 1678, which referred to a messuage, stable and plot of land being sold by Jane Leadner to Thomas Pope, a tailor. The inn was mortgaged from time to time and in 1703 John Rigden, possibly from an old brewing family, provided funds. On 19th February 1749 David Stoddard of Ash purchased a messuage going under the sign of the "Chequer" and this was sold to William Rigden in 1766. In 1778, when known as the "Four Bells", it was transferred to Isaac Kennett, who was a brewer in nearby Elham. Henry and William Mackeson agreed to purchase, on 26th May 1802, the "Four Bells" from Isaac for £300 before 5th July. At the time the house was in the occupation of Abigail Bradley. This then became one of the first houses purchased by the Mackeson brothers, shortly after they had bought the Hythe brewery from John Friend. On the death of William Mackeson in 1821 the pub was still valued at £300. Mackeson remains emblazoned in bold letters on the front of the house.

The oldest part of the building dates back to the 1600's, – most of the additions were carried out in 1839. Past landlords had a variety of "second" jobs, including Sarah Caister in 1816 who was also the village butcher, as was George Brett in 1855. The East Kent Hunt used to meet here but a past landlord did not approve of hunting so they found another venue. The pub boasted a skittles alley, and in pre-war days, the landlord would ring a cow bell to draw attention to closing time. Another little story runs that at the start of the last war a regular laid a wager that it would last no longer than the 1914-18 war. The bet was for a pint of beer a day!

The modern visitor will now find a character building sympathetically restored with an excellent restaurant where one can eat at candlelit tables. Until fairly recently, the David Burley metal map hung in the bar, but this has now disappeared. This is a lively house that hosts jazz nights – a far cry from 1946 when a Mackeson employee visited the house and made the following observations:-

There were no counters – a serving hatch being used. Ceiling – Plaster breaking away and needs repair. Walls – Damp in places and brickwork breaking away. There was no piped water to the washing up area. Comment – Rebuild or alterations. Brewery comment – Neither!

The reverse of the inn sign miniature tells us that an anker is a form of cask used by the smuggling fraternity to bring brandy into the country past the noses of the revenue men. As a vessel approached the coastline the ankers would be fastened to a length of rope which was weighted with stones with an anchor at either end. This would then be suspended below the water and when the coast was clear, usually at night, the smugglers would return to reclaim their booty.

This pub provided only a marginal living and we find entries in the Mackeson ledger for 1912 revealing a loss on working of £11/7/10 and in 1914 a larger loss of £33/19/7. However, money was spent on renovation work and in 1931 a new scullery and porch were added at a cost of £150 and that same year the forming and tarring of the forecourt cost £46. The rent during this period was modest – £3/15/- a quarter. During 1953 the pub generator was sold for £10. In 1954 a bathroom and water closet were formed at a cost of £530.

Trade remained minimal and Whitbread, on 25th March 1976, closed the pub and it was sold – fortunately with licence. It re-opened and continued to trade on a reasonable basis until the mid-1990's. At that time the owner was also running another pub on nearby Stone Street and this had got into financial difficulties. As a result he decided to sell the "Tiger". There were fears that it would either close down or be turned into a "theme" pub, and to prevent this happening the house was purchased by a consortium of villagers. It continues to thrive and long may this continue, but please could we revert back to the "Anchor" and that wonderful sign? This should not prove difficult as the old sign still hangs – the "Tiger" has been painted over it!

No 2. Artillery Arms, Ramsgate
Public House Trust Ltd, Mackeson, Whitbread, Free House

This is a lively pub and even to this day has not entirely shaken off its history. In Victorian times the house is said to have operated as a brothel and the pub has always had strong military links, as did so many Ramsgate pubs. At one time Vincent Van Gogh lived nearby. The bars and the basement, which houses the pool table, are on three levels on the ground floor, with the whole contained within a narrow four-floor building occupying a corner site. It is rumoured that a trap-door hides a tunnel that leads to the church in Vale Square, but this is now bricked off. Always popular, this is a house for serious drinkers. Unfortunately it has lost the excellent inn sign miniature and we now see mounted Hussars in battle.

The building was erected in 1812 and was initially used as a military officers' billet. On a map dated 1849 the house is called Albert Cottage. It was fully licensed in 1869, having previously operated as a beerhouse. At the time the pub had been run for several years by J. Dunt Peal with his application for the licence supported by gentlemen of the utmost respectability. Another early landlord during the 1870's was Thomas Buck.

In March 1915 when the house was owned by the Public House Trust Limited the licence was opposed. The Trust had paid £1,500 for a 72-year lease with a rent of £55/5/- and had recently spent about £70 on repairs and renovations. The house had a steady trade and was quite profitable. It was a compact place, easily worked, and a very good outdoor trade was done. If the pub was referred, it would be the first Trust house in England to suffer this fate and would be a great blow to the movement in that part of England, as the organisation was established to encourage the sale of non-alcoholic drinks and the provision of meals. Fortunately the licence was renewed. By 1932 the owners are referred to as Trust Houses Limited. On 21st October 1932 Mackeson agreed to take over from Trust Houses Limited the remainder of their sub-lease and entered into a tenancy agreement in May 1933 with A.J. Drapper who was to pay a rent of £35 p.a. On 19th August 1936, in consideration for the assignment of the head lease of the "Artillery Arms" (ex J.J. Beasley), which had 35 years 41 days to run, expiring on 29th September 1971, Mackeson paid £750. The ground rent was £5/5/-.

You really must visit this house, if only to be amazed by the spectacular bar bowed windows, which were crafted by wounded soldiers billeted next door. The coloured leaded glass depicts soldiers and cannon from the Napoleonic period. Nothing is sacred and, when I visited, a yob had smashed one of the smaller windows, which had been taken to Canterbury Cathedral to be repaired – this gives some idea of the quality of the work.

No 3. The Basketmakers, Littlebourne
(Closed 21st January 1975) Rolfe Field, Bushell, Watkins and Smith, Mackeson, Whitbread

This was a smallish house in a village boasting far grander and older pubs and, as a result, it always struggled to survive. Perhaps, for this reason, locals thought it a "clubby" pub situated on a T-junction a little distance away from the village centre.

A local resident told me that a much older house called the "Basketmakers" at one time stood in Church Road and it was about 1900 when it moved to its present site. This would have been the home-brew house of Rolfe Field called the "Two Brewers" which had been in the Field family since 1832. The firm and houses were acquired by Bushell, Watkins and Smith in about 1898 when brewing ceased. Subsequently the pub was re-named the "Basketmakers".

The house was acquired by Mackeson in a rather unusual way. West Kent brewers, Bushell, Watkins and Smith, based at Westerham, wished to divest themselves of their East Kent pubs which were almost certainly acquired when they took over Field's brewery. They exchanged this house for the "Brickmaker's Arms" and some land at Platt on Christmas Day 1925. The following year £15 was spent on erecting a new sign and a further £20 on bar alterations. In 1930 £38/18/- was spent on new inside hot and cold water and drainage and, on 27th November, the tithe rent charge of £3/17/- was redeemed. In January 1933 an application was made at the Brewster Sessions for the grant of a wine licence. In April 1934 the pub was valued in the Mackeson books at £1,900 with the tenant paying a quarterly rent of £7/13/6. Further repairs costing £120 were carried out in 1949. A "full" on licence was confirmed on 8th April 1952 when the net monopoly value of £450 was paid. During 1954 part of the pub car park was completed at a cost of £260 with a further £150 spent in 1955 to complete the job.

By modern standards the pub was quite primitive for, in 1946, all washing-up was done in a wooden tub. All beers were drawn from the wood with the cellar level with the bars making the cellar very hot during the summer months. However, the beer was always in excellent condition. In 1953 George Giles moved here from the "Plough" at Ripple and as a token of their appreciation the locals presented him with a model plough and team of horses. This kindled a life-long passion for collecting similar items and, over the years, the walls of the "Basketmakers" were decorated with bells, brasses, fringes, bridles, whips and crops – many of the items were donated by drinkers. The collection also included a schoolboy's ruler scratched Mikael Williams 1777. In 1955 the villagers attended a harvest-festival held in the public bar. So much produce was contributed that George and his wife took two days to arrange the decorations of fruit, flowers and vegetables. An interesting feature was a loaf in the shape of five small loaves and two fishes. Over £6 was raised for charity. The pub had an attractive sign and at Christmas 1959 the sign, along with 11 others, was hung outside the Innovation Stores, Rue Neuve, Brussels as part of the store's Christmas display.

After the pub closed it stood empty for a while before being sold unlicensed for about £17,000. The place was in pretty good order – the main problems being the nicotine-stained walls and ceilings and the urinals, which had to be removed from the proposed dining room. The property was further modernized in the 1980's and now provides comfortable living accommodation. It is still readily identifiable, not least because the house is called Basketmakers, with a ceramic tile faithfully copying the inn sign miniature. The river, from which the reeds were harvested to make the baskets, still gurgles past the house.

"Criticism comes easier than craftsmanship." Zeuxis.

No 4. Bouverie Arms, Folkestone
(Closed in 1997) Ash & Co., Jude Hanbury, Mackeson, Whitbread, Charringtons

This pub was named to honour the family name of the local landowner – the Earl of Radnor whose family connections with the town of Folkestone stretch back many generations. The Earl's ancestor, Jacob des Bouverie, a Huguenot, emigrated from Flanders in the 16th century and, in 1713, a descendant, with another, was elected as MP for Hythe. In April 1996 Pearl Pleydell-Bouverie died at the ripe old age of 101.

The house was opened in 1855 by James Kirby, a builder, who unfortunately was declared bankrupt in 1861. Ownership then passed to Thomas Baker, a dealer in cigars, tobacco and fancy pipes. Shortly afterwards Thomas Ash purchased the house from Mr. Banks and it appears in a schedule of his assets dated 1870. On his death on 12th March 1875, the landlady was Mrs. Tidmarsh, late of the "Martello Hotel" who paid a rent of £18 p.a. The premises were enlarged in 1898 and in 1902 Albert Hart converted the unused stables to the rear of the house into an office. In an effort to earn its keep, in 1910 the office accommodation traded as the Bouverie Stores, but this venture quickly folded. This was a house of some importance, as during the 1930's and 1940's the rent was £22/10/- per quarter – a high figure for those days. On 12th April 1957 the brewers completed the purchase of a freehold interest in land rented from Clara Sutton and others adjoining 1 Millfield for £5 plus the vendor's solicitor's costs.

One of the most popular landlords was Frederick E. Hedges, who acquired the licence on 15th October 1915. He managed a thriving Christmas savings club and was actively involved with many sports and social events. On 17th February 1931 he handed over to Frederick George Hedges – probably his son. On 8th January 1947 William G. Hoare moved here from the "Star" at Newington. Situated close to the railway station, in the 1950's the pub was a popular evening rendezvous for returning stockbrokers who would discuss the day's trades over a pint.

The following incident, narrated by a former Mackeson employee, indicates how times have changed. In the early 1950's a drunk started banging on the pub door after closing time. In so doing he broke a window. He was taken to the police cells, the brewers quickly replaced the broken glass, and when he appeared in court the next day the brewers applied for their costs, which were granted. Whether the miscreant ever paid I know not.

Towards the end, the house, now cut off by the Northern Distributor Road constructed in 1972, had acquired an intimidating atmosphere and trade declined. The pub closed in 1997 and the property was offered for sale at £75,000 plus VAT. It remained empty for some time before being purchased and incorporated into the adjoining nursery school.

No 5. Brewer's Delight, Canterbury
(Closed on 4th August 2003) Ash & Co., Jude Hanbury, Mackeson, Whitbread, Shepherd Neame

A very long while ago this house was called the "Prince of Wales Head", then "Robin Hood and Little John" and, in 1807, when trading in Dover Street, the "Malt Shovel". On 8th December 1834 it passed into the hands of George Ash, via William and Mary Ann Brett and John Gilby. By 1838 Henry Wraight, a beer retailer, had changed the name to the "Brewer's Delight" and, in 1847 he moved to the present premises, in Broad Street, taking the new name with him.

When Thomas Ash died on 12th March 1875 the landlord was Mr. Stevens who paid a rent of £13 p.a. Later, on 24th October 1878, his executors transferred the premises to the partnership Moxon, Collard and Ash later to become Ash & Co. The landlord, Herbert Rillett, on 6th June 1913, was found drunk on his own licensed premises and was subsequently fined 10/- with 19/6 costs. From November 1922 until January 1923 the house was closed for substantial internal repair work plus re-roofing at a cost of £483/17/8. Further renovation work was carried out in 1933, but during this period the rent remained static at £6/5/- a quarter. In 1956 various alterations were carried out including the forming of a bathroom and water closet at a total cost of £450.

This was a smallish house, now somewhat isolated by the Canterbury ring road, and both its success and survival depended upon a succession of good innkeepers. During the 1950's one tenant was an ex-miner, which resulted in the house being popular with the local mining community. Another landlord

during this period supplemented his income by working as a drayman for Mackeson. No doubt it gave him a good insight as to how his competitors were faring. Popular with sportsmen, a variety of pastimes were catered for, including fishing (pike, perch and roach), darts, football and cricket – bat and trap was a speciality. To the rear of the premises was a finely manicured green. In 1950 the pub teams won all of the sporting cups in the Canterbury area – a record not achieved before or since. However, custom fell away and despite Shepherd Neame, who had purchased the pub in 1972, and a number of licensees' best endeavours it could not be made into a viable economic unit. The house closed in 2003 with the intention to convert the building into office accommodation. However, this application did not proceed and in August 2004 developers submitted a planning application to the city council to create eleven bedsits as well as adding a two-floor extension at the rear. Despite local objectors, which included CAMRA, planning permission was granted in November 2004.

The inn sign miniature hung until 1995.

No 6. British Lion, Folkestone
Sankey of Canterbury, Ash & Co., Jude Hanbury, Mackeson, Whitbread, Pubmaster

This is reputed to be the town's oldest pub dating back to 1460, but no records exist to substantiate this claim and it is more likely that the "George" holds this distinction. If it was a pub in the 1400's it is thought that it was named the "Priory Arms" – after the nearby seventh-century Priory. I was told that the pub adopted its present name at the time Napoleon became troublesome – this is a possibility, as a long-lost pub, named the "Kings Head", last mentioned in 1769, had a landlord called Gibbon Ladd. Ladd had a son called John who held the licence here in 1782.

It is probable that parts of the building date back to the 15th century with the front added in Georgian times. Next door, 8 The Bayle, acts as the licensee's office. A notice of sale dated 1819 states – lot 30, a messuage called the "British Lion" with the wash-house, granary and garden near the Bail. The owner at the time was the well known Canterbury brewer M.W. Sankey who had rather overstretched his finances and been declared bankrupt. Sometime during the 1800's the house came into the possession of the Ash family. Records indicate that it "came with the Hop Poles, Canterbury". It formed part of the estate of Thomas Ash, who died on 12th March 1875, at which time H. Cooper was the landlord paying a rent of £16 for the pub and £32/10/- for the three cottages adjoining. Electric light was installed during November 1929. On 31st March 1931 Jude Hanbury conveyed two of the adjacent cottages to the Tenterden Brewery Company for £275 and, that same year, the main structure was rebuilt by Jenner & Son at a cost of £1,179/8/10.

A charming property, this house has always been popular with tourists and locals alike. It is also said to have enjoyed connections with the smuggling trade. Over the years many clubs and societies have used the snug, suitably furnished bars as their venue. Probably the most famous imbiber was Charles Dickens in 1855, who would pop in whilst writing Little Dorrit just down the road at Albion Villas. The small bar in which he sat is still called the "Dickens Room".

A very popular landlord was James Pankhurst who held the licence from 1887 until his death in 1913. He was also a bus proprietor and organized various outings for his patrons. His son, Henry, succeeded him and remained until 1929. Folkestone appears blessed with enterprising landladies and, in 1957, Mrs. Joan Hourohane and her husband Richard swept in from the nearby "Clarenden". They took over a successful, but somewhat male-oriented house, with the main diet being mild-and-bitter or brown ale. They introduced a more traditional pint and it developed into a place one visited for conversation rather than the juke box. Unfortunately, in 1974, Whitbread submitted plans to enlarge the premises, possibly incorporating the two cottages. Despite a protest and petition signed by 200 locals, the development went ahead, creating one large bar area. Richard (Gerry) Hourohane designed a pub tie, consisting of red and white stripes, with a lion on a blue background, which proved hugely popular with patrons. Joan retired in 1986.

This hostelry offers a fine menu and traditional ales. The sign has seen several changes, but the present one is easily identifiable as the original, with a Union Jack background – probably designed by Gerry Hourohane.

No 7. British Volunteer, Ashford

Tenterden Brewery Co., Jude Hanbury, Mackeson, Whitbread, Shepherd Neame

The development of the Ashford ring-road and the demolition of much of the surrounding artisan property has left this house marooned in a shopping area on the outskirts of the town centre. For a long while the land adjoining was used as a large, well-rutted car park. It is difficult to see how this pub can attract custom, and its days are probably numbered.

The house was built in the 1860's, with Mrs. Sarah Holland holding the licence in 1866. Between 1866 and 1899 the pub had eight landlords, with only

Richard Lewis, from 1874 until 1887, providing any continuity. He is also described as "a carrier to Biddenden, Tenterden and Maidstone on Tuesday, Thursday and Saturday at 4p.m.".

It was always thought that the Tenterden Brewery served half-a-dozen local houses, but this one quite definitely belonged to them as they sold it, on 25th March 1922, to Jude Hanbury for £4,000. Jude revalued all their premises on 29th July 1926, increasing the value of this pub to £4,716. During 1925 the house sold 262 barrels of beer, an above-average figure for the time. The pub was popular during this era and, possibly to reflect this, in 1938 the rent was increased from £8/15/- per quarter to £13/15/-, and, by 1948, it had increased further to £15. By 1924 the pub had passed to Mackeson and on 31st August 1956, the brewers redeemed the outstanding mortgage of £2,750.

Initially the house was named the "British Volunteers", switching to the singular certainly when the inn sign miniature was issued. At the present time it has reverted back to the plural. In the early days there were fields to the rear of the pub, which housed a large Army barracks. Typically, local publicans refused to serve soldiers, so the army converted two old cottages, which had served as a recruitment office, into the pub now called the "British Volunteer". Shades of Rudyard Kipling:-

> "Oh it's Tommy this, an' Tommy that, an' "Tommy go away"
> But it's "Thank you, Mr. Atkins", when the band begins to play".

In the 1950's there was a drill hall to the rear of the building. Substantial renovation work was carried out in the 1980's, with the original two-bar house now converted to one large room. The latest inn sign, a double-sider, shows local workmen, or the unemployed, lining up to accept the King's shilling. Hanging in the bar was the fourth series of inn signs together with a picture of Lord Kitchener. The place was empty when I called, with the landlord seeing little future for the business.

Shepherd Neame acquired the house in 2004.

No 8. Bull's Head, Adisham
(Closed 30th June 2004) Ash & Co., Jude Hanbury, Mackeson, Whitbread, Fremlins, Pubmaster

This old inn is said to have served the village since the 1500's, but I have been unable to trace any records confirming this great age. Let us just say it is very old. The original sixteenth century building, which was a simple one-bar ale house, stood at right angles to the road, but in 1932 considerable renovation work was carried out, which included the squarish building that now fronts the road. By 1870 the house, plus about five acres of land and three cottages beside the pub, was owned by George Ash, who had purchased the property, from Harrison and others, and the land, from Brettell and others. On 18th December 1890 his executors sold the pub to Collard, Moxon and Ash, who went on to create Ash & Co. On 30th March 1931 the quit rent, amounting to £7/5/10, was redeemed. In 1961 the brewers sold just less than an acre of land situated about a quarter of a mile to the south of the pub, for £150, as they had been refused planning permission to develop the site.

Over the years the house has seen some long-serving and interesting landlords. Thomas Court held the licence from about 1804 to at least 1816 and, by 1867, G. Bushell was behind the bar. Mrs. Frances Bushell served during the mid- and late-1870's, and is also described as a blacksmith. In 1882 we find Alfred J. Bushell in situ. In 1940 Mr. and Mrs. Pooley managed the house, paying a rent of £7/10/- per quarter, but unfortunately, in 1949, Mr. Pooley fell down the cellar steps and died from his injuries. He is buried in the village churchyard a short distance away. He was an ex-army man who had spent some time in Egypt. The Pooleys used the 16th century rear bedroom to store cabin trunks etc. as, with the sloping ceiling and floors, it was too uncomfortable for sleeping. On Mr. Pooley's death, his widow, her son and daughter, Phyl, managed the house. More recent characters were Charlie, who supplemented his income by driving East Kent coaches up to London whilst his wife managed the pub during the day, and in the late 1950's Major "Topper" Brown. To advertise closing time he would don his regimental cap, kept behind the bar, and march smartly up and down behind the bar shouting "last orders please". There was an interesting fellow acquiring the licence when I called for a pint in 1997. Apparently it had always been this young man's ambition to manage a pub – only one thing was missing – the cash to set himself up in business. He had taken his very old car to the M.O.T. station for its test and, not having enough money to go into town, had hung around and drifted into a sweet shop. Here he purchased a lottery scratch card and, hey presto, won £50,000! However, he proved totally unsuitable for his chosen occupation and lasted less than a year before stripping the place bare and disappearing. It is rumoured that he is now working on the ferries. As a result the pub was forced to close, but it did re-open on 3rd April 1998 when the guest of honour was Ray Butler, a former gunnery sergeant. In 1940, on his return from the Normandy beaches, Ray walked into the "Bull's Head" for a pint, was captivated by the landlord's daughter, Phyl Pooley, swept her off her feet and married her on 14th June 1941. Initially he had thought the pub had closed for good and had asked the landlady if he could pop in for one last pint.

With plenty of interesting landlords, the locals were not to be outdone. A "character" in the 1940's was Charlie Hoover, a local hop drier – skilled and thirsty work. He would buy, and arrange to have delivered to his place of work, a keg of beer (approximately thirty gallons), which he and his fellow toilers would get through during their hot and thirsty work. During the war years the place was frequented by soldiers, serving with the 16th Super Heavy Battery, who were stationed in the village. People still recall the day Winston Churchill visited the battery to give the men a pep talk. From 1940 until 1942 officers from the regiment used the upstairs room as the officers' mess. A beach hut was acquired and erected on the pub car park and was used as the cook house. After the war it was a very popular venue for the hordes of hop-pickers in the area. Miners from the Kent pits also used the pub. In 1946 the flooring was still earth covered by duck boards, although it was suggested these be replaced.

The house boasted a very popular jug and bottle, particularly with the village girls. They would slip in with local servicemen in the hope that they wouldn't be noticed by anybody else.

During 1942 the "Bull's Head" was visited by a London con man. The pub cellar was crammed full of pewter mugs, cups and plates and this gentleman, posing as an antique dealer, persuaded the landlord to part with them at a knock-down price. The articles formed part of the house inventory.

As befits an inn of such antiquity, there is said to be a tunnel linking the pub with the church, and it is stated by some that Roman mosaics lie beneath the pub car park. Both are possible but there is no evidence.

Despite its past glories, the future is bleak. It has closed for short periods, on the last occasion re-opening on 11th October 2001. During October 2002 yet another new tenant went along to a village parish council meeting to introduce himself and say what changes he had in mind, including stopping under-age drinking, to make the house more appealing to villagers. Despite sprucing the place up, and making it more welcoming to villagers, trade remained insufficient to make it a viable business resulting in the "Bull's Head" closing at 11p.m. on Wednesday, 30th June 2004. Thus another village has probably lost a valuable community service but it is hoped to sell the pub "with licence".

No 9. Botolph's Bridge, West Hythe
John Friend, Mackeson, Whitbread, Pubmaster

What a splendid sign – possibly the best in all five series. But where was the pub situated? In 1801 the area is described as Buttolph's Bridge, in 1821 Bitolph's Bridge, 1847 Buttolphus Bridge and now the present naming. The nearby bridge was known as Butters or Butlers Bridge. As there were archery butts in the adjoining field could this be how the bridge acquired its name? It is generally accepted that Botolph was a seventh-century Saxon abbot who spent a good part of his life in Lincolnshire – hence the naming of Boston and its more famous namesake in the USA. He founded a monastery possibly at Iken, Suffolk and became the patron saint of travellers. But how did this unusual name crop up in this remote spot? The most likely explanation is that the fenland farmers of Lincolnshire found the fertile soil on the marsh to their liking, resulting in some families moving into the area. It is possible that these settlers corrupted the local Butters Bridge into Botolph's Bridge to remind them of home.

The original house was a sturdy, rambling building, which some say stood on the other side of the dyke. An old photograph indicates it occupied the present site but sadly this old inn, parts of which dated back almost 600 years, fell into such a state of disrepair that there was no alternative other than to pull it down and rebuild. Mr. H.W. Alden designed the new building incorporating as many of the original features as practical and the new house opened on 23rd April 1937. The total building cost amounted to £2,091/18/8. There are no underground cellars owing to the marshy nature of the ground. For those who have never visited this isolated house close to the Military Canal it is situated at the junction of five marsh roads and has a sign advertising its presence on the main coast road, quite a distance away.

A pub has stood on this road junction since the 1700's – written records date back to 20th February 1726. A letter, written in Canterbury dated 9th May 1789, addressed to John Friend, states "I understand my brother Edward hath by my request offered you the sale of Botolph's Bridge and house for 500 guineas which is the lowest I will take for it. The rent is £15 p.a. clear of all deductions of Land Tax and Quit Rent. … another person has made application … but rather you should have it than any other person that the present tenant may continue in it". Signed R. Coleman.

On 19th October 1801 John Friend sold his brewery assets to the Mackeson brothers, with Isaac Tournay, a solicitor, as their trustee. They paid £420 for this pub, representing 28 times the annual rental of £15. At the time the landlord was Mr. Horton, who was supplied with beer to the value of £13/13/- on the following day. On the death of William Mackeson, in 1821, the house was still valued at £420. The licence was held within the Piddock family for very many years. On 11th October 1854 Elizabeth Piddock paid, to the Collector of Excise at Canterbury, £4/8/2 for her retail beer, cider and perry licence and a further £1/2/- for the spirit licence. In 1855 Mrs. Jane Piddock was managing the pub and, on 22nd

September of that year, Henry Mackeson advised her that he had reduced the price of bitter beers from £2/2/- per barrel to £1/19/- and for a kilderkin from £1/1/- to 19/6. By 1871 Henry Haywood Piddock had taken over, whilst George Piddock ran the nearby "Carpenters Arms". Henry was still here in 1899.

Due to its isolated situation, this must always have been a marginal business – this was reflected in the rent charged – £8/15/- a quarter in 1938, which sum had reduced to £6/5/- ten years later. Some additional land was purchased in 1952 and drainage improvements costing £200 were made in 1953. That same year further land adjoining the pub was purchased for £75 from Charles Donald Symonds. In 1954 £300 was spent on well drainage and a sign, probably the one sited on the main road. 1956 saw many improvements, with the construction of a water main, supplying a water closet, hot water installation and a car park for a total outlay of £500.

There is now one large bar which incorporates the dining area that serves first-class food. Thirty years ago there were public and saloon bars plus a small room. A yard of ale hung in the public bar and all the usual pub games could be played, including "Ringing the Bull". This consisted of a ring suspended from the ceiling and a hook fixed to one of the walls – the object being to swing the ring so as to engage the hook. This was appropriate as this was very much a farmers' house. The East Kent Morris Dancers met here, as did, at one time, three motor cycle clubs. These included the Cinque Ports Classic Bikes Club and the West Hythe Aschmann Cologne Motor Cycle Club. The club badge was a replica of the pub inn sign but with the monks carrying a motor cycle boot rather than a coffin over the heavenly bridge! The club came about when the "Botolph's Bridge" bikers came across a group of German bikers parked up at a nearby caravan site. They were on their way to the Isle of Man T.T. races but one member had a mechanical problem. The two groups got on famously and the Germans never did see the races.

In about 1990 the brewers hung a new sign depicting ghostly monks bearing a coffin towards the pub. Quite naturally it was not well received, with the locals clamouring for the return of the original. To their great credit Pubmaster arranged this, and I am told that the only way a replica could be created was by laser scanning the miniature inn sign. About a year ago this was amended slightly but is still acceptable.

No 10. Castle Hotel, Saltwood
Frederick Willcocks, Mackeson, Whitbread

The village of Saltwood is dominated by the castle which dates back to 1160. It offered hospitality to the Norman knights who, on 29th December 1170, planned their crime before riding on to Canterbury to put Thomas a Becket to the sword. It was the home of the late Alan Clark MP. The pub is a large imposing building overlooking the village green.

The house dates back to the 1800's and was originally three cottages. Following conversion, the hostelry was used to house the retainers of visitors to the castle. A first indenture dated 11th October 1853 was between William Rayner and Thomas Peene and the next record of note is dated 20th October 1877, when Edmund Wyles and Robert Smith Peene conveyed the pub to Fred Willcocks. On 1st June 1892 Fred sold the business, plus a cottage, to the Mackeson brothers for £3,150. Costs amounted to £50/6/- and, at the same time, the tithe of £1/0/5 was redeemed. Willcocks had been in occupation since 1877 but, on selling the pub, moved out, with George Amos taking over. On 22nd October 1897 another cottage and some land were purchased for £350. Over the years many alterations and improvements have been carried out. In 1915 a temporary bar was installed at a cost of £150, to be written off over three years. In 1921 the brewers purchased 3 and 4 Stanley Cottages for £700. Other alterations were approved on 28th April 1927 when plans were drawn up by Mr. W.H. Alden, mainly to incorporate the yard at a cost of £1,000, with a further £35 spent on a counter and cabinet. During 1928 an allowance of £31/10/- was made to the tenant in respect of electric light and gas installation and an old coal shed. During the 1930's and 1940's the rent was £15 per quarter. In August 1947 E.G. Wildin LRIBA drew up plans for additional lavatories. At that time the pub boasted a sitting room, coffee room, saloon and public bars. These two bars were ultimately combined to create a one-bar house. In 1957 Mackeson purchased from the parish council the attractive village pond in front of the pub. It was then concreted over to form a car park, for a dozen cars, at a cost of £246/18/-.

No 11. *City of London, Dymchurch*
Beer & Co., (St. Augustines Gate Brewery), Mackeson, Whitbread, Shepherd Neame

All of the signs that have hung at this house link the pub to the financial City of London, with the inn sign showing the coat of arms of the city or similar. The dagger incorporated within the arms is associated with the Wat Tyler uprising, which came so close to succeeding and ended with his death. The present, quite splendid sign shows a bird's eye view of Tower Bridge and the city. However, the name is supposed to be linked to a ship that foundered in a storm off Dymchurch during the eighteenth century. It may, of course, have been the vessel carrying the fictional character Dr. Syn, created by Russell Thorndyke in 1915, that went down. However, there is no evidence of such a casualty, but a tug-boat bearing this name saved many lives when a ship did founder further along the coast.

The building dates back to the sixteenth century and at one time was a coaching house. Henry Bean Mackeson purchased the pub from a farmer, L. Hunt, on 31st December 1885, paying £1,000 plus costs of £32/10/6. It was described as being situated to the north of Martello Tower No. 24. In 1928 the stables were converted into an order office and bar, at a cost of £200, with a further £15 spent on a counter and screen. The forge was also converted into a bar area, with the bars on split levels. The following year the quit rent was redeemed in the sum of £3/2/8. The house always maintained a regular trade, particularly during the summer months, and to reflect this, during the 1930's, the tenant paid a rent of £12/13/10 per quarter. For a long while this was a simple ale house, but, on 7th April 1948, a "full on" licence was confirmed when the net monopoly value of £1,200 was paid. A hot water system costing £100 was installed during 1955, and in 1967 electrical work to the value of £315/15/6 was carried out.

Popular with locals and holiday makers, the pub counted Noel Coward as a regular visitor. Perhaps one gentleman, reputed to belong to the smuggling fraternity, has never left the premises, as it is rumoured that his remains are sealed behind the dart board in the beach bar. The poor fellow is said to have met his end during a battle with local revenue men.

Shepherd Neame leased the pub from Whitbread on 6th May 1992 and purchased the freehold on 27th September 1996.

No 12. The Dolphin, Faversham
(Closed in 1960) Mackeson

This house is something of an enigma as, even forty years after it closed, it is still warmly remembered by older residents of the town, and yet it appears to have been a difficult house to run and was barely profitable.

It was certainly very old, with the first reference I have found being an indenture dated 2nd April 1712 between Thomas Lake of Ospringe to Peter Greenstreet of Selling (husband of Anne Dering and father of Mary). A newspaper item dated 17th July 1754 states that the gentlemen of Faversham and Ospringe will meet at the "Dolphin Hotel" at 1 o'clock to play cricket at 2 o'clock against the gentlemen of Chilham, Chartham, Bridge and Harbledown. A similar notice appeared in 1760. About this time the "Dolphin" also doubled as a theatre, seeing a week of amateur performances of "Arden of Faversham" with singing and dancing between the acts. On 25th January 1764 the landlady, Catherine Lott, offered a five guineas reward for the return of a silver tankard stolen from the hotel. Further notices appeared in the local press and, on 1st May 1854 it was reported that forty members of the town corps of the East Kent Rifles met at the "Dolphin" to

celebrate the corps' formation. An excellent dinner was provided by the landlord Mr. Pilcher. Edward Neame, the quarter master, was chairman with J.V. Barling his deputy. The gathering broke up at 10 o'clock. However, this convivial occasion was marred as one of the guests, George John Dunk, a farmer from Chilham, was killed in an accident. An employee at the "Dolphin", Alfred Lott – surely an ancestor of Catherine – told the inquest, which was held at the "White Lion", Selling, that on that Monday Mr. Dunk attended the dinner and at about 10 o'clock ordered his cart. However, although perfectly sober, he did not leave the premises until about 11 o'clock. He left alone and proceeded at foot pace with lighted lamps to his cart. As he had not returned home at the appointed time, a search commenced and his body was discovered at Whitehill under his upturned cart at 4 o'clock in the morning. A verdict of accidental death was recorded. Later that year Mr. Pilcher again provided an excellent spread for fifty of the inhabitants of the town who were entertained to supper by the Mayor to celebrate the anniversary of the Queen's birthday. In 1879 the Faversham Football Club met here and, following demobilization after the war, the local RAFA branch was founded in 1946 and selected this inn as its meeting place, using one of the rooms on the first floor. The hotel was also the favoured venue for Rotary and many other clubs and societies. One of the more renowned drinkers was A.H. (Tommy) Hopper, the England international amateur footballer who, on occasion, would be accompanied by the whole team.

At one time the "Dolphin" was a modest coaching house. Originally an Elizabethan building, over the years many alterations and additions were made. The property was largely rebuilt in 1852 with a top storey added. In its final days it boasted a fine Victorian façade. Mackeson purchased this property on 29th January 1925 from Browne and others, paying the sum of £2,250 plus costs of £49/1/-. During the 1930's tenants came and went in rapid succession. Between March 1934 and July 1937 there were four landlords, and it was not until 20th July 1942, when Mrs. D. Hills signed a tenancy agreement, that some stability was restored. Her husband was an army officer based at Folkestone. All this time the rent had remained static at £40 p.a. A Mackeson employee visiting the pub in 1946 commented "External appearance does not look like an hotel. The house and outbuildings are full of rubbish. Takings approximately £15-£20 a week". In 1954 a dining area was created and a lift was installed at a total cost of £350.

Despite locals remembering it as an excellent hospitable inn with panelled walls and a highly polished brass fender, almost worn away with use in some places, it failed to earn its keep. There was a snooker table, but the room was damp and the balls would not run smoothly. By 1960 there was such a low volume of trade that expenditure of £2,000 on essential repairs could not be justified. As a result the pub closed and Whitbread accepted an offer of £12,000 for the premises, unlicensed, from the Legal and General Assurance Society. Completion took place on 27th January 1961. The pub fixtures and fittings were auctioned off and, in 2004, a Faversham artist presented to the local museum, at the Fleur de Lys centre, a David Burley metal map of East Kent, which he had acquired at the auction. The landlord had used it to draw up the fire, so it was blackened, with parts virtually obliterated, but after much careful renovation it looks as good as new. The building was demolished in 1961 to make way for the Fine Fare supermarket, now Superdrug. Sadly the town of Faversham lost an historic inn and Preston Street will never appear the same again.

No 13. The Duke's Head, Hythe
John Friend, Mackeson, Whitbread, Pubmaster

The original building dates back to 1703 and was a dwelling house until 1749, when a licence was granted. The first landlord was Ezekiel Price, described as a beer seller and tallow maker. The place had no name and was a common ale house. In 1750 the pub was sold to the Hythe Brewery, almost certainly then owned by John Friend, and in turn he sold the property on 19th October 1801 to William and Henry Mackeson. The price was a staggering £420 – 28 times the annual rent of £15. A week later the brothers supplied the landlord, Leonard Watcher, beer to the value of £12/18/-. By now it was called the "Duke's Head", but was more generally referred to as the "Richard, Duke of York". By 1784 William Brown was utilising the stables to the rear of the premises, together with a tract of land to conduct his business of horse-trading – his wife, Mary, managed the pub. Unfortunately, in 1802, William was thrown from his horse and killed. On the death of William Mackeson, in 1821, the house was valued at £1,200. By 1871 the licence was held by Thomas Kemp, who was also a fly proprietor and operated a carriage business from the inn.

Electric lighting was installed in 1906 at a cost of £8/2/6, and that same year the brewers wrote off a bad debt of £198/15/-, a considerable sum in those days. On 31st March 1931 the Tenterden Brewery Co. Limited acquired, from Jude Hanbury, the house and shop adjoining the pub, but there is no evidence that either brewery ever owned the pub. A fire occurred at the premises in 1932, but no details are available. During the 1930's the rent paid was £10 per quarter plus £15/12/- p.a. for the stables.

The house stands close to a bridge over the Military Canal which bears its name. The town sheep and cattle market was sited close to the pub which was heaving with farmers on market days. As to be expected in a place like Hythe, the inn has strong connections with the smuggling trade – it is rumoured that a smuggler hid in a sewer beneath the inn to evade the local revenue men. In the 1950's the house provided accommodation and became a popular rendezvous for air crew and engineers working for Silver City Airways, which operated from Lympne airfield. The air crews used to bring back cans of foreign beers; the remnants of the collection are still exhibited in the bar. The landlord at that time was Hirson Robert Giffard. When I called in 1999 the landlord was David Ivory who had taken over in 1985. As to be expected from a house run by a former Whitbread employee, the place was immaculate.

In 1985 the much-loved Duke of Wellington sign seen all over Kent was replaced by a more flamboyant version. This was never accepted and, by popular demand, Pubmaster reverted to the original sign. However, was Wellington a usurper? – should it not be the Duke of York? Hanging in the bar is the first series of inn signs, together with the David Burley metal map of East Kent. The pub regularly features in the local CAMRA guide. This house is well worth a visit.

No 14. Eight Bells, Canterbury
Sankey of Canterbury, Ash & Co., Jude Hanbury, Mackeson, Whitbread, Pubmaster

There were at least two houses called "Eight Bells" in the city so care was required whilst sifting through the available information. Almost certainly this house was that initially described as being in St. Dunstans. Whitbread documents indicate that the pub was included in an omnibus conveyance, dated 1870, that revealed, at one time, the house was called the "Three Queens".

The original rambling, timber-framed building dates back to 1708 and was owned by Nathaniel Caythem during the reign of Queen Anne. It was probably a coach-house before it was demolished in 1898 and rebuilt in 1900. Sankeys, who brewed in the city in the early 1800's, owned the pub, which was then acquired by either Thomas or George Ash from the Sankeys' assignees. There was also a yard with stables opposite. The licence was held by Thomas James from about 1847 until 1880. He was also described as a timber dealer and paid a rent of £16/10/- for the total premises. An advertisement in a directory dated 1902 reads "C. Winchester, Eight Bells, 34 London Road. Horses and carriages let on hire for private parties, weddings etc". Shortly after this the stabling was converted into a skittles alley. The quit rent, amounting to £2/8/4, was redeemed on 10th October 1933.

A former landlord who deserves a chapter to himself is Jack Moat D.C.M. who sadly passed away in 2001 after a most eventful life. He served with the Royal Tank Regiment for 22 years reaching the rank of Warrant Officer II. During his war service he and his tank crew experienced a slightly unnerving experience. They picked up their tank in Birmingham and drove it to Thetford to complete their training. During this time Jack arranged for Corporal Tony Telford, who had an artistic bent, to paint on the lower side of the tank, by now named "Defiant", a young lady showing a leg. The regiment landed in France on D Day plus one, 7th June 1944. During the battle for Caen the tank was hit in the front right-hand track and ultimately the crew had to abandon the vehicle. The next day the crew took over another tank with Corporal Telford again using his artistic talents. Unfortunately, whilst advancing towards the enemy the second tank was blown up by a Teller Mine, holing the petrol tanks. Again the vehicle was abandoned, but both were later recovered. By this time the loss of life and machinery was massive and the crew were stood down until such time as a new vehicle could be found for them. After a wait, the workshops were able to provide the crew with a replacement tank and, to their amazement, they realised that the new tank was the front and back halves of their first two tanks welded together. The regiment then advanced through France and Belgium into Holland. During heavy fighting in the area of Corso on 30th September 1944 the tank was knocked out by mortar fire and two of the crew were killed. The driver and Jack were wounded and flown back to England the next day. I had the privilege of typing up the details of these heroic deeds for publication in the Tank Regiments Journal – the title was "The unique story of two Sherman Firefly tanks which later became one tank". After the war Jack married a German girl and, on 27th February 1959, became the landlord at the "Eight Bells". He was a well-built man with a large personality and soon made his mark in the trade. Hanging in the saloon bar in the 1970's was an enormous wooden spoon inscribed "Jack Moat champion stirrer of Canterbury". He was well known for his practical jokes and the pub had good darts and cribbage teams. Poker dice were played as dice were illegal at the time. The pub did a good lunch and evening trade with a sing-song to enliven the cold winter evenings. For a short while they also did bed and breakfast, but this became too successful and occupied too much of their time. A pocket diary holder advertising the pub was produced for the regulars. During the 1960's the pub Christmas club regularly paid out £2,000. In the 1980's a special bottle of wine, said to be worth over £700, was exhibited in the bar. Jack had bought the bottle in 1961 from a customer who was clearing out a cellar. It was a German white in a dusty corked bottle with a lead capsule. Part of the label was missing but it read as follows "1884 vintage Hochheim Berg dedicated to Her Majesty and His Royal Highness the Prince of Wales". Jack still had the bottle. The house was always immaculate and I am told the furniture was fantastic – it was thought to have been purchased in Hong Kong. He retired from the pub on 4th March 1984.

The house remains just as Jack left it. A traditional pub, it is gratifying to see the "Eight Bells" appearing in the CAMRA 2004 Good Beer Guide. Even the sign has not changed.

No 15. Gate Inn, Rhodes Minnis

(Closed in October 1994) George Oldfield, A.J. Beer (St Augustines Gate Brewery) of Canterbury, Sun Brewery of Littlebourne, Mackeson, Whitbread, Fremlins

The "Gate Inn" can be dated precisely. A conveyance (lease and release) dated 8th October 1756 between John Green of Stelling, carpenter, and William Oldfield of Lyminge, husbandman, and Sarah, his wife:- "All that new built Messuage with the barn, stable buildings, garden and yard and four pieces of land containing four acres being in the parish of Lyminge adjoining to a certain free Common there called Rhodes Minice near Mockbeggar Gate and pond. Consideration: £98/2/-."

On the same date a conveyance (assignment of mortgage term) was signed: Elizabeth Howell of Stowting, widow, and Richard Howell of Lyminge, yeoman, (executors of the will of Henry Howell of Stowting, husbandman), Thomas Fuller of Nackington, carpenter, and John Green to William Oldfield and Sarah, his wife, George Oldfield of Elham, brewer, and Thomas Mercer the younger of Dover, gentleman, as trustees. Property as above. Consideration: £98/2/-. However, the year 1740 is engraved in the brickwork above the fireplace.

The next document of any importance is dated Tuesday 14th October 1890 and relates to an auction by James Pledge at the Saracen's Head, Ashford. Offered for sale was the "Gate Inn". Freehold fully licensed public house plus eight acres pasture and arable land, stables and outbuildings. The property is leased to Mr. A.J. Beer brewer of Canterbury term of 14 years from 11th October 1884 at an annual rent of £35 the Lessee doing inside repairs". Mr. E.G. Glasscock was the successful bidder at a price of £485.

In November 1907 Mackeson bought out the little-known Sun Brewery, situated at Littlebourne, which came with five tied houses, one of which was the "Gate". On 31st March 1936 the quit rent of £3/1/1 was extinguished and, on 27th April 1950, the brewer sold the counter for £14/14/-. Electricity was laid on in the 1950's. On 15th January 1953 a lease of a portion of the old brick stable was granted to the Territorial and Auxiliary Forces Association of Kent, for use as an armoury by the local Home Guard Platoon, for three years at an annual rent of £10. For a time the Kings Troop Royal Horse Artillery were stationed in the fields opposite the pub and it was probably this land that was sold on 1st January 1962 for £375 less costs of £48/5/6.

This isolated pub was popular with landlords and there were several long-serving tenants. During the 1800's the licence was held for very many years by G. Couzens – certainly from 1859 until 1882. E. Roberts moved in on 11th October 1909 and stayed until 24th May 1935 when the brewers entered into a tenancy agreement with D.D. Edwards who paid a rent of £14 for the pub and £6 for the land. By 1948 the rent had reduced to £6, payable quarterly.

During the 1940's the pub did little trade with the beer described as "old". However, things improved and in the 1990's it became a rather too-lively house with much drinking the wrong side of licensing hours. After several police warnings, which were ignored, the pub lost its licence. When I called the pub had closed, but a sign propped up against a tree suggested that the traveller visit the "Rose and Crown" at Stelling Minnis. The building was ultimately taken over by the "Lord Whisky Charity" a very active animal rescue society. The lady who runs the society, Mrs Todd, was awarded the MBE for services to animal welfare in the 2004 honours list. For those who wish to visit the old pub the society runs a shop which incorporates a refreshment room.

A long while ago a gated toll road ran from Mockbeggar down to Lyminge – hence the pub name.

No 16. The Guildhall, Folkestone
*(Formerly **Guildhall Vaults**. Closed in February 1984) Cobb etc., Mackeson, Whitbread*

The original "Guildhall Hotel" stood on the other side of the road, almost opposite the town hall and dated back to the 1700's. This was demolished to make way for a more modern establishment. In its early days this house was also known as the "Guildhall Vaults". On 14th April 1846 William, Earl of Radnor, and the Right Honourable Jacob Pleydell Bouverie, Viscount Folkestone, leased the premises to Charles Andrews for a 99-year term commencing on 21st June 1844 at an annual rent of £6/5/-.

The new house opened in 1868 when Arthur Andrews was granted a beer licence; a spirit licence was subsequently confirmed on 18th October 1870. He was to remain until 1877. The lay-out here was most

unusual with one long narrow bar measuring 18 feet by 13 feet. One passed through the public bar to the saloon at the rear. In the saloon there were stained glass windows and a further entrance, via the road, to the rear of Guildhall Street. In 1871 Arthur was proud to proclaim "here is the only house in Folkestone where there is a stand-up bar like the London System". Situated close to the town centre, the pub was immediately successful and became a little rowdy. This resulted in Mr. Andrews being warned on a number of occasions to control excessive noise. However, the third licensee, James Hoad, was fined £3 with 15/6 costs for breaking a window in the Mayor's parlour at the Town Hall. (This name also crops up with the "Bouverie Arms" and "Gun Tavern".)

At some time the house passed to brewers Thomas Cobb, George Belgrave and John McGregor and it was on 7th November 1898 that Eleanor Hoad, John Banks (see also the "Jubilee") and Thomas Cobb assigned the lease to Henry Bean Mackeson for £5,900. Shortly afterwards the following expenditure was incurred:-

1902. Signboard £10 plus gilt letters. £ 7/8/6.
1904. Enlarging bar. £200
1913. Outlay on new front and enlarging billiards room. £130.

A first world war licensee, George Cozens, was fined £2 on 9th March 1916 for selling ale to a soldier, contrary to the regulations, and during the second war the walls of the house were covered with plywood, on which servicemen from all over the world inscribed their name, rank and number. A quaint note dated March 1934 advises us that there had been a change of tenant, as the former had become financially embarrassed in other quarters and the premises were now being run under management for the benefit of the incoming tenant.

During 1943 Mackeson purchased the freehold from Lord Radnor, paying a deposit of £600 on 6th July 1943, with the balance £5,400 paid on 9th August. On 5th April 1954 the brewers also completed the purchase of 6 Guildhall Street (adjoining the pub) from Mrs. Amy Rachel Sinden and Herbert Walker Barker for £4,750. They then granted a lease of the lock-up shop on the ground floor and basement to Chain Libraries Limited for seven years. The pub had a dining room on the second floor that ran the length of the building, had rooms to let, and was one of the first places to have neon light advertising. Reflecting the importance of this house, in 1938 the quarterly rent was £35/10/-.

For a very long time, from 1952 until 1984, the licence was held by a widow, Mrs. Maud Lewis, assisted by her daughter Eileen. The house was run very successfully with both ladies hugely popular and respected in the town. They were both chairpersons of the ladies' section of the Licensed Victuallers Association in their time. Eileen went on to become licensee at the nearby "Globe" in 1983 and when Whitbread closed the "Guildhall" in 1984, she re-named her house to enable the name "Guildhall" to live on. Maud came to help her daughter at the "Globe/Guildhall" until her death in September 1986 at the age of 75.

Sadly Eileen died at the young age of 58 just before Christmas 1989. As a sign of respect many local pubs closed at the time of her funeral service. If one walks a short distance to the Bayle pond and gardens a chair, dedicated to Eileen Lewis, publican for many years at the "Guildhall", can be found: it was provided by the Folkestone and District Ladies Auxiliary, of which Eileen was a founder member.

The old pub is now a Pizza Hut.

No 17. The Hope Inn, Hythe
Mackeson, Whitbread, Fremlins

This is an impressive, well-maintained, building that for a long time sat in the shadow of Hythe's windmill. The house was built in about 1790, the premises being used as canteen accommodation and officers' quarters to the army. They vacated the property in 1827, at which time the house acquired a liquor licence. Mackeson purchased the freehold in 1885, paying the sum of £1,000 plus costs of £31/11/6.

On the reverse of the inn sign miniature Whitbread dedicate this house to Victor Alexander John Hope, 10th Baronet and 2nd Marquis Linlithgow, Viceroy of India. The family presently resides at Hopetoun House near Edinburgh. There appears to be no connection between this gentleman, however worthy his credentials, and Hythe, but a man who would have been very well known in the area, at the time the pub was named, was Colonel, later Brigadier, Hope. The house was built at the time Napoleon was beginning to worry Europe, and the property had military connections. Colonel Hope, together with William Pitt the Younger, was charged with selecting the sites for the erection of the defensive Martello Towers. In all, between 1805 and 1808, 27 towers were built on the Kent coast. The pub surely honours his name.

For a long while during the 1800's the house was in the capable hands of the Cloake family. In 1855 Joe Cloake held the licence and by 1878 Miss Sophia Cloake had assumed control. She was still here in 1882. The pub appears to have traded very successfully over the years, with not a great deal of information coming to light. However, one disastrous event occurred in 1877 when a particularly high tide badly flooded the building, causing a lot of damage – the tide mark was evident until substantial refurbishment took place in 1968. It was at this time that the original brick-work was rendered and painted white. In 1926 a staircase was put in at a cost of £35 and in that same year a piece of land adjoining the pub was sold to Mrs. Dray for £50. The tenant's rent was always modest, – £8/14/- per quarter throughout the 1930's and 1940's. During 1956 £150 was spent on altering the men's urinal. The inn sign miniature has seen several embellishments over the years but basically remains the same.

No 18. King's Head, Wye
Flint & Co., Jude Hanbury, Mackeson, Whitbread, Shepherd Neame

It is stated that an inn has occupied this site since the late 1400's, but there is no evidence to confirm this. Certainly the "King's Head" is an ancient establishment with an interesting history and, at its peak, was the centre of village life and a substantial coaching inn. All manner of societies would meet here, including the village football and cricket clubs. Until 1925 the hotel was the meeting place for the Court Baron of the local manors subordinate to the Manor of Wye. The tenants of these manors had to appear to pay dues and to make an Oath of Fealty to the Lord of Wye Manor. A free lunch was provided.

During the early 1900's the stag hunt met in Church Street in front of the "King's Head". A stag was released in Oxenturn Road and the hunt sallied forth. When caught, it was rescued, comforted, and hunted again on another occasion! This stag, named Charlie, became very tame and popular with the huntsmen and would chase away the sheep when they were being fed at Little Olantigh in order to eat their food.

The hotel suffered two disastrous fires, both of which involved rebuilding the premises. The first, I am told, was in 1871 and was referred to as the great fire of Wye. The hotel was rebuilt with ten bedrooms – a further two rooms were added later. The

second, on 26th October 1889, was the result of arson and started in the Star, or Beaney's Brewery, which was sited to the rear and side of the "King's Head". Most of the ancient building behind the Victorian façade was destroyed and Wye cricket club lost all its equipment, which was stored on the premises. Another unfortunate event occurred in July 1916, but luckily the result was not so catastrophic. It was the day of the marriage of Captain Arthur Downton and Miss Joan Dunstan, daughter of the principal of Wye College. It was a happy event and to add to the excitement a colleague of the groom decided to drop confetti from his plane, but came in too low over the church and crashed into the hotel – bedroom nine. Fortunately nobody was seriously injured.

The brewers Jude Hanbury purchased the freehold on 20th August 1924 paying the sum of £2,150. They then raised a mortgage over the premises of £1,250 from Mrs. E.H. Holley and others the following month – this was discharged by Mackeson on 1st November 1956. Over the years various improvements were carried out, including, in 1930, the installation of electric light and, in 1932, a drainage system costing £62/11/9. In 1953 £300 was spent on forming a bathroom and, two years later, £500 went on improvements to the lavatory accommodation and altering the bars. During the 1930's and 1940's the rent remained steady at £12/10/- per quarter. In 1946 a Mackeson employee observed that "Jug Bar" still appeared on the door of the public bar and suggested that this could be covered by the fire screen. Also the exterior of the premises was in a very poor condition.

The first landlord that I have traced is Benjamin Ryall in 1803. Guy Ruddle was a most popular "mine host" from 1963 until 1979. He describes the house as a hybrid pub – hotel – restaurant. It appealed to a cross-section of the community, particularly the students at Wye Agricultural College. Friendly Town v Gown events occurred, including bar billiards, darts, and a beer race, for which a cup was presented to the winners. A new dining room opened on Wednesday 6th April 1966 and, in its hey-day, the hotel employed eleven full-time staff.

Shepherd Neame leased the premises from Whitbread on 6th May 1992 and purchased the freehold on 2nd August 1993. This house remains the favoured haunt of local students.

"Vows can't change nature, Kings are only men." Browning.

No 19. The Long Reach, Whitstable
Gardner & Co., Jude Hanbury, Mackeson, Whitbread, Beefeater

On 18th December 1934 the directors of Mackeson took the decision to vacate their small house on Borstal Hill and build a good-sized roadhouse on the newly-constructed Thanet Way. The locals were amazed by its style and opulence and were certain it would be a white elephant, but in time this proved to be a wise move.

The former "Long Reach Tavern" was situated just at the top of Borstal Hill and, in its early days, sat in splendid isolation on a gravel road. The original part of the building is said to date back to the 17th Century. It started life as a forge, but this was closed by Stephen Saddleton in 1858 when he moved down the hill to the "Two Brewers" and the forge opposite. It was then let as a beer-house. An early landlord was Reuben Parfett in 1882 when the pub was stated as being in the parish of Seasalter. In 1884 the inquest on Fanny Hill, known locally as the "Great Impostor", was held here. For years she had faked illness to gain sympathy and creature comforts including brandy from the locals. In 1903, during the Gardner days, the pub was described as being filthy and catering for "poachers and the roughest class of people in Whitstable". Perhaps as a result of this and the house being isolated from the other Gardner pubs in East Kent they sold it for £1,025 to John Harold and Elizabeth Jane Craven on 25th April 1903. They must have quickly on-sold as, in April 1924, Jude Hanbury raised a mortgage, from G.V. Miskin of £750 over the property. One of the last people to hold the licence was F.D. Jackson, who signed a tenancy agreement on 21st October 1932 agreeing to a rent of £25 p.a. In January of the following year an exchange of land took place whereby the brewers relinquished a piece at one end of the property for a large portion at the back of the house. Shortly afterwards the decision was taken to re-site the pub. On 26th October 1936 the premises were sold to A.E. Loudwell for £425 plus agreed value of the tenant, Mr. F.C. Neal, amounting to £21/4/6. In recent years a ladies hairdressing salon operated from the premises but this closed in 2002 and the house was offered for sale at a price of £264,950.

The directors resolved to spend between £3,000 and £4,000 on the new property. Plans were prepared by Mr. Wildin, with particular attention paid to the car-parking facilities. The building costs were on target at £4,075/13/7 with a further £682 spent on constructing a draw-in. Whilst the work was progressing, on 14th April 1935, the removal of the licence was obtained, with eighteen months allowed for the erection of the new house. The licence was transferred and the splendid new tavern opened its doors on 15th May 1936.

Mr. F.C.A.C. Neal moved from his former house, signing a tenancy agreement on 16th May 1936, paying a rent of £25 for the first year, £50 for the second and thereafter £75. The tithe of £12/19/9 was redeemed on 12th December 1940. Initially trade was poor but business picked up during the war years as many servicemen were stationed in the area. In April 1942 twenty-four-year-old Edgar Clements, who, when he became tenant at the nearby "Roman Galley", was the youngest licensee in England, took over. A popular landlord, he quickly built up trade and, amongst others, Dickie Henderson, Jack Warner, Jimmy Hanley and Lonnie Donegan would drop in for a drink when passing. The house was also a popular rendezvous for Kent cricketers during Canterbury week. Edgar remained here for over 20 years. Justification for this imposing house was confirmed during the 1950's and 1960's when it became a popular venue for coach parties visiting the Thanet coastal resorts. In 1980 the building was extended and converted to a "Beefeater" and remains very busy. During 2002 the pub was damaged by fire but was quickly renovated.

So how did the house acquire its name? One theory is that it was a "long reach" to puff to the top of the hill for one's liquid refreshment. Certainly the present sign would confirm this as the most likely explanation, but Whitbread refer to it being a nautical term, which has equal credence within the local sailing community. The most unlikely version is that the pub stood close to the town gallows from which smugglers and other miscreants were dispatched.

No 20. Lord Clyde, Walmer
East Kent Brewery, Mackeson, Whitbread, Shepherd Neame

It is said that this pub was so-named as the first landlord served in the British Army in India under Sir Colin Campbell. He was commander-in-chief in India and was the man responsible for the final recapture of Lucknow on 4th March 1858. That same year he was created Baron Clyde of Clydesdale. Story has it that, due to a misunderstanding, one particularly troublesome Indian agitator was executed by being fired from a cannon.

Built in the early Regency period, this comfortable inn sits on the seafront gazing out over the pebbled beach to where fishermen patiently bob on the waves. Walmer is quaint, with a faithful band of holiday makers returning year after year. When I called, such a couple, from Leighton Buzzard, were sitting outside relaxing in the late summer sunshine enjoying a pint. At one time the store-houses to the rear, which were owned by the pub, operated as a fish-and-chip shop.

For most of its life this was a simple ale house. It was not until February 1947 that it acquired a wine licence with a "full on" licence confirmed on 30th March 1950, at which time the net monopoly value of £550 was paid. For most of the 1930's and 1940's the rent was a very modest £5 per quarter. The pub catered for a good cross-section of the community, including miners, fishermen, Royal Marines stationed, until recently, at Deal and, during the summer months, holidaymakers. At one time a local football team operated from here – the Clyde Cosmos.

The licence has been held by some interesting tenants. One long-serving fellow was William (Billy) S. Monkton, who took over the tenancy in 1924 and retired 36 years later in March 1960. At an emotional farewell party he and his wife were presented with a silver tea service by Lieutenant-Colonel F.V. Dunn, Principal Director of Music, Royal Marines. Billy was an ex-marine and had been a member of the Royal Marine Band Service from 1914 until he was discharged in 1923. He was a practical joker and, just before his retirement, he hid a human skull in the attic with a note stating that it had belonged to the Indian found guilty of mutiny and fired from the cannon. On its discovery some while later, and following the resultant publicity, he admitted it was a hoax. His grand-children, who now live in South Africa, frequently visit the pub. Charles R. Pickford moved in on 17th August 1967 but died on 17th February 1970. He was succeeded by his widow, Ellen, who became friendly with the off-beat comedian Max Wall who, when performing at the Marlowe Theatre Canterbury during the 1970's, was a frequent visitor to the pub.

The house was sold to Shepherd Neame on 7th February 1977.

No 21. Lord Nelson, Waltham
(Closed in 1996) Mackeson, Whitbread, Free House

Land was acquired in 1793, upon which this new house was built at the end of that century. It sits high up in the North Downs in the isolated and windy village of Waltham. For a very long time the 13th Century church and pub were the centre of village activities. The local hunt met here, and there was a pool table and dart board, but the games area gave way to modest restaurant facilities. The pub bat and trap team played in the Canterbury and District League, and at one time there was a sweet shop to the side. For a long while the toilets were outside. The pub also marked the end of the journey for the infrequent bus service from Canterbury.

Villagers are of the opinion that the "new" pub replaced an older inn called the "Rose", the building of which still stands in Kake Street. More likely, in its "new" premises, it succeeded a much older tavern, the "Chequer", – formerly the "Chantry", situated a little further down the road. Records exist for this property dating back to 1658.

On 22nd August 1918 Mackeson purchased the freehold plus about five acres of land for £500, with costs of £17/7/6. Unfortunately the records do not tell us the name of the vendor. Two years later they purchased the adjoining derelict cottage and land for £55. On 18th May 1927 some of the land was leased to the trustees of Waltham Village Hall. During the 1920's the pub was valued in the brewer's books at £576/2/6. Mackeson sold approximately 4 1/2 acres to Bridge and Blean Rural District Council for £272

The coach would come to a halt by the flight of steps and passengers could step from the coach straight into the pub. The ground floor housed the bars and on the first floor were six bedrooms. Up in the attic two stout ropes were strung across the room and those patrons who were the worse for wear would be draped over the ropes to sleep it off. It was called the two-penny rope – in those days this modest sum was sufficient to purchase enough alcohol to render one comatose. There was a massive fire-place to the rear of the property where coach passengers could dry off. The pub was also used as a Customs and Excise stage posting house.

This was a substantial property standing in two acres of land with sufficient stabling to handle 20 teams of horses. There were also hen-houses and piggeries. With the decline of coaching it became a simple wayside inn and the stabling was used to store carriages and wagons. Until the start of the First World War the pub advertised "Bait and livery, horses, carriages and wagonettes for hire".

The first landlord was a fellow called James Rackstaw. A Mrs. Miller was in occupation in 1884 and on 31st January 1933 Mr. A.A. Woods signed a tenancy agreement, with his rent set at £25 p.a. He was still there at the beginning of the war. One record indicates that a full liquor licence was granted in 1845. A wine licence was obtained in February 1947 with a "full-on" licence granted on 1st May 1950 when the net monopoly value charge of £650 was paid.

In 1900 the freehold was owned by Alfred Leney, who on-sold to Jude Hanbury. On 30th April 1924 a mortgage of £750 was raised, with J. Campbell Bannerman, over the premises. This was discharged by Mackeson on 1st November 1956. During 1932 £228/19/- was spent on new sanitary accommodation, with a further bathroom formed in 1953 at a cost of £250.

In rural areas such as this the "Plough" is a common sign. It is reputed that its origins date back to the reign of Richard I (1189-1199). It is a quaint old place which is well worth a visit.

No 27. Prince of Wales, Woodnesborough
(Closed in 1966) East Kent Brewery, Ash & Co., Jude Hanbury, Mackeson, Whitbread

The "Prince of Wales" must vie with the "Cinque Port Arms" in Hythe for the title of smallest pub in all five series. Despite being a two-bar house, the "Prince" was not much larger than a double garage. Having said this, it is remembered with great affection.

The general view is that the property was built in about 1870 but if one looks high up on the front wall a brick inscribed "1854 J.J." can be discerned. A Mr. Taylor was probably the first owner and operated as a blacksmith from here. Records are sketchy, as for most of its trading days it was nothing more than an ale house and the names of early licensees are not recorded. On 15th August 1867 "about 7 acres of arable land, cottage and outbuildings at Woodnesborough" were listed in the abstract of valuation of the personal estate of George Ash deceased. In 1923 the Ash group of companies was acquired by Jude Hanbury. On 22nd July 1924 they sold, by auction, 1 to 4 Prince of Wales cottages which adjoined the pub, the purchasers being Messrs. P.L. and E.D. Gillman who paid £325. During 1923 Jude Hanbury sold, to the Tenterden Brewery Co. for £50, a forge and some land at Drainless Drove and eleven years later on 15th June 1934 the Tenterden Brewery Co. sold to Mackeson via Jude Hanbury, land at Drainless Road that was rented to W. Smallman for £6 p.a. from 11th October 1923. I am certain that the Tenterden Brewery Co. never owned the pub. Mackeson were the owners by 1935 as, on 1st November, further land was sold to Grace E. Gillman for £85. During 1947 they spent a bit of money on the place, with capital additions costing £250 and alterations £100. On 16th February 1949 the land tithe, amounting to £3/6/5, was redeemed. On 8th November 1938 a wine licence was applied for and, on 6th April 1949, a "full-on" licence was granted and the net monopoly value of £530 paid.

As previously stated, both pub and living accommodation were cramped, but over the years they were extended. Mr. Frederick Gambrill had been head gardener for a Mr. Farquer at the Grange and when the latter died he left Fred a sum of money sufficient for him to take over the pub. He signed a tenancy agreement on 5th January 1937, paying a rent of £25 p.a. and remained until about 1954. He also rented the shop across the road as well as the petrol pumps, bowling-green and tennis courts. Aunt Millie managed the shop and Fred maintained the sporting facilities. At the outbreak of war petrol became scarce and both the pumps and shop were closed. During Fred's time the pub witnessed many changes. He converted the smithy into a new kitchen for the house and the old kitchen became the sitting room, with the original sitting room becoming the pub private bar. The beer was drawn from the wood and the barrels stored in the kitchen. There was a fine collection of stuffed animals and birds, including a beautiful white African owl.

Although some way from the village, this isolated house acquired the reputation of being the premier pub in the area. Many customers worked on the local farms and Welsh miners from Snowdown visited the pub for a sing-song. They were accompanied by an elderly lady who would spend the evening smoking a pipe. The landlord's daughter can still remember the Austin family from Flemmings farm. Mrs. Austin always wore a fox fur around her neck and the head formed part of the fastening to the tail – this fascinated the little girl. Mrs. Austin's favourite tipple was port and lemon. It is said that the pub was also popular with railwaymen. When the East Kent Light Railway operated, the train would stop at the Woodnesborough crossing to fill with water. The story went that if the water-cock was set correctly there was just time for the driver to pop down to the "Prince" for a quick pint before it overflowed. During the war years it was a regular haunt for servicemen. Most were billeted at Ringleton Park and Beacon Lane farm. There were also Canadians in Nonington Woods. In peacetime one of the soldiers had been the pianist with the Henry Hall band and he attracted so much trade that some customers had to stand outside and the pub ran out of beer. The local shoot met here, with Grandma Gambrill, Mrs. Gambrill and Aunt Millie preparing lunch. Sports were popular and included cards, dominoes, cribbage and darts. There was a very strong darts team that won the local Highfield Challenge Cup three years running and, as a result, retained it. The team consisted of :-

Lionel Smith – local farmer
Toby Wheatly – miner and then a market gardener.
Bill For(e)man – farm labourer.
Fred and Ralph Gibbons – both tractor drivers.
Arthur Castle – railway worker.

Imagine my amazement when visiting the village in 2001 to find Ralph Gibbons, in his 90's, still living in his house surrounded by his family. After rummaging around in the attic he was able to produce the Highfield Cup!

Without a doubt the most famous drinker here was Squadron Leader Roland Robert Stanford Tuck, a Battle of Britain ace. A slim dandy, always immaculately attired, he owned the mushroom farm just up the road. One day he arrived accompanied by Douglas Bader for his favourite pint of Mackeson bitter. He went on to command both 92 and 257 fighter squadron. He so loved his Spitfire that it was said he could start it up blindfolded.

Mr. Gambrill was one of the first people in the village to own a television set. At the time of the Queen's coronation in 1953 the pub wasn't large enough to cope with the crowds, so those unable to gain entry watched proceedings through the bar windows. A fete was then held in the farmer's field.

The four cottages sold to the Messrs. Gillman in 1924 were ultimately demolished. Henry Farrier, who had been Fred's pot man, had lived in one of them.

Jim Stone succeeded Fred and ran the place for a few years. Another landlord then took over, but the pub could never recapture its past glories and ultimately it closed. A great pity as one doesn't find pubs like that anymore. It is now a private house called Prince of Wales Cottage.

No one can remember when the pub closed but the brewers' records would indicate 1966. On 26th October 1966 a second-hand table was sold for £1/10/- to A.R. Goulden and three days later a wall cabinet was sold for 10/- to Mr. Holloway of the stores at nearby Ash. In December 1966 second-hand furniture was sold to J. Hogbin & Sons for £1/11/3 and finally, on 31st March 1967, the fixtures and fittings were sold with the house for £138/8/9.

The old inn sign remained until the end and now hangs in the former Whitbread farm museum close to Paddock Wood.

No 28. Queen's Hotel, Herne Bay
(Closed in 1990) Mackeson, Whitbread

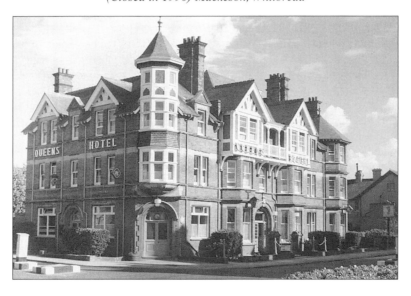

In 1900 the directors of Mackeson signed a contract with the building firm, Adcock, to erect a new hotel in Herne Bay. The town was expanding and they obviously wished to join in the ensuing prosperity as they built a very gracious hotel in late Victorian style. This must have been their showpiece as the fixtures and fittings alone exceeded the value of some of their other pubs. One would imagine it was so named to honour Queen Victoria, who passed away the year the hotel opened, but the first pictorial sign, erected in 1950, depicted the head of the Egyptian Queen Nefertiti.

The original intention was to build the hotel on the site of the old turnpike gate and cottage on the Canterbury Road. However, the turnpike cottage stood well out into the line of the road and the local council decided that this would be inappropriate and made the brewers move the frontage back 16 feet to conform with the intended road width. On 10th August 1899 H. and G.L. Mackeson purchased, for £750, this large plot of land, on which the hotel was built, from Walter C. Peacock. Peacock was a general builder residing in Clapham who had purchased a lot of land in the Herne Bay area. The total building costs slightly exceeded £5,000 and were paid in stage payments. The architect's fees amounted to £327/16/9. Initial fixtures and fittings cost £293/19/5, with a further £263/16/6 spent in 1902. In 1907 the tithe, amounting to £2/18/10, was redeemed. Further land adjoining the hotel was purchased in 1919 at a cost of £300. A large weather-vane displayed the date of the building.

In 1911 the licensee, Harold Crunden, sued Mackesons for misrepresentation of the amount of trade carried out, but lost his case. Ten years later, in 1921, the brewers received an offer from their tenant, Mr. S.D. Gordan, to purchase the hotel – he asked what price they would accept and how much of this could be left on mortgage. He was advised they did not wish to sell and certainly not by way of an outstanding mortgage, but they did enquire as to how much he was prepared to pay. They received no reply. The 1938 rental was £18/15/- per quarter – one of the highest figures in the Mackeson estate. During 1954 the static water tank was removed at a cost of £111/5/-.

Large and comfortable, the hotel was the venue for many functions and local societies, such as the Institute of Bankers. However, it was a strange decision to build such a place where they did – some way out of town and a good distance from the beach – and I would imagine that it barely earned its keep. From 1982 onwards the hotel was under company management and by February 1990 Whitbread were offering it for sale at a price of £450,000. No particular interest was shown, resulting in closure. It was subsequently acquired by the Herne Bay and Whitstable Mental Health team and was opened by the late Spike Milligan on 26th February 1993 as Durham House, a community mental health centre.

No 29. Rose in Bloom, Seasalter
Mackeson, Whitbread

It was not until the 1930's that the village of Seasalter saw any real development. Until then it was a lonely place where it paid to keep your own counsel and disregard the activities of others. An old smugglers' track ran from the beach through Scab's Acre and then crossed the road to Seasalter farm. Along this track was sited an old weather-boarded, thatched cottage, the original beer house, much frequented by the men of the night. In Turner's view of Whitstable one can see, on the right of the picture, the beginnings of this track. This area was also notorious for drinking after hours and thus received much attention from the police. A little ditty used to run:-

> "Down at the Rose in Bloom, We all got there too soon
> We felt so queer We had some beer
> For which we had to pay too dear Down at the Rose in Bloom".

Records can be traced back to 1861 when Stephen Hunt held the licence.

The ecclesiastical commissioners owned Scab's Acre and, in 1896, with the coming of the railway, this was split in two. As a result, the commissioners decided to sell this land and it was bought, in 1898, by Mackesons, who paid £800 plus costs of £16/7/6. A building is included in the deeds – the old "Rose in Bloom". It would appear that the brewers were endeavouring to improve their houses in this area as, in 1900, the old pub closed and the new house was built next door – at the same time as they were developing the "Queens Hotel". I have been unable to ascertain the building costs, but architect fees were £43/16/-. The old thatched cottage was sold in November 1900 to Mr. F. Goldfinch and the brewers received a net £600/5/2. It was restored and enlarged and given the name "Treetops", but was demolished some while ago to enable the pub car park to be extended. On 31st December 1901 the tithe of £3/14/6 was redeemed. The brewers spent £69/16/- in 1921 on installing a drainage system and, in December 1927, permanent improvements were carried out, including making up the road and fencing at a cost of £80.

The unusually named George J. Doo acquired the licence on 12th December 1927, paying a modest rent of £6/5/- per quarter. A "full on" licence was granted on 6th April 1949, at which time the net monopoly value of £675 was paid. During the 1950's the licensee was Mr. G. Hudson. He was a talented carpenter and built a model village that was displayed on a shelf in the public bar.

Until quite recently, if a lady wished to spend a penny, it quite literally cost her a penny. There was a brass machine on the door, "Cero" patented, which stated "pennies only" with an arrow indicating that the knob turned to the right, it also stipulated that "Bent or damaged coins must not be used".

The pub continues to flourish and boasts a very good menu.

No 30. Royal Oak, Margate
(Closed in 1973 and demolished) East Kent Brewery, Jude Hanbury, Mackeson, Whitbread

This was a small but popular pub domiciled in the rather seedy area of Upper High Street. The pub is first recorded in a trade directory in 1847. At that time Margate was developing as a working-class sea-side resort for Cockneys, and many cheap lodging houses and pubs were built in the area. A local map shows that herring hangs were to be found behind the "Royal Oak"; these were not removed until 1910. During 1932 the old store was pulled down and rebuilt at a cost of £148/12/9. Three years later Ross & Co., at a cost of £404/11/11, rebuilt the back addition.

Landlords, several of whom had sea-faring connections, appear to have found the place to their liking, as two in particular remained for many years. John Kemp had the house from at least 1874 until about 1923. A tenancy agreement was signed by Alfred J. Flint on 29th September 1923, and he remained until after the war. His service was interrupted during the war years as the house was closed temporarily, from 14th November 1940 until 4th October 1944, due to bombing. During this period the licence was transferred to Mr. Rawlings. In the mid-1960's the landlord was experiencing severe financial difficulties and spent £250 of thrift club savings belonging to 37 of his customers. He was prosecuted and fined £10 on each of the four charges. Although Mackeson were not responsible, an abroad cooper was despatched from Hythe with £250 to pacify the locals. It proved difficult, however, to identify how much was owed to each claimant and there was the added problem of identification. This house did a roaring trade between the wars, with 430 barrels accounted for in 1929. Following the war, trade declined and this figure was never approached again.

During 1924 there were additions costing £837 and electric lighting was installed the following year. Substantial reconstruction work was carried out in 1951 and the brewers agreed, during this period, to suspend the rent. On 19th December 1952 a small piece of land adjoining the property was purchased for £5. However, there was little point in spending too much money on updating the premises as Margate Town Council, in 1948, compulsorily purchased the whole of the Upper High Street for demolition and re-development in order to smarten up this part of town. Demolition work commenced in 1953, but the "Royal Oak" survived for a further 15 years before a compulsorily purchase order was served on 11th October 1968, but, even then, the pub continued to trade until 1973. A block of council flats now occupy the site. During the last few years Whitbread installed a manager to run the premises. In 1966 this gentleman was paid £11 per week and his national insurance contributions were £1/18/4. He spent £6/5/2 on entertaining and his rent was £18/15/- per quarter.

The story behind the Boscobel Oak is too well known to repeat here, but after Charles II gained the throne it was declared that his birthday, 29th May, should henceforth be celebrated as a thanksgiving. The day was known as Royal Oak or Oak Apple Day.

No 31. Shepherd and Crook, Burmarsh
John Friend, Mackeson, Whitbread, Free House

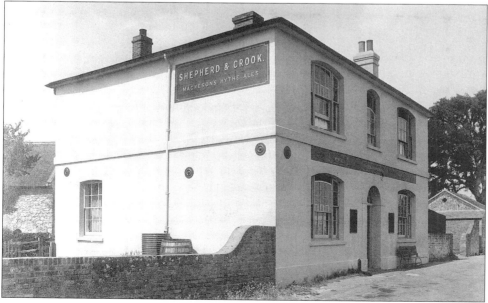

Once in a while one gets the feeling that one is ever so gently being set up. Just such an experience happened here one warm and sunny morning when the elderly gentleman, whom the landlord assured me was the village historian, patiently recounted the history of this old village inn. It is indeed old and I learned amongst many other things that the pub had traded under five different signs, as varied as the "Five Mackerels" and the "Wheatsheaf". All had rural connotations, so the story sounded plausible. And it was a very nice day.

However, the house, known as the "Shepherd and Crook", came into the possession of John Friend and it passed to William and Henry Mackeson when they purchased Friend's brewery business in 1801. On 13th November 1801, 26 gallons of beer costing £1/12/6 were delivered to the landlord, Mr. Woodsall. This gentleman's rent was £5/10/- p.a. On the death of William Mackeson in 1821 the pub was valued at £200. The place was originally built in around 1750 as a substantial private residence, acquiring a liquor licence some 50 years later. Throughout its life it was never more than a rural beer house, catering most admirably for the needs of the local community. Bits and pieces were spent on the place, including in 1872 a payment of £15/10/- to a Mr. Wood for building a rain-water tank, and during 1903 the furniture was upgraded at a cost of £55/15/-. In 1915 the pub was depreciated in the brewer's books by £70. The quit rent of £2/3/- was redeemed in 1929. Big things were afoot in 1949 as capital expenditure of £300 was incurred.

William Chambers held the licence in 1855 and by 1859 it was in the capable hands of the Piddock family, in the form of Mr. B. Piddock. By 1867 R. G. Piddock had taken over and he remained until about 1876. At around the same time the Piddock family were also at nearby "Botolph's Bridge". In 1884 that other well-known family of publicans, the Hucksteps, were here, with George behind the bar. This family were at the "Royal Oak", Bonnington for over 200 years.

The house is steeped in history and gets a mention in the Dr. Syn stories. This old reprobate tricked his foe, Mr. Merry, into delivering to the pub his clerical clothing. Whilst crossing the marsh he was shot dead! However, a much warmer welcome now awaits both local and visitor. During the last war many Army personnel were billeted here and at the nearby vicarage. Times were grim but people still managed to enjoy themselves. A story is told that on one particularly convivial night the colonel, as was his wont, crashed out in the pub's best bedroom. The privates then crept out onto the marsh and captured a lamb, which was placed in bed with their slumbering officer! The relationship between church and pub has always been close and while the church was being restored, about 100 years ago, services were held at the pub. This house was one of four local venues for the John Jones Coursing Club. This was formed before 1890 and every Monday, throughout the winter months, the members would pit their greyhounds against each other in the ancient pastime of coursing. John Jones, JP, after whom the club was named, was one of the principal landowners in the district.

During the 1930's and 1940's the rent was a very modest £2/10/- per quarter – the lowest figure I have seen. It is likely, therefore, that despite appealing to the locals the house was only marginally profitable. One lonely Sunday night in 1946 the landlord sold just two pints of beer! This may have prompted Whitbread to make one of their earliest disposals as, on 20th December 1957, they completed the sale of the house for £1,500 to William Thomas and Annie North. £1,200 was left on mortgage at an interest rate of 4 1/2% – this was redeemed in August 1958. That same year the brewers made a profit of £2/18/6 in respect of the sale of the adjoining cottage – 14 Bridge Street.

As a freehouse the place flourished. I am told that the upstairs was given over to a dance hall. The pub suffered a severe set-back in 1987 when it was buffeted in the great storm and a huge chimney toppled and crashed through the roof and several windows were blown in. The inn sign was also damaged. Fortunately, all was soon restored to good order and a local artist designed and painted a new sign – again a double-sider showing typical Romney Marsh landscapes. Included within one scene is the nearby village church.

When I arrived at the pub, about ten minutes before mid-day opening, there was not a soul to be seen. Within ten minutes of the pub opening the bars were packed, but it was impossible to say from where or how all had arrived. There was barely a vehicle to be seen. A corner of one bar celebrates the village cricket team and the house boasts a fine collection of blow lamps. Hanging on one wall is a framed collection of cigarette cards depicting RAF squadron badges, a memorial to a brave landlord who, during the last war, had served his country as a "tail-end Charlie".

The pub is just off the beaten track but well worth seeking out – if only for a tall story.

No 32. Ship Inn, Ash
(Closed on 5th April 1976) Bradly of Sandwich, Ash & Co., Jude Hanbury, Mackeson, Whitbread

The "Ship" started life as part of a Kentish Hall house, the earliest records of which date back to 1380. Unlike the other houses along The Street the "Ship" is set back from the road and this may indicate that it formed part of a farm before the development of The Street. It is a timber-framed building with a low centre and two cross wings. There is an archway through the building that carries an ancient right of way. If one walks down here a window, still etched "private bar", can be found. In 1934 it was described as the "Ship Inn" plus garden, stables and yard. The pub backed on to the churchyard wall and at one time acted as a posting house. A long while ago, on a plot of vacant ground behind the "Ship", stood a building left by the will of Henry Proud of Moat Farm, for the use of the church wardens and failing that, the owners of the "Ship". It was used for storage, but had also acted as a chapel and volunteers' drill hall. It has now disappeared. A photograph, taken in 1940, shows the local "Dads' Army" advancing down the village street past the pub. On account of the possible invasion by Hitler all sign posts had been removed.

The first reference to the house that I have traced relates to the year 1705; the parish vestry minutes frequently record "Mett at Ye Shipp". These meetings were also held at the "Chequer(s)" and "Lion". In 1798, 297 men of Ash, volunteered for the Militia (Sandwich Volunteers) which assembled at the "Ship". Queen Victoria came to the throne on 20th June 1837 and, in February 1840, a dinner was provided for the school children to celebrate the "Queen's Nuptials", and a well-attended ball took place at the "Ship".

The pub was sold at auction by Messrs. Pott and Denne at the "Bell", Sandwich, on Monday 13th February 1826 at 11o'clock. The vendors were the Bradly brewing family, who had possibly overstretched their capital resources. It is described as the "Ship" with coach-houses, stables, outhouses, edifices, buildings, yard, garden, land and appurtenances. The innkeeper was Vincent Noble Kennard. The purchaser was George Ash, who was brewing in Canterbury at about that time. The house was listed in a schedule of property belonging to his two sons, Thomas and George Ash, dated 1870, when George conveyed a moiety to Thomas. At that time the landlord was William Burton who was paying a rent of £16 p.a. There was a separate entry for stabling, afterwards erected, which was let to Mrs. Solly for £6 p.a. The Ash records state that the pub had been purchased from Bradl(e)y and others. Thomas Ash died on 12th March 1875 and by then the landlord was H. Attwood who paid a rent of £22 for the pub and stables. In May 1929 J. Ayling was paid the sum of £36/10/- to cut an external doorway to form a private bar. The brewers redeemed the quit rent of £1/7/3 on 30th March 1931.

The house does not appear to have attracted any long-serving landlords and in its final years there was a steady procession in and out. Edward Revele held the licence in 1804 and the last licensee was an ex-army man, Bill Wallace. He later became a Chelsea pensioner.

Despite its grand appearance, for most of its life it had a rather seedy reputation. It was frequented by villagers, miners, agricultural workers and, during the season, hop-pickers. A resident, who lived in a cottage to the rear of the pub, can remember late-night sessions going on till 2a.m. From time to time the police would carry out a spot check, parking their vehicle between her cottage and the pub. There were further problems during the 1950's. On a surprise visit by a Mackeson employee based in Hythe, the landlord was found to be operating a "monkey". This was a pipe that fed the slops from the bar into a cask in the cellar. A struggle broke out when the landlord endeavoured to prevent the visitor going down to the cellar. As to be expected in such a place, for a long period, almost up to the time of closure, the pub had a "knicker" bar displaying various items of lingerie.

With a brewery in the village and plenty of other public houses, the area was saturated and house closures became quite frequent. This one closed on 5th April 1976 and was advertised for sale as "in need of some modernisation but is in reasonable order throughout" at £22,500. The title was leasehold for a period of 999 years at £5 p.a. ground rent. It stood empty for a couple of years before being purchased by an architectural draughtsman who fully restored the property and investigated its architectural history. To celebrate the purchase and mourn the passing of this ancient inn, a party was held on Saturday 21st October 1978 to "Go down with the Ship. Re-opened at vast expense – bottles will be needed for messages". A fitting tribute, with the invitation showing the "Ship" sinking below the waves. Some of the original inn sign miniatures were found on the premises.

The property, now named Port House, was offered for sale in 2003 at an asking price of £285,000.

No 33. Stag's Head, Ramsgate
East Kent Brewery, Tomson & Wotton , Combined Breweries (Holdings), Whitbread, J. D. Young, Free House

The "Stag's Head" and "Admiral Harvey" are the only two houses to come into the Whitbread stable via Tomson and Wotton, the Ramsgate brewers. In 1951 this firm amalgamated with Gardner & Co. of the Ash Brewery, Ash to form Combined Breweries. This latter company was acquired by Whitbread in 1968.

The present pub is housed in a modern building but its origins are much older. It is sited in one of the town's original 18th century streets, in an area then known as the East End. It was first licensed in 1869 and by 1874 was in the hands of John Finch. It is possible that he was the first landlord. The house was described as the "Stag's Head Hotel and Commercial" inn. This sounds rather grand given that it could have been

little more than a beer house with boatmen and soldiers comprising the main source of trade. There were three cellars, with the last one, in descending order, stretching under the road. This only came to light by accident in the 1950's when builders were renovating the modern property. There was also reputed to be a passage, running from the rear of the property to Page's Off Licence, which was bricked up in 1960. During 1930 £12/2/6 was spent on providing an illuminated electric box sign. Detailed plans were drawn up in 1938 showing the proposed plan of the boundary line of the "Stag's Head" plus an amended layout of the cellars. For some reason the plans are hanging in the bar of the "Oak and Ivy" at Hawkhurst.

Landlords came and went and on 30th December 1941 Percy George Castell signed a tenancy agreement. That same month he was called up for military service. Fortunately he survived and went on to run the pub for many years. During the 1950's his daughter Beatrice spent a lot of her spare time raising substantial sums of money for various charities. Her method was to persuade customers to dip coins in beer and stick them on one of the mirrors in the saloon bar. It is pleasing to note that no attempt was ever made to steal them.

A very fine kitchen table from the "Stag's Head" sits in a private house not far from Manston. A former landlord removed it at some stage and being down on his luck sold it for £1/5/- to the present owner. He regarded the sale price as a "latchlifter" – a sum of money sufficient to get the seller back into the pub to buy a couple of drinks in the hope that he could stay all day, with others buying the rounds.

The old house was rebuilt on the other side of the alley during the 1950's as a rather ugly three-storey concrete building, out of place with its surroundings. This was badly damaged by fire in 1992 and, in 1995 was still boarded up and on the market. It was ultimately purchased by a company called J. D. Young which I believe was a small-time brewer. They changed the pub name to J. D. Young, but this did not last for very long as the house is now called "Harbour Street Bar".

No 34. Star Inn, Newington
(Closed April 4th 1978) Isaac Kennett, Ash & Co., Mackeson, Whitbread

Folkestone museum houses a fine old oil painting of the "Star" that dates back to the 1700's and depicts wooden shutters rather than windows. This house was ultimately demolished.

The property, together with garden and outbuildings, is first mentioned in the will of Sarah Nash dated 5th March 1764. She left it to her two daughters, Elizabeth and Ann. Elizabeth died a spinster in 1791 and Ann died four years later. During the early 1800's it passed to the Pain family and for a long while a chap called George Wells was landlord, from at least 1816 until 1855. He is also described as a blacksmith.

The Mackeson brothers took over the Elham brewery, which was owned by Isaac Kennett, in 1802 and as part of the contract Isaac undertook to supply no more beer to the "Star". George Ash purchased the pub for £450 on 19th November 1855 from the Warman family. In 1870 George conveyed a moiety (half share) to his brother Thomas. On the death of Thomas, on 12th March 1875, the licence was held by Henry Maycock, who paid a rent of £18 p.a.

In 1930 Kent County Council purchased a strip of land for £45 for road widening. They also undertook to assist in the levelling of a portion of land in order to provide a "pull in" and to provide fencing, which cost £261/5/10. On 27th November 1930 the brewers redeemed the tithe and rent charge at a cost of £5/10/-. Capital additions costing £500 were made in 1949 and fencing and drainage work, costing £453, was completed in 1966.

This was always a popular house with innovative landlords. At one time a pony and trap business operated from stables to the rear of the pub – these and the coach-house were converted into a restaurant during the 1950's by Mr. and Mrs. Mercer, two very able tenants of Mackeson. There was also a thriving bed and breakfast business. During this era there were no night ferry sailings from Folkestone, so most pubs along this stretch of the A20 offered this service. The pub is still mourned by local residents – one elderly lady wistfully recalled the evenings when she would pop down to the jug and bottles for her tipple. Until fairly late in the day the bars had sawdust on the floor. Despite this enterprise, it would appear that not all tenants could manage a successful business. In about 1958 the rent receivable ledger for the pub was showing a deficit of £729/11/3, with the brewers receiving a first and final dividend of just over 10/5d in the pound – £380/16/8. The local cricket ground was nearby and to the rear of the premises was an army camp. Both were reliable sources of income. The pub boasted a good-sized garden and all the furniture was chained down! One wall consisted of an attractive mural that depicted local people in mediaeval costume smoking clay pipes. One suggestion was that it was painted by an artist in settlement of his account, another that it was the work of an Irish craftsman who desired only food and drink by way of payment. When the pub was demolished this wall was left standing in the hope that it might be re-constructed elsewhere – sadly it never was. One of the barmen also acted as the village grave digger.

As late as the early 1960's The Elham Valley and District Rat and Sparrow Club met here, with the members delivering rats' tails and pigeons' feet in their shiny new cars. The club had a membership of almost 300. J. Metcalfe did the counting and Peter Fagg received 12/6 for 50 rats' tails. Jackdaws, rooks, crows, magpies and grey squirrels fetched a penny a-piece, sparrows 8d, and queen wasps 2/-.

However, progress, in the form of the Channel tunnel, was creeping up on this ancient pub. The "Star" was located on the old A20 where the name changed from Ashford Road to Cheriton High Street. The whole village was affected and in late 1973 the innkeeper of 15 years standing, Gerry Cross, was quoted as saying "one way or another the "Star" is doomed". It was subject to a compulsory purchase order in the mid-1970's and was demolished in 1978 to enable the necessary road improvements to the A20 to be carried out prior to the tunnel approach road being built. Memories of this inn remain, as close to Junction 12 on the M20 Star Lane can be found.

No 35. Sun Inn, St Nicholas at Wade
(Closed by Whitbread 17th September 1981 and re-opened as a Free House)
East Kent Brewery, Jude Hanbury, Mackeson, Whitbread, Free House, Pubmaster

The present, rather fine building standing at the junction of Sun Lane was erected in about 1900 on the site of former farm buildings. This replaced a much older pub of the same name, as records indicate that from at least 1862 to 1882 the landlord of the "Sun" was Stephen Wales. He started his professional life in 1841 as a thatcher and ten years later is described as a beer retailer, so it is likely that within a year or two he called his outlet the "Sun", possibly to retain the name of a very much older house said to have been destroyed by fire in Jacobean times. Stephen's old house stood a little way from the present property but has now been demolished to make way for a modern house.

A Mrs. Keeler was the first tenant to hold the licence of the re-built house. On 10th November 1927 Mrs. Ada Frances Kimber signed a tenancy agreement and the pub stayed within this family until 1956. John Kimber succeeded Ada in December 1946, paying a rent of £35 p.a. and, on his death on 13th

February 1955, his widow, Sarah, took over for eighteen months. Both the old and new "Sun" houses had extensive grounds. In 1920 the house had a garden, also a piece of land – 30perches with stables, barn and buildings (other than the cottage). This cottage was rented to Mrs. Ada F. Kimber at 5/- per week from 26th August 1929. A gas supply was laid on during 1931 at a cost of £19/12/6. On 31st March 1931 an exchange of properties took place with Jude Hanbury passing the cottage freehold to the Tenterden Brewery Co. The tithe of £2/4/8 was redeemed on 1st February 1951.

The main source of income was from locals, agricultural workers and servicemen, particularly during the war years. RAF Manston, with its mixture of English and American airmen, was close by. It is rumoured that during the First World War a courts martial was held at the pub, with the convicted man marched to the rear of the building and summarily shot. On a more pleasant note the first edition of the Sun newspaper was printed in about 1952. To celebrate the occasion the owners of the paper gave a barrel of beer to every pub bearing this name. This was another East Kent pub to sport a particularly fine "knicker bar" with lingerie from all over the world exhibited.

It remains a fine house in a pretty village and, with a good restaurant, is well worth a visit.

No 36. Swan Hotel, Appledore
Alfred Leney of Dover, Jude Hanbury, Mackeson, Whitbread, Shepherd Neame

The original "Swan" was housed in a fine old building erected in about 1740 and became an ale house in 1741 when Mrs. Neve obtained a licence from Tenterden magistrates. Over the years it passed through the hands of two Lydd brewers, Thomas Haisell in 1784 and, in 1839, Alfred White. The land tax was redeemed on 31st December 1803. A scandal occurred in the village in 1840 as we find "He (Jeffrey Munk) lost, fled the Country and left his wife without support. His son George was glad enough to marry Ann Saunders daughter of the landlord of the "Swan"''". It was first registered as a hotel in 1873 and a court baron was held here every year. It became a coaching inn, with the old drovers' paths from the nearby marsh passing the door. The premises were rebuilt in 1910; nevertheless much of the old stabling remains, although the original buildings were thatched.

At one time an Alfred Leney house, by the early 1920's Jude Hanbury were leasing the "Swan". In April 1924 they raised a mortgage over the premises in the sum of £1,000 and in January 1928 this figure was increased to £4,000 by including the deeds of the "Brent's Tavern" at Faversham. This was redeemed on 31st August 1956. During 1926 the public room was extended at a cost of £100 and the following year the stables were converted into garages. Two years later £15 was spent on erecting a new lavatory. The quit rent of £2/12/1 was redeemed on 30th March 1931. In November 1932 the tenant was desirous of leaving and arrangements were in progress for the tenant of the "Guildhall", Folkestone to take over the house under "supervision". Richard G. Rivers signed a tenancy agreement on 17th November 1932, paying a rent of £42 p.a. He had spent just over a year at the "Guildhall" so perhaps he still had to prove his capabilities, as this was a place of some importance. It was shortly afterwards, probably in 1933, that Jude Hanbury acquired the freehold, as that year repairs and improvements costing £125 were carried out. Fire broke out on 23rd May 1943 and caused a lot of damage – upstairs the scarring is still visible.

Most of the old coach-house and stabling have been converted, but in September 1958 the brewers sold the freehold of "Swan Cottage" to Thomas Bourne, the sitting tenant, for £325.

The hotel appears to have flourished or gone into decline depending upon the personality of the landlord. During the 1990's a very popular fellow was Danny Lynch, a wrestler for 38 years, who plied his trade under the name of the "Mighty Mongol". A big man, he must have appeared quite awesome to his opponents with his shaven head and Fu Manchu-style moustache. It is probably nothing to do with Danny, but this was one of the last pubs where one could play "ringing the bull". When he retired in the late 1990's there was a succession of landlords, all of whom failed to maintain trade and the hotel's future was in doubt. The present tenants are doing a far better job and we must wish them well.

Whitbread leased the "Swan" to Shepherd Neame on 6th May 1992 and later that year, on the 29th September, Shepherd Neame purchased the freehold.

No 37. Three Bells, Swingfield
(Closed in 2000. Sold by Whitbread in 1976. It closed for a while re-opening in 1978)
A. Langton & Co., Mackeson, Whitbread, Courage, Free House

St. Peter's, the charming village church at Swingfield Street, boasts a peal of three bells and immediately opposite one would have found this old hostelry.

One authority states that it dates back to 1684, but it is probably older – it may have been built in the 1620's. It was originally a dwelling house with stables, outbuildings and some land and formed part of a larger estate. The blacksmith's forge, to the side, was added in 1708. For a long while the forge and pub operated as one enterprise until the forge ceased to trade in 1783. For years it was a simple beer house, but in 1757 a licence was obtained. By 1849 the forge was briefly brought back into use.

A manuscript, which hung in the bar, stated that the house came into the Whitbread stable via George Beer & Rigden and Fremlins, but that is incorrect. There is plenty of documentation regarding this house. On 16th September 1742 there is an indenture between William Rolfe of Denton and his nephew John Hobday. On 6th January 1842 there is a further indenture between John Jeken, Edward Rutley and Richard Coleman all of Dover, brewers, and co-partners in trade, to William Maxted for £315. Sometime after 1863 an abstract of title was prepared for Richard Maxted with a further abstract dated 1875 for J. W. A. Dickenson. In an assignment of partnership estate and effects and dissolution of partnership between Bryan Tomblin of Folkestone (brewer) to Austin Dickenson of Folkestone (brewer), dated 30th April 1873, we find listed "Three Bells with blacksmith's shop, yard and land with two cottages". The consideration was £950. The property then passed to D. W. and J. Langton, who almost certainly traded as A. Langton & Co. at the Tontine Brewery, in Tontine Street, Folkestone. They in turn sold this pub and their business to Henry Bean Mackeson on 23rd August 1886.

In 1925 a new concrete floor was laid in the tap room. Repairs to the house and new drainage at Forge Cottage were carried out in 1930 at a cost of £38. Part of the large cat-slide roof was blown away during a violent storm in 1936 and similar damage occurred during the great storm of 1987. The pub also suffered during the war years. Planes based at nearby RAF Hawkinge were dispersed and camouflaged in the fields and woods surrounding Swingfield and, as a result, the area was bombed. The pub was hit and sustained considerable damage.

For most of the 19th century the licence was held by the Maxted family. William was the landlord in 1816 acquiring the pub in January 1842 and by 1855 he had been succeeded by Rod, who is also described as a blacksmith. The next change was in the early 1870's when William Seath took over. Another long-serving tenant, for at least twenty years, was Henry Foord who was here from 1938 until 1958. Trade was always minimal, reflected in Henry's rent of £3/10/- per quarter, and was reliant on agricultural workers, walkers and people driving out to this idyllic spot from the neighbouring towns. Whitbread sold the pub with licence in 1976 and after re-opening in 1978 it was operated by Courage for a short period. The last landlord, who took over in 1986, made substantial alterations, enlarging the bar area and creating a restaurant. Local artists were encouraged to use the pub's facilities and exhibit their paintings. This was an act of faith in such a thinly-populated area and, sadly, it was decided to close the pub. In 2000 it was offered for sale to convert into a single dwelling at a price of £345,000. Planning permission had already been obtained to convert the derelict forge into residential accommodation.

The original inn sign, built in May 1949, hung until the end.

No 38. Three Mariners, Hythe
Mackeson, Whitbread, Shepherd Neame

For a long time the "Three Mariners" was the smallest public house in Hythe. The entrance to the two bars was via an up-and-over corrugated door. Strangely it shared its name with one of the town's largest houses, the "Red Lion", which in the distant past had traded under this name.

For all of its life this modest, back-street hostelry has served the needs of the local population in a mainly artisan area of the town, and little of its past history has come to light. It is, however, a survivor, as many of the old Hythe taverns have now closed. A deed of feoffment, between G. C. Thatcher and the trustees of Benjamin Horton, is dated 8th August 1823, although the house does not appear to be as old as

this. The licence was held by Walter Higgins in 1874. Henry Bean Mackeson acquired the property on 3rd December 1879 paying the vendor, Benjamin Bassett Horton, the sum of £675. In 1930 some new outbuildings were erected at a cost of £30 and in the following year £25 was spent on remodelling the urinals and alterations to the bar cost a further £100. In 1936 Mackeson purchased the property next door, 35 Windmill Street, for £300 in order to enlarge the pub. This had formerly been Wilkins baker's shop and for years it had been possible to see a ten-oared rowing-boat tucked under the long counter of the shop. This had been a typical smuggling vessel which when fully-manned could show a fine turn of speed and easily out-run the revenue cutters. During the 1930's the landlord paid a modest rent of £5/10/- per quarter.

The pub was purchased by Shepherd Neame on 5th May 1975.

No 39. Three Kings, Sandwich
(Closed about 1963) C. F. Wacher, East Kent Brewery, Mackeson, Whitbread

This fabulous old pub served Sandwich for well over 300 years, playing a full part in the activities of the town. During the Civil War it was used as a recruitment centre for those eager to enlist. The inn sign showed the "three-portrait" sign painted by Van Dyck and sent to Bernini to assist him in fashioning the famous bust of Charles I. It was, however, Charles II who granted the town its Charter.

A carved lintel over the yard entrance indicates that the property was built in 1603 as a coaching inn. Having passed beneath this, the horses would have been stabled in Three Kings Yard, which was home to one of the oldest buildings in Sandwich, the Chantry Chapel, which dates back to Norman times. It is only recently that the entrance was resurfaced and the ring that was used to lower the barrels into the cellar, located underneath the archway, was removed. The old pump is still in position in one of the corners of the property.

One of the first brewers to own the house was C. F. Wacher who traded from the Crowhill Brewery at Broadstairs. His advert extols the virtues of his fine ales, stout and porter. The house probably passed to the East Kent Brewery before coming into the ownership of Mackeson. The licence was held by Henry

Jones from 1784 until 1803, when it passed to William Thiselton, who served for 42 years. The Philpott family, in the form of George and Herbert, remained for a long period from 1924 onwards. The forge and stabling were sold in 1927 for £250. Invicta House, 65 Strand Street, was let to Mr. Simmons at 7/- per week and the cottage in Three Kings Yard was let for a similar sum to Mr. Gambrill. In both cases the collecting agent was a local man, D. S. Foster. During the early 1900's a firewood dealer conducted his business from the yard. The cottage freehold was acquired for £138/5/- in 1928 by the Tenterden Brewery Co., via Jude Hanbury. It was on-sold on 15th June 1934 to Mackeson. Despite the pub's grand appearance, it was quite a small, narrow building, probably able to cater for only a few drinkers, as the rent in 1938 was only £3/15/- per quarter, whereas the cottage was let at £4/11/- per quarter. The brewers paid a fee farm rent of 2/8 to the Earl of Aylesford – this was redeemed on 20th June 1947 by paying 20 years' rent – £2/13/4.

Baxter & Co. of the Export Brewery, Sandwich, were taken over in 1887 by the Strand Street-based brewers East Kent Brewery Co. As a result of these two breweries, and other firms, operating in the vicinity, Sandwich possessed far too many public houses. From the 1950's onwards the number reduced from 22 to 9, with the "Three Kings" one of the casualties. The property was sold to R. H. Delves for £2,029/17/7 after costs – completion took place on 31st May 1963. The agent's charges and commission amounted to £124/10/-.

It is now a very fine private residence called, appropriately, "Three Kings".

No 40. Waterloo Tavern, Canterbury

*(Formerly the **Ordnance Arms**) Flint & Co., (Stour Street Brewery), Cobb, Ash & Co.,*
Jude Hanbury, Mackeson, Whitbread, Pubmaster, Punch

The inn, plus coach-house, stables, outbuildings and yard, dates back to 1812 and was initially called the "Ordnance Arms" when controlled by Flint & Co. Mr William Gillman was the proprietor in 1814 and the house was re-named shortly after the Battle of Waterloo which occurred in 1815. A directory issued in 1838 mentions the "Waterloo Tavern" and the landlord was listed as Richard Clark.

Flint & Co. disposed of their interest, possibly to Mr. Cobb, as Thomas and George Ash had acquired the premises by 1870, with a note stating that it was purchased from Cobb and others. At the time the landlady was Sarah Wells who paid an annual rent of £19. When Thomas Ash died on 12th March 1875, Joseph Wilson held the licence, but was paying a reduced rent of £18. The tavern passed to Jude Hanbury in 1929 and three years later they spent £11/7/9 on pulling down the sheds. On 8th March 1933 a tenancy agreement was signed by T. P. Mitchell who was to pay a rent of £20 p.a.

Repairs and improvements costing £390 were carried out in 1933, but it was not until 1955 that the bathroom and water closet were formed, at a cost of £400. In December 1969 the Mayor of Canterbury pulled a pint to celebrate the completion of further modernisation, costing £1,400. The two small bars were converted into one large horseshoe-shaped bar and there were other cosmetic improvements. The landlord, Doug Giles, was very proud of his modern house and he remained for a further eleven years, retiring after a stint of 18 years in November 1980. Further refurbishment was carried out during 1998 but this caused problems as, in early December, the pub was closed for safety reasons as there had been so many structural changes that the walls had become unsafe. The house re-opened the following January.

This is a comfortable inn, mainly frequented by locals and soldiers. A new sign was erected in 1991 depicting a French attack on a farm called "Hougemont". Unfortunately the French soldiers are shown wearing the red uniforms!

The pub closed in August 2003 for a short period and re-opened, under new ownership, on 5th November 2003. The same company also purchased the "Hop Poles" which had closed in 2003 and this re-opened in July 2004.

No 41. Welcome Stranger, Court at Street
(Closed by Whitbread on 3rd December 1974 and sold with licence on 20th May 1975.
Closed for good in 1993) Mackeson, Whitbread, Free House

Sadly one can no longer buy a pint at this singularly inappropriately named house, which after several misfortunes closed its doors in 1993.

The "Welcome Stranger" dates back to 1820 and was purpose built. For much of its life it remained a simple ale house serving a small rural community. The wonder is that it survived for so long, particularly with its poor financial history. Henry Bean Mackeson purchased the beer house on 13th September 1889, paying the vendors, Alfred and Wilmot Newman, the sum of £390. Costs of £14/12/- were incurred. In 1912 the brewers made an "allowance" of 6/- and a similar figure was paid the following year. In 1920 a new porch was added at a cost of £63 and in 1931 alterations to the bar accounted for a further £50. In August 1933 the bar counter was sold to landlord Graves for £10. He had moved to the pub that month, paying a rent of £20 p.a. The quit rent of £2/2/2 was extinguished on 31st March 1936. In 1939 the brewers wrote off £57/7/- in respect of an inflated valuation. Further problems arose on 7th October 1949 when a further £49/9/- was written off, representing the difference between goodwill and valuation on a change of tenancy.

A wine licence was confirmed in February 1947 with a "full on" licence granted on 27th April 1950, at which time the net monopoly value of £420 was paid. On 30th October 1957 a deed of exchange of freehold land adjoining the "Welcome Stranger" was signed with Robert Hugh Benson.

In the days when Kent suffered harsh winters, a three-piece band had been playing locally, but by the time the evening ended and they packed their equipment, there was about five feet of snow covering the village. The group trudged down to the pub and there they remained for several days. The landlord was most put out when one of the musicians complained that there was only one rasher of bacon for breakfast. In November 1958 Mrs. B. E. Moss entertained the employees from her four local farms at harvest supper. It was a most convivial evening with over twenty workers present.

Whitbread closed the pub at the end of 1974 and sold it with licence in May 1975. It then traded as a freehouse, possibly under the same landlord, until it closed. The premises suffered greatly in the great storm of 1987 and locals maintain that the pub never recovered from the damage inflicted. During the gale the sign was blown down and probably remains in the pile of scrap at the rear of the building. It was a flimsy structure and the roof was supported by thin branches cut from trees. Following closure the very pleasant landlord became something of a recluse and the house began to fall apart to such an extent that it is a wonder the place remains standing. For quite a while the landlord continued to serve beer to his friends who knocked on the door. However, the place was in such a state that one had to huddle in a corner of the room. He died in 2003 and the house is now boarded up. As the building is listed none of the villagers knows what will happen to it. To restore it to any kind of order will cost a fortune but even so in July 2004 the property was sold at auction. To this very day one empty beer cask sits forlornly on the pavement having never been collected by the brewers.

This had a witty sign showing a stork carrying the "happy bundle" but it has been suggested the name could have another meaning as many visitors from the continent would have landed at nearby Lympne airport on their first visit to England. This is unlikely as the "Welcome Stranger" was firmly established long before the advent of the airport.

No 42. White Horse, Bridge
Sankey of Canterbury, Ash & Co., Jude Hanbury, Mackeson, Whitbread

The Kentish Post of 10th April 1756 states that "On 14th April 1756 there will be a Auricula (a flower akin to a primrose) Feast at the "White Horse" Bridge. Best flower must have six pips. 1st prize Half a Guinea, 2nd three Half Crowns, 3rd Five shillings. 2/6 in advance, 5/- on day. Landlord William Gilbert. Very good twelve penny ordinary at 1 o'clock". First prize went to Mr. Claringbole with Don Quixote; and second to Mr. Guerard with Hobbard's Hector. The pub was owned by Stephen Beckington and Gilbert paid a rent of £14.

In 1793 Beckington sold the house to Mathew William Sankey, a brewer of Canterbury, who overstretched himself, resulting in George Ash, in 1819, purchasing the freehold plus stables, lodge and other edifices from the Sankey's assignees. In 1870 Ash's son, George, conveyed a moiety (half share) to his brother, Thomas. The licence had been held since 1859 by Charles Fortescue Hornsby Senior who paid a rent of £25 p.a. His son, C. F. Hornsby Junior, managed the "Duke of Cumberland" just down the road at Barham. Charles was still in situ on the death of Thomas Ash on 12th March 1875 and had succeeded Rod Sherrard, who was also described as a postmaster. Prior to this the pub had been in the hands of the Challcraft family with Rod the landlord in 1803 and Ann in 1816.

The "White Horse", sited on the old London to Dover road, is old and was probably built in the 17th century as a coaching inn. It is a large, square white building dominating the village street, and at one time there was an old forge next door where horses could be shod. The front is now in the Regency style and the interior is heavily beamed. On the lintel of the large Tudor fireplace it is still possible to discern the outline of a white horse painted a long while ago. On the back of this fireplace in the restaurant area is some strange writing that could be original but equally could be a hoax. It is not possible to decipher this message and there is no reference to it anywhere. It is said that the pub became the headquarters of the local Royalists during the Civil War.

William John Fairservice was a medium-paced off-break bowler who had the distinction of claiming, as his first victim in his first game for Kent, the wicket of the legendary W. G. Grace. He went on to play for the county from 1902 until 1921 and on retirement became a publican. On 31st March 1933 he signed a tenancy agreement to manage the "White Horse", at an annual rental of £30. At the same time the brewers spent the substantial sum of £912 on repairs and alterations. The quit rent of £4/19/6 was extinguished on 31st March 1936.

The pub continues to thrive and its superb food attracts customers from a wide hinterland – after dining one can enjoy a leisurely game of bat and trap. The bar sports a fine array of blunderbusses and pistols, together with several old photographs of the pub. At one time there was a billiard room. The landlord is proud of his quite splendid floral displays and again won the Bridge in Bloom trophy in 2003, a feat achieved about five times in the last eight years. A few years ago the local zoo owner, the late John Aspinall, was a frequent visitor.

No 43. White Hart, Canterbury

*(Formerly the **Cow**) Ash & Co., Jude Hanbury, Mackeson, Whitbread, Shepherd Neame*

This ancient inn, at one time called the "Cow", is first mentioned in the abstract of title of Mrs. Anne Blake, which is dated 22nd July 1768. Time passed and eventually it came into the possession of Sally Ann, Charlotte and Louisa Smith, spinsters and all living in Brighton. On 16th April 1872 Thomas Ash paid these three ladies £250 for "All that tenement used as a public house formerly called the "Cow" plus all that tenement situate near the "White Hart" formerly and for many years used as a chapel or meeting-house but then as a coachbuilders workshop in the occupation of Wm. Moyes and land that did abut to a certain burial ground". The graveyard has been transformed into a park with the tombstones re-arranged around the park wall.

It is generally felt that the "White Hart" stands very close to the site of the former church of St. Mary de Castro and was built on the rubble of the demolished church and rectory. In the cellar, which was owned by the church, there remains a chute for sliding the coffins into the mortuary below, where they were stored. The place was small and cramped with very thick walls. The public house opened on 4th March 1837 and the licence was held by George Harvey. Thomas Ash died on 12th March 1875, when the innkeeper was Mr. Holmes, who paid a rent of £19 per annum. In 1931 a new club room was formed at a cost of £280.

A double misfortune occurred in 1968 when the landlord's wife fell down the stairs and, a little while later, he was swindled out of £100, a considerable sum in those days, by a cheque fraud. This is a small, homely pub housing two bars with low ceilings and plenty of cricketing memorabilia. The mural on the wall is a faithful copy of the original that hangs at the Kent County Cricket Club and was painted in the 1970's by a customer. Kent cricketers Alan Igglestone and Brian Turner were regular drinkers at the "White Hart". By this time the pub had moved up-market, as a schedule and brief survey of licensed houses, drawn up in 1946, indicates that the clientele was mainly "Artisans and labouring – some miners". There is a well-kept rear garden and the pub is decorated with colourful hanging baskets. Good quality food is available, with the pub continuing to serve the local community – not easy these days against stiff competition. In common with most ancient inns, the house has a resident ghost, a young girl, who can sometimes be seen in the upstairs rooms. During the latter half of 2002 the pub employed a lady who had previously been a nun for ten years before pulling pints. She has now departed for New Zealand.

The inn sign remains readily identifiable, except that some background cover has been added. Shepherd Neame purchased the freehold on 12th March 1992.

"Soe the courageous hart doth fight. With fate, and calleth up his might,
And standeth stout that he maye fall. Bravelye, and be avenged of all." Hood.

No 44. White Horse, Finglesham
(Closed in 1982 having been sold by Whitbread on 20th March 1978)
Jude Hanbury, Mackeson, Whitbread

Situated on a T-junction mid-way between the village of Finglesham and Betteshanger Colliery, the "White Horse" was the coal miners' pub and a very popular place it was too.

The original house, little more than a living-room pub opposite the "Crown" in Finglesham, closed in 1930 and was then let from 27th July 1931 for 12/6 a week to S. Cope. That year Jude Hanbury transferred this freehold plus other unlicensed properties to the Tenterden Brewery Co. in exchange for two hotels. It was subsequently sold at auction on 20th June 1933 to Fred Finn of Sandwich for £145, thus creating a capital loss in the brewers' books where it was valued at £275. E. Norris was a long-serving landlord during the 1860's and 1870's.

On 14th November 1928 the brewers paid a deposit of £25 for the new site and paid the balance, £225, on 13th May 1929. The total building cost amounted to £4,909/18/-, of which £3,381/3/3 was the cost of erecting the building and £778 went on creating the forecourt. Unfortunately, whilst building work was in progress, a workman slipped off the roof and was killed. On 30th October 1929 Mrs. Mowll was paid £15/15/- for painting a horse on two sides of the sign board (I must admit that it looked like a camel to

me!) and a further £7/15/6 was spent on a light over the sign. In April 1931 the property was mortgaged in the sum of £1,000; this was redeemed in 1956. The first landlord was Bert Mantle. The original scheme had been to build the colliery houses, which opened in 1927, around the pub, but 76 houses were built in a circle nearer the pit and the remainder at Mill Hill, Deal, not far from the "Brickmaker's Arms". A "full on" licence was granted on 27th April 1950, at which time the net monopoly value of £650 was paid.

There was a hut to the rear of the pub and on 15th October 1952 this was purchased for £352, resulting in a development charge of £45. This was subsequently used as the meeting place for the 1st Finglesham and Northbourne cub pack. The pub had two large bars downstairs and a function room with bar upstairs, as well as living accommodation. The place was regularly used by the West Street hunt to meet and have their stirrup-cup before taking to the fields. A particularly popular, but unlikely, couple ran the house during the 1950's and 1960's. They were Arthur and Verida Talbot. Verida was born in South Africa, and met Arthur whilst he was completing his war-time RAF training in that country. Initially they owned an orange orchard before moving to England. Arthur had a fine singing voice that appealed, not only to the Welsh mining fraternity, but, as his fame spread, also to coach loads of drinkers from all over the county and London. Verida accompanied him on the piano. At this time food and drink were served in the hut. A previous landlord brewed something similar to lemonade for the children.

In 1979, after Whitbread had disposed of the premises, alterations took place which included knocking the two bars into one and converting the function room into a restaurant. This led to problems as the necessary planning consents had not been obtained. There was some talk that the property would have to be returned to its original state and then, early in 1982, the landlord departed. The "White Horse", still unoccupied, burned down on 6th July 1982. If one passes through the village a grassy site and the outline of the old pub can be found. There is a covenant on the land that states it can only be used as licensed premises. I cannot imagine anyone being bold enough to invest their money in such a venture so, unless the covenant can be lifted, the site will remain undeveloped for all time. Following the fire, all that remained was the inn sign swinging in the breeze – that was until one night when a collector arrived with a chain-saw and cut the sign down. All that was left was the stump. This kind of happening appears to be a common occurrence in the area, as it used to boast one of the more unusual sign-posts in the county pointing the way to Ham and Sandwich. Over the years this has been stolen on 20 occasions. In the end Kent County Council decided that to re-cast the sign-post was too expensive so it was replaced by a modern aluminium sign with Eastry inserted between Ham and Sandwich.

No 45. The Woodman, Barham
(Closed 31st August 1960) Either Rolfe Field or Alfred Beer & Co.,
Bushell, Watkins and Smith, Jude Hanbury, Mackeson, Whitbread

This substantial period house is Grade II listed and is believed to date back, in part, 250 years with later additions. During its history the property has been divided into three cottages, then a pub (reputedly owned by the then Mayor of Canterbury) and following closure was converted into a private house in 1961. For a very long period the pub was called the "Woodman's Arms".

The house was first mentioned in the will of Josiah Page, which was proved on 9th March 1761, in which he left his estate to his six children. At that time the "Woodman" was probably three agricultural cottages and it was later converted to a public house in 1847. The Page family played a very full part in the history of this modest house, with Josiah Page the first innkeeper until 1882 and possibly longer. In 1871 he was also described as a farmer. Much later, during the 1930's, an enterprising landlord, Joseph Murphy, used a photograph of the pub to advertise the house on a postcard and also produced little match-box holders advertising the sign. It was his widow in 1960 who opposed the renewal of the licence.

The "Woodman's Arms" and cottages were acquired by Jude Hanbury when, on 26th November 1925 they did a deal with Bushell, Watkins and Smith Limited, exchanging five of their West Kent pubs for five East Kent houses. It has not proved possible to ascertain how Bushell, Watkins obtained the property but I feel it was either in 1894 when they took over the failed Canterbury brewer Alfred Beer & Co. or in 1898 when the business of the Littlebourne brewer Rolfe Field was purchased.

The "Woodman" was tucked away at Derringstone Hill on the outskirts of the village. In 1923 it was valued at £365, which sum had been increased to £1,300 by 1934. The quarterly rent was £3/15/-. Perhaps to attract trade, an extra sign costing £20 was hung in 1926. The water supply was laid on in 1929 at a cost of £8/9-. The quit rent of 12/7 was redeemed on 3rd July 1931 and nine years later the tithe was redeemed. Ownership of the three cottages adjoining the "Woodman's Arms" passed from Jude Hanbury to the Tenterden Brewery Co., which paid £212/1/8 in March 1931.

After the war, in common with so many villages, there were just too many pubs – in the case of Barham five. The "Duke of Cumberland" is the sole survivor. The demise of the "Woodman" was unique within living memory inasmuch as, on 11th March 1960, an ex-licensee objected to the renewal of the licence. She was Mrs. Rose E. Murphy who, until 1957, had been licensee for 32 years. Her case was that a Fremlins house, the "Sportsman's Arms", was the next-door-but-one-neighbour and it was unfair to take a man's money for a pub that could not provide a living. She had only survived by also doing catering. Furthermore, the kitchen was also used to store casks of beer and the tenant paid no rent, rates or licence duty. During the eleven-year period from 1948 to 1959 there had been 40 official visits, with the statistics showing that the greatest number of customers at any one time was 10. The figures showed an average number of customers during the day of 2.27 and during the evenings 3.75. Since Mrs. Murphy had left there had been three tenants. Mackeson confirmed that the house gave cause for concern and its future was under review. The pub was granted a provisional licence with renewal referred to the compensation committee. In June 1960 renewal of the licence was formally refused and the "Woodman" closed at the end of August. The only person to lodge an objection was a 72-year-old thatcher, Tom Davis, who stated he had been a regular for 53 years and the pub sold the best draught beer for miles around. In future he would have to cycle a fair way to the "Black Robin". The pub and adjoining cottages remained empty for a while, until purchased, de-licensed, by Mr. C. A. Lindrige for £2,250, with completion taking place on 13th January 1961. Compensation money in respect of the licence amounting to £1,775 was received from East Kent Compensation Authority eight days later.

The property was then converted into a very comfortable private residence, within which a much later owner established a bed and breakfast business, trading as "Woodman". There is a little replica of the inn sign on the wall. Having stayed a night here, it was interesting to find the old place much as it had been described to me. At one time it had been frequented by service people and upstairs there were two large bedrooms in the front and between these there was what could best be described as a dressing room. Both bedrooms had a door providing access and the room contained a large array of wooden pegs six to eight inches long, on which to hang heavy or wet clothing. Also the original very attractive coloured glass in the front door had been extended all along the front of the building. The cellar had been converted into a den containing pub memorabilia. It is rumoured that the Duke of Cumberland stayed here whilst he was training his army on Barham downs.

The house was offered for sale in 2002 at a price of £425,000.

No 46. The Woolpack, Smeeth
Mackeson, Whitbread

Since the late 1700's there have been three houses called the "Woolpack" in Smeeth. The first was a small ale house at Stone Hill, which is now in the parish of Sellindge, but formerly was in the parish of Smeeth. This was owned by Richard Hammon, one of whose descendants still lives locally at Stowting. At the time of the Napoleonic wars, to hasten troops passing through to the coast, a new turnpike road was built that bypassed the old pub, which then closed. It was the early 1800's when the second "Woolpack" was built at the T-junction in the village, the site of which is now the modern pub's car park. It was a weather-boarded structure with steps up either side to double doors. The bars were on the second floor with stables to the rear. It was an old coaching inn, before the days of the A20, on the London-Sellindge-Dover road. For most of the 1800's this house was managed by two families – the Goddens and Epps. Francis Godden, also described as a painter, was here from 1816 until about 1860 when he was succeeded by Richard Epps, who ran a posting house and was also a job master. He remained until at least 1882. This house, plus eight acres, was leased by William Mackeson and, on his death in 1821, was valued at £900. H. and G. L. Mackeson still held a leasehold interest as late as 1898, as on 31st March 1898 they signed a new 21-year lease at a rental of £115 p.a. The lessor was the Right Honourable Lord Bra(y)bourne. Later records, dated 1905, indicate that Mackesons paid £2,000 plus legal fees of £37/4/11 for the freehold and, two years later, bought the new hall for £270. In 1912 this pub plus the "Man of Kent", Crundale and "Eight Bells", Ashford, were mortgaged to Henry Mackeson in the sum of £3,000. Mrs. Bishop, the daughter of the last landlord, recalls it being a very spooky place. Her father moved in during August 1937. It had a jug and bottle to the rear, which was used by children and housewives as they felt it "not right to use the men's bars". The upstairs was virtually uninhabitable.

This old pub was heavily involved in the smuggling trade. A story is told that a cavalcade of smugglers was attacked by customs officers close to the pub and a fight ensued. The former soon overpowered the officers, carried them to the inn, where they were bound to chairs until such time as the smuggled goods were hidden in a farmhouse at Little Chart. "They took their defeat well" commented one of the smugglers "and only asked for beer – Old Bill, the landlord, let them have plenty – three gallons each".

In the mid-1930's a rumour circulated that it was proposed to build a new road from the outskirts of Folkestone via Brabourne Lees to the other side of Ashford to provide the town with a bypass. Mackeson spotted the potential for a new and substantial roadhouse on this road and the "third" "Woolpack" was built. Unfortunately, the scheme never progressed but the villagers did acquire a fine new house.

Work on the building commenced in 1936 and the new house opened on 17th December 1937. The capital outlay was in the region of £5,800. The architect was E. G. Wildin LRIBA In 1943, 2. 569 acres were sold to East Ashford Rural District Council for £160 and on 13th April 1944 the tithe of £5/2/6 was redeemed. The first landlord was T. J. (John) Matthews, who paid a rent of £50 in his first year and £75 thereafter. He had been a good runner and an even better tandem rider. He represented his country in the 1906 Athenian games in Athens and the 1908 Olympics held at the White City. He was usually partnered by his brother-in-law. He remained until 1945. Soldiers billeted nearby kept the pub going during the war years, but even so trade was thin. During this period John also managed the "British Volunteer" in nearby Ashford. He would cycle down there every evening to lock up. Ultimately he was able to arrange for a friend from the village to live there and this chap later became the landlord.

During the war years there was always a shortage of beer. In 1938 the pub advertised at the local Ashford cinema and this attracted a lot of trade. In return the "Woolpack" advertised the cinema, and also received free admission tickets.

In November 1960, whilst the inn sign was away for repainting, a prankster arranged for a full-sized, scantily-dressed, shop-window dummy to be framed in the sign, much to the amusement of the villagers.

Originally the pub had one very large bar plus public, saloon and lounge bars but, as this wasted a lot of space, over the years it became virtually a one-bar house with a good-sized restaurant. The local British Legion still meets here.

No 47. York House, Dover

*(Re-named the **Flagship** in 1999) Mackeson, Whitbread, Flagship (re-named Nelson Brewing Co. in 2004)*

The "York House" stands close to the Dover car ferry and consequently a few years ago it attracted some notoriety as being the haunt of the modern beer and cigarette smugglers. This led to a certain amount of gang warfare, which resulted, in early 1998, in the local magistrates revoking the pub's licence to sell alcohol. The enterprising landlord then operated a tea and coffee shop from the premises, but this didn't last very long. The pub then closed for a while before new owners carried out considerable refurbishment and re-opened under a new name – the "Flagship".

This was a great shame as the "York House" was a fine pub known to seamen all over the world and had served the community well for over 200 years. The Argar family were in residence for very many years with William arriving prior to 1859. By 1878 Caroline had taken over and she was succeeded by Julia in 1882. Being so close to the port, several famous people have rested here before leaving for the continent. These include, in 1801, the Earl of Mounthaven and his entourage who were to embark for Calais the following morning aboard the spanking new vessel the Countess of Elgin. The Sultan of Zanzibar was another guest in 1898.

H. and G.L. Mackeson acquired the premises from Walter, Edwin and Ernest Pain on 4th May 1896 with a deposit of £50 paid three days before Christmas. The balance of the purchase price, £1,150, was paid on 6th April 1897. Legal costs amounted to £27/5/10. Other records indicate they purchased it on 6th April 1899, paying £1,200 to Elias Pilcher! Alterations costing £335 were carried out the following year. At that time the "York House" was one of a terrace, but the property to the left was subsequently demolished. On 24th March 1952 the brewers purchased, from Mrs. Maude Hearn, the freehold land and remains of buildings known as 116 Snargate Street for £100 and, four years later, paid the Corporation of Dover £125 for a piece of freehold land adjoining the pub, which was formerly part of 117/8 Snargate Street. It was at this time, July 1956, that the pub received a face-lift, with the tiny one-bar house expanded to more than twice its original size at a cost of £3,500. Snargate Street was a busy thoroughfare and in the past would have been the equivalent of the town high street.

All of this activity occurred during the long tenancy of the dapper, ever-popular landlord Edward Branson. He moved in on 14th March 1947 and remained until his death in 1967. The house, as to be expected, had acquired a nautical flavour. Mackeson installed, during the renovation work, a brass clock that showed the morning and afternoon high tides and Mr. Branson was also able to direct his seafaring patrons to the up-to-date weather news and tide tables displayed upon the B.B.C. weather forecast board over the bar. When I called in 1998 these items were still in evidence and the names of Mackeson and Whitbread were still engraved in the windows.

For many years the pub advertised in the Dover Football Club programme.

No 48. White Lion, Dover
(Closed in 1996) Ash & Co., (as tenants or lessee) Mackeson, Whitbread, Shepherd Neame

The "White Lion" was probably the most unassuming public house in all five series. It was situated in a modest terrace of houses built in about 1850 in the Tower Hamlets area of Dover and it came about by converting two of these properties. However, it suited the local community and its loss is still mourned today. Mackeson acquired the pub on 23rd May 1899 from Walter, Edwin and Ernest Edward paying £1,100. Costs amounted to £21/16/-. At that time Moxon, Collard and Ash were sub-tenants. That same year a new bar was installed at a cost of £100.

I have discovered nothing written about its past history and all the information gathered anecdotal. It is as if the pub never existed. However, perhaps this is not so surprising as, in the 1800's, it had been called the "Windsor Castle" and then the "Victoria". Charles Coad held the licence in 1878. At one time there was a courtyard to the rear of the premises where customers could sit and drink, but this was built over when the pub was extended to include a billiard room and toilets. There was a manhole cover beneath the billiard table.

We now move on to the pub's only claim to fame – its popular and respected landlord Percy Dawkins. He was one of the longest-serving landlords of all time and was behind the bar from 1910 to 1966. Percy left school and started work on a farm at the age of ten, earning 3/- per week. He moved to Dover to take up two jobs, one with the Dover Gas Board, a career which spanned 48 years, and the second as landlord of the "White Lion" for 56 years. I wonder how many inn sign collectors can remember him, for he was a character – a big man with a white walrus moustache. The window sills, wooden seats and doorstep would be scrubbed every day. In 1960, in recognition of his 50 years service, Charles Whitbread, son of Colonel Whitbread, visited the house to present Percy with a fine armchair. In his slack moments he could now take a rest and puff on his pipe. Whilst employed at the gas board, his wife took care of the pub during the day. She died in 1924 and his daughters, Ethel and Edith, took over these duties. He lived into his 90's. He would recall that in 1910 beer was 2d a pint and bitter 3d. In those early days he would supply beer lunches, but they are now a thing of the past. Women would not be seen in the public bar but would sit in the private bar with a drink and their knitting. In the next street one will find the "Dewdrop Inn", which had a photograph of Percy hanging on the wall. Following closure, cladding in the bar was moved up to the "Dewdrop".

Originally a two-bar house, "private bar" is still engraved on one of the windows. In its later days it was converted to a one-bar house. As befits such modest premises Percy paid a quarterly rent of £3/15/- in 1938 and ten years later it had increased to only £5.

Shepherd Neame purchased the premises on 31st January 1975 and ran the pub until it closed in 1996. The last landlords were Phil and Josie Brown. It is likely that a considerable sum of money was required to renovate the building and that trade was not sufficient to produce any kind of return. It was sold without licence on 28th February 1997. The purchaser told me that she rued the day she ever saw the place. The fabric was in poor condition and it cost a fortune to renovate. She felt sure that she would incur a capital loss.

No 49. The Red Lion, Hythe
*(Re-named **Watersedge** in 2000) John Friend, Mackeson, Whitbread*

The "Red Lion" and "White Lion" were as different as chalk and cheese. The "Red Lion" is a large, bold building, formerly a coaching inn, standing opposite the old Mackeson brewery in Red Lion Square, which takes its name from the hotel rather than the other way round. It is ancient, dating back to the early 1600's. As such it is another Hythe hostelry mentioned in the Dr. Syn stories. It was from the yard of the "Red Lion" that Mr. Mipps stole a barrow, on which to transport all of his worldly goods. In 1670 when the will of James Pashley was proved, he left the "Three Mariners", subsequently re-named the "Red Lion", to his wife.

At the time John Friend sold his brewing business to Henry and William Mackeson in 1801 this house, then named the "Three Mariners", plus cottage and stables, were included in the assets sold. The purchase price was £700 – 28 times the annual rent of £25 being paid by Mr. Watts. This sum was paid to Mr. Friend on 1st April 1802. At the time the pub plus stables were insured with the Royal Exchange in the sum of £500. Following the death of William Mackeson a valuation of his assets dated 10th June 1821 was drawn up, and this included the hotel, which was valued at £1,300. Somewhat surprisingly a valuation dated 28th May 1829 shows a figure of only £393/18/2, which sum included fixtures and fittings plus £50 for goodwill.

During the mid-1800's the licence was held for some time by Thomas King. In 1879 the sum of £675 was paid to Mr. Vile "on account" in respect of building works with legal costs totalling £17/10/6. In 1894 the brewers paid £15 to remove the old tram shed. Garages were erected in 1929 at a cost of £350 and by 1938 the landlord was paying the substantial rent of £20/10/- per quarter plus an additional sum of £13 per quarter for the garages. The bars contained a fine array of mementoes of the Mackeson brewery.

Despite much local hostility, the house was re-named the "Watersedge" in 2000. I am told, but have discovered no evidence to support the claim, that this was the name the hotel first traded under all those years ago.

In September 2004 the leasehold interest and contents were offered for sale at £175,000.

No 50. Swan Inn, Great Chart
Mackeson, Whitbread

There is a marked Dutch influence on the architecture of this pretty village and the "Swan", with its gabled end, sits comfortably in the main street. All is now tranquil again following the building of the village bypass.

This is another ancient inn, dating back to about 1650. It has a long sporting tradition, supporting the village cricket team and is also the assembly point for the Ashford Valley Foxhounds. A good crowd would gather to watch them move off at the traditional Boxing Day meet. The hounds were kennelled at nearby Goldwell. At one time there were stables to the rear and it was quite probably a coaching house.

The pub was obviously popular with landlords as several stayed for a while. In 1803 the licence was held by Stephen Durtnall and by 1816 he had given way to John, possibly his son. Henry Smith held sway in the 1830's followed by Leonard White, in 1846, who was also described as a shopkeeper. By 1859 Giles Grist was in residence and was still here in 1871.

For years the pub plus a good part of the village was owned by the Toke family of nearby Godington Park. Leslie A.St.L. Toke sold the pub to Mackeson on 11th December 1919, when a deposit of £200 was paid; the balance, £1,800, was settled early the next year. Legal fees amounted to £106/15/6. They quickly set about improving the property, with £300 spent in 1920 on installing new bays and a bedroom, and the following year the premises were extended at a cost of £610. The pub had been quite small and the extension swallowed up the family accommodation. A new bathroom costing £100 was added in 1930. It was suggested, in 1946, that a new separate lavatory should be built for ladies, as the house was attracting a large number of charabanc parties. By now the "Swan" was very much the focal point of village life, the quite high quarterly rent of £12/10/- reflecting the volume of trade. There was one slight aggravation – at one time the next-door neighbour, who had been the village butcher, made a regular habit of parking on the busy pub car park. It was frequently necessary to ask him to move on.

The pub now boasts fine restaurant facilities, the quality of which attracts both residents and visitors alike. One's meal comes with the resident ghost who, if he doesn't appear while one is eating, can be seen whilst drinking one's coffee. I am told he has been captured on tape.

Special Series of Four issued in August 1951

(Card)

1   William Caxton, Tenterden   2   Ordinary Fellow, Chatham

3   G.I., Hastings   4   Queen's Head, Maidstone

No 1. William Caxton, Tenterden

This is a name change, as the "William Caxton" was formerly called the "Black Horse". See Series 1, Number 15. The re-naming ceremony took place on 19th July 1951 as part of the town's Festival of Britain celebrations. Several very attractive signs have hung here since.

No 2. The Ordinary Fellow, Chatham
F. Leney, Fremlins, Whitbread

A comfortable old pub called the "Brown Jug" stood in Whittaker Street, Chatham, for many a long year. Leney rented the premises in 1881, when they valued the house at £900, and they went on to purchase the freehold for £1,200 in 1890. However, the pub was unable to resist the march of progress and in 1937 was demolished to make way for new council houses, the site having been presented for this purpose by Frederick Leney & Sons Limited.

The pub regulars may not have been too displeased as a fine new pub in Palmerston Road, "The Ordinary Fellow", was built to replace their old home and this opened in March 1937. It was so-named in memory of King George V who, being totally overcome by the warmth of his subjects' greeting during his state drive through London on the occasion of his Silver Jubilee, remarked to the Archbishop of Canterbury, "I like to think of myself as just an ordinary sort of fellow". Unfortunately, whilst the pub was being constructed the King passed away, so it was King George VI who was on the throne at the time the house was officially opened. A message of loyal greetings was despatched to the monarch stating "Your Majesty's subjects assembled here at the opening of "The Ordinary Fellow" send loyal greetings on raising this new sign bearing words spoken by his late Majesty King George V, in whose honour it was so named and respectfully dedicated. His late Majesty's self description as "just an ordinary fellow" has already taken its place amongst historic sayings, and it is hoped that the sign, "The Ordinary Fellow" will perpetuate his words in a traditional English manner".

The naming of this house inspired a leading article in The Times newspaper. The inn had been built upon the site of the old Palmerston Stores, purchased in 1929 for £2,400, which were named after the great Victorian statesman. By coincidence the late King was born in the year of Palmerston's death – 1865.

One of the first landlords was George Morgan Philo, from 1939 until 16th November 1942, when he was succeeded by John Snape who remained until 1958. A coming-of-age party was held in 1958 and to celebrate the occasion an inn sign was issued overprinted in red "1937-1958 Coming-of-Age re-issue". These are now extremely rare and command a high price.

It is a busy house which caters well for families. A bouncy castle and swings are provided in the beer garden for the youngsters.

No 3. The G.I., Hastings
(See Series 1, No 1.)

No 4. Queen's Head, Maidstone
(See Series 1, No 23.)

These are repeats showing the same sign.

Series Four issued 27th March 1953

(Card)

1	Bat and Ball, Leigh, near Tonbridge	26	Mitre, Tonbridge
2	Black Horse, Headcorn	27	Nevill Bull, Birling
3	Bowl Inn, Hastingleigh, near Ashford	28	Nottingham Castle, Westgate-on-Sea
4	Bull Hotel, Tonbridge	29	Old House at Home, Edenbridge
5	Camden Arms, Cranbrook	30	Palm Tree, Wingmore, near Elham
6	Castletons Oak, Biddenden	31	Plough, Westfield, near Hastings
7	Chequers, Tudeley	32	Queen's Head, Canterbury
8	Cinque Port Arms, Hythe	33	Robin Hood, Upper Halling, near Rochester
9	City of Canterbury, Canterbury	34	Rose and Crown, Stone Street, near Sevenoaks
10	Coach and Horses, Eastry	35	Royal Oak, Gillingham
11	Eight Bells, Wingham Well	36	Royal Oak, Newingreen, near Hythe
12	First and Last, Burham	37	Shakespeare, Sittingbourne
13	Gun Tavern, Folkestone	38	Ship Hotel, Dymchurch
14	Hope Inn, Lydden	39	South Eastern, Tonbridge
15	John Jorrocks, Frittenden	40	Sugar Loaves, Hollingbourne
16	Jubilee Inn, Folkestone	41	Swan Inn, Wickhambreaux, near Canterbury
17	Kentish Rifleman, Dunks Green, nr Tonbridge	42	Three Chimneys, Biddenden
18	King Ethelbert, Reculver	43	Two Bells, Folkestone
19	Kings Arms, Sandwich	44	Vauxhall Tavern, Canterbury
20	King's Head, Shadoxhurst, near Ashford	45	Von Alten, Chatham
21	King's Head, Wateringbury	46	Walnut Tree, Ditton
22	Locomotive Inn, Ashford	47	Warren Inn, New Romney
23	Lord Cornwallis, Tunbridge Wells	48	Wheatsheaf, Swalecliffe
24	Man of Kent, St. Michaels, Tenterden	49	White Hart, Hythe
25	Mitre Tavern, Canterbury	50	White Horse, Chilham

To celebrate the launching of the fourth series a luncheon was held on Monday 23rd March 1953 at the "Royal Star Hotel", Maidstone, which was attended by over 300 tenants of Whitbread Inns. They were told that the signs were collected all over the world and collectors included former American presidential candidate Thomas Dewey and ex-King Farouk of Egypt. Over four million cards were in circulation.

The menu was:- Cream of Tomato Soup, Fillet of Sole Princess, Chicken Favorite, Garden Peas, Marguerite Potatoes, followed by Iced Pudding Elizabeth, Petits Fours, and Coffee.

No 1. Bat and Ball, Leigh
B. Baker, F. Leney, Fremlins, Whitbread, Shepherd Neame, Free House

With both cricket balls and bats manufactured locally, what other name could this ancient ale house take? This is a smallish, two-bar pub in the centre of the village of Leigh – pronounced "lie" – built on the site of an old ale house that was closed down and demolished. The place has changed little in recent years with Whitbread and Fremlins still engraved in the windows. There is a pleasant rear garden.

The house is first mentioned in the church register of 1740 and, thirteen years later in the Register of Alehouses, the landlord is listed as John Carpenter. This was one of a large number of houses leased in 1892 by the Tonbridge brewers Baker to Leney, at an annual rental of £30. They purchased the freehold on 16th November 1905.

Many local residents were employed by the Duke family bat and ball factory, and cricket balls were also manufactured just down the road at Chiddingstone Causeway. The Eade family were well-known bat makers and Amos Eade, a member of this family, was the publican until his death in 1903. The brewers valued the house at £2,000 in 1922.

W.G. Wells and Samuel Harris were the tenants in June 1942, paying a rent of £26 p.a., the brewers holding a deposit of £25. It was not until April 1941 that the house acquired a beer and wine licence and at that time the landlord's inventory was valued at £94/13/-.

Because the sign shows a winged bat shielding a ball it has been suggested that this could allude to an 18th century hell-fire sect which wreaked havoc in the locality. Certainly the ale house would have been trading then, but I feel the cricketing claim is the more likely. The old sign has given way to a muscular Kent batsman smiting a six from an unseen bowler who probably played for Sussex. The house has always had close links with local cricketers and it is said that during the 1960's Colin Cowdrey would spend a few hours coaching the local youths on the pitch next to the pub.

The main entrance was formerly the jug and bottle where, I am told, two seats were provided for little old ladies to take a tipple and have a rest and chat. The serving hatch is still there. Drinkers consisted of the local working men, in particular those employed on the land. During the war years the pub was a popular venue for RAF personnel stationed at the Penshurst airstrip. Boom time was the hop-picking season, but this died out in about 1956. Surrounded by popular walking country, the "Bat and Ball" is a welcome haven in which to quench one's thirst. During the 1990's the landlord played for the village cricket team and other activities still enjoyed are football, pool, darts and rounders. A welcoming house, long may it continue to flourish.

Shepherd Neame leased the premises on 6th May 1992 and purchased the freehold on 27th September 1996. They sold on to the licensee on 11th June 1999.

"An early Spring by heaven sent Proclaims the majesty of Kent,
Whose blossom takes the April air, Before the county batsmen dare." Anon.

No 2. Black Horse, Headcorn
(Closed November 1988 and demolished the following year) H.T. Wickham & Co.,
Jude Hanbury, F. Leney, Fremlins, Whitbread

A fine old weather-boarded house, with a rather engaging hand-painted sign, once stood in Wheeler Street at the Biddenden end of the village of Headcorn. A nice photograph of the pub includes a local, Tom Longhurst, pushing his cycle.

This was a Wickham house. Their brewery was in the village of Yalding and on 22nd March 1921 Jude Hanbury and Frederick Leney purchased the business at auction for £20,000 and divided the eleven pubs between them. Jude attributed a book value of £2,371 to this house. The following year the old pub was demolished and was replaced by a basic two-bar house at a cost of £2,319. For most of its life it was a simple ale house, not acquiring a beer and wine licence until 9th April 1941. At that time the landlord was Thomas Wolvey who arrived in 1939, paying a rent of £40 plus his inventory costs of £74/5/-, he remained until 1957. Eli Cooper in 1880 is the first tenant that I have traced and he was also a farmer. The last landlord was David L. Monks, who acquired the licence in 1981 and remained until the end in November 1988. In November 1960 land adjoining the "Black Horse" was sold for £1,861/2/3 after costs.

Situated on the edge of the village, the "Black Horse" can best be described as the "Cinderella" pub in the area. It was always in the shade of its larger rivals and struggled to survive. In its later days it provided first-class fish and chips, but relying on a few loyal locals its days were numbered. It did well during the hop-picking years and wartime: being the nearest pub to the airfield, it received another boost – 2,800 men of the Canadian and American Air Forces were stationed in nearby Shenley House and its grounds. Headcorn suffered greatly from bombing during this period, mainly from bombs jettisoned by returning aircraft unable to reach London. Huge excitement and relief occurred during the First World War when an aircraft carrying a young Winston Churchill made a forced landing.

Close to that long, straight railway line up to the capital stood Little East End Cottage and for a short period early in the war this was occupied by two mysterious foreigners. It was strongly rumoured that they were spies and the locals accepted this as fact when they suddenly disappeared and soon afterwards the notorious Lord Haw Haw announced on German radio that the railway line close to East End would be bombed. And so it was. This shadowy couple used to drink at the "Black Horse".

The pub sat on a good-sized plot and when it was demolished in 1989 the "Black Horse" housing estate was built.

No 3. Bowl Inn, Hastingleigh
Sankey, Ash & Co., Jude Hanbury, Mackeson, Whitbread, Free House

High on the windy North Downs above Wye one will find the "Bowl Inn" housed in a solid, squat, white-painted building. The original sign still swings in the breeze.

Records date back to the 1700's, at which time the old ale house was almost certainly housed in the property now known as Myrtle Cottage, which was built by Thomas Newport. It was this house that was mentioned in the will of John Sankey proved in 1744. It crops up again in the will of Richard Sankey dated 4th January 1805, at which time the pub passed to Edward Scudamore and Edward Tournay as trustee, with the licence held by Mary Moreland. The house must have passed back to the Sankey family as in the 1840's Samuel John Sankey leased it to Stephen Hayward and on 27th December 1853 sold an ale house called the "Bowl Inn" to the brewer George Ash and others. George died in 1867 and his estate passed to his sons Thomas and George. The pub is listed in a schedule of the brothers' assets compiled in 1870 and includes those appurtenances erected and built by Stephen Hayward. This would be the present pub. The landlord at the time was Stoddard Fagg who was paying a rent of £18 p.a. Stoddard must have been here for a long time as he is listed in the 1861 census and retired in 1882 when he went to live at Crabtree Farm, another property built by Thomas Newport.

The pub, church, and just opposite, the Tappenden stores, which has served the surrounding villages for over a hundred years, were the hub of village activity. The present building probably started life as two agricultural workers' cottages with many alterations carried out since. In 1856 the Reverend Prideaux founded the Elmsted Friendly Society to provide a very modest income when a worker fell sick. Subscriptions and benefits varied, but it is interesting to note that a death payment of £7 was made on the demise of a man, yet only £3 on the death of his wife! As late as the 1950's this society still had 77 members. The annual general meeting was originally preceded by a church service that one missed on pain of death – actually a fine of a 1d was levied! Members then adjourned to the "Bowl" where a good time was enjoyed by all. The society held two meetings per month in the pub tap room. A similar society sprung up in Hastingleigh, as we find an article in the April 1899 Parish Magazine stating " on Saturday May 15th Divine service was held in the Parish church when the rector preached. The dinner took place at the "Bowl" where Mr. Cobb had prepared an excellent repast. The members were congratulated on their great musical ability. The club is also to be congratulated that, although the share-out rule was abolished only last year, there is now a substantial balance in hand of £20".

The pub was also the meeting place for the Rat and Sparrow club and each week members would gather, bringing with them their haul of sparrows' heads and rats' tails to be counted. Members of the committee would later dispose of these grisly items by burying them in the pub garden. At the end of each year a cold dinner would be prepared by the landlord and a modest reward given to the member with the highest tally.

Tuesday was market day at nearby Ashford. Although mainly an animal market, other produce, such as eggs, was sold. The pub landlord was the eggler, collecting eggs and taking them with a mule and van (a four-wheeled cart) to be sold at the market.

The village was a good place to live and landlords generally remained for a long period. Besides Stoddard Fagg, on 11th October 1909 Mr. R. Kerr succeeded Mr. Cobb who had arrived in about 1895 and remained until his death in 1932. His widow then managed the house for a few years. A Mr. Newport took over in May 1948 and remained until his death on 13th February 1962, after which his widow Margaret carried on for a further year.

Mains water was laid on in 1928 and electricity came to the pub in 1951. In 1946 two pull-beer engines costing £40 were installed by A. Kerr. Shortly afterwards, in 1950, repairs and alterations costing £1,200 were carried out. For a long while the pub boasted a skittle alley next door to the house, which, as far as I know, still remains.

Trade at the best of times could only have been modest and this was reflected in the rent charged. In 1938 no rent at all was payable and ten years later the sum was a very modest £6/5- per quarter. In 1946 a Mackeson representative called at three in the afternoon to be told by the landlord that he had not seen a customer all day! On 25th October 1979 Whitbread installed a manager to run the inn and on 25th April 1980 they sold the premises with licence. One of the villagers, Colin, purchased the house in 1986 managing it most successfully for the benefit of villagers and the walkers tramping this lovely part of the county. Egg and chips were his speciality and for some time the pub featured in a good food guide. Sadly Colin died in 2001, but his widow continues to run a first-class house.

"Come, fill the bowl ... the bird of time has but a little way to fly
– and lo! the bird is on the wing." Fitzgerald.

No 4. Bull Hotel, Tonbridge
(Closed in 1960 and demolished in 1962) B. Baker, F. Leney

This fine old commercial hotel and posting house traded from 65 High Street, Tonbridge. It was once called the "Horse Shoe".

The history goes back a long way, with Edward Walter running the place in 1732. Long-serving landlords were Richard Montague from 1839 until 1866 and Herbert Huntley who traded from 1886 until 1903. To advertise his house he produced a snuffbox bearing his photograph. Each Tuesday at one o'clock this gentleman provided a market dinner for 1/9. He also offered vintage wines and old bonded spirits. One could play billiards and there was good accommodation for motor cars. During his era the hotel was the headquarters for the Tonbridge Angling Society, the Equitable Friendly Society, the Gardeners' Society, Ancient Order of Druids, Royal Arch Chapter, Tonbridge Football Club and Skating Club. He was a busy man. It was during his reign, in 1892, that B. Baker of Tonbridge leased the hotel to F. Leney for an annual rent of £130. They purchased the freehold on 16th November 1905. Another long-serving landlord was Herbert Cecil Vaughan who died on 7th May 1944 aged 68. He became the tenant on 24th February 1925, paying a rent of £100 p.a. – the inventory valued at £1,101/8/-. He was a member of a family who had been hoteliers for generations, and prior to running the "Bull", he had been at the "Swan Hotel", Horsham, and the "Railway" at Burgess Hill.

To the rear of the property there were stables and a cobbled yard and at one time these were let to local traders to store their goods. They were also used by the last of the town horse-cabbies. Situated close to the River Medway, the place was prone to flooding and suffered greatly in 1880 and the November 1911 flood. It was here that the murderer Daniel Good was arrested in 1842. A great favourite at the bar was a Mr. Ware who laid claim to his own seat. If this was occupied when he arrived it would always be offered to him. He would sit there all evening but he only ever drank half-pints.

A feature of the main bar was a huge oil painting on oak, dating from about 1830, of a prize bull in John Deacon's park in Mabledon. As a gesture of friendship towards the pub's landlord Mr. Deacon allowed the beast to model for the artist, Ben Herring, son of the more celebrated horse painter John Herring. When the "Bull" was demolished the painting hung for a time above a meat counter before being rescued by Tonbridge Urban District Council and hung in the guard room of Tonbridge Castle. Its whereabouts are now unknown.

The hotel was valued in the brewers' accounts for 1945 at £5,090 – this was increased to £7,312 in 1951. Despite its prominent position trade declined to such a point that Whitbread sold the hotel, de-licensed, for £60,000 on 15th June 1960. The premises were demolished in 1962 to make way for a Marley D-I-Y store which became Payless and more recently Peacocks. The loss of this fine old building was not mourned at the time and few residents now know of its existence.

No 5. Camden Arms, Sissinghurst
(Closed in 1997) Isherwood, Foster & Stacey (Leaseholders), B. Baker, F. Leney, Fremlins, Whitbread

This modest hostelry, serving the tiny hamlet of Wilsley Pound, commenced life as a couple of agricultural cottages and following a disastrous fire in 1997 was renovated and converted back into three cottages.

The original buildings date back to the late 1600's and it was during the early 1700's that it became an ale house. The first reference seen is in a deed of gift in 1859 from John Beadle, a yeoman, late of Yalding then Maidstone, to William Fancett and his wife, Mary Ann (nee Beadle), of "A freehold public house at Cranbrook known as the "Camden Arms" in the occupation of Messrs. Isherwood, Foster & Stacey of Maidstone, Brewers". Mary died on 29th March 1876 and shortly afterwards Fancett and John Beadle Fancett, born 11th February 1851, and the only surviving grandson of John Beadle, mortgaged the property. This was redeemed in 1884 and after this John B. Fancett of Rochester obtained a judgement against William Fancett for over £5,000. As a result of this John Beadle and his wife Caroline Ann became sole owners of the pub. They did not retain it for long, selling it and adjoining land in March 1885 to Benjamin Baker of Tonbridge for £830. In 1892 Baker leased the premises to F. Leney at a rent of £60 p.a. to include two acres of land and premises adjoining the pub. They went on to purchase the freehold on 16th November 1905. It remained nothing more than an ale house – until acquiring a beer and wine licence in April 1937. A full licence was confirmed on 28th April 1950, at which time the net monopoly value of £900 was paid. The following year a loss of development value, relating to the land, amounting to £425 was settled, and in June 1963 land was sold for £140. When Fremlins, in 1960, acquired the Leney estate, included within the package was land at Camden which was let at 25/- per quarter to R.L. Woolliams of Mill Farm.

A very long-serving landlord was Oliver Curtis who became host on 1st December 1927 and was still here at the end of the war, handing over to Stanley Pollard Hope on 31st July 1946. In 1939 his rent was £20 p.a. and the inventory was valued at £169/7/11. The pub was valued in 1922 at £1,950, which had increased to £3,439 in 1950.

An old resident of the area told me that he could remember the outside toilets and the well to the rear of the premises and that it was a well-frequented pub in Oliver's days. Certainly the December 1931 payout to the 46 members of the thrift club of £170 exceeded that of the much larger "Kings Head" and "Bull", both of which were close by.

Sadly the fire in 1997 destroyed this welcoming, old inn.

No 6. Castleton's Oak, Near Biddenden
(Closed 2002) Tenterden Brewery Co., Jude Hanbury, F. Leney, Fremlins, Whitbread, Free House

It is said that this house dates back to 1614 and formed part of a farm estate. Some while later it became an ale house, brewing its own ale, but it was not until 1867 that it was first registered as an inn. Back in 1740 the land and house were purchased by E. Cassleden who was described as a joiner and coffin-maker. His story is on the reverse of the inn sign and he now rests in Biddenden churchyard. The pub acquired its name in 1895.

An old photograph, probably taken during the 1914-18 war, shows that the pub has changed little over the years, except that the road has been raised thereby eliminating the four steps up to the bar. In those far-off days the house stood on a sleepy crossroads, but with increased traffic this is now a very dangerous spot.

At one time the house formed part of the estate of the Tenterden Brewery Co. with Jude Hanbury purchasing the property in March 1922 for £2,500. During the 1940's the pub, together with the "Bull", Rolvenden and "This Ancient Boro'", was mortgaged in the sum of £4,500 to Miss K.N. Champion who received interest at 4% p.a. The mortgage was redeemed in October 1956.

A very long-serving landlord was Owen Watts who signed a tenancy agreement on 6th April 1925 and remained until after the war. His annual rent was £37 plus 10/- for water and £1/10/- for electric light. His inventory was valued at £225 and he held a full licence. It was obviously a popular rendezvous as during 1925 the barrelage was 233 barrels and the pub was valued at £2,510 – this was increased to £4,194 in the following year. The landlord ran a slate club and the Christmas 1934 payout of £108 was shared between the 100 members. During 1933 Tanner's Orchard, close to the inn, was sold for £180.

The pub is isolated and at best could only have provided a precarious living. It closed for a while in 1995 but fortunately re-opened eight months later under the stewardship of a friendly and enterprising young landlord called Laurence Blake. By a strange co-incidence a gentleman of this name ran the pub from 1835 until 1847.

Sadly the pub closed again in 2002, although the original sign still hangs and Whitbread is still engraved in the windows. It became a freehouse in 1988.

Opposite the pub stands Castleton's Oak Cottage which was a former toll-house on the edge of the Earl of Cranbrook's estate.

No 7. Chequers, Near Tudeley

(Please see Series 1, Number 42.)
A new sign was erected in 1951 and as a result this house again appeared in a series of inn signs.

No 8. Cinque Port Arms, Hythe
(Closed 23rd March 1961 and now a solicitors' office) Mackeson

The loss of this fascinating old pub is still mourned by the older residents of Hythe. It was one of the smaller pubs in the town and at the best of times was only a marginal business.

The building dates back to the first half of the 18th century and it traded as an ale house from about 1830. It was originally called the "Chance" and Thomas Pilcher was the landlord. The name change occurred in about 1880 whilst the pub was in the ownership of the Maycock family. George, who had run the place for several years, died on 21st January 1880, and his wife, Jane, then managed the house until her death on 7th April 1891. William and George Maycock then carried on for a short while before selling it to Henry Bean Mackeson on 17th May 1891 for £1,310. The sale probably came about as the estate was to be divided between seven children. In 1901 legal fees of £185/18/- and £16/16/- in respect of C.P. appeal were incurred and two years later the furniture was upgraded at a cost of £30. To reflect the marginal nature of this business, in 1919 the rent was a nominal £13 and the rateable value of the premises £24. The brewers decided to increase the rent by raising the price of beer by a 1/- a barrel up to a maximum of 200 barrels.

The place obviously appealed to Edgar C. Flack who signed a tenancy agreement on 28th December 1939, by now paying a rent of £20, and he remained until March 1954. The last landlords were probably Albert and Joan Measday who took over in October 1958.

This was a quirky house that in its early days was the haunt of smugglers, who stored their wares in the cellar, and, as to be expected, local fishermen. Its claim to fame is that locals never used it because it was so rough! It was the kind of place a respectable drinker would pop into to "have a crafty pint" – safe in the knowledge that nobody was likely to come in and find him. Wedding receptions were catered for, and I am reliably informed that there used to be a stuffed two-headed lamb in a glass case in the bar. That gives some idea of the flavour of the place!

Sadly all this came to an end in 1961 when the pub closed. The premises were placed on the market and the shopkeeper next door was interested in purchasing the place, but on survey it was found to be in a poor state of repair with the toilets a particular problem. It then went to auction but failed to reach the reserve price of £3,000, although it was subsequently sold, de-licensed, for this sum to a local solicitor.

"The Royal Navy of England hath ever been its greatest defence and ornament." Blackstone.

No 9. City of Canterbury, Canterbury

(Closed in May 1970. Now run as a bed and breakfast establishment)
Flints Brewery, Stour Street, Canterbury, Ash & Co., Jude Hanbury, Mackeson, Whitbread

This pub, which served the St. Thomas's Hill area of Canterbury, closed over 30 years ago when it was felt that the heavy cost of repairs could not be economically justified. Initially there were three bars and a shop, the roof of which was thatched. To the rear of the building, in the kitchen, a slab was discovered beneath which was a well. Today the reason for closure would not be readily apparent as there is no local competition and the pub is opposite the entry road to the University. People living in the locality would welcome a new house yet, in January 1983, a proposal to re-open the pub as the "John Bull" was rejected by the city planners.

This ale house commenced trading in 1803, although some say its origins are earlier. It had been purchased by Mr. Thomas Flint and he went on to sell it, by way of auction, on 26th June 1849 to George Ash. It was described as an "Old established roadside public house with a brick built and thatched shop in front". Almost certainly at a later date this was incorporated into the pub. In addition there were also a yard, orchard and gardens which were formerly hop ground. Thomas Ash died on 12th March 1875, at which time the landlord was E. Hopper who was paying a rent of £19/10/- p.a. This gentleman had rents and loans outstanding amounting to £134/5/6 and the Flint land tax was 12/-. Prior to this John Martin had held the licence from at least 1838 until 1848. Not much else is known about the pub, other than a door to the urinal was added in January 1930 at a cost of £3/12/-. The tithe rent of £6/5/2 was redeemed on 22nd June 1939 and a full-on licence was granted in 1949.

Following closure the building has been used for several purposes. In 1971 the local council granted planning permission to convert the pub into student accommodation.

St. Edmunds Residential School then took the building over and more recently it has been converted into very nice bed and breakfast accommodation.

The original inn sign still hangs with the dates 1803-1971 added.

No 10. Coach and Horses, Eastry

(Closed on March 28th 1968. Now a restaurant) Mann family, George Beer (Leaseholders),
East Kent Brewery, Jude Hanbury, Mackeson, Whitbread

This ancient building stands on the edge of the small town of Eastry. The property dates back to 1749. It is believed that Thomas Mann (1792-1869) enlarged the premises, as the north end is older than the rest, and opened it as a beer shop. It is so described in the tithe schedule dated 1841, and the first entry in the

rate book is a year later. The Mann family were in occupation for a long while, probably from 1841 until about 1880 – Mrs. M.A. Mann took over after the death of Thomas.

George Beer leased the premises from 6th April 1898 paying an annual rental of £72 and on 30th July 1919 the house was sold by auction, the purchaser being the East Kent Brewery. It passed to Jude Hanbury and we then discover that the Tenterden Brewery had an indirect interest as, on 31st March 1931 they purchased four cottages, three of which were ultimately demolished, next to the pub at a cost of £175. Whether or not this was a book-keeping exercise I do not know for the records then indicate that these cottages were sold to Mackeson via Jude Hanbury on 15th June 1934. The rental income from one cottage, let to Mr. Setterfield, was 3/- per week, and F. Dustnall of the Eastry Cash Stores was the collecting agent. At about this time alterations to the bars costing £35 were carried out and drainage was installed at a cost of £198/14/-.

P.W. Roberts signed a tenancy agreement on 15th February 1933 and paid a rent of £25 p.a. During his tenure life must have been pretty tough. In 1945 the floor was chalk and very uneven, the engines were worn out and required renovation and the tenant asked for electric light to be installed. This came about the following year. We then move on to the era of Albert Brooks who was landlord from 1951 until 1957. This gentleman was an amateur boxer and quite capable of looking after himself. His children can vividly remember the comings and goings during this period. In 1953, during the dreadful floods, the pub was submerged. The children rowed a rubber dingy around the car park to amuse themselves. The house had no cellar – the barrels were stored in a little place to the side of the building. The toilets were outside. A band played every night of the week and again this was, in part, a family affair. The Royal Marines were based in Deal and would play jazz to earn a bit on the side; they would be accompanied by Mrs. Brooks on the piano and Rod Brooks played the drums. Up to six coach-loads of people, about 200 customers, returning from a day out at Margate would descend on the pub – the driver would be slipped a pound plus drinks. When the coaches departed they would be supplied with four crates of brown or light ale. Margate had a bye-law in the 1950's that all coach parties had to leave the town before six o'clock. There was a public, saloon and cosy bar and the children were provided with a little room adjacent to the car park. The beer was delivered to the pub by a steam lorry that was based at Wingham Engineering. The level of activity attracted the attention of the authorities and at the end of one evening a rather quiet customer introduced himself as the representative of the performing rights authority and demanded that the landlord pay £25 for infringing the act! Located close to the former Kent coalfields, the pub was frequented by a few miners, but due to its cosmopolitan nature they tended to rendezvous at more insular houses such as the "Brickmakers" at Deal. The pub was very quiet over winter and it was during this period that the landlord devoted much of his energies to rearing the 50 or so pigs that he kept.

This period was the pub's hey-day and it then settled into gentle decline. On 19th April 1958 a strip of land 34 feet by 4 feet, forming part of the front garden, was sold to Ellen Louisa Pointer for £10. The place struggled on until closure in 1968. A most unusual event then occurred which caused some confusion at the Wingham and Sandwich Division Justices. Following closure the pub was offered for sale by auction, de-licensed, on 14th May 1968, but bids failed to reach the reserve price. The following day Robert M. Maxstone Graham, a local estate agent who had not attended the auction, saw the auctioneers and agreed to buy the property for £3,250. He then applied to the Divisional Justices to have the licence transferred from Gerald A. Rouse. Rouse was the last tenant and his licence had been renewed for a year in February. This application was opposed by Mackeson. Mr. Maxstone Graham freely admitted that he hoped he had found a loop-hole in the licensing laws and that he had a partner who wished to re-open the old pub, even though it needed a lot of money spent on it for redecoration. Mackeson had written to the court on 6th September 1968 regarding the de-licensing and, despite the fact that this was after the former pub had been sold, the justices found against him. I am told that for a while it was a private house then, in 1972, it was converted into a licensed restaurant which it remains to this day. It is a pleasant building and still gives the impression of being a public house. It is quaint in its coat of green with black shutters and white slap-board sides. The two outdoor lavatories are still present. There are tales of smuggling activities and secret tunnels but I found no evidence to support this assertion.

The old inn sign remained to the end and now hangs in what was the former Whitbread farm museum near Paddock Wood.

No 11. Eight Bells, Wingham Well

(Closed and sold by Whitbread April 1976. Re-opened to close in 1998) Either Alfred Beer & Co., or Rolfe Field, Bushell, Watkins and Smith, Jude Hanbury, Mackeson, Whitbread, Free House

This house was built in 1779 and over the years was considerably extended to include a good-sized restaurant. The inn could have been named the "Six Bells" as, back in 1719, this was the number hanging in the church belfry. However, the parishioners then decided to re-cast the six bells and increased the number to eight musical bells.

Rumour has it that it started life as a malthouse, became a brewery and then an inn. In those far-off days it was the haunt of fishermen casting on the Little Stour which was famous for its great pike. In fact this area is riddled with dene holes. The seams from the former Snowdown Colliery snake under the pub, but a dene hole is far older – indeed possibly dating back to 2,000 B.C. A good while ago a landlord was disturbed by a great rumbling and, on going to his back door, he found, just outside, a vertical shaft, with footholes, about 18 feet deep cut into solid chalk. This was found to lead into a main chamber about 20 feet long. Seven smaller chambers were also discovered. One would imagine that the local smugglers were aware of this phenomenon. From time to time small indentations had been spotted and apparently locals would comment on the way that people approaching the pub could be heard as if their footsteps were coming from under the floor of the bar. During the 1950's a pig rummaging around in the back garden fell into a dene-hole.

On 26th November 1925 Jude Hanbury exchanged, with Bushell, Watlins and Smith Limited, five of their West Kent houses for a similar number of pubs in East Kent and, in so doing, acquired the "Eight Bells". It has not proved possible to trace how Bushell, Watkins acquired the house but I feel it likely it was in either 1894 when they took over the failed Canterbury brewer, Alfred Beer & Co., or four years later when they purchased the business of the Littlebourne brewer Rolfe Field. Jude Hanbury redeemed the tithe, amounting to £2/13/6, on 27th November 1930.

The first landlord I have traced is John Holney in 1804. For most of its long life the "Eight Bells" was a modest ale house and consequently little information has come to light.

W.A. Rilstone signed a tenancy agreement on 26th January 1939, and paid a rent of £20 p.a. A wine licence was granted on 15th April 1947 and a full-on licence following on 27th April 1950, when the net monopoly value of £575 was paid. During 1949 repairs costing £100 were carried out. In September 1961 the licensee wanted to use about an acre of land adjoining the pub as a holiday caravan site to house 25 caravans. This met with stiff local opposition and planning permission was refused.

Whitbread sold this remote house in 1976 and it then re-opened on Monday 1st August 1977 as a freehouse. Despite having substantial restaurant facilities it provided a very modest income and closed for good in 1998. Locals tell me that it was not really missed as towards the end it moved down-market with such things as "Page 3" girls displayed in the bars. It is now a private residence called Bell House which was offered for sale in 1998 at a price of £285,000.

"They went and told the sexton and The sexton tolled the bell." Hood.

No 12. First and Last, Burham
*(Now the **Golden Eagle**. Sold by Whitbread on 2nd September 1977 and re-opened as a Free House) F. Leney, Fremlins, Whitbread, Free House*

Perched high on a hill with widespread views over the Medway valley and surrounding countryside, the "First and Last", a substantial building, is to be found at the very edge of the village.

The property was built in about 1850. The three Leney brothers held this beer house and the adjoining cottage under a 14-year lease from July 1875 and on 22nd January 1880 they bought the freehold for £975 from William Colegate. In addition to the "Beerhouse known by the sign of the "First and Last" and the cottage adjoining then or late in the occupation of Mr. Eagles" the sale included the roadway separating them from the three cottages still remaining in William Colegate's ownership and the right to draw water from the well on his property (the Leney brothers bearing half of the repair costs). In return the three cottages had a right of way over the roadway and also right of use of the "tank" on the land sold.

In 1881 Leney valued the premises at £1,000 but thirteen years later this figure had reduced to £975 and the annual rent was £40. Clifford A. Kemp took over the tenancy in May 1927 and in 1939 he was paying a rent of £25 p.a. He had lodged a deposit of £100 and his inventory was valued at £161/11/6. He was obviously attached to the place as he didn't retire until December 1948. It was during his tenure that a beer and wine licence was granted in April 1942. Whitbread appointed a manager in December 1976 and then closed the business on 10th June 1977. The premises were sold in September 1977 and re-opened as the "Tudor Rose" for a couple of years. It was then purchased by a Malaysian businessman who re-named it, in 1979, the "Golden Eagle" – a bird of good fortune.

Due to its splendid setting this pub was a popular venue in the 1950's for local coach parties and those who could afford a car. It still flourishes and boasts an excellent restaurant.

No 13. Gun Tavern, Folkestone
(Closed 19th August 1974 and ultimately demolished in 1982) Ash & Co., Mackeson, Whitbread

This comfortable house was well-served by a succession of first-rate landlords but unfortunately it stood in the way of the town re-development plans and was closed down in 1974 and was compulsorily purchased on 6th January 1975.

Ash & Co. purchased the house in 1867 from a Mr. Hoad. At the time of the sale the tenant was Will Elliott who paid a rent of £25 p.a. It was described as an unfinished house, which is strange given that it first opened in 1843 – perhaps it was being extended. On the death of Thomas Ash in March 1875 the landlord was William Hunt who paid the same rent. It would be interesting to learn more about Hoad as he

and a Mr. Banks also sold the "George". Banks was also the vendor of the "Bouverie Arms".

It was a blacksmith, Thomas Cock, who first opened the pub next to his forge no doubt hoping to entice his customers in for a drink whilst their horses were shod. The original property formed part of the Gun Brewery on the other side of the road and was referred to as "Gun Cottages". The brewery took its name from an Elizabethan gun that stood on the corner of Guildhall Street and Cheriton Road. In about 1910 it was placed on a wooden carriage at the east end of the Leas. A brass plaque stated "An iron demi-culverin of rare type of the late 16th century, part of the muzzle shot away. This gun is believed to be part of the armament of the church battery, one of the two batteries which formerly existed on the cliffs to the east of this spot". Later it was moved to the East Cliff Corporation works and finally in 1940 it was melted down to assist the war effort. The brewery was built in 1846 by Mr. Ham Tite and was initially known as the Steam Brewery, changing to the Gun in 1887. In 1898 control passed to Alfred Leney & Co. Limited of Dover and brewing ceased. It then became a bottling plant, but in 1922 all brewery connections ceased and the site was converted into shops. The whole area was demolished in 1972 to make way for the one-way traffic system.

I digress – Thomas Cock had a brush with the law in 1855 and William Hunt was declared bankrupt in March 1877. Tragically, Donald Cook, who was tenant from 1922 to 1929, committed suicide after being fined £5 for keeping his house open during prohibited hours. Despite this landlords settled in well and over its 131 years' history it had only 12 licensees. Thomas Frederick Green established the record, serving from 23rd November 1929 until 4th May 1965. Shortly after he had taken over, Mackeson carried out alterations to the bars and a new urinal and lavatory were built at a cost of £490. Thomas had an aversion to his house being photographed as he considered it would bring bad luck.

Jude Hanbury and the Tenterden Brewery were in the habit of exchanging properties and on 15th April 1931 the latter company acquired the cottage and forge next to the "Gun", paying £275.

Following Mr. Green's retirement trade slackened and then Whitbread were notified of the town council's decision to re-develop this area. The pub closed in 1974 and was sold in 1975. However, the building was not immediately demolished and traded for a while as a post office before serving, from 1976 until 1982, as headquarters for the sea scouts. It was then demolished. The site is now a car park.

"How much I owe. To the defences thou hast round me set." Emerson.

No 14. Hope Inn, Lydden
Mackeson, Whitbread, Pubmaster

The standard pebble-dash applied to all Whitbread houses here masks a pleasant flint and brick frontage which contained the old Mackeson signage. The pub stands on the former London to Dover road.

The building dates back to the early 1800's and was called Horn's Ashes house. The owner was John Childs. It was a beer house in 1847 when Charles Golder leased the premises from Thomas Reeves. He also established a general provisions store that sold a wide range of goods and was managed by Anne Golder. Charles was to remain for quite a while as in 1882 he was described as a beer retailer and shopkeeper. It was well into the 1900's before the store ceased to trade. In about 1900 the property came into the hands of the Parkes family but they did not retain it for long, as on 5th March 1902 Mackeson purchased this beer house at public auction paying £1,150 with legal costs of £19/18/-.

They then set about improving their latest asset and quickly added a new back portion to the house at a cost of £200. In December 1927 the tenant wished to sell five acres of his rough pasture to the brewers for £275 to liquidate his debt. Mackeson considered this price too high and finally agreed to pay £200 and take £100 in reduction of the debt. The tenant then hired the land at £10 p.a. In 1932 a "draw-in" was formed at a cost of £35 and on 25th April 1945 the tithe rent of £26/7/7 was redeemed. A wines and spirits licence had been granted in the early 1900's and a full-on licence was confirmed on 27th April 1950, at which time the net monopoly value of £420 was paid. In March 1963 land was sold to Mr. L.M. Stephen for £900.

The pub always did a good trade with this boosted in about 1968 when Squadron Leader Dutch-Stewart became the tenant. He transformed the pub into a top-quality eating house and this tradition continues today.

This is another old inn with a resident ghost but to date it has never been seen. It can, however, turn on taps and hand dryers, open and close doors, and switch on lights. The closest it came to being discovered was when it tapped two members of the staff on the shoulder.

No 15. John Jorrocks, Frittenden
(Formerly the New Inn. Closed 14th February 1969) Sharpe & Winch, F. Leney, Whitbread, Fremlins

This welcoming, white weather-boarded pub sat comfortably in the pretty village of Frittenden just a few hundred yards from the "Bell". The pub attracted local agricultural workers, the younger generation and, in season, the hop-pickers, whilst the "Bell" appealed to the more traditionally-minded. As fashions changed it became obvious that the village could only support one house and sadly the "John Jorrocks" closed in 1969 when the tenant moved down the road to the "Bell". However, the villagers were determined not to forget the old place and we now find the surviving house re-named the "Bell and Jorrocks". That should give any stranger food for thought! The "Bell's" sign at one time was a simple bell and to emphasise the name-change Jorrocks' head was superimposed on the Bell and a hunting scene was added. It looked quite attractive.

The house dates back to the mid-19th century and it is a sturdy structure with a beautiful walled garden. Benjamin Hodges held the licence in 1891 and lived there with his wife, Annie, and their four daughters. They must have been cramped as they had taken in two lodgers who were both agricultural labourers. Benjamin was also described as a carrier and coal man. At the time the property was owned by the banker, Charles Hoare, who, in 1892, sold it to William F. Winch, auctioneer and brewer. On 18th July 1928 Sharpe and Winch sold out to Leney and the "New Inn" was described thus:- "All that messuage tenement or Beer House and premises … with the gardens and land and separate urinal (it was across the alley way) … Subject to the right of said W.F. Winch to pass and re-pass etc. over the land coloured green.".

This was another house that ran a slate club with a payout taking place on 22nd December 1914: after the share-out a most enjoyable evening was spent, capital songs being sung by Messrs. Murrell, Butcher, Evenden, Grigsby, Bud, Standen, Ward and Martin, Mrs. Standen and Mrs. Bud accompanied at the piano.

Robert W. Harmer (Jim) was a long-serving, versatile and popular landlord – he moved in on 23rd February 1928 and remained until his death in January 1948. His initial rent was £15 p.a. plus a further £1 for electricity and the inventory was valued at £53/9/5. His widow, Catherine, remained for her "widow's year" as was allowed by the tenancy agreement. Jim acquired a beer and wine licence in 1947, but it was not until 1957 that a full licence was obtained. Jim's son, Fred, can vividly recall his early days here. His father's real name was Jim, but in his youth he had used his younger brother's birth certificate to join the sea cadets and continued to use his brother's name for the rest of his life, although he was always known as Jim in the family. He went on to spend 22 years in the navy. He possibly ran the village butcher's shop before taking over the pub and carried on this trade using the room to the left as his shop. The old shop was used as a larder in the winter but during the summer months, and in particular at "hopping time", it became the living room in order that the existing living room could be used for storing casks. These were kept cool by covering them with jute sacking that had been soaked in the well just outside the back door. Not liking pumps, the only available method of dispensing beer was direct from the cask at the back of the servery, which meant that the temperature varied and affected the quality of the beer. At hop-picking time the beer was emptied direct into galvanised baths so that the jug or glass could be dipped in for speed of service. The area converted to a kitchen was called the fish house as Jim also ran a fish business for some time and stored his stock here. The old butcher's shop was converted into the gents' toilets in 1948 and 1949 when mains water was laid on. Prior to this a well existed in the yard at the corner of the butcher's shop and water was supplied to the old kitchen via a water pump. During the war years, in 1940, a Heinkel was brought down in the village. The name change occurred on 14th April 1948. In 1950 major alterations took place.

Phil and Dolly Oliver took over in 1958 and were particularly lively landlords with their zany advertisements bringing a lot of trade to the house. They always made one welcome and could offer hot pies, snacks, and sandwiches. Their era was probably the pub's last carousel as it was to close in 1969. At the time it was valued in the brewers' books at £7,600 but it was sold, unlicensed, on 28th April 1969 for £6,320.

This old pub is now a most comfortable private residence aptly named "Old Jorrocks".

"'Unting is all that's worth living for …
Tell me a man's a fox-hunter, and I loves him at once." John Jorrocks (Surtees).

No 16. Jubilee Inn, Folkestone
*(Formerly the **Jolly Sailor** then **Skylark**. Re-named **Carpenters** (1988)*
*then the **Mariner** in 2000) A. Langton & Co., Mackeson, Whitbread*

The original, rough, old beer house dated back to 1862 and was one of several Folkestone pubs to be called the "Jolly Sailor". Surprisingly it was housed in a quite handsome three-storey building. As to be expected, most of the clientele came from the seafaring community. Old records tell us that there was a boat builder's shop and store to the rear and one could enter the pub from either the Stade or Radnor Street.

The original owner would appear to be William Cockett, but on his death the estate was insolvent and the house was offered for sale by public auction in October 1865. The likely purchaser was Arthur Langton, a partner in the local Tontine Street Brewery (see the "Three Bells"). Just prior to this it had been re-named the "Skylark" after a local fishing boat. The change of name did little to improve the pub's reputation as,

in 1865, landlord Richard Bayley was fined for the non-payment of fines and, two years later, his successor, William Spearpoint, was sentenced to a term of imprisonment for assaulting his wife. Despite these events the house was granted a spirit licence in 1869.

On 6th June 1879 Arthur Langton was in possession and sold the house to Augustus Frederick Benwell for £450. However, Henry Bean Mackeson acquired the pub on 23rd May 1886 from John Banks (see "Guildhall") and the following year the landlord, John Ollington, applied to the local magistrates to change the name, yet again, to celebrate Queen Victoria's jubilee. In granting the request the bench wryly remarked that perhaps the name change might improve the character of the house. The new owners carried out several improvements which attracted a better class of drinker, but it could not entirely escape its past as, in 1889, Mackeson spent £6 on replacing damaged furniture. In 1893 Folkestone police opposed the renewal of the licence on the grounds that the house was not required, but their application was rejected.

A report prepared for the brewers stated that the pub was in a slum area, and the cellar was unclean, containing the dust-bin, coal, and rubbish. It was suggested that the premises be rebuilt. Folkestone town council published, on 16th January 1934, a slum clearance scheme which included the "Jubilee", and Mr. Mowll, of solicitors Mowll and Mowll, was instructed to act on behalf of the brewers. The hope was to demolish the pub and rebuild on a better site. Almost one year later to the day, Commander Findlay of Mackeson was able to report that it was proposed to exchange the present site for a larger and cleared site a little way to the east of the present house. It was felt that new premises could be built at a cost not exceeding £4,000. On 15th April 1935 Mr. Ingram was appointed as architect, agreement having been reached with the council to exchange sites a month earlier. The deed of exchange was actually signed on 10th May 1937. The rebuilding estimate proved to be optimistic, the final figure being £5,505/11/3, but this did include the cost of fixtures, of which £427/15/2 was charged to the incoming tenant. In addition the architect was paid £200. Mr. Chawner, previously the tenant at the old "Jubilee", opened the new house in 1936 and paid an annual rent of £45. However, on 9th April 1936 this was amended to £25 in the first year, £50 in the second and thereafter £75. Mr. H.W. Rice signed a tenancy agreement on 24th October 1938, by which time the rent had increased to £100 p.a.

Trade in the new and impressive house expanded rapidly, again based around the fishing fraternity and holiday makers. During the 1960's Don and Mary Mayne were the tenants. As a little surprise for his wife, Don purchased a fishing-boat built at Whitstable for a local fisherman, Reg Noble, on the understanding the vessel was named after his wife. When I visited the pub in April 2001, at anchor in the harbour, was vessel No. FE 73 – Mary Mayne!

Another name change occurred in 1988 when Leslie Carpenter moved from the nearby "Oddfellows Arms". He expanded the food side of the business – the whole of the first floor was used as a restaurant. The final change of name occurred in 2000.

In May 2004 the leasehold interest in this popular pub was offered for sale with a guide price of £65,000.

No 17. Kentish Rifleman, Dunks Green
(Formerly the **Red Lyon**) F. Leney, Fremlins,Whitbread, Free House

Set in the rolling West Kent countryside, this 16th Century house is indeed a sight to behold. It probably started life in 1552 as a farmhouse and formed part of the "Hamptons" Estate, which came into the hands of the Dalison family through the marriage of Maximilian with Frances, granddaughter of John Stanley, who was the owner during the reign of Elizabeth I. The Dalison connection was a long one stretching from 1668 to 1957, when the estate was sold after the death of M.D.P. Dalison, the last member of the family to live there. At the time of his death Leney had been renting the property for very many years and at auction purchased the freehold for £3,250. The rent was paid to Dalison's agent, H. & R.L. Cobb. From a "Change Statement" of 1927 it can be established that there would have been land in addition to the pub, as the valuation includes £220/12/6 for "Live and dead farming stock".

The pub was initially called the "Red Lyon", with Richard Brown the first known innkeeper in 1680. In 1851 the pub was re-named the "Kentish Yeoman" but this name was short-lived, changing to the "Kentish Rifleman" when John Jury became landlord in 1867.

This house was the papermakers' local being only a stone's throw from Roughway Mill. Apart from this, its main sources of income were the local agricultural workers and, in season, hop-pickers. The fine, beamed premises, with a distinctive original cellar which is partly sunken with a barrel ceiling, boasts a good restaurant which attracts customers from the nearby towns. Cricket is played on the green opposite.

The original Corporal Jones sign hung for many years, but during the 1990's it was replaced by an altogether smarter figure silhouetted against a painting of the house. However, by 1999, Jones was back, thank goodness.

This freehouse was offered for sale in April 2004 at a price of £735,000.

No 18. King Ethelbert, Reculver

*(Formerly the **Hoy and Anchor**) William Gurney, Ash & Co., Mackeson, Whitbread*

King Ethelbert (560-616) was the first Christian King of Kent. He was of Frankish descent and in about 581 married Bertha (see No. 32). Bertha was born in 562 and was the daughter of the King of Paris. It was a political marriage that enabled Ethelbert to gain a foothold in Europe. We don't know what Bertha thought of the marriage as she was an educated lady, able both to read and write, whereas her husband was only semi-literate. She brought her own chaplain to this country and it was agreed within the marriage vow that she could retain her own faith. Ethelbert succeeded to the Kentish throne in 585 and was converted to Christianity in 597 by Augustine, the first Archbishop of Canterbury. Ethelbert is credited with founding both Rochester Cathedral and St. Paul's Cathedral. Bertha died in 606 and was buried at St. Augustine's Abbey, Canterbury, as was Ethelbert ten years later.

Ethelbert was an enlightened and far-sighted ruler. He wrote the first laws of the English legal system which were observed by all his people. Fond of a drink, his third law stated "If the King drinks at anyone's house, and anyone there do any evil deed, let him make two fold compensation".

The pub has a long and interesting history and is probably the only hostelry in England built on the remains of an old Roman wall. The first pub had a variety of "Anchor" names and by 1800 was established as the "Hoy and Anchor". Not long after, it either collapsed into the sea, or was in imminent danger of so doing, like the church nearby, and a new site was purchased some way inland. Following the death of the Reverend Richard Morgan in 1804, the ancient vicarage south-west of the church was unoccupied. Despite its poor structural condition, by 1808 the licence of the "Hoy and Anchor" had been transferred to the vicarage pro tem. The vicarage did not become the inn but merely held the licence until the first part of the new inn was built. A local wit stated "it has now exchanged its inhabitants and the jolly landlord revelled with his noisy guests, where late the venerable Vicar smoked his solitary pipe". One source indicates that, on transfer, the house was re-named the "Sun" while the new house was being built. The "Gentleman's Magazine" of October 1809 informs us that the vicarage was no longer an inn, a new house having been built for that purpose some distance to the south of the church. This was the new "Hoy and Anchor", built by William Gurney; it retained its name until about 1838, by which time the pub is referred to as the "King Ethelbert". A Whitbread article indicates, however, that initially it was called the "Ethelbert Arms". Richard Morgan, who was mentioned earlier, led an interesting life and his career started at sea. He was the last parson to live in the old vicarage at Reculver and on his death he was buried by the towers and somewhat ironically the sea was to claim both his grave and last mortal remains. The original building is now the south-facing limb of the inn and at one time was called the Hoy and Anchor bar. In about 1870 a substantial block of coastguard buildings was erected within the fort. It may well be that the consequent additional trade led to the building of the west-facing arm of the building. The difference in the height of the roofs quite clearly indicates the two parts.

Records indicate that Henry Monger was the landlord of the old inn in 1803 and by 1809 it was in the hands of the Gurney family, with the builder of the house, William, registered as the landlord. He was followed by John Holman (a relative) from at least 1848 until 1882 when Walter Brewer took over.

An old deed of 1906 refers to the "King Ethelbert" formerly the "Hoy and Anchor" plus land called "Under Wall Marsh Field". Perhaps it was part of this land and sheds that were sold for £150 on 20th December 1939 to Herne Bay Urban District Council. On 12th February 1941 the tithe of £6/4/10 was redeemed. During the 1950's many improvements were carried out. These included, in 1953, extensions to the kitchen costing £500; a year later alterations to the bars and paving the rear cost £250; and finally in 1956 connecting drainage and alterations to the cellar amounted to £100. It was just as well that the bars were modernised, as a visitor from Mackeson in 1946 commented "Bars – all very old fashioned – including tenant! Mostly summer trade only". Numerous servicemen looked to the brewery trade for employment immediately after the war and in 1954 Wing Commander C.E. Mitchell was the landlord here as well as being a local councillor. He had a Roman vase on display in the saloon bar, and in addition a number of Roman coins of the Constantine and Antoninus Pius era – all of the items had been found in the vicinity of the house.

By the time of the late 1950's Reculver had developed as a holiday resort, mainly for Londoners, and a large caravan site had sprung up to provide the necessary accommodation. To take advantage of this additional seasonal demand, in 1960 a new summer bar was built to the side of the pub and an enterprising landlord created a mini-market to meet the needs of the holidaymakers. During the first part of the last century the inn was a favourite haunt of wildfowlers stalking widgeon, curlew and brent-geese.

The great storm of 1953 almost washed the pub away and a new sea wall was built enabling the house to re-open its doors once more. This really is a remote spot and well worth seeking out. The house stands in the shadow of the great Reculver Towers, a landmark for miles around. The towers fell into disrepair and were purchased in 1809 by Trinity House. They were rebuilt to act as a landmark for ships hugging the treacherous coast. Also due to its isolation the local beach was used to fine-tune the Barnes Wallis bouncing bombs which were used with devastating effect on the Ruhr Dam.

No sign has hung here for a long while.

No 19. Kings Arms, Sandwich
East Kent Brewery, Mackeson, Whitbread, Free House
Despite its reputation as one of the premier taverns in Sandwich, not a great deal has come to light about

the Kings Arms' history. The house was originally called the "Queens Arms" and the inn sign still depicts the Royal Arms of Elizabeth I. I am told that the name change occurred in 1687. The peculiar gargoyle or corbel, dated 1592, on the corner of the house had its "nose" removed during a collision with a large lorry that was trying to negotiate the bend.

The pub is housed in a fine jettied, timber building which probably dates back to early Tudor times. For a long period the "Kings Arms" was a coaching inn and it has always played a full part in the activities of this historic town. An old notice tells us that on 29th July 1846 Mr. Francis Crosoer and John Hicks were to sell by auction freehold estates, farms, lands, dwelling houses and cottages, in all 21 lots, at the "Kings Arms". Tenants found that this house provided a comfortable living and tended to serve for long periods. Mr. Horn, 1803-1828; Thomas Pearson, 1828-1847; the Wareham family, 1882-1913; and Arthur Elgar Ames, from 1924 until at least 1938, were all long-serving tenants.

Electricity was installed in 1932 at a cost of £21/10/6 and we see the redemption of the tithe, £9/1/-, on 3rd May 1939. The Tenterden Brewery Co. had acquired the freehold to the adjoining property, Invicta House, and in 1934 this was transferred to Mackeson.

The house offers accommodation and remains a popular rendezvous for both locals and tourists.

No 20. Kings Head, Shadoxhurst
Tenterden Brewery Co., Jude Hanbury, Mackeson, Whitbread, Shepherd Neame

A cursory glance would indicate just another village inn, of some antiquity, but nothing special. However, one needs to park and walk to the rear to find the most ancient part of the pub, which dates back to 1776. The additions to the front were carried out in 1840. The original village pub, standing close to the church, was called the "Green Man" and closed in the 1800's. A farmhouse with about 30 acres of land was then converted into the new hostelry. It was a registered small-holding and has a daton line – a trig point for map-making. On the door there is a crest which states "Militia Mea Muliplex" and displays the Whitbread hind and a dog, and a Toke sign indicates that it once formed part of a large estate. There are stables to the rear.

Landlords can be traced back to 1803 when John Mills was the tenant. He was still here in 1816. A most popular and long-serving fellow was Doug Royel who retired from the house in about 1995 after serving 42 years. At one time he bred horses on the smallholding and from time to time the pub had problems with gypsies camping on the land. Doug was a big man and had been a marine. Unfortunately he suffered greatly with a knee problem which he sustained by jumping from the deck of a destroyer on to the quay-side in Madagascar during the last war.

For a while the freehold was owned by the Tenterden Brewery Co. but on 25th March 1922 it was sold for £2,000 to Jude Hanbury. This was always quite a busy pub – 118 barrels of beer were sold in 1925. At that time the house was valued in the brewer's books at £2,000 and it was suggested that this be raised to £2,124. There are several outbuildings and at one time there was an army camp in the barn. The Captain of the Fleet, who was a King's Officer, lived in a large house nearby. In 1932, £13/7/- was spent on adding a window to the coach-house. On 27th June 1944 C.A. Naylor signed a tenancy agreement which contracted him to pay a rent of £20 p.a. plus £2 for the land. Major refurbishment work, costing £2,600, was carried out in 1954. The place was further extended in 1995. During the 1930's this house plus the "Rose and Crown", Old Romney, were mortgaged in the sum of £1,500. This was subsequently redeemed on 1st November 1956.

Shepherd Neame leased the premises from 6th May 1992 and purchased the freehold on 29th September 1995. For a short while a new "King" appeared on the inn sign – to me he appeared to be the brother of the "King" hanging at Wye – but public demand quickly restored the portrait of King George II. This is a comfortable house with a very fine restaurant.

No 21. Kings Head, Wateringbury
(See Series 1, No 30.)

Courtesy of the Kent Messenger Collection

Harvey James designed a new sign in 1951; as a result this house appears twice in the inn sign series.

No 22. Locomotive Inn, Ashford
Star Brewery, Wye, Mackeson, Whitbread, Fremlins

The "Locomotive", during the 1950's, was one of the most popular taverns in town. In those days Ashford had an important locomotive and carriage manufacturing industry which had been established in 1847. It was thus very much a railway town, with up to 3,000 people employed within the industry. The South

Eastern Railway Company's works had their own shops, school, bathhouse, pub, mechanics' institute and library, a social and educational club, and the company contributed towards the cost of a church. About 1,000 locomotives were built or rebuilt at the works. This pub was one of the closest to the works and at lunch-times great swarms of thirsty employees would descend on this and neighbouring pubs for refreshment.

The land on which the "Locomotive" stands was purchased by the South Eastern Railway Company on 22nd October 1846. They in turn sold 38 perches to John Maytum, an Ashford builder, on 29th September 1859. Maytum sold the "Locomotive" and cottages, 33 days later, to William Elliott Long Buss. On 11th October 1860 Buss leased the premises for a term of 999 years at a rent of £5 p.a. to Thomas Beaney

of the Star Brewery, Wye. On 5th February 1876 Thomas assigned the lease to John Allard Beaney, possibly his brother, but more likely his son. In any event it would appear that John overstretched himself, resulting in Beaney's Brewery at Wye being offered for sale by way of auction on 24th June 1879. The leasehold interest was assigned by John Beaney to Henry Bean Mackeson on 14th October 1879 for £1,300 plus legal costs of £28/13/6. The company purchased the freehold in 1964 for £200. The Star Brewery was destroyed by fire in 1898. Over the years improvements were carried out, including, in 1895, to "Vile – on account" in respect of building which cost £250. Electric light was installed in 1931 and a year later alterations to the bar, a new garage and conveniences were added costing, in total, £363/10/3. The quit rent of £1 was extinguished on 31st March 1935.

The earliest landlord that I have traced was Edward Quested who was the incumbent in 1866. By 1870 Daniel Rolfe was the tenant and during the 1950's F.E. Biggs was a popular mine host.

It is probable that in its early trading days this was a coaching inn. It stands on the junction of Beaver Road and Torrington Road – Lord Torrington was a director of the South Eastern Railway. At one time the pub's recreational facilities included a bowling alley and other activities enjoyed by the locals were such pub games as darts, dominoes and cribbage. During the 1950's there was a private bar for the use of two local shopkeepers, the Ealham brothers, and their friends. Alan and Mark Ealham, who both played exciting cricket for Kent, were related to the shopkeepers. Mark went on to represent England. This private bar was ultimately converted into the jug and bottle. The cellar runs the full length of the building.

Over the years the house has been extended to the rear where, in the 1950's, there was a narrow strip of land about five feet wide. There was then wooden stabling which has been converted into bed and breakfast accommodation in the form of five very pleasant double bedrooms. The new Ashford International station is but a short step up the road. The original three bars have been converted into one and this houses a fine collection of railway engine photographs, including one of the "Golden Arrow" which daily passed through the station on its journey to Paris. For a time during the 1990's the inn sign showed this train, but fortunately it has been replaced with the original, but certainly less streamlined, Stephenson's Rocket.

No 23. Lord Cornwallis, Tunbridge Wells
(Closed October 1988 and demolished August 1989) F. Leney, Whitbread, Fremlins

The "Lord Cornwallis" was a short-lived pub. It occupied the western part of the "Carlton Hotel" and it opened its doors during April 1937. Situated on the Eridge Road, it was a couple of minutes' walk from the Pantiles, on the edge of the common and just a minute away from the Southern Railway Station. It was the last pub in Kent before one crossed the border into Sussex.

It was named in honour of Captain the Right Honourable the Lord Cornwallis, MC, DL, JP, the then holder of the title and Lord Lieutenant of the County. He had served with distinction in the military, was a member of Kent County Council and had played for Kent County Cricket Team. He was also a director of rival brewers Fremlins. The family is better known in Suffolk and this is the only licensed house in Kent displaying the arms of the Cornwallis family.

A private gathering on the evening preceding the opening was attended by, amongst others, J.E. Martineau and John Marchant. The only wall decoration in the saloon was a bronze commemorative tablet with portraits of the patron and of the late Lord Cornwallis. There was a frieze in the bar, executed by Major V.H. Seymer, DSO, which showed the "Veritable Origin of the Tunbridge Wells Chalybeate Springs". Legend has it that Saint Dunstan, in his youth, was a skilled blacksmith and, being tempted by the devil in his own forge, seized Old Nick's nose with his red hot pincers and threw him through the roof. Nick's spring, coupled with the smith's impetus, resulted in a prodigious leap ended close to a stream on what is now the common. To alleviate his pain Nick bathed his nose in the cool water. Dunstan's pincers had left scales on Nick's nose and it is said that traces of iron in the waters are the result of this sequence of events. The properties of the waters were accidentally discovered in 1606 by Dudley Lord North and the rest is history – Tunbridge Wells became famous for its medicinal waters.

This was another house where a military man, Captain S.C.M. Sharpe, was the licensee for a while, but the best-remembered landlord was Mr. H.J. Pursey. He had been the tenant of the "George and Dragon", Speldhurst, for 13 years before moving into the town in 1945. Sadly, he was to die in harness in September 1952. He had been a member of the Queen's Yeoman of the Guard and been present at a number of historic state occasions, including the 1935 Jubilee celebrations, the Coronation of King George VI and the ceremony at St George's Chapel, Windsor, when Queen Elizabeth and the Duke of Edinburgh received the Order of the Garter. He had joined the Grenadier Guards in 1907 and served with distinction during the 1914-18 war, for which he was awarded the Belgian Croix de Guerre. Mr. Pursey was given an impressive farewell and amongst the numerous mourners were several representatives of the armed forces.

The inn attracted a good cross-section of the local community, but really this was the railwayman's pub. In common with the mining fraternity, there was a strict hierarchy within the industry – the engine drivers were the top of the heap and therefore had their own bar, whilst the "oily rags" had to make do with a separate room!

In April 1958 John Marchant and his guests celebrated the coming-of-age of the house. Lord Cornwallis recalled that he was pleased to allow the brewers to use the family arms and name and his only proviso had been that he and his family would be entitled to free drinks. He remembered the occasion when his son and friends had enjoyed this privilege after a hectic day's harvesting. As a result of this birthday party Whitbread re-issued the inn sign with more comprehensive background detail on the reverse. They were also overprinted in red on the reverse "1937-1958 Coming of Age re-issue". Only a few of these miniatures were issued and they are now very scarce. Advertisements placed by collectors can often be seen in publications such as the Kent Messenger offering to pay up to £400 for this rarity.

Unfortunately, the house stood in a part of town that was undergoing rapid re-development and, following closure, it was demolished in 1989 to make way for a car park at the recently-completed Sainsbury supermarket. By this time the nearby West station had also closed and the licence of the "Lord Cornwallis" was transferred to a new Beefeater pub which had sprung up where the station had once been. Appropriately, it was named the "Old West Station".

No 24. Man of Kent, St. Michaels, Tenterden
(Closed July 1998 and converted into a dried-flower business and bed and breakfast establishment)
Sharpe & Winch, F. Leney, Fremlins, Whitbread, Free House

This half-tiled house with its red pantile roof stands a mile or two from the town of Tenterden on a very dangerous bend in the road. Built in the late 17th century, it probably started life as a private farmhouse and it still retains an acre of land. Some time later a blacksmith's forge was incorporated and more recently it was converted into a public house. For a long while it was a simple beer house before acquiring a beer and wine licence in April 1936; a "full-on" licence was granted on 28th April 1950. At that time the net monopoly value of £750 was paid.

Little about this pub's history has come to light. At some time it came into the hands of Sharpe & Winch, the Cranbrook brewers, as, when Leney purchased the business in 1928, this was one of 13 houses included. It was in the hands of the Milton family for over 90 years. The licence was held by E.G. Milton prior to 1932 and his son, who had the same initials, took over on 15th November 1948. He was still in occupation at the end of 1960. In 1939 Mr. Milton Senior paid an annual rent of £20 plus £1 for electricity and £2 for the water closet. The brewers held a deposit of £25. During the war, on 15th September 1940, a Messerschmitt 109 was brought down close to the pub, but fortunately no damage was sustained. In May 1957 the brewers dedicated a small strip of land, 372 square yards, to Kent County Council for highway improvements. In return the council made good the drains and services and agreed to maintain the boundary fence.

Despite the poor visibility when approaching the house, it was popular with locals and visitors, particularly with families and coach parties going down to coastal towns such as Hastings. It was approximately half-way to the destination and a good spot for a little liquid refreshment. It was always busy during the summer months and ticked over in the winter. However, trade dwindled and the pub closed in June 1994. Some refurbishment took place; this included a new kitchen and an extension to the cellar, and it re-opened in June 1995. Nonetheless, trade was insufficient to provide a living and it closed for good in July 1998. The freehold of the now retail and residential property, re-named Forge House, was offered for sale in 2003 at a price of £435,000. It is now an Indian restaurant.

In 1948 this house had a similar sign to the Ashford pub of the same name, but this changed in 1951 to the Bishop Odo sign, which also hung at Crundale. Perhaps to avoid another double-sider the Bishop Odo sign appeared in this series together with the mounted figure from Crundale in series 5.

No 25. Mitre Tavern, Canterbury
*(Re-named **Canterbury Tales** in 1981)*
Ash & Co., Ash's East Kent Brewery, Jude Hanbury, Mackeson, Whitbread, Enterprise Inns

Sited close to Canterbury's great cathedral, the "Mitre" was a very appropriate name for this welcoming hostelry. It also stands opposite the town's Marlowe theatre and thus gains additional patronage from this source.

In the mid-1600's an inn of this name stood in the High Street but this closed in about 1760, at which time it was called the "Mitre and French Horn". The present house, a three-storey building, probably dates back to the middle of the 17th century. The site or dwelling is mentioned in the will, dated 21st June 1688, of Robert Sutton of Canterbury, gentleman. The house was rebuilt sometime between 1820 and 1840. At about this time it was in the ownership of James Warren, a watchmaker, and in 1846 it was sold to Charles Goodwin, who owned the Eagle Brewery in Longport. Thomas Mason held the licence until at least 1848. The house is mentioned in the licensing lists of 1845 and 1846. By 1861 it had passed to Peter Lyle Truefit of Sturry and Osmond Augustine Beer of Canterbury, brewers. On 31st December 1875 it was sold to Richard Moxon, but in-between there had been three other owners. On 24th October 1878 the partnership Moxon, Collard and Ash were operating the pub and they in turn sold the whole site to Ash's East Kent Brewery for £21,000 on 31st August 1920. Ash's were taken over on 25th July 1923 by Jude Hanbury.

On 24th April 1936 Jude Hanbury mortgaged the property in the sum of £750 to Mr. G.V. Miskin and his mortgage over the old "Long Reach Tavern" was redeemed. Miskin's mortgage over this house was repaid on 31st August 1956. Control passed to Mackeson, who purchased the cottage adjoining the pub, in December 1956 for £400.

The quietly-spoken Reg (Bill) Sladden ran the house for a period of 36 years from 1942 until he retired in October 1978. Prior to this he had worked for the East Kent Bus Company. It was his custom, each Christmas, to give the visiting Mackeson abroad cooper and the company directors a large box of Kentish apples. In those early days this was a busy place and it is interesting to note that, in 1946, it was frequented in the main by artisans, shoppers and traders. When Bill left, the pub closed. It remained empty until 1980 when it was purchased for £47,500 by an off-the-shelf company called Piphome Limited. The company directors were 12 local business men who were often referred to as the dirty dozen. They decided to acquire a public house when one of their number, on complaining to a local landlord about the quality of his beer, was told that if he felt he could do better to go and buy a pub of his own. This he did with spectacular results. Each director brought his own particular skills to the business, and it was at the time of the grand re-opening in December 1981 that the name was changed. Various local concerns and individuals contributed items of interest: contributors included Greenfields, the gunsmiths; Sladdens, the jewellers; and Derek Minter, the Isle of Man T.T. winner, who donated a signed photograph. There were also paintings hung, which depicted the 12 directors. Les Cook, formerly of the "Dolls House" in the Elham valley, was brought in to manage the house, and needless to say it was hugely popular. The company's annual general meetings were held in a different country each year. The pub was ultimately sold to a local business man, Mr. Blackman, in 1987. In 1988 ownership had passed to the Friends of Frobishers, a restaurant and wine bar company, which on-sold in 1989 to Steve Graham, who extended the premises into the next door cottage to form a restaurant.

It still provides good bar food and is a popular lunchtime meeting place. When I visited, one regular drinker still harked back to the good old days. He used to take his girl friend to the cinema opposite, now the Marlowe Theatre, and then pop over to the "Mitre" for a drink after the show. At that time the pub had a splendid bar, but the new one reminded him of a butcher's shop and it took him a long while to get used to the décor. He does, however, remain a very good customer. Regular features include morris dancing, quiz evenings, wine-tasting and jazz.

No 26. Mitre, Tonbridge
(Closed 1996 and demolished a short while afterwards) B. Baker, F. Leney, Fremlins, Whitbread, Free House

The "Mitre" was a solid, well-built property constructed in the mid-1800's standing some way from the town centre in Hadlow Road. Due to the various activities carried on here it is remembered with some affection by many Tonbridge residents.

The first landlord, who only remained for a year, was C. Jones (1864 to 1865). Like so many houses in this area, this was a B. Baker pub. In 1892 it was leased, together with the coach-house, stables, assembly room and premises, to Leney for £80 per annum. The freehold was purchased on 16th November 1905. On 7th April 1913 the stables were leased to J. Burgess and he operated a soda-water factory from the site. In September 1918 a Mr. Smith took over the factory, paying an annual rent of £25. At this time the house was described as the "Mitre Hotel". For a long time the assembly rooms, situated on the upper floor and accessed via an outside staircase, were called the "Oast Theatre" and were home to the Tonbridge Theatre and Arts Club. I met several locals who could still remember their excellent productions. This building fell into disrepair and the thespians then moved on to a new "Oast Theatre" located between Tonbridge and the village of Hildenborough. In October 1960 the Leney estate was acquired by Fremlins. This included the hall at the Mitre buildings, which was let to the landlord, A.S. Goodwin, at a weekly rent of 11/-.

Initially, for some reason, there was a very rapid turnover of tenants: nine served during the first 37 years of the pub's life. H. Dray then held the licence from 1902 until 1914. He was succeeded by various members of the Catt family (possibly related to the family of the same name at the nearby "Chequers" at Tudeley) who remained until 1938. Mr. Arthur William Catt, who had previously run a house in Lewisham, arrived in 1919 and died in harness on 16th July 1934. A.S. Goodwin signed a tenancy agreement on 9th August 1938 and remained until 1957. In 1939 he paid a rent of £50 for the pub plus £30 for the factory. The brewers held his deposit of £75 and the inventory was valued at £644/3/6. Besides the private and public bars, there was also a well-frequented jug and bottle.

Public houses have been called the "Mitre" since the 15th century and many such houses have ecclesiastical connections. However, this one is probably the exception to the rule, as it is said the name is a corruption of a much older name – The Martyr. Certainly this district, at one time, held many Royalist sympathisers, as witnessed by the presence of the Church of King Charles the Martyr just a short distance away.

The pub and the inn sign altered little over the years – the main difference being a change in the background colour. The pub sat on a good-sized plot and the remorseless demand for new housing and a steadily-dwindling customer base brought about the pub's inevitable demise. The house was demolished and the site is now occupied by a small housing development known as Mitre Court. One of these properties is virtually identical in design to the old pub.

"Vanquished in life his death by beauty made amends;
The passing of his breath won his defeated ends." Johnson, on Charles I.

No 27. Nevill Bull, Birling
Jude Hanbury, F. Leney, Fremlins, Whitbread

An inn has occupied this site for centuries but it was known to past generations as the "Bull". There is no doubt, however, that the new sign derived its name from the famous crest of the Nevill family, whose associations with Birling Manor and the surrounding area are well-documented. The re-naming was out of respect to Michael Nevill, grandson of William Nevill the 4th Earl of Abergavenny (who lived in the village from 1816, when he came as vicar, until his death in 1868). Michael Nevill was killed in action in 1943 whilst serving with the Scots Guards in North Africa. His two sons still live in the village. On 30th November 1951 Mrs. J.V. Balfour of Birling Place unveiled, on behalf of the family, the new inn sign which depicts the crest of the Nevills, Lords of Abergavenny. The opening ceremony, at which John Marchant was present, was interrupted by a tweedy woman complaining about the design of the new sign. Incidentally, the pub was about the only place in the village not owned by the Nevill family.

The "Bull" is first mentioned in 1628 with William Tanner the first recorded owner in 1647. By 1783 William Jupp was running the house and he was succeeded by Richard Higgins in 1789 who stayed until 1813 when William Jupp returned. The Kentish Gazette of 20th May 1814 tells us "A few days since, a gormandizer, for a trifling wager, exhibited what he was equal to, in performance at the "Bull" in Birling, by eating in half an hour, one hundred eggs, to the great astonishment of all present". The Jupp family controlled the house for many years. Ann Jupp took over in 1836 and remained until her death in 1845. By 1851 Frederick Capon was the landlord and he handed over in 1875 to Alfred Capon. Of his 16 children 11 were born on the premises.

A photograph of the inn taken in about 1880 shows a very different property to the one we see today. It was constructed of red brick (there are two brickfields in the parish), with a diaper pattern of blue headers. It probably dated from the 17th century and likely hid an earlier structure. This was probably the building acquired by Jude Hanbury in 1888: the brewers paid a deposit of £100 in that year with the balance, £2,900, paid in 1889. Shortly afterwards the pub was gutted by fire. A new "Bull" sprang up in 1892 when £350 was paid for "building on account" followed by completion of building costs, amounting to £1,016/4/7, in the following year. At the same time £700 was spent on purchasing two messuages and premises. These new premises were quite grand as, in 1903, a maintenance charge of £22/15/- covered the house, stables, carriage shed, water closet, gates and fences. The Mid Kent Water Company, in 1900, was paid £7/11/- for laying on a water supply.

At one time the "Bull" came with a large area of land which was farmed by the landlord. Over the years much of this land was sold. In August 1959 the cottage adjoining the pub was disposed of for £400 and in September 1963 land was sold for £2,870 with a further sale at a price of £3,250 four months later.

The pub was modernised in the early 1980's and remains a popular venue with a first-class restaurant.

No 28. Nottingham Castle, Westgate-on-Sea
Mackeson, Whitbread, Fremlins, Thorley Taverns

This was one of the larger Mackeson houses. It was situated in Beach Road close to the sea shore. Fifty years ago, with its ivy-clad original brickwork, it was an impressive building – it is now somewhat tarnished by being painted a creamy-yellow colour. During this era Thanet was a bustling and popular holiday area and the "Nottingham Castle" was a busy hotel with a wide range of beers that included Bass pale and Burton ales. There were ten bedrooms together with a comfortable billiards and coffee room.

The house is of no great age. It was listed in a local directory of 1874 but with no landlord mentioned. Mackeson acquired the property for £2,700, plus legal fees of £59/17/4, in 1920 from Mr. E.A. Mann. Could this be a branch of the Mann family that owned the nearby "Coach and Horses", Eastry? They then spent a further £600 on improvements. During 1924 the tithe, amounting to £4/11/3, was redeemed. Business boomed and to cater for this much rebuilding work, costing £450, was carried out in 1931 and a year later a new wing was added at a cost of £1,750. The original pub occupied the corner site.

On 25th June 1923 Mr. L.L. Jones signed a tenancy agreement and moved into the hotel. His daughter is still alive and when sorting out the old family papers came across a bundle of documents relating to her

father's purchase of the business. The previous tenant, Mr. G. Enderby may have paid rather too much by way of inventory – this resulted in a lengthy correspondence with the agents acting in the sale, C. Hebden Phillips & Son, of Franklyn House, 47 St. George's Place, Canterbury before a price of £2,000 was agreed. The agents, in confirming the trading figures, rather cryptically refer to a couple of items stating "it will be noticed there are two amounts showing very small profits, this is accounted for by something which need not be mentioned here". F.A. Braithwaite of 2 & 3 West Street, Finsbury Circus, prepared a statement of settlement, dated 25th June 1923, amounting to £1,368/18/10. During these negotiations Mr. Jones had enquired into the possibility of leasing the premises from Mackeson, but was told that this was not the brewer's normal practice. However, on 30th May 1932 they did lease the premises to him for a five-year term at a premium of £250 and an annual rent of £150. He also paid £100 towards rebuilding work. These were considerable sums in those days, so Jones must have been confident in his ability to manage the establishment. On Thursday 15th April 1926 he prepared the fourth-anniversary banquet for the Ancient Order of Druids, the "Queen of Thanet" Lodge No. 450. The meal consisted of thick tomato soup, filleted soles in roxiana sauce, either roast beef or pork and Christmas pudding or raspberry cream. An abroad cooper visiting the pub in 1945 described it as "the best kept house I have seen". Mr. Jones continued to run the hotel successfully until 1951 when he handed over to Thomas Joseph Shutler, who paid £481/17/- for the valuation.

During the First World War a sea-plane base was located at the end of the road and it is said that there was a tunnel linking the base to the pub which acted as a short cut and saved having to cross the road. The officers' mess of the Royal Naval Air Service (float sea-planes) was based in the "Nottingham Castle" and airmen were also billeted on the premises.

During the 1920's a much-loved resident, Dr. Summerskill, known as the "Shilling Doctor" because of the fee he charged per visit, lived close by at 7 Beach Rise. Whether or not he dropped into the hotel for a pint I know not, but his daughter, Edith, went on to become Minister of Health in Clement Attlee's Labour government formed immediately after the War.

In 1961 money was spent on eradicating dry rot and during 1962 and 1963 major alterations were carried out, which included creating Friar Tuck's Grill Room where one could enjoy a 9/- family luncheon on a Sunday, having sipped a sherry in the Maid Marion Bar.

This is an unusual name and, as to be expected, both explanations for it involve a ship called the "Nottingham Castle". The first is that this ship was wrecked on the nearby Goodwin Sands over a century ago, the other that a local seafaring man claimed to have sailed "all the seven seas" in the old "Nottingham Castle". It is appropriate that these naval connections continued until the end of the Great War.

No 29. Old House at Home, Edenbridge
(Re-named **Old Eden** in about 1984) B. Baker, F. Leney, Fremlins, Whitbread

This was the most westerly of the Whitbread inn sign houses, situated very close to the Surrey border. Probably for this reason it was omitted from the David Burley metal map – the only pub excluded in all five series.

The oldest part of the building dates back to the 15th century and the original property is best described as a smallish Kentish hall house. It was probably used as a farmhouse and over the years it would have seen many changes, including the replacement of the ancient stone cladding with Kentish clay tiles. Substantial additions were carried out in the 19th century, among which was the building of a cross wing. It was in about 1865 that the property was converted into a modest beer house with three cottages to the side.

Despite its great age, manuscript records date back to 1800 and no further. James Alexander of Edenbridge, timber merchant, at the time of his death in the early 1800's owned land and properties within the town. He left his assets in equal shares to his two sons, Thomas and John. Thomas bought his brother's inheritance and, at the time of his death in 1871, he was the sole owner. As was common in this era, the mortgage was obtained from individuals, not from a building society, as would be the norm to-day. The first description of the property was recorded in 1818 and is set out as follows:- "… All that messuage or tenement commonly called by the name of Heads then divided into six several tenements … On the east of the road from Westerham to Hartfield …". A similar description is found in another conveyance dated 1844. It is not until 1876, when the creditors of James, who had inherited the property on the death of his father Thomas in 1871, put all of the assets up for sale, that it is described as "… All that beer house and garden known as the "Old House at Home" situate at Edenbridge in the County of Kent with the two cottages outbuildings and gardens … occupation of Alfred Beer …".

The pub was bought by Benjamin Baker of Tonbridge, who in 1892 leased this house to Frederick Leney & Sons Limited at an annual rent of £25. Leney purchased the freehold on 16th November 1905. Only the "Hop Pole" at East Peckham commanded a lower annual rental, which gives some idea of how modest a property this was. During July 1928 £100 was spent on new cellars and lavatory accommodation.

The first landlord that I have traced was J. Draper in 1867 and he remained until at least the mid-1880's. Records are sketchy because it was no more than a beer house (it did not acquire a wine licence until 1937). A full licence was granted on 7th April 1949 when the net monopoly value of £725 was paid.

During 1960 Frederick Leney & Sons Limited sold their estate to Fremlins, and included within this sale were two cottages, 121 and 123 High Street. Both were let at a weekly rent of 17/1 – 121 to A. Warner and 123 to Mr. Horlock. A third cottage was purchased late in 1962 for £1,250. Later two of these cottages were incorporated into the pub and the third was demolished to make way for a car park. The following year £980 was spent on improving the facilities.

Standing close to the bridge that spanned the River Eden (hence the new name), the pub was prone to flooding, but over the years the flood defences have been considerably improved resulting in no major disasters since 1968. The pub was not to everyone's taste and during the 1990's a landlady moved here from the "Windmill" at Hollingbourne but found she could not settle and after a short while moved back. At the time both houses had been designated as Wayside Inns. On 5th March 1985 the pub became a Whitbread-managed house and at about that time the pub was again refurbished.

At Christmas 1959 the sign, along with eleven others, hung outside the Innovation Stores, Rue Neuve, Brussels, as part of the shop's seasonal display.

A couple of locals told me that they thought, for a while, the premises acted as the town "doss house". Perhaps this explains the jokey name and sign.

No 30. Palm Tree, Wingmore near Elham

Shepherd Neame, Mackeson, Whitbread, Free House following closure by Whitbread on 24th January 1975

The "Palm Tree" is said to date back to 1728 and was initially a farm dwelling. It was of pretty basic construction and over the years much renovation has taken place so that one finds today a building of very solid appearance. The first major refurbishment was carried out by Edward Jawell, a yeoman. In 1735 Edward leased the premises to Isaac Sweetlove, who was granted a licence to sell ales and cider. At that time the property was simply called the "Ayle House".

Time moved on and by 1749 records indicate that the inn was referred to as the "Whyte Hause", amended in 1763 to the "White Horse". During this period the inn relied for its custom upon local agricultural workers and a few travellers on the Canterbury to Folkestone road. In the late 18th century it is recorded that striking farm labourers marching upon Barham stopped here for refreshment.

There are smuggling connections aplenty and the pub is said to have been a haunt of the Ransley gang from Aldington. It was either used as a meeting place, (certainly the house is remote), or to celebrate a successful run. Ransley was convicted in 1827 and transported to Australia where he was subsequently joined by his wife and nine children. These events would have occurred whilst the house was in the ownership of Josiah Cressy, a seaman and victualler from Folkestone who purchased the property in 1806. He is credited with sailing to the South Seas with Captain Cook and, probably to remind him of those balmy days, he re-named the pub, in 1812, the "Palm Tree". Another explanation for the name is that thirsty navvies building the railway through the Elham valley saw it as an oasis of beer in a dry and parched landscape. I prefer the former explanation. Josiah remained until his death in 1845.

By the late 19th century ownership had passed to Charles Fagg. Shepherd Neame had been supplying the "Palm Tree" with beer since at least 1893 and this arrangement continued until one year into the Great War. It is likely this arrangement was under an "estate lease". A photograph showing the pub in its

Shepherd Neame days can be seen in the bar. Mackeson purchased the pub in 1920, paying £1,100 plus legal fees of £38/3/-. They created a tea-room and their initial outlay amounted to £342/18/7. An old inventory lists a kitchen cow and in the cellar was a milk maid's yoke. The animal was kept to provide for the family.

Typical of many rural pubs it came with three acres – the plot is now used as a caravan park and for parties, rallies, boot fairs and fetes – all useful sources of income. The place is also popular with walkers and cyclists using the picturesque Elham valley way. The pub boasts a roomy and comfortable restaurant, built in 1991, which incorporates a floodlit 90-foot well that makes an impressive focal point. The food is excellent, especially the grilled sardines.

The pub retains much of its old charm, and pinned to the timbered ceiling is a fine array of old and new banknotes, including one from the Falkland Islands.

Whitbread closed the pub for a brief period and it was then sold, with licence, in 1975. Since then the property has been renovated and considerably enlarged. The original inn sign still hangs.

No 31. Plough, Westfield
Smiths of Lamberhurst, Jude Hanbury, Mackeson, F. Leney, Fremlins, Whitbread, Fremlins, Shepherd Neame

We now cross the county border again into Sussex to visit the "Plough" which appears to have passed through more brewers than any other pub in all five series. We commence with Alan Simpson, the managing director of Smiths of Lamberhurst, who retired in September 1921, which event resulted in the assets of the company being sold. Jude Hanbury purchased this property at a price of £900. Mackeson then appear to have paid £2,750 for the pub plus all fixtures and fittings, completion taking place on 27th September 1926. Costs amounted to £51/10/6. Mackeson placed a value of £2,471/12/- on the property as at 30th September 1926. The following year repairs costing £250 were carried out and in 1929 electric light was installed at a cost of £21/10/-. Two years later £46 was spent on cesspool drainage and the following year £18/10/- was incurred on emptying it. This latter work may have been carried out in response to a neighbour suing the tenant at the "Plough" for contaminating his land. A lengthy court case ensued and the end result was that the tenant had to pay the substantial sum of £1,000 by way of compensation. This was in part funded by Mackeson. On 24th August 1934 the house passed to Leney, who agreed to pay £21,476 to acquire eight Mackeson properties including the "Plough" which was valued at £2,196. Leney carried out further drainage work in 1937, at a cost of £250, together with other property improvements and alterations.

In October 1960 Fremlins took over the flat at the "Plough" – the flat had been occupied by the landlord, E.A. Borg, rent-free. Also during the 1960's a series of land transactions was executed. On 19th March 1965 land was purchased for £1,200 and in January and May 1966 two plots of land were sold for £2,500 and £2,379. A further smaller sale took place in July 1968 at £325.

A long-serving landlord was E. Pierce. He signed a tenancy agreement on 19th June 1939 and remained until 27th August 1951 when he was succeeded by Roland Enoch Pierce, probably his son. Father was paying a rent of £40 when he took over and his inventory was valued at £136/14/-. The brewers held his deposit of £25.

The final change of ownership occurred on 6th May 1992 when Whitbread leased the premises to Shepherd Neame. They went on to purchase the freehold on 29th September 1995.

There are good restaurant facilities here and ample car parking.

No 32. Queen's Head, Canterbury
*(Reverted back to **Three Tuns** in 1981) George Beer and Rigden (as Leaseholders), Jude Hanbury, Mackeson, Whitbread, Trumans, Scottish and Newcastle, Spirit Group*

This ancient inn was built within the area of the old Roman amphitheatre and, as an inn, dates back to about 1600, although the property is older. At this time an iron cross called the "Tierncrouch" stood in the centre of the road junction. The house is situated on what was the old Watling Street. The inn sign is dedicated to Queen Bertha (562-606), wife of King Ethelbert, a brief history of whom can be found under the sign of "King Ethelbert".

In fact we have here one of the first pubs to change name. Initially the house was known as the "Three Tuns", changing to the "Queens Head" in about 1797, at which time the licence was held by John Clements. It reverted back to its original name in 1981.

The hotel, (it still offers accommodation), has played a very full part in the social life of the city. It is recorded that in 1679 the Prince and Princess of Orange stayed here, and on 26th September 1687 the Woollen Drapers Company held a meeting at the house of Mr. Will Hart at the sign of the "Three Tuns". The billeting list of 1693 listed the "Three Tuns" for twelve men. It is said that the hotel was the venue for illegal Cathedral masses at the time of the civil war.

We now move on to 1889, 1st of February to be precise, when George Pilcher of the "Queens Head" and George Beer & Co. of the Star Brewery, Canterbury signed a memorandum of agreement. Mr. Pilcher agreed, from time to time, limited to five days per week, for a period of one year from 6th February 1889 "to horse with good sound and suitable horses and turn out in a complete and proper manner with all necessary harness and other appliances the dog cart or other two wheel trap the property of the said George Beer & Co. for use by them or their travellers in the course of their business". He was to be paid £75 p.a. for this service by quarterly payments. The tenant further agreed that during this period he would purchase from George Beer wines, spirits, liqueurs and cordials to the value of £100. Unfortunately problems soon arose. On 20th December 1893 a dispute occurred concerning two broken kegs. The relationship then deteriorated, resulting in a letter from Mr. Pilcher dated 7th January 1894, stating that the contract expired on 7th February 1894 "… and that I shall not supply horses and traps after that date. I wish I had never let traps to your firm for if Biston (a traveller) has a horse for a day I am obliged to rest it for two days … Biston is not fit to drive a donkey much more horses like mine. He races them up and down and at the end of the day tethered them for an hour to cool down". I was unable to trace the brewer's reply. Mr. Pilcher obviously ran a thriving business, offering, in 1894, livery and bait stables, dog carts, pony carts, open and closed carriages and brakes for hire. Further troubles arose in the 1960's, when mention is made of rapid staff turnover. "They are again getting overwhelmed by the pace of work here. The cause is obvious:- he is too rude to staff, therefore they leave and he does the work".

George Beer & Rigden decided to dispose of the "Queens Head" by way of an auction held on 29th April 1926. Tomson and Wotton bid up to £6,500 but the hotel went to Jude Hanbury for the sum of £6,600. In November of that year they raised a mortgage over the premises in the sum of £3,000 at an interest rate of 5 1/2 %. In June 1933 the brewers re-negotiated all of their mortgage rates down to 5%. The only person to hold out held a mortgage over the "Queens Head" so this was redeemed three months later.

In the dining room there is a priest hole which drops down to the cellar, and it is rumoured that there are other tunnels in the pub.

The hotel suffered during the last war and was badly damaged during air raids in 1942.

No 33. Robin Hood, Upper Halling
*(Re-named **Pilgrims Rest** in 1991. Closed Christmas Eve 2001) F. Leney, Fremlins, Whitbread, Free House*

In days of old pilgrims would have crossed the River Medway at nearby Burham, en route to Canterbury, and would then have made their way to the old city passing close by this hostelry. The house in fact sits on the Pilgrims Way, and Pilgrims Road runs to the side of the pub. Although I never like a re-naming, at least the new name had some relevance.

This beer house, plus six cottages, was purchased by the three Leney brothers from Mrs. H. Mills and mortgagee on 25th October 1881 for £1,560. On 17th January 1896 Augustus Leney transferred his brewery estate to the limited company and the pub, plus six cottages, was valued

at £1,000. The agreement for sale was drawn up by Messrs. Godden, Son & Holme of 34 Old Jewry. By 1908 the rent charge was £40 p.a., of which the cottages accounted for £35.

This is another house that proved popular with landlords. T. Topley held the licence from at least 1859, when the pub was in private hands, until about 1867. The long reign of the unusually-named W.H. Ife commenced on 7th December 1926 and ended in approximately 1945. In 1939 he paid a rent of £20 p.a. plus £2 for the bath with his inventory valued at £107/1/-. Throughout this period the place operated as a simple beer house and it was not until 1947, when Lily Heath was landlady, that a spirit licence was obtained and on 20th April 1951 a full-on licence was granted. The net monopoly value of £500 was then paid.

The "Robin Hood" was built in about 1800, probably as a modest beer house selling ale, wine and port wine, mainly from the barrel. The place boasted a tap room, private bar and a small jug and bottle. The pub housed an oven, in which the landlord baked bread and pies, mainly for family consumption, but some were sold to customers. In the Leney days this was a smart house which displayed the company's name surrounded by green terracotta tiles. The pub was originally flanked by six cottages but now only two survive. In December 1922 three were sold for £65 to W.G. Brown. In addition to the purchase price he was also responsible for assuming liability under the sanitary inspector's order. In common with many small houses during the period between the two wars the pub was referred to as the "Shant".

In the early 1900's landlord Paris, as a side-line, ran a little cottage industry, to the rear of the premises, making chestnut fencing. From about 1900 until the outbreak of the Great War the Rat and Sparrow club met here. The locals took things one stage further than their counterparts at other hostelries as the sparrows were netted and then released at the rear of the pub to be shot by paying customers using muzzle loaded guns with percussion caps. Fortunately a fair number of birds made good their escape. At this time the beer was stored and served from the cellar. If very busy the landlord would bring up a flagon of ale. One can still see the steps, bowed from this constant use.

The pub housed a set of batteries and generated its own light using an old converted Morris Cowley engine that acted as a generator. The landlord at the time of the makeshift generator, about 1934, was Bill Ife, an ex-marine, who sported a large moustache. Bill ran a tight ship – there were bare boards and spittoons, which were black-headed, and the place was spotless. It was one of the first buildings in the village to have electricity installed.

Although the pub remained open during the war, both beer and cigarettes were in short supply and regulars often turned up to find the landlord had nothing to offer.

The fortunes of Upper Halling and this part of the Medway valley relied very much upon the cement, quarrying and paper industries, which at their peak employed thousands of workers. Reasonably well-paid, the workers had money to spare for luxuries and the local pubs did a roaring trade, particularly at lunchtimes – owing to the hard and thirsty work. The pubs were also supported by a smattering of agricultural workers. Before the spirit licence was granted, an elderly resident, who enjoyed his mild ale at 4d a pint in the 1930's, can remember the landlord, if he ran out of beer, cycling to the brewery at Wateringbury with an empty barrel and returning with a full one carried in a little cart.

During Gordon Smith's era, circa 1991, the pub underwent considerable renovation. It now consists of just one large bar and a small room for children to the rear. Before this work was carried out the bars only occupied the area up to the pillars; behind these was the landlord's accommodation. It was at this time that the name change occurred.

With the decline of the three major local industries and the introduction of modern labour-saving machinery, trade dwindled. When I called at lunchtime in 2001 I was the only customer. Shortly after my visit the pub closed during the day, opening in the evening and weekends only. It closed for good on Christmas Eve 2001 and was sold de-licensed. The freehold was offered for sale in July 2004 for £310,000.

The inn sign is credited as the work of M.C. Balston. However, on the death of Kathleen Claxton all of her design work was discovered, including the sign of the "Robin Hood", so it appears likely that the information on the reverse of the inn sign is incorrect.

The pub was always referred to as the "Robin".

No 34. Rose and Crown, Stone Street
*(Re-named **The Snail** in 1995) Green family, Jude Hanbury, F. Leney, Fremlins, Whitbread, Free House*

The Rose & Crown, Stone Street, Seal.

Sited in the rolling, heavily-wooded, West Kent countryside the "Rose and Crown" is the archetypal Kentish ale house. It is built partly of Kentish ragstone, and partly rendered, topped with a red Kentish-tile roof. The gardens were a special feature which brought forth articles and photographs in national magazines.

The building dates back to the early 1600's. It is a solid structure and I would surmise that originally it had farming connections. It was certainly a beer house in the early 19th century – James Hackets and two sureties held the licence in 1816. By the mid-1840's the pub was being run by the Green family with Ann Green, wife of Thomas Green, a farmer, in possession. The Greens were a well-established Stone Street family and one can still find Greens Cottages in the village. At this time the building was used as the village beer house, a farmhouse, and the village store.

This was one of the first properties bought by John Beale Jude in 1854 when he started as a brewer in Wateringbury. He purchased the house from John, Francis, William and Henry Green. The family connection remained, as William Green was the tenant in 1855, followed in 1859 by J. Ongley. Various deeds of the 1870's describe the property thus "… All that messuage or tenement formerly called Goosemarsh with the buildings and land … and for many years passed used as a public house called the "Rose and Crown" … at Stone Street, formerly in the occupation of Thomas Cooper afterwards of Joseph Buss since of Robert Barrington afterwards of George Hills since of Thomas Cooper afterwards of John Green then of Ann Green and then of William Green …". The rent in 1874 was £19/10/-.

The Moore family took up residence, possibly in 1891, but it was not until 22nd November 1893 that Edward Moore signed a tenancy agreement. He died from tuberculosis a year later on 8th September, aged 50. He was succeeded by his wife Catherine (Kate) who died at the pub on 5th April 1912. A note in the register indicates that Mrs. Moore got into some form of trouble, so the licence was transferred to her son James Henry in April 1908, although he did not become tenant until 17th April 1912. He remained until March 1934 and died three months later. A Mr. Stein, a member of the Zoological Society, rented a room on a long-term basis and he would give the Moore children pictures of lions and tigers. Twice a week he attended meetings in London. At this time the car park was a grass field where the chickens foraged. In the back field stood a massive mill-stone used for sharpening scythes and other farm implements.

During the early 1900's facilities were upgraded. In 1900 £8/17/6 was spent on repairs to the well and pump. Three years later the well was sunk three feet deeper and repairs to the curb and the supplying of well tackle cost £6/17/6. In 1906 piped water was laid on at a cost of £8/10/-, and in 1909 alterations and general repairs were undertaken for £119. A piece of land adjoining the pub was sold in 1922. That same year the tithe was redeemed as was the land tax in 1950.

On 10th December 1923 Leney made an offer of £6,000 for three of Judes' West Kent pubs, including the "Rose and Crown", on which they placed a value of £2,600. The other two were the "Green Man" at Hodsell Street and "Black Horse", Stansted. The directors said that they would accept £8,000, but would also include within the package the "Plough" at Trosley. Alterations were carried out in 1935 and architect's fees of £36 were incurred. Herbert Sutton was the tenant in 1939, paying a rent of £30 p.a. plus £2 for the bathroom. The brewers held his deposit of £25.

Many clubs and organisations used the premises, one of the most active being the renowned Rat and Sparrow club. During the War years 28,000 creatures were dispatched; they included rats, sparrows, wasps, jays, squirrels and many song-birds, indeed anything a farmer considered a pest. Exhibits would arrive in a brown paper bag. A new barmaid opened such a package which had been left by mistake on the counter and to her horror found it was full of rats' tails. At meetings the members would enjoy a meal – invariably steak and kidney pie. At one time the club records were maintained by the honorary secretary , B.G. Norris – I wonder if any of his relatives remain in the village. The pub was also the venue for the Volvo car club.

The inn was the favourite haunt of the squires of Ightham Moat and Ivy Hatch. Their staff would deliver them to the pub and either sneak away to a corner for a drink or return very much later to collect them.

During the 1950's this was a two-bar house with a little off-sales area that also acted as the village store. The pub was famous for its children's room where one could obtain crisps and coke, but it was necessary in winter to wear three coats to keep warm! With linoleum on the floor, the place could be icy cold. There was a billiard room on the first floor and the pub had a strong bar-billiards team.

The "Rose and Crown" always boasted a good restaurant and slowly the place moved away from being a traditional village pub. To reflect this change it was re-named the "Snail at Stone Street" and will probably remain so owing to the goodwill the fine restaurant facilities have built up.

Just as an aside, the Wilkinson family owned the nearby Frankfield Estate. On the death of Horace Wilkinson in December 1908 he decreed in his will that the embalmed head of Oliver Cromwell, which was in his possession, be returned to its proper resting place in Westminster Abbey. However, his wishes were not complied with and it was retained by the family. It was not until 25th March 1960 that it was returned and buried at Sydney Sussex College, Cambridge; Oliver Cromwell's alma mater.

No 35. Royal Oak, Gillingham
(Closed mid-1999) F. Leney, Fremlins, Whitbread

This town-centre pub stood within easy walking distance of the "Samuel Pepys" and the "Woodland Tavern" – only the latter, a few yards away, survives. The pub is named after a screw battleship launched in 1862 at Chatham. As late as 1900 the address is given as Green Street, New Brompton.

The original beer house, dating back to 1860, was quite small and occupied a corner site. Over the years it expanded into the adjacent cottages. Leney rented the premises from George Maplesden of King Street, Rochester who had purchased the house in 1880. The initial term was for 30 years but this was extended to 40 years to expire on 24th June 1928. The annual rent was £45 payable quarterly. The freehold was purchased for £1,870 in 1904. The original letting included a garage and cottage and, as recently as 1929, the rent for these was more than that for the pub.

John Whitehurst was the tenant in 1866 and is described as a beer seller. The house played an active part in the social life of the area as is witnessed by the following events. In 1871, at a bagatelle match which attracted a good crowd, the favourite, Mr. Wooley, of Old Brompton, was soundly beaten by Mr. Boucher, of New Brompton, by 87 points. On Christmas Eve 1873, the police were called to the premises but were refused entry. Henry Rule was named on the licence but the house had been kept for some time by John Hughes, who stated that he had not seen the defendant since the summons was served. The case was dismissed. In January 1887 an inquest was held at the "Royal Oak" on Amelia Ann King, aged 66, who died from injuries received after falling down stairs. A verdict of accidental death was recorded. The death of Mr. T. Blake, licensee for 12 years, was reported in 1906. A naval man, he is credited with having fashioned the coffin in which the remains of Dr. Livingstone had been brought back to England.

An interesting court case arose in 1920 when the landlord of 16 years, Charles Cokayne, was charged with selling in the public bar one pint of bitter at 8d per pint instead of 7d and failing to exhibit a price list. Defendant pleaded "not guilty" to the first offence, but "guilty" to the second. Part of his defence was that at least half of the bitter had to be removed from the premises for analysis and the drink was sold at 8.15p.m. Apparently it was illegal to buy beer to take off the premises after 8p.m. and therefore there was no case to answer. The magistrate over-ruled this point and Charles was fined £2 and £1 respectively and paid £2/2/- costs. There are a couple of coincidences here. Prosecuting council was Mr. F.C. Boucher – could this have been the underdog who won the bagatelle match? The second is that on purchasing the unlicensed premises from Leney in 1960, Fremlins also acquired Royal Oak Cottage, 44 Canterbury Street, which was let at a weekly rent of 16/10 to Mrs. C. Cokayne. Could she have been the widow of Charles?

The licence was held by G.L. Cooke for a ten-year period from April 1936 and by 1939 he was paying a rent of £75 – the cottage was let separately. During 1937 building works were carried out at a cost of £750, and that same year, in April, a beer and wine licence was obtained. A full-on licence was granted on 7th April 1949, at which time the net monopoly value of £1,500 was paid. In common with many Leney properties, the tithe at the "Royal Oak" was not redeemed until 1944.

This was always a busy house but over the years trade declined and this, coupled with structural defects in the property, led to closure. The house stood empty for a while and has recently opened as a kebab house.

No 36. Royal Oak, Newingreen
(Closed in 2000) Mackeson, Whitbread

Mackeson purchased this substantial property from George Hardy and others for £2,100 plus costs of £48/6/- on 2nd December 1885. However, it would appear that John Friend, who sold his brewery business to Mackeson in 1801, was trading with this house as, on 19th October 1801, he supplied the landlord, John Gilbert, with two butts of beer costing £12/15/3.

The original building is said to date back to 1560, but I would suggest the early 1600's, with numerous modifications taking place during the reign of George III. The property was initially built as a farm building and drover's cottage and the first owner was Thomas Finche of Canterbury. The house then passed through several hands until, in 1775, it was purchased by Caleb Buss, a farmer and brewer of Hythe. Three years later Buss obtained a licence to sell ales and cider. The Buss family ran the house for many years and

we are told that Thomas Buss registered the name of the "Royal Oak" in 1797.

A long-serving landlord was Thomas Divers who arrived in 1873 and remained until his death in 1902. He also carried on his original trade as a coal merchant. On his death his widow, Jane, ran the house for a short while.

The "Royal Oak" was destined to become the first American-style motel in this country. An enterprising Canadian, either George or Graham Lyon, had noticed that this country had nothing to offer the motorised traveller who required a cheap and cheerful place to stay overnight. Thus was the concept born. For a period of 21 years from 29th September 1953, at an annual rent of £200, he leased from the brewers 7.87 acres of land on which were built log cabins. Two months later, by way of mortgage over the premises, the brewers advanced Lyon £4,000. This must have been one of the shortest mortgages on record as it was repaid on 2nd October 1954. The motel opened in June 1953 initially during the months of March to October. It could accommodate up to 50 people in 27 units and there was an 80-seat restaurant. The suites were grouped in three wings with each unit having a private bathroom and lock-up garage – some had a separate sitting room. Charges ranged from 21/- to 27/6d per person per night. Much capital expenditure was involved, including £3,200 spent on internal alterations, lavatories and a new kitchen during 1953. Further substantial improvements were carried out in 1966 at a cost of £4,345/9/-.

This house was sold off by Whitbread in the 1980's but was taken over again in the early 1990's.

Business boomed, but an establishment such as this had to be regularly updated and the associated costs as well as falling trade caused by severe competition led to the inevitable. When it closed in 2000 it was hoped to preserve the motel units, but these had been built using asbestos and the walls were packed with straw so they had to be demolished. The place remained empty for a long while before the motel area was developed into most futuristic office accommodation housing a company called Holiday Extras which must employ about 200 people. Anyone who has booked such services as airport car-parking will probably have been routed through the former "Royal Oak". The pub itself now houses Oak Creative.

There were several changes of inn sign but, to my amazement, in January 1999 the original had again appeared. On making enquiries I was told it had been found in the backyard, the manager quite liked it, and decided it should be re-hung.

No 37. Shakespeare, Sittingbourne
(Re-named the Pied Piper in 1974 and the Shire in 1982) F. Leney, Fremlins, Whitbread

This is a large house abutting the A2 on the eastern edge of the town. Sittingbourne has seen more redevelopment over the years than most towns of its size and of the six inn sign pubs in the area, this pub is the sole survivor.

The building dates back to about 1860 but little is known of its history. The first reference that I found relates to 1874 when Francis Bower was the landlord. Initially Leney rented the premises from Mrs. Black. The first lease expired on 24th June 1895 – the annual rental had been £115 payable quarterly. However, this was re-negotiated on 9th May 1891 for a 21-year term ending on 25th March 1912, at an increased rent of £140. Leney purchased the freehold at about the turn of the century and in 1921 the hotel was valued at £4,250 – a considerable sum. Hot water was installed during July 1928 at a cost of £30.

Situated as it was, on the main road to the coast, it was a good stopping-off point for the numerous coach parties pouring out of the capital. In the house advertisements for 1938 it offered a "Room quite apart from the main building for coach drivers". At that time the landlord was Herbert A.B. Spooner who had previously managed the "Plough" at Westfield.

S.J. Sidders took over on 29th April 1940, paying a rent of £30 and providing the brewers with a deposit of £200. However, the rent was suspended during the operation of the supplemental agreement. The brewers also agreed to pay the rates and licences etc., and Sidders paid slightly more for his beer.

On 26th June 1972 the pub became a Whitbread-managed house and a couple of years later the name changed to the "Pied Piper". During March 1982 considerable renovation work was carried out costing £26,000 and the house was then renamed the "Shire". Latterly it has been restyled as a theme pub. From then on name changes came thick and fast. In addition to the above it has also be known as "Hotspots" but now appears to have reverted to the "Shire".

No 38. Ship Hotel, Dymchurch
John Friend, Mackeson, Whitbread

This ancient hotel, (there is a title deed dated 1618,) was one of eleven houses owned by the Hythe brewer John Friend. On Monday 19th October 1801 John sold his business to William and Henry Mackeson, late of Deal. The purchase price was 28 times the annual rental of £68, i.e. £1,904, yet the property was insured

with Royal Exchange for just £350. This was the most prestigious of all the Friend houses – the "King's Head" in Hythe commanded a rental of only £14. The hotel came with 22 acres of land. At the time the landlord was Mr. Beck and during December 1801 and January 1802 he took supplies of two butts and a small firkin at a price of £13/5/- and £13/13/- respectively – obviously inflation was a problem even in those far-off days. In November 1802 he paid his rent of £70/10/-. William Mackeson died on 10th June 1821 when the house was valued at £1,500, dwarfing the value of £200 placed on the "Shepherd and Crook".

A bold building facing the sea, the hotel had strong smuggling connections – an activity carried out by gangs on a vast scale, supported in general by the majority of the locals. The cargo usually consisted of brandy and wool. During some renovation work a secret hiding-place was found in the chimney breast that still contained a store of smuggled spirits. Standing nearby is the "New Hall", rebuilt in Elizabethan times, where the lords, bailiffs and jurats of Romney Marsh met annually for the Grand Lath on the Thursday after Whit Sunday. After their business had been transacted they would adjourn to the "Ship" for their annual luncheon. Many a lord was well acquainted with the activities of the "free traders". The pub has low beamed ceilings and walls with secret stairs and cupboards and naturally there are strong connections with the Dr. Syn stories.

The hotel was used for a variety of functions and on Monday 12th September 1842 an auction was held here by Messrs. Whites and Goulden at 12 o'clock precisely for "37 acres of valuable fresh marshland at Burmarsh now in the occupation of Mr. Hammerden Major".

John Stokes was the tenant during the 1850's and from the 1890's until 1905 Frederick R. Binskin was behind the bar. An inscription written with a diamond ring on a window reads "My friend Binskin likes a drop of whisky and hare soup".

In 1921 the place was extended at a cost of £1,178/0/10 and in 1925 an amusement hall was erected – the tenant agreed to pay 5% interest on the capital outlay of £710/5/2. The hall became known as the "Bowery" and the adjacent land was used by campers, who provided custom for the pub. Dances were frequently held on the premises. Land at the rear of the hall was sold for £850 in April 1961 with outline planning permission for the erection of four houses. Redemption of the quit rent of £3/2/- occurred in 1929 and the tithe of £16/5/3 was redeemed on 6th March 1942. 1955 saw the upgrading of the lighting system and hot and cold water was supplied to the bedrooms at a cost of £250.

A much-loved landlady, Mrs. Dorothy Saunders, retired on 11th February 1965 having taken up the tenancy in 1927. She was the lady who handed out the inn sign miniatures. The following year extensive renovation work was carried out at a cost of £4,267. This included a new kitchen and a dining room that could seat 30 customers. The brewer's contribution towards the installation of the "Call Order" system amounted to £346/7/-. Finally £31/10/- was spent on refreshments on launching these new facilities and £20/12/6 on photography.

In its new form the hotel offered accommodation with central heating throughout. Terms were bed and breakfast 32/6; full board 42/6 – the minimum stay was three days. The hotel was now under the personal supervision of Mr. and Mrs. T.J.A. Burden who were renowned for their excellent grilled Scotch beef and steaks. The hotel continues to flourish.

"Every ship is a romantic object, except the one we sail in." Emerson.

No 39. South Eastern, Tonbridge
(Re-named **Station House** in 2000) B. Baker, F. Leney, Fremlins, Whitbread

Without a doubt one could state that the "South Eastern Hotel" (as it was known in its early days) is the house that the Breeze family built. The first traceable landlord was Henry Backhurst back in 1874 and he was succeeded by Luther Breeze senior in 1878. Luther was elected a town councillor in 1897 and served continuously until 1918 when he ceased his membership for a while before being re-elected in 1921. He was to serve behind the bar for a period of 41 years but in his later days he was assisted by his wife and son, Luther junior. He died in November 1926. He had passed the licence to his brother George Henry in 1919, as he had returned home after a spell at the "Angel", Strood. George passed away in April 1925. The licence then passed to his widow, Rachel, who managed the house for a short while before handing over to their son, George Reynolds Breeze on 29th November 1927. His reign lasted for 30 years, with a short break from 10th March 1942 until 14th August 1945 whilst he was away on war service. During this period the hotel was run by his wife, Alice Dorothy. In 1939 he paid an annual rent of £70 plus £2 for the ladies' water closet. The brewers held his deposit of £100. This was the usual practice of the brewery in respect of all houses as a guarantee for debts.

So, what of the pub's history? The property stands on a plot which, along with other land that originally belonged to Elizabeth Banes, was acquired after her death in 1738. The whole was purchased in two lots by Benjamin Andrews, who in turn sold it in 1770 to William Vinten. However, in 1804 Vinten sold part of the garden to John Snelling. On the land which was situated next to the turnpike gate at the lower end of the town Snelling built seven cottages in a row. In 1865 Benjamin Baker, a brewer in Tonbridge, bought the four cottages nearest the road and built the pub in their place, and as the remaining three cottages became available he bought them to incorporate into the pub. The Vinten family had meanwhile retained ownership of the area fronting the High Street to the east of the premises, but in 1882 Benjamin also bought this and, after demolishing the two houses, extended the pub to its present size. Benjamin Baker then leased the premises to Frederick Leney & Sons Limited in 1892 for £70 p.a. and they went on to purchase the freehold on 16th November 1905.

During the 1920's and 1930's this was the favourite watering-hole for the local railway workers. Also many members of the armed services will remember drinking here during the war years. For a long while it was a popular house and when I called one winter evening it was very busy. Customers were playing pool and other bar games and I spent a little while listening to a sprightly old lady telling me about the good times she had enjoyed during the hop-picking season at the "Merry Boys". This era was obviously a memorable part of her long life. However, the place went downhill and, on a subsequent visit, I found it quite intimidating. Shortly after this the pub was spruced up and, in 2000, the pub was re-named "Station House".

There is no longer a pub called the "South Eastern" in Kent.

No 40. Sugar Loaves, Hollingbourne
F. Leney, Fremlins, Whitbread

The "Sugar Loaves" stands just a couple of hundred yards from the "Windmill" in the pretty hamlet of Eyhorne Street, but the two pubs are very different. The "Windmill" is a "Wayside Inn" with very popular restaurant facilities, whereas the "Sugar Loaves" is the friendly village local. Nonetheless it also serves very good food.

As to be expected it sits comfortably in its surroundings and dates back a very long time. The property was built in the early 18th century probably as a beer house, as Mary Rumfield was the landlady in 1720. By 1753 another lady, in the form of Sarah Symonds, had taken over and in the early 1800's Thomas Smith was the landlord. He was still here in 1816 and at this time the pub was called the "Three Sugar Loaves". In 1855 John Farmer, who probably succeeded his father, Richard, was the tenant and he remained for about 15 years. During his tenure the name changed to the "Sugar Loaf" and then "Sugar Loaves". I am told that during the 1930's it was called the "Sugar Loaves and Railway Inn". Certainly there is an alley-way nearby that runs down to the village railway station. During this period it acted as a small hotel, with accommodation to the side, but in the late 1930's the building was split up. By the 1940's the house was simply known as the "Sugar Loaves".

The pub was the venue for village societies and sporting clubs and late in the 18th century the churchwardens met here. An advertisement in the local press of 1860 informs us that the dean and chapter held their manorial court baron and court leet here. On these occasions tenants were expected to come and pay their quit rents. The "Sugar Loaves" was also the meeting place for the United Men of Kent Benefit Society, and in 1901 over a hundred members, who were still paying into the society, sat down to a meal provided by the landlord, Mr. Peerless. The food was followed by music, entertainment and dancing. Richard Thomas owned the property in 1850 and when his son, Richard, married, he provided a great dinner for all his father's tenants, entertaining over 40 people at the pub.

Frederick Leney and his two sons purchased the property plus the stables and gardens for £950 from I. Charsley and others on 1st July 1878. In 1881 they placed a value of £970 on the property – this figure was subsequently reduced to £950 in 1890. The quarterly rent was £10.

With plenty of local competition, pubs of this type depend for their survival on the capability of the landlord. In recent times it has been threatened with closure but at the moment it is in very safe hands.

No 41. Swan Inn, Wickhambreaux
*(Re-named the **Hooden Horse** on 21st July 1956. Closed in January 1979)*
Gardener & Co., Mackeson, Whitbread

The original "Swan", a thatched cottage serving one of the prettiest villages in the whole of Kent, was destroyed by fire in 1880. It is first mentioned in the will of Edward Spickett West, dated 31st December 1862, in which he left his assets to his wife, Jane, and on her death to their son, who shared the same initials as his father. Included in his estate was the "Swan" beer house at Wickhambreaux, let at £28 p.a. on lease to Gardener & Co. for 21 years expiring 6th January 1903. The licensee was responsible for all repairs. The place was valued at £800. This would have been the new property erected on the same site as the cottage. It would appear that Mackeson acquired the leasehold interest in 1899, when they paid £22 for the proportion of premium for the lease of 21 years to 6th January 1903. They installed a new cellar in 1903 at a cost of £25.

In July 1923 Mr. West decided to dispose of the pub, advising Mackeson that he would settle for £1,500. The brewers decided to make an offer of £1,400, but would pay the asking price if this proved necessary. They ultimately agreed to the asking price, paying a deposit of £150 followed by the balance of £1,350 on 1st November 1923. Costs amounted to £44/12/3. A valuation had been carried out, prior to purchase, on 3rd October 1923 when the pub was described thus:- "There was a tap room two cellars and upstairs three bedrooms and club or dance room, yard with a corrugated iron stable. Water is from a well and is raised by pump. Small quit rent of 1/- or 2/- a year is paid to Manor of Wingham of which the Marquis Conyham is the Lord. The pub was valued at £1,200". Shortly after purchase the brewers arranged a mortgage over this property and the "Chequers" at Biddenden with Messrs. R.H. Green and C.E. Mumford to secure £1,950. On 21st June 1932 the mortgage was transferred to R.H. Green and Arthur Penn. 1930 saw the redemption of the tithe which amounted to £3/13/4, and on 31st March 1936 the quit rent of £4/5/- was extinguished. The house is included in the Coal Holding Register as it sits above a coal mine. The West family were coal merchants and it is likely that early tenants carried on the trade.

During 1945 the "Swan" was visited by an abroad cooper from Mackeson at Hythe, who commented "All beers drawn from the wood. On the day of my visit the landlord missed the delivery man and ran out of beer. Entrance to cellar for delivery of casks is through the bar".

For such a modest property, quite large sums were spent on the place. It did not acquire a full-on licence until 23rd April 1951 when the net monopoly value of £550 was paid. The bars were altered in 1953 at a cost of £200 and in 1955 kitchen alterations and the installation of an upstairs toilet cost £300. In 1963 the "Swan" was selling mild ale for 1/4 a pint, bitter ale at 1/6 and tankard for 2/3.

For very many years the pub had been associated with morris dancing. On the first Saturday evening in September the morris men, with their hooden horse, would dance in front of the inn as a finale to the "Blessing of the Hops" ceremony. The procession commenced in the morning at Canterbury Cathedral and then wound round the villages. When it was decided to re-name the pub, the "Hooden Horse" was a natural alternative. The new sign was designed by Tony Gosby and was unveiled on 21st July 1956 by Sir Stephen Tallents.

Trade held up well for a while but gradually the house went into slow decline. By this time the pub was in Whitbread's hands and they also owned the other local, the "Rose", which was situated only a few yards away on the village green. The "Rose" was very dilapidated and closed in 1977 for a refurbishment that lasted 18 months. The "Rose" appealed to tourists and coach parties whilst the "Swan" was the villagers' pub – a spit and sawdust place with linoleum floors. It is likely that James Frederick Gowers was the last true landlord, for on 27th April 1977 a manager was appointed, and the rest is history.

It was intended to sell the old place by way of auction but before this could be arranged a private buyer came forward to purchase what is, after all, a very desirable residence. The house was sold on 25th September 1979 and is now called Hooden Horse House.

In July 2004 £425,000 was being asked for the freehold.

No 42. Three Chimneys, Biddenden
Sharpe & Winch, F. Leney, Fremlins, Whitbread, Free House

On Thursday 22nd June 1893 at the "Star Hotel", Maidstone at 3 o'clock in the afternoon Messrs. Day & Son auctioned several freehold properties, one of which was the "Three Chimneys" beer house. Almost certainly it was purchased by Sharpe & Winch, the Cranbrook brewers, for when Frederick Leney & Sons Limited acquired this firm in 1928 the "Three Chimneys" formed part of the estate.

The pub is housed in a gracious old building said to date back to 1420. The inn sign miniature tells us that the house was so-named because, during the Napoleonic wars, French officers were imprisoned at nearby Sissinghurst Castle and whilst they were allowed the freedom to exercise they could walk no further than this spot – the intersection of three small lanes. The officers referred to the area as the "trois chemins", which the locals corrupted to Three Chimneys. This may be so but it has to be said that very old local maps, which pre-date this era, refer to the area as Three Chimneys. One of these small tracks leads to Bettenham Wood where, in 1667, twelve victims of the plague were buried. To this day the pub is still relatively isolated and in recent times the brewers paid £1/5/- to M.P. Savill to erect a sign-post on his land, abutting the main road, to advertise its whereabouts.

George Sivyer was the landlord in 1884 when the pub was on the Sharpe's mailing list. In November 1887 the inquest into the death of Thomas Moore was held here. This unfortunate gentleman left the pub late at night and walked straight into the pond opposite and drowned. A drinker, on leaving the house, heard a gurgling noise, realised what had happened, and raised the alarm, but sadly too late. The pond was dragged six times with grab hooks before the body was recovered. It was agreed that to prevent such an unfortunate accident in the future the pond would be fenced off.

Despite its present popularity, for much of its long life the pub was nothing more than a simple beer house serving the local agricultural workers. Wages were low and this was reflected in the December 1934 slate club pay out of £1/3/11 to each of the 68 members. J.J. Hunt was the tenant in 1939, and paid an annual rent of £20 with a modest deposit of £25. His inventory was valued at £40/10/-. A wine licence was acquired in 1947. During 1951 the brewers accepted the sum of £160 in respect of the loss of development value on land to the rear of the inn.

During a brewery consolidation Whitbread decided to dispose of this outlet and on 25th May 1976 it was sold to Mr. Carter, the tenant. Over the years the original building has been tastefully extended and it is now a traditional country pub with an excellent restaurant which draws customers from all over the county. The original sign still hangs.

No 43. Two Bells, Folkestone
Ash & Co., Jude Hanbury, Mackeson, Whitbread

The "Two Bells" was built in 1828 in open countryside to attract custom from those using the Folkestone to Canterbury road. It consisted of a dwelling-house, stables, outbuildings, garden and land in the ownership of Elizabeth Selden, who had inherited, in 1830, from her husband John, a Folkestone auctioneer. She then sold it to Mr. Claringbould, a millwright, who in turn disposed of it in 1833 to Jacob Fagg, a tea dealer. He is listed as landlord from 1841 until his death in 1855, at which time his widow sold to James and William Walker, brewers of Dover. They were the forerunners of Alfred Leney & Co. Limited. They improved the property, obtained a full licence, and then leased it to William White, who is credited with naming the pub the "Two Bells" after the naval custom of ringing a bell every half hour during a watch. A schedule of the assets of Thomas and George Ash dated 1870 lists this house, stating that it was purchased from Spicer "with cottages". The tenant from 1863 until 1871 was Lewis Furminger who paid a rent of £9/10/- plus 6/- for insurance. He proved to be something of a problem and in April 1871 was fined £1 plus 11/- costs for keeping the house open during illegal hours and was asked to leave the premises. He was succeeded by Charles Sinden who, on the death in March 1875 of Thomas Ash, was paying the same rent as Mr. Furminger plus £9/15/- for the cottages adjoining. In March 1931 these cottages were acquired by the Tenterden Brewery Co. following an exchange of assets with Jude Hanbury. The pub was damaged during the war and in June 1961 the brewers entered into a deed of exchange with Folkestone Borough Council whereby the war-damaged site of the nearby "Wheatsheaf" was exchanged for the sites of 4 and 6 Bridge Street, adjoining the pub, plus a payment of £15. 1955 saw a major redevelopment here with alterations and additions costing £3,500.

In 1941 Violet Rutter designed the inn sign, engraving on the two bells "Corfu". This led to speculation as to why this ship had been selected, but the simple answer is that the commanding officer of this armed merchant cruiser had been Lieutenant Commander N.C.M. Findlay – managing director of Mackeson. It was simply nostalgia. The ship had been built in 1930 as a P&O cruise ship and in 1939 it was requisitioned for war service. At the end of the war it was returned to P&O and was ultimately broken up in 1961. Later the name Corfu was replaced by SS Mohegan, but why the change? As far as I can ascertain the Mohegan sank in 1898 after being wrecked on The Manacles rocks off the Cornish coast with the loss of over a 100 lives. Many bodies were never recovered but there were 45 survivors. Divers reported that they received electric shocks when approaching the vessel and it was also said that it gave off a low moaning noise. The wreck is of some historical importance but it would be interesting to learn why its name is commemorated here.

Over the years the house has had a succession of first-class landlords but of late there have been frequent changes. In 1984 the licensee was Ron Mercer. He suffered from heart problems and decided, in an endeavour to raise funds for the British Heart Foundation, to have painted, by local artist Ken Fisher, a huge mural at the back of the house detailing people and events associated with the town. The mural was named "Heart of Folkestone" and was unveiled on 31st August 1984 in the presence of the Mayor of Folkestone. Over £80 was raised for the charity. Unfortunately it was subsequently covered with white-wash.

The "Two Bells" remains a busy, two-bar house serving a mainly artisan area of town. It boasts well-respected pool, darts and football teams.

No 44. Vauxhall Tavern, Canterbury
*(Formerly known as the **Halfway House**. Closed June 2,000 now a Burger King Restaurant)*
Ash & Co., Jude Hanbury, Mackeson, Whitbread, Inn Business

The present house was built in 1861 but it stands on the site of a much older inn.

Matthew Martin of Canterbury, Edward Pillow of Harbledown and William Sutton of Boughton Corner were the named devisees in the will of William Newport. William drew up the will on 25th February 1870 and died shortly afterwards. On 8th April 1871, the three devisees conveyed the "Vauxhall", together with outbuildings and garden ground to Thomas Ash for a consideration of £530. The abstract of title of the same date tells us that the pub was situate at Vauxhall in the parish of Northgate. The pub was in the occupation of Edward Vincer, who had acquired the licence in 1859. Since 1855 he had been the landlord at the "Royal Dragoon" just down the road. The "Halfway House" dated back to at least 1769. In November 1899 a parcel of land was sold for £10 for an intended new road.

The "Vauxhall" stands on the site of the 18th century Vauxhall Gardens which were modelled on the famous pleasure gardens of the same name in London. The first Lord of the Manor of the London gardens was Baron (and Bandit) Falkes de Breaute of Faux Hall – now Vauxhall – whose arms are reproduced on the inn sign. In 1949 the landlord of the nearby "Waterloo Tavern" had in his possession a ticket for the Vauxhall Gardens. It was dated Thursday 16th August 1753, was numbered 432 and cost 1/-. Perhaps due to its proximity to the gardens the customers here would hold "Hoods and Bissets" shows. I understand these were flowers, something akin to a carnation, which had wavy lines on the petals.

Situated on the eastern edge of the city on the main road to Margate, the tavern was a popular stopping-off point for coaches heading for the coast. This was particularly so during the 1930's when L.T. Seymour was the landlord. He made good use of advertising material – a photograph of this era shows a very busy pub forecourt with a fine array of charabancs which belonged to the East Kent Road Car Co., Premier Line and C.H. Betts. Another source of income was from the military, as the local barracks was situated opposite the inn.

Electric light was installed in July 1924 at a cost of £15 – the tenant paid half of this sum. During 1931 a draw-in and chain fencing were provided. The "Vauxhall" appeared accident prone as, in January 1930, G. Browning was paid the sum of £1,094/11/- to carry out alterations and re-instatement following a fire; whilst in October 1933 disaster struck again when the "Vauxhall" was largely destroyed by fire. This time Mr. Browning was paid £10/12/6 to board the place up. The tenants, Mr. and Mrs. Seymour, were quoted in the Kentish Gazette as saying that "the interior of the inn was gutted and in the main part of the building on the ground floor the only part that seemed intact was the bar counter". It was also reported that after the firemen had been playing water on the blaze for some fifteen minutes the family cat walked out the front door! However, a marquee was erected in the garden in order that trade could continue whilst the damage was repaired. The "Vauxhall" was altered during this restoration, which cost £1,480, and also received a more radical face-lift in the 1980's.

The city council's survey of licensed houses tells us that by the end of the Second World War the clients using this house were "artisan and labouring residents and passing drivers". In December 1952 C.F. Barber left the house and received £538 for his inventory. A month later this was sold to the incoming tenant, P.G. Beckett, for £555 less shortages overcharged which amounted to £17. In 1953 a new counter was installed. On 10th June 1966 the brewers installed a manager to run the premises. The manager was paid a weekly wage of £14/10/- and his National Insurance contributions amounted to £1/4/8. He was provided with a cash float of £20 and an entertainment allowance of £11. At the same time a new dart board was purchased at a cost of £4/12/6.

A plan to add a licensed restaurant was given the go-ahead in April 1974, despite the protests of customers who merely wanted a friendly local. To cope with the project the premises would have been extended to include a new kitchen. However, it appears that the locals won the argument as this proposition was shelved. Nevertheless, the house closed from April to June 1978 for a £26,000 face lift. Prior to this the tavern was purely a men's pub and the saloon bar was rarely used. The intention was to lift the house into the family-friendly category. A new beer store was built and the old one was converted into a modern, well-fitted kitchen for the preparation of bar snacks.

In recent times the whole character of this part of the city has changed and, although a few residential streets remain, the area is now home to motor vehicle show rooms and D-I-Y establishments. The pub always appeared busy but it closed in 2000. It stood empty for a long while and began to look very dilapidated. When I called in February 2001 a young Australian called Shay gave me a conducted tour of the premises and told me that he was being paid £100 a week to sleep here and protect it from intruders. Prior to his arrival the place had been wrecked by squatters who had removed just about everything that could be piled into a white van. I was told that a previous landlord had committed suicide and the house was haunted – certainly a door closed of its own accord whilst I was there!

Permission was given in July 2001 for the place to operate as a Burger King outlet. The original inn sign gave way many years ago to one showing an old Vauxhall car.

"The knight's bones are dust, and his sword is rust: His soul is with the saints – I trust!" Coleridge.

No 45. Von Alten, Chatham
*(Changed from **Alton** about 1895) F. Leney, Fremlins, Whitbread, Free House*

In 1861 this beer house was named the "Alton Ale House" and was in the ownership of Mark Barnes. I am told that the inn was opened by a one-armed soldier who had served at the Battle of Waterloo. It is possible that it replaced a much older inn called the "Sun Tap". Wall's brewery operated at the rear of the pub but this closed many years ago.

Augustus Leney rented the house from Barnes, paying an annual rent of £100, payable quarterly, and the lease due to expire on 25th December 1897. However, he purchased the freehold for £2,000 from Mrs. Barnes on 2nd July 1891. During January 1894 he also purchased 43 High Street, Chatham for £875 and spent a further £950 on redeveloping this acquisition. The following year new building work costing £730/18/4 was carried out. By this time the house was named "Von Alten".

An early reference to the pub tells us that in 1859 a small fire damaged the tarred woodwork. A subsequent fire caused considerable damage. In January 1862 J. Bridges was charged with assaulting Mark Barnes, landlord of the "Alton Ale House", Hammond Place. He was found guilty and fined 1/- with 17/- costs. There were more problems in November 1868 when James Connelly, a hawker of nuts etc., was charged with wilfully breaking a square of glass. He was ordered to pay a fine of 7/6 and expenses or face 14 days' hard labour. In 1872

the pub was simply referred to as "Alton" and was to sell by retail beer and cider to be consumed on the premises. In 1877 it could sell by retail wine, beer and cider to be consumed on or off the premises.

In those early days the pub stood hard by the "Empire" Music Hall which was renowned throughout the Medway towns for the quality of its concerts which attracted amateur entertainers throughout the district. In October 1918 the directors of the "Empire" approached the brewers on the subject of diverting the right of way. After some correspondence it was agreed that a three-foot right of way be walled in. Concerts were also held at the "Von Alten" most evenings, providing another outlet for local talent.

For most of its life the pub was a simple beer house, only acquiring a full licence on 20th April 1951, at which time the net monopoly value of £850 was paid. In November 1962 Leney paid a deposit of £350 in respect of the purchase of the adjoining property, 61 High Street. Completion in the sum of £3,150 took place on 11th April of the following year.

The pub name is dedicated to Karl August, Graf Von Alten, a German General who fought with the British against Napoleon in Spain. He served with great distinction, which was recognised by Wellington who placed him in command of large numbers of English soldiers at Waterloo. A statue of the General can be found in Hanover Square. When the sign was produced it aroused great interest in Germany – a copy is now owned by Von Alten's descendants. In October 1983 Rainer Von Alten, a direct descendant and keen yachtsman, was sailing in the Medway with his club members and they all descended on the pub for a drink. Despite the General's great service on behalf of this country, memories and knowledge of history are lacking. As a result the "Von" was deleted from the name in 1914 and was not reinstated until about 1930. It was deleted again for the duration of the Second World War.

By the early 1990's the house had become a popular rendezvous for the "gay" community and during this period it was decorated and furnished in a quite splendid fashion. It was felt that a change of name was called for and on 7th December 1994 it became the "Gaslamp Ale and Wine House". However, this didn't last long and it has now reverted back to its original name and the familiar sign.

One can only assume that in fairly recent times part of the pub has been demolished as it now has a very narrow High Street frontage but it does extend back a reasonable way.

"By strangers honoured, and by strangers mourn'd." Pope.

No 46. *Walnut Tree, Ditton*
(For a while in the 1990's re-named **Spatts***) F. Leney, Fremlins, Whitbread*

George Humphreys, a carpenter, of Ditton, bought land from John Golding in 1846 and built a house thereon. To finance this venture he borrowed money and when he sold the house for £1,070 to the three Leney brothers on 1st November 1865 the mortgage was still outstanding. The place was used as a beer house but had no name. George remained in occupation, but by 1869 his son held the licence. An old photograph gives the impression that the pub was semi-detached, with one half brick and the other weatherboarded.

Henry George Tassell signed a tenancy agreement on 16th November 1925 and during his tenure of at least 20 years witnessed several changes. During 1928 gas was installed at a cost of £30/14/7. In 1939 his annual rent was £25 plus £2 for gas, £1/10/- for electricity (this was installed in January 1929 at a cost of £29/2/6) and £7 for the land. His inventory was valued at £133/2/-. A beer and wine licence was granted in April 1938 and a full licence on 7th April 1949, when the net monopoly value of £1,050 was paid. Additional land was purchased in November 1934 for £900. In 1951 the brewers were paid £752 in respect of loss of development value on land adjoining the pub.

The house stands a little way back from the main A20 road in Bradbourne Street and in October 1947 the brewers paid a rent of 1/- p.a. to East Malling Research Station to lease a small piece of land adjoining the pub in order to create a little outside patio area for the use of customers. In 1963 substantial improvements were carried out at a cost of £600 and an extension was added in about 1970 to the west of the building. Much of the land fronting the A20 was sold off in 1972 for housing development.

The "Walnut Tree" was taken over as a managed house in 1976 and for a period of approximately 10 years in the 1990's it was re-named "Spatts". In about 1998 it reverted back to the original name.

A local of some age told me that it used to be a lovely old pub and then became "all dolled up". He felt that it didn't quite know to whom it wished to appeal – the regular drinker or the night-club set. In the end the regulars won.

The pub was so-named as a large walnut tree stood in front of the house but this was struck by lightning in about 1960 and now only the stump remains.

No 47. Warren Inn, New Romney
Alfred Leney, Jude Hanbury, Mackeson, Whitbread, Shepherd Neame

Isolated, a little way out of New Romney and built on reclaimed warren land, this inn has experienced more characters and excitement than most. At one time the coastline came up to the rear of the house. The pub is so-named as it stands close by the warren, on the outskirts of New Romney, where the townsfolk kept rabbits for meat. The inn sign miniature shows a horse galloping past the winning post, thus revealing that hereabouts was situated the famous Romney racecourse.

Initially the building was semi-detached with a brick cottage to the left and the pub was the weather-boarded half. These have subsequently been amalgamated to create a good-sized inn. During the 1870's the pub was in the hands of the Cobb family, with William holding the licence prior to 1874 and, probably taking over following his death, Mrs. Frances Cobb was listed as licence holder in 1882. The freehold plus three acres of land, a coal yard, wheelwrights and forge were sold by auction at Ashford in 1879 for 800 guineas – Alfred Leney was the likely purchaser as Jude Hanbury paid Leney the sum of £1,325 for the inn on 20th August 1924. Jude Hanbury raised a mortgage of £800 over the premises 13 days later and this was redeemed by Mackeson on 1st November 1956. After a couple of years they spent £44/14/6 on external painting, repairing the roof, and fixing three signs. The same year a gas supply was connected at a cost of £9.

1887 provided some excitement when a ship was wrecked nearby and two Norwegian sailors struggled ashore. Seeing in the distance the lights of the inn they were able to reach the door to be provided with succour. During the late 1940's and early 1950's "Roguers" used to lodge here. These people were employed by seed firms and it was their task to walk the growing crops to remove "rogue" or stray varieties of seed heads from the growing corn. As late as the 1950's the "Warren Inn" was a pitch and tar house with a dirt floor. A well-remembered landlord of this era was "Flat cap Sid" who kept a donkey and a cat. For a prank he would take the donkey upstairs and it was said that his cat would fight anything that moved. Sadly one morning the pub failed to open and on calling out the brewers from Hythe, who broke down the door, Sid was found dead in bed. During the war years ENSA would put on shows here and it was a popular rendezvous for servicemen stationed in the area. One day in about 1950 Hughie Green, of Opportunity Knocks fame and father of Paula Yates, popped in for a drink after landing at nearby Ferryfield airport. Landlords generally stayed for a while – for example Cyril Harding, who owned a parrot, held the licence for 21 years and when I called in 2001 the landlord Ben Tree had served for 18 years.

Shepherd Neame purchased the pub on 5th May 1975; included was ten acres of land, which at one time had been let off as a market garden. There is now a good-sized car park and a large play area for children. For some reason the American flag was fluttering in the breeze when I visited. The pub can provide accommodation and is supported by locals, visitors to the caravan parks, and tourists. It provides a good living during the summer months, at one time seven staff were employed, but difficult times are experienced during the winter. The house used to put out six darts teams.

The pub is a friendly place which is well worth a visit. Despite its isolation it can be found on the main coast road, the A259.

"Slow 'uns on four legs and fast 'uns on two – they're the trouble." Kimber.

No 48. Wheatsheaf, Swalecliffe
Ash & Co., Jude Hanbury, Mackeson, Whitbread, Greene King

Towards the end of 1933 the directors of Mackeson thought that the time had come to rebuild the old "Wheatsheaf" to create the kind of premises that could comfortably cater for the population of this expanding area. Detailed plans were sought from an outside architect and on 24th September 1934 it was resolved to accept a tender in the sum of £4,389 submitted by J. Wiltshier & Co. to carry out this work.

There was a cost over-run but the splendid new premises were completed mid-way through 1935.

The old "Wheatsheaf" can be traced back to 1705. At that time a six-acre plot of ground containing two cottages was sold by Thomas Grigg to Charles Fairway, a mariner. A blacksmith, John Blackman, purchased the site in 1746 and in 1806 it passed to Andrew Hunt. By the 1830's the tenant, Stephen Halliday, had established a beer house in one of the cottages and it was rumoured that the other cottage had smuggling connections. On Monday 21st September 1840 the "Wheatsheaf ", large garden, two brick houses and superior arable land, in all five acres situated at Swackliff, were offered for sale by auction held at the "Falstaff Inn", St. Dunstans, Canterbury. Two-thirds of the purchase money were allowed to remain on mortgage. Stephen was the purchaser and as he took £800 by way of mortgage we may assume that he paid £1,200 for these assets. He didn't retain the freehold for long, selling it in 1844 to George Ash for the same price that he had paid. He did, however, stay on as tenant until about 1870. The brewery listing for 1855 tells us that he was also a farmer but it is more likely that he used the five acres of land as a modest small-holding. Mentioned within a schedule of property owned by Thomas and George Ash dated 1870 is the "Wheatsheaf" with Stephen, as the tenant, paying an annual rent of £43/5/6. His loan at this time amounted to £128/3/-. It is possible that the very high rent he paid related in part to the land or it was inflated to include loan repayments. Again mere speculation, but it is interesting to note that the Ash brothers purchased at about the same time the "White Horse" beer shop at Chilham from "Halliday" – was this the same person? Jude Hanbury acquired the premises in 1923 and paid the balance of the purchase price for the pub plus three cottages; this amounted to £427/1/-. The place suffered some damage in July 1928 which resulted in an insurance claim of £150. In June 1929 the brewers paid £7/10/11 for the installation of a water service. Just before demolition in 1932 the brewers considered renting the land to the rear of the pub for the purpose of dog-racing. Tentative draft terms were submitted to the prospective hirers but matters did not proceed, due mainly to possible future legislation which would have a bearing on dog-racing tracks. The old pub was demolished in 1935.

Mackeson decided that the existing tenant would not take over their spanking new investment. He would be paid off with the same sum that he paid to go in – £200. The new rent was to be £30 p.a. plus £20 for the field. The trade fixtures were valued at £511. A tenancy agreement was signed on 24th April 1935 by F.H. Clements, agreeing to a rent of £20 in the first year rising to £50 in the second and £70 in the third year plus £30 for the land. Another strange coincidence arises here as ten years later, at the nearby "Long Reach", we find that E.F. Clements was the landlord.

In 1956 about four acres to the rear of the pub were sold off for £600. Also a further small plot adjacent to the house went for £66. This was to be used for an entrance roadway. The inn has a very large car park and some time in the 1950's a travelling circus stopped here for a short while. Unfortunately an elephant took a small step backwards and dislodged one of the pillars! A further rumpus occurred in February 1961 when a 57-year-old "writer and poet" standing over six-feet tall banged his fist on the bar counter so hard that the counter cracked. A few days later he returned causing more damage and then started a fight with the landlord. A quick-witted female member of staff hit him on the head with an ashtray and knocked him out. This necessitated a trip to hospital by ambulance. When he recovered he was gaoled for two months. It is hard to imagine now, but in the 1960's the pub forecourt was the rendezvous for the Thanet and Herne Foxhounds.

Like the rebuilt "Long Reach" locals thought the brewers had miscalculated growth within the area and indeed it did take quite a while before the population grew to a sufficient size to justify the capital outlay. However, the place is now very busy. In 1998 the pub had an image change and there is now a special corner for sports fans, featuring action pictures, memorabilia, a pool table and dart-board. Food is served all day and there is seating for about 90 people.

The inn sign miniature, now embellished, is still recognisable. The design is taken from a Southern Railway poster of 1935 advertising rambles in the county organised by the railway company. The Wheatsheaf promoted the material for the October and November rambles and the poster was designed by Audrey Webber.

No 49. White Hart, Hythe
John Friend, Mackeson, Whitbread, Free House

Debate still continues as to the oldest pub in Hythe – some say the "White Hart" others the "Bell" but most probably the "King's Head".

The building would appear to date from the 15th century. Whitbread date the hotel back to 1648 when we know that one Ferdinando Bafsooke (later changed to Bassett) paid the sum of £241 to acquire the "White Hart" plus stable, barn and two gardens". In 1665 John Bafsooke succeeded his father and went on in 1670 to issue token coins. There was a shortage of small coins in those days and most responsible merchants issued their own tokens. By 1684 this establishment had become the principal hostelry in Hythe. It remained within the Bassett family's control until 1733. The inn abuts the town hall and there is a door linking the two and a room in the "White Hart" was used for a long period as the robing room for the mayors, aldermen and councillors of the day. The landlord received a fee for this service. By about 1750 the hotel was in the hands of Julius Deedes who owned a malt-house at nearby Newington, so it is possible that the landlord brewed his own beer.

The Hythe Session book of 1801 records the "White Hart". This was the year that the Mackeson brothers purchased the brewing interests of John Friend. They agreed to pay 28 times the annual rental of £40 and £1,120 was duly paid over on 1st April 1802. However, the property was only insured for £600 with the Royal Exchange. A Mr. Foreman was the landlord. By now this was a commercial and posting inn and travellers could enjoy the luxury of both hip-bath and shower. At 9 o'clock every morning the Times coach would call on its way to London via Ashford, Charing, Lenham and Maidstone. William Mackeson died in 1821 and when his estate was wound up the hotel was valued at £1,200.

Improvements were carried out and £28 was paid to Bailey to install a water closet and partition in 1825. In later times a new bar, bathroom and water closet were installed at a cost of £200 and, in 1932, £99/1/6 was spent on converting the cellar, which would have been on the ground floor, into a bar and new entrance. There was no underground cellar – this gave rise to speculation that the property was built as a waterfront tavern before the sea receded. By the late 1950's the hotel advertised rooms with hot and cold water and electric fires.

In January 1933 the brewers were approached by Messrs. Geering and Colyer, estate agents, enquiring whether the company wished to dispose of the freehold for business purposes, for which the licence would not be required. Mackeson responded by saying they did not particularly desire to sell the property but what would the potential purchaser give? There was no further correspondence.

Over the years many famous and interesting people have stayed here. In 1804 Major General John Brown, said to be the master-mind behind the building of the Military Canal, held a meeting here with the consultant engineer, John Rennie. 1914 saw the inaugural meeting to form the local branch of the Association of Men of Kent and Kentish Men. During the Second World War the hotel played host to many RAF pilots based at the nearby Lympne and Hawkinge camps and amongst these very brave men was Flying Officer Douglas Bader. Following the doodlebug attacks Field Marshall Montgomery and the American Ambassador John G. Winant stayed here to view the earliest examples of this new weapon. Ultimately American anti-aircraft artillery and radar were moved into the area. The hotel remained open throughout the war. Lympne airport was also the venue for many record-breaking flights. Jim Mollison to the Cape, Charles Scott to Australia, Tommy Rose to South Africa and Jean Batten to New Zealand, all rested at the "White Hart" before setting off on their epic adventures.

Whitbread sold the premises on 31st August 1977 and since then the place has continued to prosper. Further major refurbishment was carried out in 1992 and in 1994 a German landlord took over and an interesting range of beers was offered.

No 50. White Horse, Chilham
Ash & Co., Jude Hanbury, Mackeson, Whitbread

Chilham lays claim to be the prettiest village in Kent – and it probably is. The "White Horse" sits in a corner of the village square, hard up against the ancient church, and boasts a pedigree stretching back to 1422.

Deeds can be traced back to 1632 when William Bayles was in occupation, but for a long while it appears to have been used as business premises. An indenture dated 28th November 1701 conveyed the property (no mention that it is a beer house) with the backside garden, easements, commodities and appurtenances from Stephen Osman of Headcorn, a carpenter, to Stephen Dines of Chilham, a cordwainer, for £35. In 1789 William Halliday of Chilham, bricklayer and grocer, bought the premises and they reverted to a single hereditament, and so they remained for the next 50 years. William died in 1832 leaving the property to family members. Three of his children sold the "messuage or tenement" to George Ash on 17th September 1839 for the sum of £310. On the death of Thomas Ash in March 1875 the house was in the possession of Samuel Palmer who paid an annual rent of £12. The insurance premium was 6/-.

Like most houses of this antiquity the "White Horse" is said to be haunted. The story goes that during refurbishment carried out in 1956 an old inglenook fireplace, circa 1460, was discovered and when it was opened up there appeared a grey-haired man in a long black gown standing with his hands behind him and his back to the fireplace. Originally the property belonged to the clergy – in the adjacent church there is a list of rectors dating from 1293. From 1655 to 1662 the incumbent was Sampson Hieron M.A. In 1662 he had been deprived, for some reason, of the living. This date is important as it coincides with the Third Act of Uniformity, on the enactment of which 2,000 ministers of good repute had their livings removed for failing to use the Book of Common Prayer. At the time of the refurbishment the landlord's name was Mr. Sampson. Mr. Hieron still puts in the occasional appearance. To add further spice to these ghostly stories two complete and preserved bodies were discovered buried in the kitchen area. It is thought that they were soldiers who took part in Watt Tyler's uprising – their bodies are now buried in the local churchyard.

Mackeson redeemed the tithe, amounting to £1/2/-, on 27th November 1930 and on 31st March 1936 the quit rent of £1/5/5 was extinguished. During 1931 the stable was converted into a urinal.

In April 1933 the brewers held a conversation with Sir Edmund Davis' agent who suggested the removal of this house to a main road site which he was prepared to place at the disposal of the company. After due deliberation the agent was advised that the site was not considered equal to the present one.

One gets the impression that for a long while this was quite a primitive place and in 1935 a Mr. Gray was invited to look over the pub with a view to becoming the tenant. He refused because it has "Oil lamps and no proper sanitation".

The "White Horse" did not acquire a wine licence until February 1947 and a full-on licence was granted on 6th April 1949 at which time the net monopoly value of £600 was paid. A cooker and hot water system were installed during 1955 at a cost of £150 and the following year £1,500 was spent on the bathroom, water closet and lavatory accommodation and alterations to the bars. Ten years later a gas supply was installed costing £34/13/- and further capital improvements amounting to £1,084/10/9 were carried out. It was at this time that the two skeletons were unearthed.

Despite its great age and picturesque setting the "White Horse" has had its ups and downs. In 1968 it was reported that the spirit trade was down by 10 gallons during December 1967 and the following January, and the landlord was complaining about some of the university students. Various village organisations such as the football club meet here and the 100 Club draw to raise money for the new recreation ground sports centre is held here every week.

In 2004 the leasehold interest was offered for sale at a guide price of £65,000 "all at" with a rent of £31,000 per annum.

Series Five issued in April 1955

(Card)

1	Admiral Harvey, Ramsgate	26	King's Head, Hythe
2	Army & Navy, Lower Rainham	27	Man of Kent, Crundale
3	Bailiff's Sergeant, St. Mary's Bay	28	Nag's Head, St. Leonards-on-Sea
4	Bell Inn, Hythe	29	Nelson's Head, Hythe
5	Brent's Tavern, Faversham	30	Newcastle Inn, Ewell Minnis, near Dover
6	Brickmaker's Arms, Deal	31	Old Golden Cross, Hastings
7	Britannia, Milton Regis	32	Pier Hotel, Herne Bay
8	Bull, Sissinghurst	33	Railway, Gillingham
9	Burnt Oak, Gillingham	34	Red Lion, Stodmarsh, near Canterbury
10	Cardinal's Error, Tonbridge	35	Royal Dragoon, Canterbury
11	Carpenter's Arms, Canterbury	36	Royal Oak, Bonnington, Romney Marsh
12	Cecil Arms, Strood	37	Royal Oak, Iden Green, near Benenden
13	Chequers, Biddenden	38	Ship Centurion, Whitstable
14	Chequers, High Halden	39	Ship Hotel, New Romney
15	Clarendon, Sandgate	40	Shrew Beshrewed, Hersden, near Canterbury
16	Clothworker's Arms, Sutton Valence	41	Spread Eagle, Chatham
17	Denmark Arms, Rochester	42	Trafalgar Maid, Chatham
18	Duchess of Kent, Dover	43	True Briton, Folkestone
19	Duke of Cumberland, Barham	44	White Horse, Tonbridge
20	Falstaff Tap, Canterbury	45	Windmill, Cranbrook
21	George Inn, Folkestone	46	Woodland Tavern, Gillingham
22	Grapes, Milton Regis	47	Woodman, East Malling
23	Green Man, Shatterling, near Wingham	48	Woolpack, Winchet Hill, near Goudhurst
24	Harp, Tunbridge Wells	49	York, Chatham
25	Hop Poles, Canterbury	50	Ypres Castle, Rye

This series was launched at a Tenants' Luncheon held on 28th March 1955. The inn signs were available to the general public on 2nd April 1955.

No 1. Admiral Harvey, Ramsgate
*(Re-named **Harveys Crab and Oyster House** in about 1982 then plain **Harveys**)*
Bradly family, Tomson & Wotton, Mackeson, Whitbread

A long while ago a small brick-built tavern stood overlooking the town harbour in which the masts of schooners lying at anchor bobbed up almost as high as the pub roof. It abutted Dyason's Royal Clarence Baths which were frequented by King William IV. This was the former "Admiral Harvey".

The pub was first mentioned as lot 14 in an auction held on 13th February 1826 at the "Bell", Sandwich. The vendors were the Sandwich-based Bradly family who were brewers. The inn sign miniature tells us that the house was named after Admiral Sir Thomas Harvey (1775-1841) of Eastry in Kent. He was the son of an admiral, father of two admirals and brother-in-law to two more! Two of the Harvey family, of consecutive generations, had married daughters in the Bradly family. However, John Land, in his well-researched book "Ramsgate Pubs Past and Present", states that it commemorates Admiral Henry Harvey (1737-1810).

The property, together with two small shops, was purchased by Thomas Hogben. In his will dated 21st July 1886 he states that he had always used his mother's surname, Parnell, but his real name was Hogben. He owned several properties, including the "Admiral Harvey", and they were all registered in the name of Thomas Parnell. His primary occupation was that of a sea-man. His life style obviously suited him as he ran the pub until he died in his nineties. He was succeeded by John T. Williams. The place was sold on by his heirs and was ultimately purchased in 1887 by Tomson and Wotton. They in turn, on 4th July 1898, sold the house for £4,600 to Ramsgate Corporation who almost immediately on-sold it to J.B. Hodgson. However, the council wished to demolish the premises in order to improve facilities in this attractive part of town. By 1901 re-development was under-way and to facilitate progress a resolution dated 9th November 1901 was passed by Council of the Borough of Ramsgate to the effect that "sale of the surplus land belonging to the Corporation at the junction of Harbour Parade and York Street … that any building to be erected on the side will be deemed by the Corporation an extension of the existing buildings and therefore exempt from the bye-laws with respect to new buildings".

Stanley H. Page auctioned the pub plus 34 and 36 York Street on behalf of Mr. Hodgson on Wednesday 25th September 1901. Mackeson were the purchasers, paying a deposit of £340 at the year-end, with the balance, £3,060, paid a fortnight later. Legal costs amounted to £64/10/-. Certain conditions applied, the main one being that part of the property be pulled down for street widening. Mr. Hodgson had entered into a contract with a Mr. Martin of Ramsgate to demolish the pub and 36 York Street and build on the remaining land a new house at a cost of £1,787/10/-. This estimate was not far out as £1,060 was spent during 1902 and the following year there was a further outlay of £809/0/3 to complete the rebuilding work. Architect's fees totalled £73/6/-. A further £69/3/9 was spent on gilded lettering. This has always been a "prestige" house and was one of the first in Kent to advertise its presence by means of neon lighting.

Charles Holyer was the last landlord at the old house. A former cigar importer, Jules Richieux, took over the spanking new tavern in January 1903. Jules was to father, on 9th September 1903, a son named Emile who was born on the premises. He went on to become the famous impressario "Prince Littler". Ernest John Parsons took over in 1907. He remained for a long while but in 1927 was suspected of adulterating his beers and overcharging. An agent was employed to gather evidence but the tenant suspected he had been rumbled and ran the place immaculately thereafter. The brewers decided not to proceed to forfeiture of the lease as they had no hard evidence and Mr. Parsons remained in situ until 6th May 1931, at which time he was succeeded by his wife, Ivy Muriel Parsons.

In February 1925 it was perceived that stiff competition could be faced from the recently completed "Popular Hotel and Restaurant" owned by a Mr. Marzeth. On behalf of the brewery company and the tenant it was decided to oppose the granting of a full licence to this upstart and the application was duly refused.

The pub was prone to flooding when water backed up the drain in the pot house and a particularly bad incident occurred in 1945. It was not until 1957 that 34 York Street was properly incorporated into the pub – this and bar alterations cost £2,000.

Whitbread appointed a manager to run the premises on 11th May 1982 and shortly afterwards it and the "Pearson's Arms" became Crab and Oyster theme houses. It remains a very busy place with a large and popular restaurant called the Harbour View. In 2003 the leasehold interest was offered for sale at a price of £150,000 "all at" plus stock at valuation.

"It is indeed a desirable thing to be well descended." Plutarch.

No 2. Army and Navy, Lower Rainham
(Closed in April 2003) F. Leney, Fremlins, Whitbread, Famous Pub Co.

The "Army and Navy" was built on desolate marshland flanking the Medway. This area was enclosed in about 1800 and was used as a nursery ground called Cherry Garden. One of the occupiers, Robert or John Rains, built a row of cottages here and the easternmost was subdivided sometime before 1856. It is probable that shortly afterwards it reverted back to one house and became a beer shop. In 1898 Leneys purchased the premises for £2,000; by this time it was named the "Army and Navy". In 1921 the pub was valued in the company books at £2,030 – this figure was reduced to £1,730 in 1926.

One of the first tenants was T. Platts in 1867 when the house was said to be in Old Brompton and T. Blake arrived in 1878 when the address was River Street, Old Brompton. William J.A. Dolling signed a tenancy agreement on 14th November 1938, paying a rent of £30 with the brewery holding his deposit of

£50. One former landlord had been an ex-speedway rider. During the 1940's the pub may have experienced trading difficulties as £62/8/11 of rent arrears was written off as a bad debt. A beer and wine licence was obtained on 8th April 1940 and a full one in 1954. The tithe was redeemed in 1944.

Early in 1963 land adjoining the pub was purchased for £500 and the following year the next-door cottage was bought for £600. At the same time land was sold for a net figure of £2,610/1/-. In 1966 another cottage was purchased for £800 and two years later the pub was extended to incorporate all three cottages.

In common with most houses that remain within a family for a long while it was spick and span and was welcoming to visitors. The pub appeared to be caught in a time warp, even as late as the 1990's. It was popular and had a strong sporting tradition. However, local competition always felt that as far as darts was concerned the "Army and Navy" had a definite advantage as players had to avoid an enormous clock hung on the wall at shoulder height, making it virtually impossible to move to the right.

By 1995 all reference to Whitbread had been removed and the sign slightly altered. It traded on for a few more years before it passed into the annals of history. There was talk that it could be converted into a restaurant but it reverted back to the original three cottages.

"I'm a jolly – 'er Majesty's jolly – Soldier an' Sailor too!" Kipling.

No 3. Bailiff's Sergeant, St. Mary's Bay
Mackeson, Whitbread, Shepherd Neame

The "Bailiff's Sergeant" is the second pub in the inn sign series not to appear on the metal map of East Kent produced in 1950 by David Burley, not because of any omission on his part – quite simply there was no pub here.

During the 1940's St. Mary's Bay was a small rural hamlet sitting on the edge of Romney Marsh but after the war its expansion was rapid but unplanned. It suddenly blossomed into a fair-sized community, somewhat lacking in social amenities – especially a public house. Mackeson spotted the opportunity to open a pub in the area and whilst there was no shortage of sites the difficulty was that it would be many years before building materials could be spared for such a purpose. It was necessary therefore to find premises that could be easily converted. The "Jesson Stores" in Jesson Lane, built in the 1930's, fitted the bill and the justices gave permission for this grocery and off-licence shop to be converted into a public house. The freehold was purchased from Mr. Harold Robert Hollis for £5,750 and completion took place on 2nd February 1951. Mr. Hollis then carried on in business as the first landlord of the new pub. The Ministry of Works, however, would not grant the necessary building licence in view of the national emergency. Mackesons' architect, E.G. Wilden, set himself the task of providing the best sort of inn he could within the narrow limits imposed by the restrictions on building. He divided the shop into two bars, made the side entrance into an off-sales department, and turned the garage into lavatories and a beer store.

The ceremony of unveiling the sign of the "Bailiff's Sergeant" was performed on 8th July 1951 by Major M. Teichmann-Derville, the Bailiff of the Lord's Jurats and Commonalty of Romney Marsh. The Jurats date back to 1216. It is his sergeant who is depicted on the sign and who accompanied the bailiff on this occasion in the full uniform of his ancient office. On 8th May 1952 the company paid the net monopoly value, £2,250, for a "full on" licence.

A year later Mackeson purchased the freehold of the adjacent property, May Cottage, from Mrs. Victoria Alexander Mary Hopker for £1,350. Much later the cottage was incorporated within the pub and the place was rebuilt. A less lavish re-opening ceremony was held in February 1968 to celebrate the imposing new premises and Chris White, an abroad cooper with Mackeson, visited the premises prior to the ceremony reporting "Due to the upheaval bitter cold and over conditioned but cleared in time for the opening".

The pub remains busy with both locals and holiday makers, mainly Londoners, who have a second home or caravan down here.

Mr. Hollis the first landlord was a kindly man. I can remember one bright, but very windy morning cycling across Romney Marsh from Hastings only to find on arriving at the "Bailiff's Sergeant" that he had no inn signs to offer. He took my name and address and very promptly posted one on to me.

Shepherd Neame leased the premises from Whitbread on 6th May 1992 and purchased the freehold on 27th September 1996. Clearly a very good investment.

No 4. Bell Inn, Hythe
Mackeson, Whitbread

Three houses claim to be the oldest tavern in Hythe – the previously mentioned "White Hart", the "Bell" and the "Kings Head". It is probably the latter by a short head.

The "Bell" dates back to the late 1500's and some state that it was built from ships' timbers salvaged from the wrecks near Romney Marsh. At one time the inn fronted the sea-shore but the build-up of shingle from the west resulted in the pub being stranded a little way inland on the main Hythe to Folkestone road. As is to be expected, the place has close associations with smuggling. There is a tunnel that runs under the floor of the pub close to the millstream which was used as a hiding-place for brandy and gin. This contraband was floated up the millstream by way of "Ankers" (see the "Anchor" series 3, No 1.). When the coast was clear the items were hauled up into the inn by means of a windlass, installed in a partitioned portion of the attic, which could be lowered into the water. It is stated the landlord's young son could get into the stream and wade down to the canal.

Henry Mackeson and Scrope Hutchinson, his trustee, purchased the "Bell" on 26th November 1829 from J.B. and C.E. (his wife) Brockman and the Reverend W. Brockman at a possibly inflated price of £900, as they did not wish to see it fall into the hands of a competitor. By 1855 Charles Horton was the tenant and he was succeeded by his wife in 1867 who carried on until 1874 when she handed over to Charles R. Nelson. A much later landlord, A.F. Ridley, advertised the pub as five minutes from the sea, station and golf links. He stated that it was a noted port house using dock glasses.

During 1921 a new bathroom was installed at a cost of £57/3/11 and 1930 saw the redemption of the tithes, amounting to £2/15/-, payable to the vicar of Newington. Three years later land was sold for £40. Considerable renovation was carried out during the 1960's and this led to the discovery of an ancient fireplace that contained an assortment of keys, mugs, bones and clay pipes. The new bar was built around this attractive feature.

The "Bell" is a much more sedate place now and well worth a visit.

No 5. Brent's Tavern, Faversham

Delmar and Pierce, W.E. & J. Rigden, George, Beer & Rigden (all as Leaseholders),
Jude Hanbury, Mackeson, Fremlins, Whitbread, Free House

The "Brent's Tavern" occupies a handsome three-storey building in the Regency style perched on a small knoll rising above Faversham creek – locally called a Brent. It commands splendid views over the marsh and the pub is often referred to as the "Rock".

The house is listed and, according to Whitbread's records, was built in about 1800 and is one of the town's oldest licensed houses. It is said that it was built as a mansion for one of the owners of the local gunpowder factories and later became a top-hat factory. Renovation work was carried out in the 1930's and a number of dusty top-hats were found in the attic: this led to speculation that the owner of the coffin factory, situated opposite, had lived here.

The major landowner in this area was the Sondes family and their properties included the "Brents Estate", which was leased out. The "Brent's Tavern" formed part of this estate. One source of information indicates that the house was first licensed in 1809 but there is no evidence of this and it is more likely it acquired a licence about 1831, when the occupant was George Springett, who was supplied with beer by Delmar and Pierce, brewers located at Beer Cart Lane, Canterbury. In about 1849 Delmar and Pierce took over the tenancy and sublet it to tenants. In 1875 the firm was taken over by W.E. & J. Rigden Limited who in 1922 were acquired by George, Beer & Rigden Limited – a fine photograph taken in 1926 shows the house in their colours. They in turn were swallowed up in 1949 by Fremlins. Mrs. Elizabeth S. Hall (the Whelers of Otterden Place and the Buttens family) inherited the "Brents Estate", the tenancy was formalised to a yearly tenancy of £40 p.a. and this arrangement continued until 1926, when the heirs of Mrs. Hall sold 14 acres of the "Brents Estate". Jude Hanbury records for January 1928 indicate that they were the purchasers paying in September 1926 £1,157/17/6 including costs and then mortgaged it and the "Swan" at Appledore in the sum of £4,000. The pub later passed to Mackeson, the Hythe brewers, who redeemed the tithe of £2/8/4 on 11th January 1940. During June 1929 Chittenden and Simmons were paid the sum of £3/1/- to dig out the signboard and re-erect it in a more prominent position.

The war years were turbulent times and I have no doubt that local inhabitants were pleased to have such a solid building in their midst, particularly as they were able to use the pub cellar as an air-raid shelter. Perhaps to cheer everyone up, in 1941 a piano was purchased for £3. An abroad cooper despatched from Hythe in 1945 reported "there was a large rambling cellar … full of rubbish … mattresses etc". The place had obviously been put to good use.

In May 1952 Mackeson purchased 43 Upper Brents, a bungalow adjoining the "Brent's Tavern", from Mrs. B.M.L. Hensher for £120. In 1953 the bungalow was incorporated into the pub and other substantial renovation work was carried out at a total cost of £3,300. Whilst this work was going on a number of old farthings and pennies were found lodged in the massive beams that remain a feature of this house. The front wall of the property was also rebuilt. The pub closed for the duration of the building work and officially re-opened in July 1953. Further work was carried out in 1962 at a cost of £3,650.

All kinds of local organisations have used the "Brent's Tavern" as their meeting place. The Workers Education Association held lectures here in the early 1960's, and in 1967 the local Amalgamated and Engineering and Foundry Union switched to the "Brent's", having met at the "St. Ann's Cross" since 1893. The prowess of the pub's various sports teams was legendary.

Landlords came and went and for some reason none stayed for very long. W. O'Brien moved in on 29th June 1938, and paid a rent of £25 p.a. When he was succeeded by A.T. Playford in 1941 the rent had increased to £26 and was held at this level for a long while. Probably the longest-serving was Ernest Edward Darby from 28th January 1959 until 1980.

At one time the pub was surrounded by rather mean bungalow-type buildings but these were demolished and were replaced by the North Preston estate. The people living here form the base of the pub's clientele.

The rather splendid sign showing the Brent Geese is relevant as these birds can be seen on the nearby marshland but I feel the pub really took its name from the part of Faversham in which it is domiciled – the Brents.

The bars contain a fine array of pictures of railway engines and a strong RAF and Naval presence is evident. There are also Fremlins maps and the David Burley metal map of East Kent.

No 6. Brickmaker's Arms, Deal
East Kent Brewery Co., Jude Hanbury, Mackeson, Whitbread, Free House

On 21st February 1862 the Archbishop of Canterbury sold just over seven acres of land for £498 to Edward Hobday. Following the death of Edward his executors auctioned the land on 28th June 1877; the purchasers were Thomas Tuff Denne and William Denne. Between 1877 and 1885 they developed the site and on 7th July 1885 they sold this property to G.C. Stapleton of Sand-wich, a brewer, as trustee for William Henry Pitt Draffon, for £500. This gentleman, on 3rd June 1899, sold his entire estate of twenty pubs to the East Kent Brewery Co.

The "Brickmaker's Arms" is an extended, end-of-terrace house on a corner site. At one time it was surrounded by brickfields, hence the pub name. The area was and remains mainly residential and most of the customers were either from the brickworks or the nearby Kentish coal fields. A good number of licensees were ex-miners.

Jude Hanbury acquired the "Brickmaker's Arms" in 1920 when they took over the East Kent Brewery Co. and they in turn passed it on to Mackeson, which in September 1930 purchased land for £700 in Mill Road. It was upon this land that the extension was built.

This is a modest house which now caters for the local community and boasts good darts, pool, bar billiards, football and cricket teams. In 1926 the bar was partitioned at a cost of £20. During November 1928 W. Maple was paid £5/8/- to renew the cellar flaps and to repair the guttering. Ten days later he renewed the fencing at a cost of £3/10/-. In 1932, £11/10/- was spent on concreting the yard and pathway. Other minor expenditure was incurred over the years. A report carried out for Mackeson in 1945 stated "Needed money spent … generally wants cleaning up". Initially there were three small bars but these have been amalgamated to form good-sized and comfortable accommodation.

The pub was granted a full-on licence on 30th March 1950, at which time the net monopoly value of £450 was paid. The following year £200 was spent on alterations to the bars.

The Cox family held the licence for a long while. Fred W. Cox arrived in about 1918 and by 1930 Errol C. Cox had taken over. In 1972 the new landlord was Ernie Kemp, a big man, a bit of a boxer, and an ex-miner who had walked from Newcastle to Kent seeking work. He remained for at least 20 years. When I called in 2002 the owner was another former miner, Alan Garton. Alan's father, Arthur, had been landlord at the other local miners' pub – the "White Horse" at Finglesham.

At the time the fifth series of inn signs was issued I was living at Lenham, a good distance from Deal. I relied for my supply of signs on the Deal Beach Parlour ice-cream man who visited the village every evening during the summer months.

In 2002 the freehold was offered for sale at a price of £150,000 "all at".

Shall the clay say to him that fashioneth it, "What makest thou?" Isaiah.

No 7. Britannia, Milton Regis

(Closed in 1994. Now the Charcoal Grill Take Away) Milton Brewery, F. Leney, Fremlins, Whitbread

£63/2/11 was incurred in respect of the cost of a lease and mortgage. The hotel appears to have run into financial problems in 1920 when the sum of £113/11/4 was written off to "goods" and £8/11/3 to rent. That year a glazed partition was installed at a cost of £18/18/-. The lease expired at the end of 1934 but when the company applied for renewal they received no response and had to seek out the owner's agent to progress matters. A new lease was granted on 8th July 1935, from Mr. Birch and others, for a 21-year period at a premium of £750 and an annual rent of £65. The following year saw an agreement to fix a sign-board on a bungalow owned by A.C. Hayes at a peppercorn rent of £1 p.a. Mackeson finally purchased the freehold in January 1946 for a consideration of £3,500.

The present house stands on Brewers Hill, formerly known as Camp Road, which leads to Shorncliffe Camp. It was here that Richard Hills established the Sandgate Brewery in 1836 with the "Clarendon", as it became known, standing near by. It is likely the inn was the brewery "tap". The present pub dates back to the mid-19th century and probably started life as a private house. It is likely that when it converted to an hotel it replaced a much older house that had traded in the vicinity. In 1946 it commenced to style itself an inn rather than an hotel in order to avoid confusion with a place bearing the same name in nearby Folkestone.

Immediately after the war an abroad cooper from Hythe inspected the premises and reported "Ceilings and wood joists were covered with cobwebs ... walls dirty ... concrete floor uneven and very dirty ... cellar full of rubbish and in a filthy condition". Because of the pitch of the slate roof there were problems with damp in the bedrooms. At one time the house had a marble cellar but this was broken up some time ago.

Mackeson entered into a deed of grant on 1st January 1953 with Frank Shaw as owner of land adjoining the "Clarendon", whereby he gave permission to the company to erect a second window immediately below the existing window in the south wall of the pub subject to payment of £1 per annum for five years for the enjoyment of the access of light.

From 1960 a highly-regarded couple, James Joseph Dymoke-Byrne (Smokey) and Edy Dymoke-Byrne, ran the house. Smokey, said to be descended from the King's Champion of Tudor times, had served in the Royal Navy and subsequently, during the war years, was appointed a liaison officer in Trieste, where he met his wife, a Yugoslavian national. He fought with Marshall Tito's partisans and was awarded the George Cross, although there remains some doubt as to whether he agreed to accept this award. Indeed his life was shrouded in mystery. On his death in 1969 Edy continued to run the pub until 1989. During this period "time" was called on a bugle played by Chris McNally. The "Smokey" Byrne clock still hangs above the bar, but unfortunately a previous landlord removed the mechanical workings and it is now battery-operated. Outside one will find a bench dedicated to Edy.

The "Clarendon" remains a popular rendezvous for serious drinkers and those who enjoy good food. It has the added attraction of replicas of the various sets of Whitbread inn signs adorning the walls. One landlord crafted a fine array of bar tables incorporating draughts, back gammon and cribbage sets. At one time the Mackeson Brewery Dinner Club used to meet here. The local CAMRA branch awarded this house their "Pub of the Year" award in 2002 and it also appears in both the Good Pub Guide and Good Beer Guide.

At one time Edy Byrne made an offer for the house but this was never taken up. In 1977 Shepherd Neame purchased the premises.

No 16. Clothworkers Arms, Sutton Valence
(See Series 2, No 27.)

Again there is no particular reason for this identical sign to appear in two series. I wonder why Whitbread didn't select such signs as the "Royal Sovereign" at Chatham or the "Black Horse", Stansted.

No 17. Denmark Arms, Rochester
(Closed 28th January 2001) F. Leney, Fremlins, Whitbread, Free House

The "Denmark Arms" is a smallish, end-of-terrace house, which, for about 140 years, provided a comfortable haven for those people living in this artisan area, well away from the tourist haunts of the city. This was a traditional house and right to the end Mackesons Milk Stout was engraved on the windows. I do hope these have been preserved.

The row of houses was built in 1863 with it likely that the pub plus forge and stables were purpose-built. It was so-named to honour the then King's marriage with the beautiful Princess Alexandra of Denmark who went on to found the Queen Alexandra Rose Day. Having rented the pub for some time, the three Leney brothers purchased it from I.G. Naylor on 23rd October 1877 paying £600.

Landlords can be traced back to 1874 when Mrs. Jane Humble was in possession and the address was in Maidstone Road. In 1877 William Letley took over, he was succeeded in 1899 by George E. Chaplin and the address was now given as Albert Road. A variety of social functions took place and in 1893 the landlord applied, through his daughter, for three hours' extension of time on Bank Holiday for a dance. Six years later a further extension for five hours was applied for, on the occasion of a soiree to be held on a Friday by the attendees of the dancing class held at the house. Both applications were granted which would indicate that this was a well-managed house. In January 1899 an inquest was held here on a 55-year-old who had fallen from a cart and died as a result. Sidney J. Pye signed a tenancy agreement on 20th September 1920 and he stayed until after the end of the war. In 1939 he was paying the modest rent of £20 plus £1/10/- for electric light. Perhaps because of his length of service no deposit was held and he had a full licence.

In 1927 plans for alterations to the premises were passed by the justices and the work, costing £90, was to commence after Christmas. Further building work valued at £150 was carried out in 1936. Everything connected with this house was on a very modest scale.

It did, however, remain a good old-fashioned pub. The locals would raise large sums of money for charity and in 1987 a goodly sum was raised for Guide Dogs for the Blind by way of tramps' suppers and fun walks. It was also a CAMRA real ale pub providing a good pint of Fullers London Pride.

Unfortunately times and tastes change and the inevitable occurred in January 2001. The "Denmark Arms" was just another back-street pub that will be mourned only by the locals.

No 18. Duchess of Kent, Dover
*(Amalgamated with **Walmer Castle** in 1964 to form the **Elephant and Hind**)*
East Kent Brewery Co., Jude Hanbury, Mackeson, Whitbread, Fremlins

The "Duchess of Kent" is ancient – very ancient. Standing close to Butcher's Lane it traded as the "Butcher's Arms" as early as 1690. By 1822 the structure was in such a parlous state that the property had to be re-fronted. The pub was re-named the "Duchess of Kent" in 1835, the year she visited the town. Its next-door neighbour was the "Walmer Castle" and as a result their histories have become entangled.

The "Walmer Castle", established in 1729, had previously been known as the "Hare and Hounds" and the "Dolphin", yet legal documents relating to the "Duchess of Kent" could indicate that this pub had traded under these names. A document dated 10th November 1783 refers to the "Hare and Hounds", but by 29th May 1802 the house is called the "Dolphin". In this deed Benjamin Jelly Worthington, Thomas Gover and Thomas Horn convey to Kingsford Wood premises in Market Place, Dover for a consideration of £300. A subsequent conveyance dated 11th August 1846 was made between the late Kingsford Wood and James Webb whereby the property changed hands for £600. The following day Webb mortgaged the property to James Kingsland in the sum of £400. In 1858 Webb conveyed the house to William Harding. In 1890 Mrs. Harding offered the "Duchess of Kent" to the highest bidder but it was withdrawn at £1,100.

The "Duchess of Kent" was a small but busy house situated in the Market Square. It held a licence to open at 3.30a.m. with this privilege renewed in 1874 and 1900. During the late 1800's coaches would depart from the inn for St. Margaret's Bay at 4.30a.m. each day except Sunday. At the start of the First World War all licensed premises and clubs were prohibited from selling alcoholic drinks after 9p.m. with the exception of the "Duchess of Kent" and "Walmer Castle" and the buffets at the town and harbour stations. In the 1920's it was still an "early house" offering accommodation with the bar windows plastered with advertisements including a prominent one for Martell's Three Star Brandy. The pub passed to Jude Hanbury in 1920 when they acquired the share capital of the East Kent Brewery based in Sandwich. In the late 1920's a circular electric sign costing £13/15/- was installed. The pub was acquired by Mackeson in 1929.

A visitor from the Hythe brewery, in 1945, described the house thus "… very poor cellar … ceiling mains very bad and require renewing". Alterations to the bar were carried out in 1954 at a cost of £160. It would appear that as late as 1961 the brewers still only held a leasehold interest as on the 7th January the company entered into a lease of 25 Market Square from the National Provincial Bank (their neighbours) for seven years at £100 p.a. plus a service charge of £40 p.a.

In 1962 Whitbread and Fremlins, the owners of the "Walmer Castle", obtained planning consent to amalgamate the two houses – this involved an almost total rebuild. The licence of the "Duchess of Kent" was surrendered with the new house opening in 1964. The two brewers held equal shares in the new pub which was named the "Elephant and Hind", the Elephant being the trade sign for Fremlins and the Hind Whitbread's emblem. About the turn of the century the pub was re-named "Bar Elle" before changing again to "Ellies Café and Bar".

It remains a busy town-centre pub.

No 19. Duke of Cumberland, Barham
Ash & Co., Jude Hanbury, Mackeson, Whitbread, Free House

Indentures dating back to 1640 refer to this house as a staging inn with stables at the rear. Prior to this it was an old ale house. In its early days it was simply named the "Dukes Head". Whitbread state the pub takes its name from Ernest, Duke of Cumberland (1771-1851). However, William, the third son of George II, born in 1721, was created Duke of Cumberland in 1726 and became a soldier in 1745. It was he who led the English army against the Scots at Culloden on Wednesday 16th April 1746 when the English scored a resounding victory. He trained his troops on Barham Downs and, it is said, used the nearby "Woodman" as his headquarters. I think it more likely the house honours his memory.

The first reference that I have traced to the pub being called the "Duke of Cumberland" is dated 1812. George Ash and others purchased "a piece of pasture land and Heredits" on 30th December 1843 for £500 from Charles Fortiscue Hornsby and his mortgagees. This description is something of an understatement as the pub came with: *60 acres of land; 60 acres of pasture; 60 acres of meadow, which flooded in winter; ten acres of woodland; four orchards; four hop gardens; oast houses; and four stables.* There is a contradiction in the documentation as the Ash records of 1870 indicate that they purchased the property from Hudson. By this time Hornsby Senior had moved on to the "White Horse" at Bridge and had been succeeded by his son who had the same initials. He paid a rent of £25 and insurance costs amounted to £1/13/6. William Stevens was the tenant at the death of Thomas Ash in 1875. At about this time the pub was brewing its own beer which was served in tankards – in order, it is said, that the drinkers could not see the contents!

In the early 1800's the front of the property was extended and this now comprises the bar area. These comfortable and appealing rooms are full of memorabilia, including the David Burley map of East Kent. There is also an advertisement for the regular Thursday 11a.m. coach to London – as the pub was sited on the old Folkestone, Canterbury, London stage coach run. This was priced at 50/- in 1761 – an enormous sum given that the average labourer's wage was about 6d per week. The horses were changed here and gentleman travellers were advised to carry arms. This may well be because of local highwaymen – in the village of Kingston, just down the road, is a pub called the "Black Robin" which commemorates the exploits of one of their number.

In May 1925 Jude Hanbury entered into an agreement with Major G.A. Meakin regarding a door at the hall that opened on to the premises known as the "Duke of Cumberland". In January 1937 the brewers leased, for a term of 21 years at a nominal rent of 1/- p.a., land to the South East Kent Electrical Power Co. Limited for a transformer to be sited next to the pub. The tithe was redeemed on 5th June 1940 and repairs were carried out in 1949 at a cost of £100.

The pub closed for a short while during October and November 1998 whilst an incoming owner carried out much-needed renovation work. It is now a one-bar house boasting good restaurant facilities and is popular with walkers in this splendid part of the county. One can play bat and trap and the house still offers accommodation. The pub also acquired a nice new inn sign showing the coat of arms of the Duke.

At one time, not so long ago, the village was blessed with five public houses but this is the sole survivor. It became a freehouse in 1992.

No 20. Falstaff Tap, Canterbury
*(Re-named the **Tap** in 1996. Closed in September 1999) Ash & Co., Jude Hanbury, Mackeson, Whitbread*

This small house which dates back to the early 1700's was the overflow house for the much larger and older "Falstaff Hotel" which itself can possibly be traced back to 1403. Until 1783 the hotel had been known as the "White Hart". Both houses are situated outside the Westgate and catered for pilgrims and other travellers who arrived late in the evening after the great gate giving access to the City had been closed. The upper echelons would spend the night at the hotel whilst the coach drivers and servants would go round the corner to the "Falstaff Tap" or other beer houses.

Henry Green was the landlord in 1838 and was followed by James Strutt who, in 1854, was convicted for opening his house before hours. In 1855 Mrs. Mary Harrison was listed as the landlady of the "Sir John Falstaff Tap". It would appear that the hotel also held the licence for the "Tap" as we find in December 1863 that Richard Spendiff, landlord at the "Falstaff Hotel" including the "Falstaff Tap", transferred the licence of the "Tap" to Charles Lott. However, the house was owned by Clara Kelley Croasdill of Westgate House, a spinster. Her will was proved in 1897 and she left to her friend, William Samuel Perry Patterson of Canterbury, a surgeon, "... All that messuage known as the "Falstaff Tap" with the yard, stables, outbuildings being situated in North Lane then let to William Burton". She hoped Patterson would add the surname of Kelley to his. This he did as, on 22nd July 1919, Mr. Kelley-Patterson sold the pub to Ash & Co. for £2,300. William Burton was still "in situ".

During 1924 alterations to the bar were carried out and new gates and electric light were installed at a total cost of £144/7/0. Three years later a bowling-green was constructed, costing £23/3/- and a further £264/9/8 was spent on garages and a new fence. During 1930 a new scullery, which included a new sink, was built at a cost of £106/16/6. W.S. Gibson signed a tenancy agreement on 18th October 1945, paying a rent of £25. The place was obviously in good order as a visitor from the Hythe Brewery that year reported "all clean and well kept". The pub suffered during the war and on 1st October 1953 a claim in respect of chattels at the "Falstaff Tap" garage was settled under the War Damage Act 1943 in the sum of £100/3/11. 1952 was a busy time as we find both garages were provided with a lean-to and covered way, also electric cable and casing were purchased, and a water supply and tap were laid on – all completed for £29/7/-. In 1956 the garages were rebuilt at a cost of £200. In about 1960 a large upper-storey extension was added to the side of the building.

A Whitbread Ladies Luncheon meeting was held here during 1954 at which the guest speaker was the celebrated cooking television personality Philip Harben. He challenged any lady present to prepare a sandwich quicker than he could cook an omelette. The pub landlady, Mrs. Violet Chappell, rose to the occasion and swiftly produced a superb offering. However, a brewery employee told me that it was not really a fair contest as the landlady was permitted to use cut bread etc. whilst making her sandwiches in a specially prepared "mock" kitchen. The object of gatherings such as these was to encourage landlords to be more adventurous in the variety and quality of food they had to offer. Violet and her husband Bob, who died in 1961, moved on to the "Two Brewers" in Canterbury from whence she retired to enjoy a good old age before she died in a Herne Bay nursing home in March 2004.

A problem arose around 1960 when the police objected to a proposed new licensee. The gentleman in question had served in the Light Infantry and his credentials appeared impeccable. The brewers asked for an adjournment of the proceedings and obtained the services of a solicitor who had known the man during his army days in Italy. It transpired that he had been charged, whilst a landlord in London, with receiving a large consignment of corned beef which was discovered in the pub cellar. Apparently he had been storing this for a supposed friend who had endeavoured to frame him. The police application failed and he went on to manage the house most successfully.

The pub closed for a while in 1983 whilst renovation work costing £36,000 was carried out. It was taken back to its original beams and bare bricks to become a traditional drinking house and it re-opened on 26th August. It was again part of the "Falstaff Hotel" with an inter-connecting car park and the food was prepared in the hotel kitchen.

One wonders if tenants who make name changes, as in 1996 to the "Tap", have any idea of the long pedigree of these houses. Probably not, as it did not survive for very long. Towards the end the bar takings failed to cover the cost of merely opening the premises for business.

On closure I was told that the six bedrooms would once again provide overflow accommodation for the hotel, but to date the property still appears empty although the car parking to the rear is being used.

Falstaff: *"A tapster is a good trade;*
                    it is a life that I have desired;
                    I will thrive."   Shakespeare.

No 21. George Inn, Folkestone

*(Known as the **Cheker** until the early 1700's when re-named the **George**. Became the **Cheker** again in April 1988 then **Thistle and Shamrock** in 1997) Kennetts of Elham, Marsh, Ash & Co., Jude Hanbury, Mackeson, Whitbread, Free House*

If we rely on written records the "George" is probably the oldest house in all five inn sign series. Even in the 16th century a man's status decided how he would be welcomed when visiting an unfamiliar town. If the traveller was important enough he would be entertained by the mayor in his parlour but people of more humble origin would be taken to an inn. Thus in 1525 we find the mayor entertaining a group of travelling players at the "Cheker" as follows "Yevon in reward unto the prences players in expense upon them at Master Kennettes att the Cheker, 3s 4d". The pub stood in Cheker Lane which was subsequently renamed George Lane. Over the years it has occupied three sites and could date back to 1426.

In his will dated 1545 Master Kennett left "his chief messuage in the Mercery" (one of the former sites and now called Church Street) "call the "Cheker" to his son John". We know that the pub had been renamed the "George" in the early 1700's as a report dated 1729 states "that two mares were stolen from the George's stable", which fact gives rise to the possibility that it was a modest coaching inn. The place was also referred to as the St. George on occasion. At about this time the inn was relocated to Rendezvous Street, occupying the present site of the Merchant Chandler shop. It was then owned by the Marsh family who operated the adjoining brewery. A little ditty ran the "George" was situated where George Lane met Grace Hill in Rendezvous Street.

At some time the house was acquired by the Ash family as it next appears in a schedule of property belonging to Thomas and George Ash dated 1870. It was in the possession of Will Wilson who had succeeded his father T. Wilson and was paying a rent of £23. He also had a loan of £90 outstanding with the brewers. Their records indicate that they purchased the property from Hoad and Banks.

The "George" became a well-patronised popular public house not far from the town centre. It also benefited from the close proximity of the Central Cinema as, at the end of the film, patrons would pop into the "George" for a quick half before making their way home. One of the upstairs rooms was used as a meeting place by several local organisations, including the Order of Oddfellows and the "George Inn" Cork Club, many members of which were said to be abstainers. For most of its long life this was a well-run house and landlords became part of the furniture. The last to stamp his authority was Dennis Chapman, an ex-wrestler, who was here from 1966 to 1986. Sadly on his departure trade declined; this coincided with the closure of the cinema and the pub became one to be avoided, indeed it closed for a short while in 1987. Fortunately this decline was halted in 1997 when the property was purchased by Caroline Andrewartha who set out to improve its image by renaming the place, painting the outside purple, and totally remodelling the interior on an Irish and Scottish theme. The toilets are to be found in the cellar.

In 2002 the freehold of the "Thistle and Shamrock" was offered for sale at a price of £265,000 plus stock at valuation. In 1996 the asking price was £55,000.

No 22. Grapes, Milton Regis
(Closed 24th January 1977) Milton Brewery, F. Leney, Fremlins, Whitbread

On 25th May 1899 Frederick Leney & Sons Limited passed a resolution to purchase from Mr. E. Hartridge the Milton Brewery together with residential and trading properties for a consideration of £27,000. Thus the "Grapes" came within the expanding Leney portfolio of houses. On 30th August 1901 Leney agreed to the release of a right of way adjoining the "Grapes" to Mrs. C. Emptage.

The "Grapes" was a small, low, two-up, two-down terraced cottage fronting a narrow pavement serving an artisan area of town. The inn sign was too large to be affixed to the building and was hung on a high stanchion which abutted the pub close to the entrance to the public bar – the sign was almost as high as the chimney stack. This was never more than a simple beer house right up until the 1950's and all beers were drawn from the wood.

George Whitehead was the licensee in 1908 and was succeeded by Henry Saddleton. On 28th June 1926 Herbert J.L. Adams signed a tenancy agreement and he remained until after the war. In 1939 he was paying the modest rent of £25 plus a £1 for electricity and the brewers held his deposit of £50. His inventory was valued at £53/12/-.

The house was always on the hit list for closure but the brewers gave it one last chance, appointing an experienced landlord who, to their surprise, expanded the business to such an extent that the premises next door were purchased in order to cater for the increased trade. Ivor Lowry was the last landlord and a very good one. His widow could still recall all too vividly the happy ten years they had there. The cottage walls were bowed and a tall man could not stand up straight in the saloon bar. The upstairs floor sloped to such an extent that the bed had to be levelled up with books. Ivor was a freemason and after meetings all would retire to the "Grapes" for a drink. An empty beer crate would be placed to the side of their table and during the course of an evening this would be filled with empties. The landlady collected key rings and her large collection was strung across the serving bar. The pub had no cellar and the barrels were stored in the back garden – when required they were rolled into the back of the bar. The beer was always in first-class condition, leading to a popular and lively house.

The pub stood at the bottom of Chalkwell Road where it meets Crown Road. Unfortunately this area has been re-developed and a roundabout now occupies the site of the old pub.

This was one of my favourite cycle rides, from Lenham up over the Downs to this warm and hospitable house, where a plea for an inn sign was never refused.

"I wonder often what the vintners buy. One half so precious as the stuff they sell." Fitzgerald.

No 23. Green Man, Shatterling
(Re-named *Frog and Orange* in 1997) Gardner & Co., East Kent Brewery Co., Jude Hanbury, Thompson & Wotton, Whitbread, Free House

Although situated on the A257 Canterbury to Sandwich road, the "Green Man" remains an isolated house and as a result the inn sign was never easy to obtain in other parts of Kent. At one time the pub was surrounded by hop gardens and apple orchards and whilst the former have disappeared this remains a very rural area. The present house was built in about 1820. It replaced an old thatched cottage originally built in the late 1720's as a farm dwelling with approximately ten acres of land. The cottage was converted to an ale house but, as a result of an infringement of the licence, was closed down. For a long while it was in the ownership of the Kien family.

In 1820 the owner was Sophia Russell and the property was occupied by Filmer Larkins, a farmer. He went on to acquire a licence to sell ale and in 1826 was granted a full licence. In 1841 the house was sold to John Dadds of Wingham who almost immediately on-sold to George Collard, a victualler of Staple, at a price of £450. One cannot be certain, but Sir George Collard was a partner in Ash & Co. hence it is possible that this house passed through their hands. On the death of George in 1863 his widow, Clara, sold the pub to Gardner Godden Brewery of Ash. This firm merged, in 1951, with Thompson & Wotton which in turn was acquired by Whitbread in 1955. In 1972 it was sold as a freehouse.

Apart from a few travellers making their way to or departing from Sandwich the pub's only source of income would have been the local agricultural workers. As a result any landlord needed a second occupation to supplement his meagre income from the pub. We find Robert Lloyd (1827-38) described as a tobacconist and the first tenant in 1863, Thomas Wyborn, was also a market gardener, George Mercer (1886-1896) was a shoe maker and Mrs. Matilda Hood (1916-1925) a milliner. The Oakley family remained for a long while with George Harry (also a market gardener) listed in 1907 and by 1934 Thomas had taken over. He was succeeded on 4th March 1935 by F.G. Perkins who was paying a rent of £20 plus £11/10/- for the land – about 30 acres.

The quit rent amounting to £2/18/4 was redeemed on 30th March 1931 and the following year a new porch and lavatory were fitted and the west wall was cemented to match the new structures. The work was carried out by Jude Hanbury at a cost of £304/5/6. The cellar was prone to flood, and in about 1950, the cellar walls were lined with bitumen and cement, but this never really solved the problem.

The pub closed for a short while in 1971 for refurbishment and it was at this time that the original ornate stone enamel sign showing a Robin Hood character was discovered behind the barn. Further refurbishment occurred in 1997 when the pub was re-named the "Frog and Orange" – thus much of its past history relevant to the area was obscured. Several small local businesses took their name from the "Green Man" including the Green Man Kennels. The lovely old sign also came down. It is now part pub, part restaurant and is a pleasant place to eat.

"Art may make a suit of clothes, but nature must produce the man." Hume.

No 24. Harp, Tunbridge Wells
(Closed 6th September 1978) B Baker, F. Leney, Fremlins, Whitbread

This was a lively, noisy house situated in St John's Road. These kind of places live on in people's memories and when the local paper the "Courier" kindly published my article seeking information about the pubs in Tunbridge Wells almost every correspondent had fond memories of the "Harp".

The original "Harp" was built in about 1830 and was first licensed in 1832. Henry Goodwin was the innkeeper from 1839 to 1845, but for some reason no one stayed for very long. Between 1832 and 1912 there were 15 tenants. In 1892 B. Baker, the Tonbridge brewers, rented the "Harp Hotel" plus coach-house and stables to F. Leney at an annual rent of £70, although the tenant paid the brewer a rent of only £50. On 29th September 1903 the brewers assigned the lease to Mrs. Reeves and she remained until 1912. Frederick Leney & Sons Limited purchased the freehold on 16th November 1905.

The goings-on here appear to have kept the local police force quite busy. A report dated 13th April 1862 refers to drunkenness and customers slipping out of the back door when officers arrived. During this era there were several other police raids.

The "Harp" was reconstructed in 1912 and as a result lost some of its character. The original was a charming old Georgian establishment with old oak beams and a large oak, gothic-shaped, front entrance door with iron ringed handle, a domed outside with a gilded wooden harp measuring at least five feet in height and the brickwork overgrown with ivy. The exterior was illuminated with two candlelight horse carriage lamps. The stables were rented out but these were demolished in 1912. The last landlord was W.H. Downs.

William Robert Smith was the first tenant in the remodelled house and he remained until 1919 and was succeeded for a very short period by his wife. It remained a popular house but in the late 1960's and early 1970's trade dwindled and the "Harp" closed in 1978. The property stood empty for a while before re-opening as a Victorian Stone Fireplace display centre.

No 25. Hop Poles, Canterbury

(Closed in September 2003 re-opening on 16th July 2004) Rigden & Delmar,
Ash & Co., Jude Hanbury, Mackeson, Whitbread, Pubmaster

Opinions differ as to when the original "Hop Poles" opened but it was sometime between 1692 and 1723. It is likely a dwelling-house occupied the site, possibly with a licence to sell ale.

Records for 1803 tell us that the pub was called "Three Hop Poles" and that the inn keeper was Thomas Scott. The name had not changed by 1817 when George Stubberfield was the landlord, but appears to have altered a little after that. Daniel Gann, succeeded by his wife, ran the house for a long period in the mid-1800's. Records dated 1870 show that Thomas and George Ash owned the premises: the Ash family had purchased the pub, private house and land adjoining from Rigden and Delmar. John Roalfe was the innkeeper and paid a rent of £15 and the house was occupied by William Impett who paid £10/8/-. However, other Ash & Co. records state that this house, together with the "British Lion", was purchased from Parnell. They both quote Roalfe as the landlord paying a similar rent. By 1888 Mrs. J. Wraight was the landlady whilst her husband, Henry, ran the "Brewer's Delight". During this period the pub offered for sale Dunvilles V R Whisky.

The old house fell into disrepair and was rebuilt in 1904 in a style bearing a remarkable similarity to the "Eight Bells". On 26th July 1929 S. Terry installed electric light at a cost of £19/14/- and in November 1930 Bateman & Sons were paid £289 to rebuild the skittle alley in order to make a new club room. During 1925 the cottage and yard next to the pub, known as 108 Wincheap, were sold for £450, but 22 years later they were re-purchased from Mr. E.J. Smith for £1,750. The premises were occupied by the Thanington Dairy which vacated in 1951 when the "Hop Poles" was extended. In October 1963 a new bar to provide a social club atmosphere was opened by the Reverend A.E. Blake who had recently retired as vicar of Thanington. At the ceremony he commented that his former boss, the Archbishop, was attending a teetotal event in the city! In 2001 the walls of the games bar were adorned with a mural depicting countryside scenery.

The pub was aptly named as, believe it or not, until the late 1950's the place was surrounded by Lillywhites hop gardens growing the famous Canterbury Goldings hops and an oasthouse was located close by. It remains a pleasant place on the outskirts of the city as one approaches via the Ashford Road.

In September 2003 the pub closed with the freehold and contents offered for sale at a price of £175,000 plus stock at valuation. It was some little while before a buyer, who also acquired the nearby "Waterloo Tavern", came forward and the house re-opened on 16th July 2004.

No 26. King's Head, Hythe
John Friend, Mackeson, Whitbread, Shepherd Neame

When I weigh up all the evidence I feel there is little doubt that the "King's Head" is the oldest pub still trading in the town. In 1583 it was known as the "George", changing to the "Sun" in 1714 and it took its present name in 1750. It is the only inn mentioned in "Gleanings from the Minute Books" of the town. On the proclamation of Oliver Cromwell as Lord Protector in 1653 the members of Hythe Council celebrated at the "Kings Head" spending the princely sum of £3/14/6 on wine and beer plus 2/6 for a drummer.

There is much conjecture concerning the reason for the changes of name but a possible explanation for the most recent change could be new ownership – it was about the time that the house was acquired by John Friend, – the forerunner of the Mackeson brewery. He had been in business for a long while when on Monday 19th October 1801 he sold his total portfolio to William and Henry Mackeson, late of Deal. They paid the surprisingly high price of 28 times the present rent – in this case the rent was £14 which resulted in a purchase price of £392. The house was insured for £250. At the time the innkeeper was a Mrs. Smith and on the day of purchase she took delivery of 106 gallons of beer at a cost of £6/8/-. On 3rd November 1801 there was a further delivery of two butts costing £12/12/- and a kilderkin of porter at £1/7/-. Her annual rent fell due on 6th November. At the time of William's death in 1821 the house had increased in value to £1,000.

For many years after 1850 the pub was in the hands of the File family – firstly in the form of Henry, then Mrs. D. File, followed by Henry again, and finally Edgar. The house possessed many interesting architectural features, including a minstrel's gallery with a rounded ceiling for acoustic effect in the upper room. In 1921 the billiard room was extended at a cost of £167/19/5 and in 1955 improvements to the lavatory accommodation and alterations to the bars were carried out at a cost of £400. Numerous in-house functions were held here, including the Wateringbury Brewery annual dinner and the Hythe Brewery Sports and Social Club dinners and dances. The place was also well patronised by local organisations.

Shepherd Neame purchased the freehold on 11th February 1977. It remains a very atmospheric place and offers fine food to the discerning traveller. In 2002 I had the great pleasure of meeting Miss Eve Wild who had been secretary to Commander Findlay all those years ago. She was well into her nineties and living in a local nursing home. I asked her where she would like to go and was told – to her favourite pub, – the "King's Head". She had a bite to eat but did drink two gin and its and then asked me to purchase for her 20 cigarettes, as the home had banned her from smoking after she nearly set fire to the place. To anyone familiar with the large photographs of the Mackeson pubs taken in the 1950's it is Eve's copperplate handwriting that identifies each house. Sadly she died a year later and is greatly mourned. A more recent visitor in November 2003 was Michael Howard, the local MP who took time out from planning his shadow cabinet to sup a glass of Spitfire ale and pull pints behind the bar to raise money for the Royal British Legion.

No 27. Man of Kent, Crundale
(Closed in January 1957) Mackeson, Whitbread

The "Man of Kent" is another of those small village inns which closed years ago yet is still fondly remembered by villagers of a certain age who can vividly recall the happenings and personalities of the place.

The property dates back to the 18th century and probably started life as a farmhouse or three agricultural cottages. The first indication that it was being used as licensed premises was in 1908 when Mackeson paid £905 for the property plus £45/0/3 for the fixtures, so it had probably traded since the 19th century. In 1930, £150 was spent on building a new garage and bathroom, and the following year a water supply was laid on to the cottages at a price of £11/9/6. The quit rent of £3/14/4 was also extinguished. A record dated 9th June 1932 indicates that the company was unable to find a suitable tenant and was compelled to take over the house and place it under management. On 28th August 1933 the three cottages were sold at auction to J. Knight who paid £250 – £39 over the brewers' book value of £211.

During the early period of the pub's existence life in this charming village must have been idyllic although somewhat spartan. Each landlord played a very active part in the community in a variety of ways. The village post office and shop formed part of the "Man of Kent" and sold everything from meat to home-made bread. In 1922 Tommy Pilcher, having been discharged from the army in 1921, returned to the village of his birth to take over the tenancy – indeed he had spent most of his formative years here as his father had run the establishment during the 1860's and 1870's. Once a fortnight he would kill a pig to satisfy the villagers' bacon requirements and behind the pub was a brick-built smoke house used for curing the bacon and smoking herrings. The licensing hours in those days were 10 o'clock to noon and 6 o'clock to 10 o'clock during the week and slightly shorter hours on Sundays. His wife, Emily, did much of the work in the bar while he was busy baking bread that was delivered to all the surrounding villages. Emily's work was hard as Tommy reported "She had to carry all the beer up from the cellar with the glasses. There wasn't enough trade to make it worthwhile using the pumps although we had the engine for it – not worth the trouble of cleaning the pipes".

From time to time lodgers were taken in – quite often students from nearby Wye College who, during their holidays, worked for Mr. Berry at Crundale House Farm. Other casual residents included a gentleman who went in the evenings to catch moths.

The pub also sold shoes supplied by Darnells of London. A quarter of beef was purchased from Weddell's and the groceries were supplied by Reynold's of Orange Street, Canterbury or Headley's of Ashford. His father would buy a cant of wood in Marriage Wood for faggots to use in the smoke-house or the bakery, but the pub never sold wood.

The house was the rendezvous for most local societies and the goal runners were particularly welcome and thirsty guests after a contest. A report in the Kentish Express dated 9th April 1921, when the Crundale Goal Runners hosted Sellindge, states "A very even run was recorded, both teams showing good play. The referee Mr. S. Sharp finally pronounced it a draw, both teams scoring three strokes three points. After the run a smoking concert was held at the "Man of Kent" when there was much singing and quaffing of Ale". In April 1924 the pub darts team played a home match against Godmersham's British Legion Hut members, defeating them by four games to three.

The landlord at the time also enjoyed the privilege of being treasurer of the Slate Club. Members paid a subscription each week, then, just before Christmas, came the big payout. The local newspaper describes the 1923 distribution thus – "The "Man of Kent" Slate Club had their share-out on 21st December. The year had been a very successful one and each member received £1/7/-." It then lists the officers elected for 1924, the chairman being Mr. W. Cozens. There was then a sing song followed by the Sole Street Minstrels giving several excellent turns.

Ill health caused Tommy Pilcher to leave the "Man of Kent" in 1925 and he died in April the following year and was buried in the village churchyard.

On 1st April 1930 Anthony Thomas, aged 22, was granted the licence by the chairman of the Ashford Bench. By this time the old brick oven had collapsed but Anthony decided to rebuild it and to revive the baking part of the business. All that was required was a skilled baker and one came forward, namely Albert Blake. Albert was a young Welshman, lodging at Sole Street, who arrived in the area seeking work in the coalfields. He had, however, trained as a baker and soon the renovated ovens were producing 160 loaves a day to be sold in the surrounding area.

These were the depression years and times were hard but trade did perk up when a darts match took place. A landlord stated "All the beer was drawn from the wood in the cellar where it kept beautifully, but involved a great deal of exercise in running up and down the stairs! On busy nights such as when there was a darts match we would draw gallon jugs. I stocked only two varieties of draught beer – mild known as beer, and bitter, known as ale, priced at 4d and 6d per pint". During the winter months a cask of "Old" was added to the selection and apparently a mixture of old and mild was very popular with the locals.

Evening sing-songs were a regular feature and an old chap called Jones always contributed a song. Almost invariably the words would include "bugger", but if the landlord's wife was within earshot he would carefully omit the offending word. A regular visitor to the shop was the local postman who arrived each day on his motor-bike and sidecar for the 5 o'clock delivery each day, having travelled from Canterbury via Penny Pot and Sole Street. By tradition he was always provided with a mug of tea and sandwich or slice of cake.

Albert Blake continued to run the bakery and lodged just across the road at 2 Well Cottages with Mrs. Fairbrace whose husband had died in the Great War. Mr. and Mrs. Thomas gave up the licence in June 1932 and it was at this time that the company was unable to find a new tenant. They therefore appointed Mr. Blake to manage the pub for them. Shortly afterwards he married Mrs. Fairbrace and they both ran the house until 1937.

In spite of all these rural activities there was a violent side to the village. Close by a vicar was murdered in the 16th century, but a more tragic tale is that of George Wood. George had served his country during the Great War and undoubtedly had suffered some mental trouble as a result of his experiences. He returned to the village and worked at several odd jobs, including providing a hand at the "Man of Kent". On 23rd April 1923 the landlord, Mr. Relf, discovered that George was providing pub food to a down-and-out living in a derelict property opposite and decided to dispense with his services. On hearing this news George rushed off to get his gun but found the bolt had jammed. He chased the fleeing landlord and on catching him bludgeoned him about the head with the butt of the rifle. Thinking he was dead and realising the consequences George climbed into the pub water tank and drowned. Mr. Relf survived this ordeal and later bought a shop in Ham Street. In the meantime the hunt was on for George and his body was ultimately discovered by a lady who was working in the pub. It was recovered from the water tank with grappling hooks. Initially villagers were horrified at this savage attack, but on reflection couldn't reconcile the facts with the George they had known before the war. After a while they came to the conclusion that his mind had been so affected by the dreadful scenes he must have witnessed that they could forgive him. As a sign of good faith his name was ultimately added to the village war memorial commemorating those brave village boys who had lost their lives in defence of their homeland.

Sadly all good things come to an end. Despite the best endeavours of several landlords, trade dwindled thus rendering the pub uneconomic to maintain. It closed in 1957 and on 28th February of that year was sold de-licensed to Frank Harvey for a £1,000. The agent's selling commission amounted to £39/6/1. The selling price failed to match the valuation in the company's books, resulting in a write-off of £470/4/7. The licence was transferred to the nearby "Lord Nelson".

On closure the old wooden partitioned bench-seating was moved up to the "Compasses" at Sole Street. By coincidence, John Bartlett, who subsequently lived in the house after the pub closed, painted the sign for the "God Encompasses All", which can still be seen at the "Compasses" near the grindstone. Mr. and Mrs. Gerolemou purchased the property in 1977 when it was in a pretty dilapidated state. They spruced it up and for a long while have been operating as a bed and breakfast establishment, appropriately named the "Man of Kent". The bar was converted into a self-contained twin bedroom with en-suite facilities.

In 2002 the freehold of the "Man of Kent" was offered for sale at a price in the region of £400,000.

No 28. Nag's Head, St. Leonards-on-Sea
(See Series 1, Number 10.)

This is another duplicate but possibly because of the splendid sign.

No 29. Nelson's Head, Hythe
(Closed 10th October 1974. Now trades as Sotirio's Restaurant) Mackeson, Whitbread

I am told that in its early days this house possibly traded as the "Shoemakers Arms", as it stood close to Shoemakers Bridge which crossed a stream long before the Military Canal was built.

For a long while the "Nelson's Head" was in the hands of the Nelson family and it was James Nelson, in around 1840, who decided to leave his name to posterity by re-naming the pub. He was described as a beer seller, grazier, dealer and chapman. Mackeson took an interest in the premises in 1847, possibly by advancing mortgage monies to Nelson, although records indicate Nelson held only a leasehold interest. Following his death on 28th April 1849, his executors, Henry Bean Mackeson and Joseph Wilson, proved the will on 20th March 1850. Nelson bequeathed the pub to his son John and daughter Jane. It is reported that Henry Bean Mackeson went on to acquire the pub on 31st December 1880 from Henry Nelson in a somewhat acrimonious manner when John Nelson died in 1880 owing the brewer, by way of mortgage, £1,200 – a figure roughly equal to the value of the pub and adjoining house. It appears that Mackeson repaid the mortgage owed by Nelson and another by taking over the premises. However, the family remained in possession and Henry Nelson, probably a son, retained the licence until 1882, when Daniel Brett took over.

In 1922 the tenant suggested that improvements be carried out to both the private and saloon bars, but only the private bar received attention. The pub does appear to have had a rather chequered past. It had two staircases – one at either end of the building. At some time the house adjoining had been incorporated into the pub, resulting in one of the staircases leading to a single bedroom. For some reason the pub, from time to time, was placed out of bounds to local army personnel!

Hythe suffered quite severe bombing during the war and in August 1942 a decorator painting the exterior of the building was killed by the blast from a nearby bomb. The brewers always had trouble with the drainage here and in the 1960's decided to excavate to try to find what was causing the problem. They had gone down quite a way when they discovered an unexploded bomb! About this time seven or eight regulars were running a little club whereby all paid the landlord a certain sum and he then invested the total in premium savings bonds. They won a few prizes, but on the death of the tenant Mackeson experienced problems when the club was wound up as they had cause to suspect that members were claiming more than they had subscribed.

The inn sign was a quite splendid portrait of Lord Nelson which hung from 1938 until 1966 when a Miss W.M. Gandell wrote to the chairman of Mackeson, Colonel W.H. Whitbread, pointing out that the patch covered the wrong eye – it was his right eye which was blinded; and furthermore the colour of the greatcoat was not the royal blue depicted on the sign. The problem was how to re-design the patch over the right eye and give him a new left eye! After much thought a simple solution was found. By undoing the rivets of the star and bust itself you merely had to reverse the bust, re-engrave it on the back and weld over the right eye, and the only difference is that Nelson will be looking to his left instead of to his right. The greatcoat was then painted in dark royal blue the same colour as appeared on the "Lord Nelson" sign at Waltham.

Inevitably trade in this over-pubbed town declined and the "Nelson's Head" was particularly badly affected by the departure of the military from the town. Following closure the place re-opened shortly afterwards as a restaurant called the Nelson Griddle, which in turn gave way to an Italian restaurant – Sotirio's.

No 30. Newcastle Inn, Ewell Minnis
(Closed in April 1995) Mackeson, Whitbread, Free House

I am still not entirely certain whether the name of this house is the "Newcastle Inn", as the inn sign indicates, or the "New Castle Inn". In any event it is incredibly difficult to locate, being situated down endless narrow country lanes. As a result, in my part of Kent, the sign was always hard to come by.

I am told that the old thatched "Castle Inn" dated back to the 1700's but by 1874, when William Keeler was the innkeeper, and the house was said to be situated at Alkham, it had taken its present name. In 1899 it is more accurately stated that it was domiciled at Ewell Minnis and William was still the landlord.

On 25th October 1912 Mackeson purchased the property, paying a deposit of £62/10/- plus a further £39 for additional land. Legal costs amounted to £14. About this time a disastrous fire ravaged the building, resulting in rebuilding costs of £769/8/10 being paid on 30th September 1913. Worsfold and Hayward drew up the plans for the new pub and were paid £44/9/9. That same year the balance of the purchase monies, £562/10/-, was paid and the fire insurance claim of £480 was settled. £48/15/- was spent on fixtures.

Many villagers still miss the old pub and put forward the following explanations for its name. The first was that Geordies carrying merchandise to Dover for shipment to the continent would leave their horses stabled at the inn and then descend upon Dover. This is a rather unlikely scenario, but certainly the inn sign shows the coat of arms of that great city. I feel the more likely explanation is that the far older "Castle" inn, destroyed by fire, was re-named as the "New Castle" inn when rebuilt. Apparently the old thatched pub stood just behind the new building. At some time the new name was corrupted to its inn sign form, but by the time it closed it had reverted back to "New Castle".

The pub is remembered as a friendly local, particularly during the war years when managed by Mr. and Mrs. Herbert G. Putland. Drinkers would come from all over the area and the house was very popular with walkers. There was a jug and bottle and in the late 1930's the place also housed the village shop. It was one of the few pubs in this area to boast a darts team and when matches were played the bars were full to over-flowing. Good simple food was provided. Just up the road stood a flint-built house, which at one time acted as the coach-house for the pub. The "Three Bells" at Swingfield Street was not so far away and it was not unusual for bar staff to be employed by both houses. The pub is surrounded by heath land which made it popular with travellers who could park up their caravans. However, there was a strict rule that all customers must wear a shirt. Many of the odd jobs that needed doing were carried out by a local character called Fred the Shed. Because of its isolation the pub closed when the last customer left the premises. During the early 1970's patrons would place their surplus pennies around a pole in the bar to raise money for charity. Each year a well-known personality, such as Henry Cooper, Jenny Agutter or Susan Hampshire, (who had a holiday home at nearby Sandwich) would arrive to demolish the tower into a blanket held by the locals. Over a three-year period innkeeper Percy Board and his customers raised almost £1,000 for the Cancer Research charity. Around the bar were photographs of the celebrities who had attended the great knock-down. The back bar housed a piano. It tended to be a young persons' house and the Young Farmers met here.

In 1954, £450 was spent on the bathroom, drainage and paths and two years later mains electricity was laid on, new lavatories were installed, and alterations were made to the bar for a similar sum.

Whitbread closed the house on 28th March 1977 and shortly after it was sold it re-opened trading as a freehouse. In its later years trade fell away and in 1995 it closed for good when it failed to attract a trade buyer. In 2001 the freehold was offered for sale at an asking price of £395,000. A canine beautician business now trades from Newcastle house.

No 31. Old Golden Cross, Hastings
(See Series 1, Number 5.)

This is another repeat but this time showing the sign designed by Violet Rutter in 1954. Personally I preferred the Series 1 sign designed by Prudence Rae-Martin. The same sign still hangs but against a red background.

No 32. Pier Hotel. Herne Bay

(See history for name changes and dates of closures) Mackeson, Whitbread, Bass Charrington, Free House

The "Pier Hotel" occupies a classic building situated on the seafront almost opposite the town pier and pavilion. It has an interesting history and a somewhat chequered past.

It was originally an extension of Oliver Lee's Billiard and Assembly Rooms and "Brunswick Hotel". It can be traced back to the 1830's when it adjoined the "Royal Pier Hotel". It was an immediate success. An advertisement in a local paper states "Pigeon Match will take place prize a massive silver tankard to be shot for by 20 subscribers at 15/- each on Wednesday 23rd September 1840 at 21 yards their guns to be loaded with 1¹/2 ounces of shot. Dinner provided by landlord T.M. Skrymsher after the match at 2/6 per head." By 1855 George Steer was the landlord of the "Royal Pier and Posting House"; he was succeeded by J. Steer in 1859.

The "Brunswick Hotel" failed in around 1875 and the last licensee transferred next door – the establishment was called the "New Pier Hotel". The word "New" was dropped in about 1898, probably at the time when the "turn-of-the-century" brick frontage was added to create the public bar area. This massive restructuring cost £2,085. At the time Mackeson owned a leasehold interest, having paid a premium of £150 to Mrs. Eliza Ann Handford of Kentish Town for a 70-year lease dating from 24th June 1896 at an annual rent of £140. Mowll and Mowll were the solicitors acting and their costs amounted to £72/13/5.

During 1907 £15/16/4 was spent on furniture and the following year improvements were carried out at a cost of £118/2/4 and a further £24/13/- was spent on refitting the billiard table. At the same time it would appear that there was a total spring-clean as furniture to the value of £575/13/- was sold and new additions were made at a cost of £440/19/7. During 1928 a garage was erected for £650. Mrs. C. Peck, in 1935, advertised: ""The Pier Hotel and Restaurant" with Residential and Commercial First Class Accommodation. Luncheon and Teas. Moderate Terms. Garage attached." I would imagine it would have been a very nice place to stay. In 1955, £100 was spent on the installation of a hand-powered lift.

Mackeson finally purchased the freehold of the hotel and garage plus 61A, 62 and 63 Avenue Road from H. Teesdale and A.W. Matcham, the trustees of Alice Mary Marlow deceased, for £9,250: completion took place on 23rd November 1948. Ten months later the three properties in Avenue Road were sold to Mr. Maurice Ezra Philp for £1,400. The garage was sold to Robert John Root for £2,250 on 18th November 1958.

Aubrey Dix was landlord from 1967 and was the last licensee under Whitbread. The place then closed for a short while before being sold to Bass Charrington. In 1986 they sold it to Peter Woods and Roy Hanslow who changed the name to the "Welcome Inn". This name didn't last long as in 1990 Garry and Sue Edwards bought the house and reverted back to the "Pier Hotel", but unfortunately they traded only until August 1992 when the place again closed and was placed on the market at an asking price of £100,000. In 1993 it was acquired by Mr. M.W. Thompson who, on being advised by the police that the house had a bad reputation, re-named it "Constables". The hotel was subsequently offered for sale at a price of £150,000 in January 1999. It no longer traded as an hotel but was sold as a pub plus three one-bedroomed self-contained flats. The following year the leasehold interest in flat one was placed on the market at £32,500.

To bring the wheel full circle the original "Royal Pier Hotel" became a convalescent home for London children and was ultimately demolished in the 1960's: it was replaced by a ten-storey block of Greater London Council flats.

No 33. Railway, Gillingham
(Re-named *Southern Belle* 20th June 1979) F. Leney, Fremlins, Whitbread

The "Railway Hotel" was erected in 1850 at the same time as East Kent Railway came to Gillingham. The station was built close by.

A post office directory dated 1866 indicates that the licence was held by Edward Dalton and records show that in 1872 the property was owned by James Budden. The licence was to sell by retail excisable liquors to be consumed on the premises. That same year Margaret Smith was accused of stealing some sheets from the landlord, Robert Henry Clark. However, Chatham magistrates discharged her. The Chatham Observer stated that on 3rd May 1873 the incoming landlord, Stephen Hibbard, held an opening dinner and later that month he applied for an hour's extension on the occasion of a foresters' supper.

D. Barnard was the tenant in 1878 when the place was described as the "Railway Tavern and Concert Hall". In 1892 an advertisement was placed in the local paper stating: "Wanted good general and plain cook, about 22, all found." Barnes. "Railway Hotel". By 1889 Austin Frederick Budden of Gads Hill Place, Higham, had acquired the hotel and it was he who sold the premises to Augustus Leney for £5,700 on 29th September 1893. This was the initial value of the house in the company books and it was re-valued at £6,900 in 1908. In 1905 Leney leased the hotel to J.T. Winter for a period of 7 years commencing on 24th June 1905 at an annual rent of £130. The lease was subsequently extended to 24th June 1915.

In 1893 a meeting of builders, landowners and other interested persons was held here with a view to obtaining some modifications to the bye-laws. Two years later the inquest on the body of George Fagg, a platelayer, also took place here. He had fallen down the cliff at Brompton Cutting on leaving work and was killed instantly. A verdict of accidental death was returned. Many years later, in 1945, a petty officer had a few drinks and on leaving the pub stooped down and rolled up a rubber mat which he put under his coat. He thought the mat would look nice in his new house. It had been a silly thing to do and he was sorry: he was fined £2.

This was always a busy and popular house. It was well frequented by railway passengers and, as it was on the main road to the dockyard, for many years its chief custom was from sailors. Its drinkers could possibly have downed more pints of beer than those in any other pub in Kent – just after the Second World War it was recorded that it sold about 1,250 brewers barrels of wet trade. This was an enormous through-put.

In 1937 building works to the value of £700 were carried out. It received a further facelift in the summer of 1956 when the rambling and unconnected bars gave way to a centrally-served bar and saloon. At this time Marjorie Hutton designed a delightful new inn sign showing a station scene. An unwanted part of the ground floor was converted into separate premises and was then let to F. Woolgar (Medway) Limited for a period of 21 years commencing 15th April 1957 at an initial rent of £300 p.a., rising in the second year to £600. These premises were acquired by Fremlins in October 1960.

There can be little doubt that the "Railway" was the premier pub in the area and local tenants aspired to manage the place. In 1922 Mrs. B.F.E. Crumbie came here from the "Samuel Pepys"; we then see John Pollard arrive from the "Worlds End"; and lastly, in January 1944, Charles F. Denyer from the "Spread Eagle". On 14th August 1974 it became a Whitbread-managed house but in about 1990 it reverted back to a tenancy.

The pub was re-named in 1979, and acquired a southern states steamboat theme, but the last sign I saw was a quite splendid Merchant Navy-class locomotive hauling an express through the town.

No 34. Red Lion, Stodmarsh
Ash & Co., Jude Hanbury, Mackeson, Whitbread, Free House

One can find this excellent house far off the beaten track down by the local nature reserve. After having tramped through the marshland admiring the views and identifying the numerous bird species, one can return to the pub for a splendid meal and sparkling conversation. Those who do so will be following in the footsteps of King George VI, who visited after a duck shoot, and the RAF ace Douglas Bader. When I called one Wednesday evening in 1994 the pub was so full that I was unable to park my car in the village, let alone in the pub car park.

The original weather-boarded building stood sideways on to the road and dates back to the 15th century. Originally it was a simple agricultural cottage and formed part of the Stodmarsh Court Estate. Over time the estate was broken up and this property came into the possession of Isaac Griggs, described as a grazier and brewer. It was he who obtained the first licence in 1685 and named his house the "Lion". During the 1720's tithe suppers were held here. A full licence was obtained in 1749 when we see the first reference to the "Red Lion"; from time to time it reverted back to the "Lion". The house licence was revoked for six months in 1899 for unlawful gaming. John Clark ran the pub from about 1800 to 1817.

Over the years the original house has doubled in size and has been swung round to front the road. In 1933 further additions took place, including bringing the toilets within the building for the first time. During refurbishment an old clay bread-store was unearthed. Capital additions costing £500 were made in 1949 and on 8th September 1950 a deed of exchange between the brewers and Mr. H. W. Twyman was executed. Twyman acquired a parcel of land at the rear of the pub, subject to his paying £35 and also undertaking to erect and maintain a three-foot-high, 4 1/2 inch brick wall with nine-inch piers at intervals of ten feet along the line of the new boundary. The legal fees amounted to £17/2/4.

In 1962 the landlord, Pat Featherby, spent three months crafting a bar in his well-equipped workshop behind the pub. He used chestnut from the Earl of Guilford's estate and heavy-gauge copper. Although this started as a hobby, his bar was installed at the "Bell" in Hythe and he had other orders in the pipeline. Ultimately, in 1967, he installed one in the "Red Lion" and operated a very successful small restaurant, but unfortunately beer sales went into rapid decline. As a result he was given 12 months' notice to quit – clearly he was a man ahead of his time. Another interesting feature in the car park was a gypsy caravan which gradually rotted away.

At some time this house passed into the hands of the Ash brothers – probably towards the end of the 19th century as there is no mention of the place in a list of their assets dated 1870. It would have then taken the usual route through to Whitbread who sold the house on 21st January 1977.

Over the years both of the inn sign miniatures have hung here, as at one time we saw a red black lion, as appeared at the "Black Lion", Mereworth. However, all is well as we are again back to the original, which also advertises Greene King Fine Ales.

A visit is a must if you are in this area.

"A still and awful red." Coleridge.

No 35. Royal Dragoon, Canterbury
(Formerly Waggoners Arms. Closed in April 1998) Ash & Co., Jude Hanbury,
Mackeson, Whitbread, Shepherd Neame

The first mention of this house is on 6th November 1807, although the building is probably a little older. It was built as three grave-diggers' cottages and the cellar was used as a mortuary and it was "set close by a barracks for hussars". This description is probably accurate as the rear garden certainly includes part of an old cemetery. As a result the licensee needed permission from the Church Commissioners as headstones had to be removed but "mortal remains shall lie beneath". By about 1830 it was in the possession of Thomas King, a victualler, and in his will, dated 10th July 1831, he left the property to his wife Jane. At that time the pub traded as the "Waggoners Arms". It is interesting to note that at about this time there were many name changes and all of the former names had connections with the countryside thus indicating that the City, in those earlier days, had been a fairly modest rural town. The will of Thomas was proved on 12th January 1832. Jane died on 31st March 1842 and her executors, Mr. King and Mr. Underdown, sold the house plus a buildings yard for £100 to George Ash. It was still called the "Waggoners Arms".

George Ash died on 16th August 1867 with his will was proved on 29th October 1867. He left his estate to his two sons, Thomas and George. By now the name had changed to the "Dragoon" and it was so named in a list of the brothers' assets drawn up in 1870, at which time the landlord was James Stroud who paid an annual rent of £10/8/-. The first recorded innkeeper was George Kidman in 1839. He was followed in 1848 by Edward Vincer who remained until 1855 before moving down the road to the "Vauxhall". On the death of Thomas Ash in March 1875, Henry Castle was in possession. By now the house was listed as the "Royal Dragoon" and had probably been so since about 1870.

During the war years financial problems arose and in 1940 a bad debt of £18/18/1 was written off. The following year fixtures were sold for £69 less £20 for the beer engine. The roof of the "Royal Dragoon" was badly damaged during the blitz of 1942 and was subsequently restored with a higher pitch. An abroad cooper from the Hythe brewery reported on the place in 1945 and conjures up a sorry image. He states: "Ceiling wood joists full of cobwebs. Walls damp and dirty. Floor – earth covered with sawdust – filthy condition. Bad!". Things must have improved, however, as in November 1952 the outgoing tenant, E. Wilsher, was paid £164 for his inventory, which the incoming man W.G. Styles took over for £163/2/-.

The pub was often under the threat of closure and the ideal opportunity arose in April 1980 when a car smashed through the wall into the saloon bar. However, this is a building of architectural importance – and a great deal of money was spent on repairs. When I called shortly before the pub closed it was being run by two students and catered mainly for young people. It only opened in the evenings but it was thought that with low overheads it might survive. Unfortunately there were problems with after-hours drinking and the pub ultimately lost its licence.

The house took its name to honour the Royal Dragoons stationed at the nearby Cavalry barracks. Their main task was to combat smugglers on Romney Marsh. In battle they rode to war but then dismounted to fight on foot. However, unless they were well acquainted with the ways of the marsh and its inhabitants, one would imagine they were not very effective down there. A report in the Kentish Gazette dated 25th June 1802 states: "Two troops of horses belonging to the Royal Dragoons were sold by public auction at Canterbury cattle market. They were bought up with great avidity; some of them being knocked down at upwards of £40 and the whole averaged at above £25 per horse".

Shepherd Neame purchased the pub in 1972. Following closure they sold the freehold on 10th July 1998 and after much renovation work Royal Dragoon House was offered for sale in July 1999 at a price of £147,000.

No 36. Royal Oak, Bonnington
(Closed in 1971) Mackeson, Whitbread

A visit to the village churchyard will reveal the history of this fine old inn. There may be found gravestones recording the passing of numerous members of the Huckstep family who ran this house for about 200 of its 231 year history. Perhaps this is not so surprising as one Huckstep sired nine children, most of whom were born at the inn. From time to time it was referred to as the "Bonnington Oak". It took its name to commemorate the restoration of King Charles II following the puritanical era of Cromwell.

Records date back to John Skewer's will of 12th April 1748 in which he left the house to his wife, Mary, for life then to his son, John, and heirs in perpetuity. The will was proved on 19th May 1763. The inn then

passed through several hands until 21st December 1813 when Richard Marsh (a brewer from Folkestone) and his wife, Alice, sold the house to Henry and William Mackeson; John Hughes of Dartford, acted as trustee. Prior to the transfer Richard and Alice, in 1810, had extended the property forming a two-bar house with the public bar occupying the original building and the saloon situated in the extension. On the death of William Mackeson it appears, valued at £500, in a schedule of his assets dated 10th June 1821. During 1872 Mr. Edwards was paid £15/10/- to install a new tank and pump. In 1929 the brewers redeemed the quit rent of £2/18/6.

Money was spent on improvements on a fairly regular basis. During 1953 lavatories were installed and this, plus drainage, cost £450. The following year £880 was spent on the bathroom, kitchen and staircase and a few years later in 1966 unspecified work was carried out at a cost of £255. Electricity was laid on in 1968. In December 1955 a strip of land, about one-fifth of an acre, adjoining the pub was purchased from Romney Marsh Farms Limited for £40.

However many times I visited the pub I always had to ask directions from local farmers. When I read the well-crafted Whitbread publication of 1948 "Inns of Kent", I discovered that the author never found the pub and he could only be certain it existed as beer was delivered from the nearby Hythe brewery and the account was subsequently settled. Its past history therefore must be intertwined with the local smuggling fraternity – no less than the notorious Ransley gang based at nearby Aldington. One crisp morning, very early, these villains were returning home after a fruitful night spent transporting wool across the marsh to Littlestone, for onward transmission to France, and on their return they were hauling kegs of brandy back to their village. This was hard and thirsty work and when they arrived at the small triangular green opposite the "Royal Oak" (now a road junction) they shook up whichever member of the Huckstep family was then running the house and demanded he serve them breakfast, which they consumed whilst sitting on the brandy kegs on the green. Naturally the landlord could recall nothing of this encounter when the Dragoons later paid him a visit.

At best this house could provide only a very marginal living. Until the end of the Second World War it relied on local agricultural workers and some military personnel, but from the 1950's onward things became more precarious. During 1943, 133 brewers' barrels were consumed, but by 1951 this had dropped away to 27 barrels: one of the lowest figures I have seen. An abroad cooper from Hythe reported in 1945, whilst PC Huckstep was the landlord, "two weeks has run out of beer – none left in stock. Water is delivered here. All very clean. Very little winter trade". The "Royal Oak" was one of four Mackeson houses where, since 1890, the John Jones Coursing Club would gather, with their greyhounds, every Monday during the winter months to indulge in the ancient pastime of coursing. This house was always popular with villagers from Aldington. They followed in the footsteps of the Ransley gang and most weekends would make the three-mile pilgrimage to the "Royal Oak" to enjoy some well-earned entertainment. Amongst the maze of lanes in this remote spot one wonders how they found their way home. An old-timer supping ale just down the road at the "Shepherd and Crook" could recall playing darts at the "Royal Oak" by paraffin light. Another local remembers the days of Mrs. Woollett, a small lady, who during the 1960's was famous for her pickled eggs.

Even as early as the 1970's it was next to impossible for such an isolated house to survive and sadly it closed in 1971. It was converted into a quite charming private residence named the Old Oak. The present owner has a fine array of photographs of the house and past landlords.

This is another of those small country inns, the passing of which is still mourned by local inhabitants.

No 37. Royal Oak, Iden Green
(Closed early 1997 and subsequently demolished) Sharpe & Winch, F. Leney, Fremlins, Whitbread, Free House, Shepherd Neame

Thomas Wenman was the innkeeper here in 1884, advertising for sale Sharpe's Fine Ales. The Cranbrook brewery continued to supply ale until 1928 when the business was purchased by Frederick Leney & Sons Limited. The first document that I discovered was a mortgage deed dated 5th July 1842. On 21st January 1848 William Barling Sharpe took an interest in the house by advancing by way of mortgage £2,500 to Thomas Neve and George Farncombe. On 10th October 1890 Frances Mary Elizabeth Rush conveyed the pub to William Sharpe. Sometime in the past the original house would have been demolished.

Not a great deal of the pub's early history has come to light but an epic event occurred in July 1931 when the police constable from nearby Benenden was summoned to the "Royal Oak" to arrest an armed man. The miscreant, 38-year-old George Williams, a general servant of no fixed abode, appeared at Cranbrook police court before Colonel A.S. Barham and Captain V. Dampier. He was charged with being drunk whilst in possession of a loaded firearm and pleaded guilty.

PC Oakley told the court that on receiving a complaint he visited the "Royal Oak Inn" where he saw the accused. On asking him if he had got any firearms he replied in the negative. The accused then put his hand into his right hip pocket, and the witness, seeing he had a revolver, immediately closed with him and forced his hand down towards the floor. The accused called out "Let me go, or I'll shoot you", and then became very violent. The constable called to the landlord, Mr. Bridgland, for assistance and he at once went to his aid and they succeeded in disarming the accused who was then handcuffed. There was one live cartridge in the revolver. The cartridge had contained shot, but, being too big for the revolver it had been adapted by cutting away the shot – the powder and wad remained in the cartridge. A quantity of similar ammunition was found in the pocket of the accused. The constable added that when the accused went into the public house he ordered a drink, which the landlord served, and then, on noticing his condition, immediately took away. The accused had been discharged from the service of Colonel Morony, but whilst he had been in the army he had been a good worker, although drink was his downfall. The prisoner was sentenced to one month's hard labour.

The pub sat on a large plot and in September 1946 a portion was sold for £112/10/-. The house was granted a full licence on 28th April 1950, at which time the net monopoly value of £625 was paid. The following year the brewers accepted the sum of £250 in respect of the loss of development value over the remaining land. In October 1960 Fremlins acquired the Frederick Leney estate – this included the cottage at the "Royal Oak", which was sub-let to Mrs. E. Butler.

Whitbread sold the premises to the Drewitt family on 10th September 1973 and it then traded as a freehouse. David and Rita Drewitt expanded the restaurant side of the business and the décor adopted a British Raj theme. There was a splendid choice of food and they boasted one of the finest cold-cabinet selections in the county. The restaurant could seat 30 and won "the best pub in the South East" award on two occasions. In November 1983 Stephen and Rita Kent took over and continued to maintain the pub's high reputation. A later owner was Roy Hannaford who carried on in much the same vein, but he renamed the pub the "House of Hannaford" – it was said that he stocked as many brands of champagne as one would find in the West End.

Shepherd Neame acquired the premises in 1996 and the name reverted back to the "Royal Oak". However, their tenure was short-lived as a disastrous fire, early in 1997, virtually gutted the building. Trade was insufficient to warrant the capital outlay necessary to restore the house, so the brewers sold it, de-licensed, on 20th June 1997. Owing to the size of the plot it was not long before the pub was demolished to be replaced by a couple of houses.

No 38. Ship Centurion, Whitstable
*(Now **Ship Centurion Arminius**) Fenner & Flint of Canterbury, Sankey of Canterbury, Ash & Co., Jude Hanbury, Mackeson, Whitbread, Shepherd Neame, Free House*

The original "Ship" was first licensed in 1750 and was built by Fenner and Flint who were described as either coal merchants or brewers – more likely they were both. At that time it stood a little out of town and was probably built to attract trade from the increase in horse-drawn traffic on the Whitstable to Canterbury road. To the rear of the premises were a group of weather-boarded store houses, a stable and a coal-yard. William Waddington was registered as the first innkeeper. The house was sold in 1801 to Matthew Sankey who brewed in Canterbury and he in turn sold it to George Ash in 1827. Thomas Ash senior died on 12th March 1875 and the inn and four adjoining cottages were listed amongst his assets.

W. Wallace was the landlord, paying an annual rent of £19 and the four cottages were let to Cooper and others for £36/8/-. These cottages were to be developed into a row of shops. Jude Hanbury purchased the share capital of the Ash brewery in 1923.

Edward Foad was a well-known local business man in the early 19th century and he and his partners, Nutt and Salisbury, were responsible for building Island Wall and draining the salts behind. Against the advice of business colleagues he then went on to sow wheat on the new land, but inevitably the crop failed. In order to recoup some of his wasted capital he moved into the "Ship".

The pub adopted its present name in about 1840 but the reason for this addition is not known. In 1899 the landlord fell on hard times and, at his second attempt, managed to do a runner to avoid his creditors. A very popular landlord of the early 1900's was William Gammon, who also acted as the town crier at 1/6 a shout. Bill was a large be-whiskered man and his other claim to fame was that he had been bos'un on the "Great Eastern" steam-ship. The ship was built at Millwall and, at the time, at 18,915 tons, was the largest steam-ship afloat. During his tenure there was an advertisement painted on the wall offering oysters at 2/6 a dozen. Local mariners heading for home would sing:-

> *"We crack on all our canvas, boys, and for Whitstable town we sail,*
> *And all the thought that's in our head, Is old Bill Gammon's ale."*

The old building, snug, and several steps down from street level, was rebuilt in 1913 and 1914. The new house was designed by a local architect A.A. Kemp.

The quit rent, amounting to £4/19/8, was redeemed on 10th October 1933. In December 1947 Mackeson sold a piece of land in Skinners Alley, at the rear of the premises, to Whitstable Urban District Council for £50.

Shepherd Neame leased the house from Whitbread on 6th May 1992 and went on to purchase the freehold on 29th September 1995. They quickly on-sold on the 4th December of that year to Armin Birks who had sailed in from Germany. It was he who added the "Arminius" to the pub name. "Arminius" is the God of Strength, so maybe the new name is appropriate as the fellow certainly sells a strong brew. In 2000 the house won the much-acclaimed CAMRA Cask Marque certificate and this was renewed the following year.

The house is now affectionately referred to as the U-Boat.

No 39. Ship Hotel, New Romney
John Friend, Mackeson,Whitbread, Shepherd Neame

In early 1793 Elizabeth Rolfe, the landlady, had delivered to Mr. John Friend at Hythe a handwritten note requesting "a 15 gallon Barrel of strong beer be delivered to the "Ship". Last one exceedingly good". Later on 3rd June 1793 she penned: "I have sent a 16 gallon barrel to be filled with your best strong beer which I beg may be quite fresh and new as it will be kept some time before it's tapped. I want it to settle before the weather gets hot. The cask you sent will be on the draft a few weeks longer. That proved exceedingly good and hope this will be the same. Don't fail to send it soon, and we beg to have the bill sent with it. Your obliged friend". However, this stone and timber building is much older, dating back to about 1495 and can show records of all its landlords since that date. It was once a coaching inn.

John Friend sold his brewing business to William and Henry Mackeson on Monday 19th October 1801. The purchase price for each pub was 28 times the annual rental. In this case the rent was £40 and the brothers therefore paid £1,120 for the pub plus cottage, stables and four acres of land: they insured the premises for £500 with the Royal Exchange. By now the innkeeper was a Mr. Gibbs who took delivery of beer to the value of £3/12/- on 27th October 1801 and a month later he purchased two small firkins at a cost of 5/-. His rent fell due for payment on 6th November 1802.

William Mackeson died in 1821 and as a result a valuation of his assets was carried out on 10th June of that year – the "Ship" was valued at £1,400. During the 1850's Henry Rayner held the licence. In 1872 Mr. Edwards built a new clubroom at a cost of £138/10/-. The "Ship" was one of the more important houses on the marsh and as a result the place was refurbished on a regular basis. In 1910 new furniture costing £436/3/7 was provided, but in 1915, probably as a result of the war, the value of the building was depreciated in the brewers' books by £300. At the end of the war fixtures and fittings were sold for £367/16/-. A new kitchen was installed at a cost of £357/4/8 in 1920, and in 1931 new lavatories were added costing £100. In 1957, £1,200 was spent on a further re-vamp. During the 1920's a small cinema, run by a couple called Toner and Bloom, operated from the premises.

Needless to say, the "Ship" was frequented by "free traders", despite the fact that it was the meeting place for the local coroner's court. A good landlord knew when to look the other way. Some legal activities took place here, including regular sheep auctions.

When the man from the Hythe brewery inspected the place in 1945 he reported "Cellar is a stable. Very cold in winter, hot in summer. Riding school attached".

Shepherd Neame have run the house since 6th May 1992 when they leased the premises from Whitbread. They went on to purchase the freehold on 31st March 1993. The "Ship" was renowned for its restaurant facilities and it specialises in fish dishes. This fine tradition continues to this day. The hotel can also offer eight comfortable bedrooms to visitors touring this interesting part of the county.

No 40. Shrew Beshrewed, Hersden
*(Re-named **Raggs** in 1980. Closed by Whitbread 20th April 1980 and re-opened as a Free House. This closed in about 1988) Jude Hanbury, Mackeson, Whitbread, Free House*

So what can we make of this short-lived house? Its early life as a miners' institute was bedevilled with problems and when the pub closed its presence was missed by virtually nobody. Like the "Bailiff's Sergeant" it does not appear on the David Burley metal map; however, unlike the "Bailiff's Sergeant" this house did exist – nonetheless it didn't become a pub until 1952.

The "Shrew Beshrewed" was first conceived on 7th July 1930 when the board members of Jude Hanbury decided to build, at a cost of no more than £2,500, a permanent club to provide leisure facilities for this rapidly-expanding mining village. There was a slight financial over-run as the final building costs came out at £2,750/9/5. The new premises were to be called the "Westbere Social Club and Institute". On the second floor was a large club room. It had been a long time coming as the brewers had purchased the site for £240 in January 1927. In December 1931 Jude sold the club premises for £3,890, probably to a committee of people who managed the running of the Institute. By about 1934 Mackeson had a financial interest and unfortunately, by 1939, the club was experiencing severe financial problems which resulted in £1,500 of the outstanding mortgage being written off. Following this, on 14th April 1939, Mackeson became mortgagees in possession and promptly closed the club.

The place stood empty during the war years. After the war the Thanet sea-side towns became a mecca for Londoners tired of dreary post-war life. These premises situated on the main A28 road to the coast were ideally located to benefit from this passing trade. An added bonus was that Margate Corporation had passed a bye-law stating that all coach parties had to be out of the town by 6 o'clock, so passengers would need somewhere to slake their thirst. Early in 1952 the club buildings were remodelled at a cost of £1,457, the development charge of £640 was paid on the late Westbere Club, and the "Shrew Beshrewed" opened for business on 30th July 1952.

The re-naming was topical and was inspired by the old ducking-stool which exists in nearby Fordwich. The splendid inn sign, designed by Violet Rutter, paints the scene. The first landlord was Mr. H.W. Neale and it was his daughter, in front of a good-sized party of invited guests, who unveiled the sign. In the early 1970's jazz evenings were held, which attracted the likes of George Melley.

Hersden was very much a mining village and the majority of the men worked at Chislet just to the south of the village. Development work had commenced in 1914 but it was not until 1918 that the first coal was winched to the surface. The mine, at its productive peak, employed 1,600 men, but sadly, the workings became uneconomic and the pit closed in 1969. As miners received concessionary coal, no gas supply was laid on and electricity was supplied from the colliery power station, but the service was very limited.

Shortly after Whitbread disposed of the premises the house was re-named "Raggs". As the attractions of the Thanet towns faded when compared to a cheap holiday in Benidorm, trade dwindled. Locals tell me it played little part in village life. Live sex shows were held in its later days and one old gentleman remembers the miners diving out of the windows when the police raided the establishment. On closure the premises were sold and a garage now operates from here. A villager made the plaintive comment "It slipped from pub to garage without anyone noticing".

"Every man can tame a shrew but him that hath her." Anon.

No 41. Spread Eagle, Chatham
(Closed early in 1969) F. Leney, Fremlins, Whitbread

The "Spread Eagle" was a large pub, dominating its terraced neighbours. It stood at the corner of Jeyes and Frederick Street in a largely artisan part of town. It was sited within the Chatham town centre re-development plan and as a result the building was demolished in about 1970.

The house was built in the early 1870's and the first owner/occupier was Henry William Balcombe. He remained innkeeper until at least 1874, but by 1884 ownership had passed to Walter Hickmott of Maidstone Road, Chatham. In about 1894 one of the Leney brothers, probably Augustus, purchased the pub for £5,400, a considerable sum in those days. The house held a licence to sell, by retail, excisable liquors to be consumed on the premises, but by 1878 all intoxicating liquors could be consumed on or off the premises. In 1922 the pub was valued at £5,680 in the brewers' accounts.

On 20th January 1913 A.W. Jordan signed a tenancy agreement but he didn't stay long, being replaced eleven months later by Ernest A. Goord who was to pay an annual rent of £50. By the time C.F. Denyer

moved in, during April 1933, the rent had increased to £60 and the brewers held his deposit of £100. His inventory, in 1939, was valued at £411/6-. In 1945 Charles E. Selden, tontine secretary for the public house, was charged with wilful intent to defraud. Bail of £50 was granted. The result of the charge is unknown.

Not a great deal else is known about the place except in 1960 four tables were purchased for £18! There was some excitement on 24th August 1962 when Fred Trueman, the Yorkshire and England fast bowler, visited the pub to demolish a pile of pennies which amounted to £36/12/- – this was donated to the British Empire Cancer Campaign. Fred had been invited by Ernie Morgan, the Chatham Town football club manager, who had got to know Fred when they both played football for Lincoln City.

The years slipped by and the end approached. In 1969 the house was valued at £11,000 and was sold on 10th April of that year for £11,350. The pub was demolished the following year when Chatham Magistrates Court held the licence in suspense.

"You cannot fly like an eagle with the wings of a wren." Hudson.

No 42. Trafalgar Maid, Chatham
*(Formerly **World's End**, Chatham) F. Leney, Fremlins, Whitbread, Free House*

As far as landlords were concerned the "World's End" was bad news and the brewers therefore decided to re-name it. The new name was chosen by a panel of judges from more than 10,000 entries in a competition. One of Chatham's older pubs, the "New Inn" in nearby John Street, had been badly damaged by enemy bombs, was closed by removal order, and the licence was transferred to the "World's End". The "New Inn" served the locality where sailors and shipwrights, during Nelson's day, would have lived.

Next door to this old pub had dwelt for quite a while a woman who had served at Trafalgar in the look-out frigate, Euryalus. However, the Euryalus was no ordinary look-out frigate. She carried 36 guns and was among those ships that were the eyes and ears of the fleet. On 19th October 1805 the British fleet was positioned 50 miles to the west of Cadiz with only the frigates Euryalus and Sirius keeping watch. At dawn the frigates saw that the enemy ships were hoisting their topsails and preparing for sea. By 9.30a.m. Nelson had been informed and had set course for the straits to intercept, but with rain and fog the enemy remained out of sight. Before dark Nelson sent a signal to Blackwood of the Euryalus ordering him to keep the fleet in touch with the enemy during the night. This he did guiding Nelson ever closer to the enemy and when dawn broke on 21st October the British ships could see the silhouette of the enemy fleet against the eastern sky.

As the fleets closed Blackwood went aboard the Victory and urged Nelson to transfer his flag to the Euryalus "the better to control the fleet out of the gun smoke and confusion of battle". Nelson refused but asked Blackwood to witness the codicil he had just made to his will; that done Blackwood returned to his ship and action was joined at about noon. Nelson died at 1500 hours, and the victory was complete by 1630 hours.

After battle, command passed to Admiral Collingwood, but with his own ship and the Victory dismasted, and unable to make the necessary signals to control the fleet, Collingwood was forced to shift his flag to the Euryalus.

So this lady must have witnessed history in the making. Her adventures were chronicled in "The Mirror of Literature, Amusement and Instruction" issue dated 26th January 1837. It was decided therefore to commemorate the new name to honour this worthy lady. Violet Rutter designed a sign based on the description given by the London lady who won the competition. One interesting entry was the "Green Parachute" – a note of explanation was scribbled on the reverse of the design stating "the bomb what done the damage at the "New Inn" had a green one".

The result of the competition was announced on 31st December 1952 when the new sign was unveiled by the Right Honourable A.G. Bottomley, OBE, MP. The ceremony was performed by floodlight and many local dignitaries were present, including John Marchant.

The design has stood the test of time and can still be seen. The pub itself was offered for sale in January 1999 at a price in excess of £175,000.

"It's vain to think or guess at women by appearances." Butler.

No 43. True Briton, Folkestone
*(Formerly the **Cock**. Amalgamated with the **Harbour** in 1982) Ash & Co.,*
Jude Hanbury, Mackeson, Whitbread, Fremlins

Once upon a time three houses lined the western side of Harbour Street by the inner harbour – the "London and Paris", the "Cock", and the "Harbour Inn".

The "True Briton" started life as the "Cock" and is first mentioned in 1741 when the licence was held by Richard King. The name change, possibly the result of the patriotic fervour whipped up by the Napoleonic Wars, occurred in 1799 when the house was acquired by Stephen Golder. An abstract of title dated 13th September 1870 refers to the ""True Briton" lately rebuilt, formerly known by the sign of the "Cock" but for some time past been known by the sign "True Briton"".

For most of the nineteenth century the "True Briton" traded as a small but comfortable hotel catering

for the average traveller. Its main entrance was from Harbour Street but one could also obtain access to the rear of the property via South Street. By 1843 Ash & Co. had acquired the premises from Parnell and his wife, and in 1870 the landlady was Mrs. Andrews who paid an annual rent of £25. The title was copyhold. On the death of Thomas Ash, in 1875, the tenant was W. Keeler, paying a similar rent. His tenure stretched from 1855 until 1877, although during this period he did pick up two convictions. The first occurred on 10th April 1861 when he was fined 1/- and 9/- costs for having a defective man-hole cover to his coal hole, which had resulted in an officer of the 17th Regiment slipping over and hurting his leg, whilst on 5th October 1872 he was fined 20/- plus costs for remaining open during prohibited hours.

Another colourful licensee was Miss Mary Pearson (1882-1901). Whilst running the "True Briton" she was also part-owner of a number of schooners which plied their trade from Folkestone. The crew were regular imbibers at the pub and it was customary for their beer to be "put on the slate". Any sums outstanding were settled on payment of their wages, which were paid over at the pub. Just off the public bar was a small room known as the "Captain's Room" used by Miss Pearson and the masters of the ships to transact their business.

In 1903 the first motor-coach outing ever to be arranged sallied forth from the doors of the "True Briton". The place attracted many sporting personalities including the boxers the Sixth Duke of Wellington, a well known amateur when he was Earl of Mornington, Larry Gains and many others. Probably due to its situation Channel swimmers liked the house too. Derham used it as his base whilst training for his great swim for which the News of the World awarded him £1,000, and Fahmy Attalla, the Egyptian champion, planned his second attempt on the Channel in the public bar in 1947. The house also boasted strong darts teams which were winners and runners-up in the News of the World Individual Darts Championship for the Folkestone and Dover Area in 1937.

Like so many houses in this area the pub was damaged by German shells. Fortunately neither the landlord, Gladstone Martin, nor any of his family were injured when the rear of the inn was hit on 2nd March 1943. The pub remained closed for the remainder of the War, but emergency renovation work was carried out and it re-opened on 29th May 1946. The refurbishment was completed six months later. A new inn sign commemorating the bravery of local airmen, particularly those based at nearby Hawkinge, was unveiled depicting a Battle of Britain pilot on one side and a woad-covered ancient Briton on the other.

Further restructuring occurred in 1952 – this involved closing the house for a while. Most of the work was internal and included the installation of a bath. The total cost was £1,000. A party was held in the saloon bar at the re-opening and to mark the occasion Marjorie Hutton designed a new sign featuring the great East Indiaman, "True Briton", built at Deptford in 1790. Outward-bound on her eighth voyage, having exceeded her original "safe" charter of six, she disappeared with all hands. The original sign lay forgotten at the Hythe brewery, but on re-discovery in 1965 it was presented to No. 11 Squadron HQ at RAF West Raynham, Norfolk.

Probably a portent of things to come, in August 1957 Fremlins, the owners of the neighbouring "Harbour Hotel", were granted a licence to carry out alterations and reconstruction of their premises, which entailed the execution of certain works affecting the "True Briton". In February 1982 the brewers, as a commercial decision, decided to extend the "Harbour" by incorporating the "True Briton" and thus create a very busy house appealing mainly to youngsters.

*"They love their land because it is their own,
And scorn to give aught other reason why."* Halleck.

No 44. White Horse, Tonbridge
(Closed in 1970) B. Baker, F. Leney, Fremlins, Whitbread

The "White Horse" was a small, narrow three-storey pub fronting the High Street with a rear entrance in Bank Street. This was a decided advantage to under-age drinkers or other miscreants as they had two means of exit should parents or the local bobby pay a surprise visit. An inn sign hung in both streets. Despite its modest size there were public and private bars plus a jug and bottle.

The building dates back to the mid-18th century but we do not know its original purpose. There is a reference in 1790 to a religious group called the Brethren who met in the backroom at the "White Horse" until their chapel was built opposite the pub. This inn comprised one of a large group of local houses leased by the Tonbridge brewer, B. Baker, to F. Leney in 1892; the rent for this house was £65 per annum. They purchased the freehold on 16th November 1905. The first recorded landlord is Rhoda Bately in 1856. Following her there was a succession of tenants, none of whom stayed for very long until Edward R.J. Allen arrived on 13th January 1931 – his predecessor had been paid an allowance of £5 on leaving the premises. He was to remain until 1963 and was the man who handed out the inn signs. In 1939 he paid a rent of £30 plus £2 for electricity. His deposit was £75 and the inventory was valued at £272/16/-. At this time repairs were carried out at a cost of 185/9/9. Christmas 1950 witnessed a happy re-union at the "White Horse" when Edward entertained his brothers and their wives. This gathering was probably unique in the history of the trade, for the three brothers were married to three sisters (née Willsher). Edward was a keen bowls player, whilst his wife was well-known within the Tonbridge tennis fraternity. As trade fell away, one of the last landlords supplemented his income by working as a printer, serving behind the bar at lunchtime and in the evenings, and leaving his wife to manage the place during the day.

The "White Horse" was a popular watering hole for the town's firemen and on market day it was crammed with farmers, as the cattle market was directly opposite the back of the pub. The farmers would drive their livestock to the market, pen them up, and then clump into the rear of the pub in their dirty old boots. This was on a Tuesday, when the licence was extended until four in the afternoon.

Two events coincided to seal the fate of the "White Horse". The cattle market closed down in about 1970, and Whitbread decided to consolidate their interests in West Kent and East Sussex and it was decided the place had to go. The last time I passed it was being used as private employment offices.

No 45. Windmill, Cranbrook
Jude Hanbury, F. Leney, Fremlins, Whitbread, Shepherd Neame, Free House

Sitting high on a bank at the northern end of town, the "Windmill" dates back to about 1550. It was extended a hundred years ago and further improvements were carried out at the end of the war. The extension now houses the excellent restaurant facilities which can seat 30 people. Viewed from the road the old cottage is at the right-hand end. The garage occupies the site of the town's original windmill that was demolished early in the 19th century. The building probably started life as a miller's cottage. The cellar is still in use but is small and damp and must provide inhospitable facilities for the resident ghost.

The pub obviously takes its name from the demolished windmill. The "new" one is said to be the highest mill in England and is acknowledged to be the finest post-mill extant. A new inn sign was erected in 1995 but had to be quickly replaced as local residents complained that it didn't depict the town mill, not even a Kent mill, but the type one might find in Norfolk.

The Swattenden trustees normally held their meetings in a town-centre hostelry but in 1760 they moved a little out of town to meet here. For most of the first half of the nineteenth century the "Windmill" was in the capable hands of the Wimsett family. Richard was here in 1816 and either his wife or daughter, Elizabeth, in 1848. C. Waghorne had taken over by 1859.

Jude Hanbury purchased the property in 1887, paying the sum of £1,000 plus legal costs of £31/15/-, but we do not know from whom. Three years later a porch was added at a cost of £30. On 16th June 1902, £12/18/6 was spent on laying on water from the mains and the following year the signboard was repaired and re-written at a cost of £4/17/-. In March 1912, 6/- was spent on the carriage of two loads of clinker.

Shepherd Neame leased these premises from Whitbread on 6th May 1992 and purchased the freehold on 29th September 1995. In 2003 the pub was offered for sale at a price of £300,000 all at plus stock at valuation.

No 46. Woodland Tavern, Gillingham.
*(Re-named **Canterbury Tales**, 1996) Woodland Brewery, F. Leney, Fremlins, Whitbread*

The "Woodland Tavern" has an interesting history. Anybody going about their business today would find it hard to believe that 200 years ago this area was largely woodland and supplied much of the timber required to build the great naval ships of yesteryear. This area of Gillingham takes its name from Woodlands house and premises which were built sometime before 1840 by John Lock, a local landowner and brewer, as a country residence. The area expanded rapidly in the mid-19th century and was acquired

by the British Land Company. On 8th October 1862 they sold, by auction at the Sun Hotel, Chatham, 50 plots of land: the auctioneer was a Mr. Whittingham. Plots 47 and 48 on the corner of Canterbury Road and Paget Street were purchased by a brewer, George John Sayer of Almond Place, Rochester. He erected a house and brewery, called the Woodland Brewery, and about three years later took into partnership Theophilus Foster of Wainscott.

However, the brewery's finances must have been in a parlous state as, in the following year, Charles Baker obtained a court order against Sayer and forced the sale of the brewing plant etc. This was bought by Jesse Clark Foster of New Road, Rochester, who was described as a gentleman, and was probably a relative of Theophilus, as his name appears previously in a lease dated 9th October 1867. At this time the pub had a licence to sell, by retail, excisable liquor to be consumed on the premises. The house plus garden ground behind the adjoining cottages remained in his ownership until 1877 when he in turn sold it to the three Leney brothers for £1,750.

They immediately ceased brewing and in the following year sold the old brewery buildings to James E. Lines. The buildings fronted Canterbury Street, and have since been used for a variety of trades, including that of a furniture depository in about 1930.

The pub was an important social venue for the local community. The first innkeeper was the same George John Sayer who had built the property in 1863 and he remained until 1867. In September 1872 Richard Mutton applied to have his house open until 1 o'clock on account of Sanger's Circus performers staying here. Permission was granted. Four years later he applied for an extra hour on Saturday night for the occasion of the anniversary dinner of the Lodge of the Manchester Unity of Odd Fellows, but the bench granted half-an-hour and the house was to be cleared by half-past 11 o'clock. In March 1877 a smoking concert took place and in November 1893 an enquiry into the death of the illegitimate child of Elizabeth Matilda Hicks, a single woman, was held. The jury went on to return a verdict of death by misadventure. Towards the end of the 19th century the "Woodland Tavern" was the regular monthly venue for the Ancient Order of Foresters of Court "Pride" No. 3089 and in April 1899 a meeting of the New Brompton Amateur and Cottage Gardeners Mutual Improvement Society was held here. By now the pub could sell all intoxicating liquors to be consumed either on or off the premises.

Times moved on. In January 1957 Miss Jean Kennerley, daughter of the landlord, William Hadlow Kennerley, entered a competition for the title Queen of the Barmaids. Although not the winner, she did reach the finals, held in London, and recalled to the local newspaper that she had enjoyed the night of her life. Whilst this event must have delighted her father, he did have one big problem. The pub's telephone number was one digit different from that of the town's municipal building and Medway Ambulance Station. Mr. Kennerley received, on average, four "wrong numbers" a day and contacted the press in desperation when he was called at 3a.m. one morning to be asked to send an ambulance.

By 1988 the pub was firmly established as the "biker's pub" and a tough tavern to manage. However, the incoming tenant, a young mum called Linda McClean, vowed to restore the pub's reputation. Her application had been opposed by the police on grounds of under-age drinking, motor-bikes parked on the pavement, and excessive noise created by the live bands on music nights. This last complaint led to the house being forced to install adequate sound-proofing, and to assist with meeting the cost, which ran into thousands of pounds, four bands – The Absolute, Anyone's Gods, Rough Diamond and Mean Mr. Mustard – put on a concert in the Historic Dockyard, the first rock concert to be staged here.

The house closed for a while in 1995 but was revamped, painted bright yellow and re-opened the following year as the "Canterbury Tales".

No 47. Woodman, East Malling

(Closed 29th December 1971) F. Leney, H.T. Wickham & Co., Jude Hanbury, F. Leney, Fremlins, Whitbread

In 1810 a plot of land, a good way out of East Malling on the Mereworth road, was sold for £200. The purchaser was Jane Smith and by the following year she had a property built, called the "Woodman", which she sold for £200. Perhaps she retained some of the land. Over the years the pub has been extended on two occasions and is now a substantial family residence with well-manicured gardens.

The house was first licensed in 1867 and took the name of the "Woodman" almost certainly because chestnut coppicing was an important source of employment in this isolated and heavily wooded area. Prior to 1867 the property was referred to as the house at Malling Heath. Even to this day the area is quite remote and the old cottage opposite has long since been demolished.

Due to the pub being nowhere in particular, its past history is unusual as it appears to be the only pub in the inn sign series within the Leney empire which they failed to retain. Leney entered into a yearly tenancy agreement dated 4th January 1881, to take effect from 29th September 1880, with Viscount Falmouth over the "Woodman" at Mereworth – the annual rent was £50. This agreement remained vested in Mr. Augustus Leney, subject to a declaration of trust by him in favour of the company. This was given up on 29th September 1915. The house came with just over five acres of land. As far as I can ascertain there has never been a pub called the "Woodman" at Mereworth. It appears likely that the house then passed to the Yalding brewers H.T. Wickham & Co. as when that brewery was acquired by Jude Hanbury and Frederick Leney on 22nd March 1921, the "Woodman" formed part of the Wickham estate. The houses were split between the two parties and the "Woodman" was acquired by Jude Hanbury, who attributed a book value of £1,050 to the property.

The first landlord was G. Jarrett in 1867 and he remained until about 1876 when Thomas Iden Newman took over. At this time the pub was described as being at the Heath. In 1926, £2/10/8 was paid to F. Pierce for painting out and re-writing the sign. By 1932 the house was referred to as the "Woodman's Arms", and at the end of the year Ernest A.H. Moreby took over the tenancy. He paid a rent of £20 plus £1 for electricity and the brewers held his deposit of £50. He was succeeded by his wife in February 1941 and she remained until 1947. Unusually, on transfer of the tenancy, no valuation of the inventory was taken. In

1951 the brewers accepted the sum of £237 in respect of loss of development value in respect of land at the "Woodman".

This was a rustic house catering mainly for agricultural workers and those employed in the woods and orchards. The barrels were laid on staunters and placed under the windows and all beer was drawn from the wood. Moreby's brother, who lived at the pub, kept turkeys for the Christmas trade and when their time had come they were plucked in the pub cellar. He also stored his Newton Wonder and Monarch apple crop down there.

Records indicate that this was a two-bar house: one room was approximately ten foot by ten foot; and the other was about eighteen by eighteen. There is some evidence that the rear room may have been used as a snug. One gained entry straight from the road, as a door has been partially blocked up leaving just a central window.

A correspondent recalled the day he cycled out to the pub to collect an inn sign and his delight at being proffered dozens, with the landlord's comment that he was sick of young kids asking for lemonade and the quicker he got rid of the inn signs the better. However, despite the trade generated by these young lads, and £320 spent in 1964 on improvements, income fell away. As part of the disposal policy following the amalgamation of Whitbread and Fremlins, this house was closed down and sold unlicensed to George Bull. There is a little plaque by the door showing the "Woodman" inn sign.

"Woodman, spare that tree! Touch not a single bough!
In youth it sheltered me, and I'll protect it now." Morris.

No 48. Woolpack, Winchett Hill
(See Series 2, Number 43.)

Another repeat, but this time we have the new inn sign designed in 1952 by Marjorie Hutton. This depicts a rather weary horse carrying an enormous woolpack, which appears to weigh almost as much as the animal.

No 49. York, Chatham
*(Also known as the **York Tavern** and **Railway Inn**, **York Hotel**, **York and Grapes**,*
***Bullseye**, and **O'Connell's Bar**) F. Leney, Fremlins, Whitbread*

In about 1840 the Richard Watts charity, which owned a large area of land in the Medway towns, was given permission to lease parts out for building. Richard William Dadd acquired a lease for 99 years from March 1844 at £14/14/8 per annum. There was a condition that within twelve months building took place subject to their approval of the plans.

Accordingly a public house was built and called the "York Tavern". In 1855 the lease was bought by James Budden, a canteen keeper, who lived here and ran the business until he died on 6th January 1866 when it was taken over by James Breeze. Almost certainly it was James Budden's son, also called James, whose wine and spirit business was amalgamated with the brewery operated by the Biggs Brothers to form the Strood brewers Budden and Biggs operating at the Steam Brewery in Strood. The following year the pub was known as the "York Tavern and Railway Inn", probably to pick up trade as the town railway station was close by. At this time a licence to "Sell by retail, excisable liquors to be consumed on the premises" was held. By 1886 the hotel could sell "All intoxicating liquors to be consumed either on or off the premises". James continued to run the pub until he retired in 1881. He sold his interest to Charles Frederick and Augustus Leney and the freehold was bought in 1923 when the whole of this area was put up for auction.

Fred White took over the tenancy of the "York Hotel" during 1882 and unfortunately lost his wife, Cecelia Louisa, who died at the hotel on 18th July 1884 at the young age of 29. In 1884, besides the rental payment of £3/15/-, the company paid an insurance premium of £1/10/6, this figure increasing to £1/18/- in the following year.

The house suffered a couple of convictions in 1892. First, in March, James Constable received a summons for having his house open during unlawful hours and, on pleading guilty, was fined 10/- and 9/- costs. Later that year Walter Myall was charged for a similar offence and also for allowing an unlawful game, namely banker, to be played on his premises at the same time. He was fined £2 and 9/- costs in each case. 1900 saw the hotel landlord, Mr. Mulder, advertising for a strong girl and a lad of about 17. Boys will be boys and, in January 1920, a heavily loaded brewers' dray, unattended, outside the "York Hotel" attracted the attention of two small lads. One of them, on mounting, startled the horses and they dashed towards Chatham Station. A soldier managed to control the horses. The dray driver reproached the boys needfully (if not too delicately) and rewarded the soldier with refreshment of the drayman's stock in trade. That same year the hotel advertised for a "Cook, General, no Borders, wages £46/10/- p.a. References required". In January 1922 the Chatham Centre Instructional Class (S.E. & C. Railway) held a successful New Year concert here, and in 1925 Henry Bradford was fined £5 for selling intoxicating liquor out of hours. A sad occasion occurred in August 1946 when the funeral of the late Jasper James (Jess) Wright, who died in service aged 46 after taking over the tenancy on 7th March 1931, was held at Chatham cemetery. Over 100 wreaths were laid by the graveside.

In December 1915, at which time the house was called "York Grapes", the board of Leneys had to consider the desirability of alterations, but deferred making any decision pending further information. The ground rent and reversion interest came up for auction on 2nd October 1923 and the board left it to the discretion of the managing director as to what action to take. In fact they purchased this interest at a cost of £1,600. The company went on to purchase the freehold for £10,000 on 4th January 1924.

The pub name commemorates a victory of the Duke of York at sea in the 17th century. The house was re-named the "Bullseye" on 9th February 1983 – this name lasted until 1995 when it became "O'Connell's Bar".

No 50. Ypres Castle, Rye
(See Series 1, Number 13.)

This is the final repeat. There is no obvious reason as the sign remains identical. However, perhaps it is due to the fact that we started this saunter through the Whitbread houses with a visit to the "G.I." in Hastings and should therefore finish our journey in the same county.

A BRIEF HISTORY OF
THE FORGOTTEN BREWERIES THAT SUPPLIED THE ALE

FREDERICK LENEY & SONS LIMITED

This company developed from humble origins into a substantial brewing concern based in Wateringbury at the Phoenix Brewery.

In 1778 land at Wardens Hill, Wateringbury, was purchased by Richard Crow and in the early 1800's he and Mr. Crow (probably his son), built a brewery, which, quite naturally, was called Wardens Hill Brewery. The business prospered and a few years later Mr. Crow employed Edmund and William Pontifex "to install a steam-powered installation". It took a while to negotiate an acceptable contract, possibly because the Pontifex brothers had doubts about the Crows' ability to finance the venture. If this was the case their concerns were well founded as the Crows' finances were such that, on completion of the work, they were unable to pay. Litigation commenced and this dragged on until 1836, when Messrs. Pontifex took possession of the brewery. Brewing ceased for a couple of years and during this period the brothers negotiated a lease with Abraham Leney and his son Charles, who was running the "Bull" at Wrotham. However, this was not progressed and, on 25th December 1843, a new lease, for a term of 21 years at a rent of £100 p.a., was executed with Charles alone. Possibly in view of past financial problems the brewery was re-named the "Phoenix". Charles was born in 1814. At the age of twenty he married Naomi Evenden from Wrotham and a year later their eldest son Charles John was born, to be followed by Alfred in 1837.

Charles' brother Frederick was probably born at the "Bull" where he remained until 1853 when he moved to Wateringbury to join his brother as a partner in the business. By this time Frederick had three children – Charles Frederick, Charlotte and Augustus. Charles retired on 4th February 1859 and Frederick bought his half-share and became the sole proprietor. During 1861 Charles' youngest son, Alfred Charles Leney, together with his father-in-law James Evenden, purchased a brewery in Dolphin Lane, Dover, from the Walker Brothers' trustees which was re-named the "Phoenix". The following year Alfred married Catherine Fremlin, the girl next-door-but-one, whose brother was Ralph Fremlin. Frederick was now managing the Wateringbury brewery and Pontifex & Co. were the owners. In March 1862 the company sold it to Samuel L. Lucas. Seven months later the freehold was finally purchased by Frederick Leney for £3,150, and by August 1864 his eldest son, Charles Frederick, become a partner. On 1st January 1872 Augustus was made a partner for a period of 14 years. The eight company shares were allocated as follows:- Frederick and Charles Frederick three each, and Augustus two. At the same time sixteen-year-old Richard Tapply, who was to rise to joint managing director, joined the firm. Frederick drew up a will on 15th July 1875 and appointed three of his sons, Charles Frederick, Augustus and Herbert as executors. In 1880 Herbert, a farmer, was replaced by his brother-in-law, William Tapply. Frederick died on 26th May 1881 leaving his two sons and their brother, Edward, who was also a partner, running the firm. On 30th December 1882 Charles Frederick and Augustus became sole proprietors. During 1885 Charles Frederick sold his 9/16 interest to Augustus who for a while had been the driving force behind the firm's expansion, ably assisted by Richard Tapply as manager.

By the time the firm was registered as Frederick Leney & Sons Limited in the spring of 1895, Augustus held 158 licensed houses, 71 of which were freehold. Included within the leaseholds were 36 pubs plus the Royal Victoria brewery and Quarry Hill brewery, both in Tonbridge, leased from the Tonbridge brewer, Benjamin Baker. The lease was dated 1st August 1892 for a 30-year period from 24th June 1892, at a rent of £3,100 apportioned amongst the various properties. By a memorandum of agreement dated 17th January 1896 Augustus sold, for a total sum of £235,000, all of his properties, plus the family home, to the newly-created company – completion took place on 25th March 1896. Almost all of the licensed premises were then charged by way of a trust deed, dated 11th June 1896, in favour of the debenture stock holders – houses were withdrawn if they were sold and acquisitions were charged.

Augustus was a man of many interests and sadly his love of horse-riding was to lead to his untimely death. He was master of the Mid-Kent Stag Hounds and whilst hunting at Boughton Monchelsea on 30th October 1915 his horse failed to clear a fence and he was thrown to the ground. He died from his injuries four days later. His eldest son, Frederick, who died in July 1921, was company chairman until about October 1919, at which time Major Percy Jude joined Richard Tapply as co-managing director. By the mid-1920's no member of the Leney family was associated with the company.

Regular board meetings were held and the minutes provide an insight as to how the company was managed.

17.1.1896	*First board meeting held at 34 Old Jewry, London EC4. Present Augustus Leney in the chair plus Edward Leney, H. Green and Richard Tapply. Bankers to be Wigan Mercer & Co. of Maidstone. Secretary – A. Starmer. Registered Office – Phoenix Brewery, Wateringbury.*
11.6.1896	*Conveyance and assignment of the properties owned by Augustus Leney to the company. Almost all were charged to the debenture trustees, who provided the finance.*
25.5.1899	*Resolve that the company purchase from Mr. E. Hartridge the Milton brewery with residential and trading properties for £27,000 with £15,000 left on mortgage at an interest rate of 4%. Completion to take place on 31st July 1899. There were five local freehold houses.*
16.11.1905	*Purchase of the Benjamin Baker of Tonbridge houses. Conveyance B. Baker Junior to the Devisces in trust for sale under the will of the late J.T. Baker.*
15.5.1913	*The Milton brewery sold to the guardians of the poor of the Milton Beacon.*
3.10.1918	*Managing director, Bertram Leney died at Exeter. Richard Tapply to succeed.*
10.1919	*The eldest son of William Jude deceased, Major Percy Jude, joined the company when he was appointed co-managing director with Richard Tapply. (See Jude Hanbury & Co. Limited.)*
27.1.1921	*A proposal was put forward to amalgamate with Jude Hanbury. Leney would appoint four directors to the new company, Jude three. It was agreed that amalgamation would take place on 31st October 1921. Whilst the proposal was accepted by Jude Hanbury on 20th April 1921 negotiations were abandoned in December 1922.*
2.1921	*Noted advertisement for sale by auction of H.T. Wickham & Co. brewery at Yalding and would look into the matter. Decided, in conjunction with Jude Hanbury, to bid no higher than £30,000. The firm was purchased at auction on 22nd March 1921 for £20,000 and completion took place in August. The eleven public houses acquired were split five to Leney, six to Jude Hanbury. In January 1925 the brewery, to the rear of the "Two Brewers", was sold for £650.*
8.1921	*Smith's Lamberhurst Brewery was offered for sale by auction on 9th September 1921. The directors agreed to bid up to £12,000 for various houses but were unsuccessful owing to "the excessive prices ruling". The business was purchased by the Dartford Brewery Co. Limited which in turn was acquired in 1924 by the Maidstone brewers Style and Winch.*
8.1921	*Discussed amalgamation with Hadlow brewers Kenward & Court Limited. Negotiations ceased in November.*
1.1922	*As a result of the sale of the Tenterden Brewery Co. Limited and houses, would consider making an offer for the "Crown" Cranbrook. The business was subsequently sold as one lot so no offer was made. Had decided not to bid for the whole company.*
1.1923	*Made a joint offer with Jude Hanbury for the licensed houses and trade of Maidstone brewers Isherwood, Foster and Stacey. Rejected.*

5.1923	Offered Isherwood, Foster and Stacey £105,000 for their Chatham and District houses. Offer again rejected.
27.10.1927	The Company was acquired by Whitbread.
11.1927	The directors agreed signs should be pictorial where suitable.
18.7.1928	Purchase of Sharpe and Winch, Cranbrook brewery at Bakers Cross, Cranbrook for £20,000. This comprised 13 houses, all in the Weald of Kent.
27.6.1929	Board meeting held at Chiswell Street, EC1. A contract was drawn up between Whitbread & Co. Limited and Jude Hanbury & Co. Limited for the sale to Jude Hanbury of all the ordinary shares in Frederick Leney. By now Jude Hanbury had been acquired by Whitbread.
21.3.1930	Heads of agreement between Jude Hanbury and Frederick Leney for a working arrangement.

Judes were to hand over to Leney the group of about 50 houses in the districts of Wateringbury and Maidstone and elsewhere in West Kent and the following arrangements would apply:- Leney to undertake, without remuneration, the general supervision of the houses, to see to the collection of rents from tenants, the insurance, repairs and payment of outgoings and to act generally on behalf of Judes as landlords and, with full authority on Jude's behalf, to do anything necessary in respect of the houses and in all the dealings with the tenants.

Leneys to have exclusive rights of supply to the houses of all beers, ales, stout etc. Leneys to collect their own accounts for goods supplied and to take the risk of their own bad debts.

Leneys to account to Judes quarterly for all tenants' rents collected, less statutory charges. Leneys to pay to Judes, as agreed, royalty on beers etc. supplied. The arrangement was to commence 1st April 1930.

3.10.1946	The last company board meeting was held.
18.6.1947	W.G. Daish appointed assistant secretary to the company. This gentleman was the acknowledged expert on Inn Signia and carried out research into names and signs.
1.11.1960	Effective from this date, but ratified at a board meeting held on 14th December 1961, Fremlins acquired the share capital of Frederick Leney & Sons Limited together with 189 public houses. The signs remained, but with Fremlins replacing Whitbread. Whitbread acquired control of Fremlins in 1967.
31.1.1970	The company ceased trading.

Although the Leney houses traded under the Whitbread name, the title deeds remained in the name of Frederick Leney & Sons Limited.

JUDE HANBURY & CO LIMITED

This company was also domiciled in Wateringbury and traded from the Kent Brewery in Bow Road just a short walk from the Phoenix brewery.

John Beal Jude, born on 22nd February 1807, founded the firm in about 1839, although in November 1833 he was paying rates on a brewery in the name of John Jude & Co. In 1850 Ralph James Fremlin, who went on to establish the famous brewery business in Maidstone that bore his name, was employed by his uncle, J.B. Jude, as brewer's assistant clerk at the Kent Brewery. John rapidly expanded his interests and by 1851 he was also a coal merchant and farmer employing 18 men. In about 1861 his nephew William Jude moved from Hollingbourne to the village and was employed as a brewer's clerk and by

1870 he was the manager of the Kent Brewery.

John Beal Jude died on 2nd September 1871 and his 22-year-old son, Thomas William, was the main beneficiary of the estate. Thomas and his cousin William worked well as a team – Thomas was more interested in farming activities which left William to run the brewery in the name of Jude & Co. In June 1873 the brewery was extended. Thomas died at the early age of 25 in 1874 and his sister Elizabeth Ann inherited his estate. Elizabeth married a farmer, William Wigram Blest, in June 1875 and went on to have five children. By prudent management and the shrewd purchase of public houses, William expanded the business and in 1876 took into partnership Ernest Osgood Hanbury, a nephew of Robert Hanbury, who was a senior partner of Messrs. Truman, Hanbury and Buxton. The firm was then re-named Jude Hanbury & Co. William Jude died on 4th November 1918 and shortly afterwards the business converted to a private limited company and Major Philip Hanbury was subsequently appointed managing director. In October 1919 William Jude's eldest son, Major Percy Jude, joined Frederick Leney & Sons Limited when he was appointed co-managing director with Richard Tapply.

3.11.1919   *First board meeting held at 19 Eastcheap, London EC3. Present:- J.Q. Rowett, J.D. Whitehead, Major P. Hanbury (the Major was the driving force for future development), and A.G. Whitting, of Messrs. Hanbury, Whitting and Ingle, solicitors.*

22.3.1921   *Purchased, in conjunction with Frederick Leney & Sons Limited, the H.T. Wickham & Son brewery at Yalding with the tied houses split between the two companies.*

13.4.1921   *Received details from Frederick Leney regarding a proposed amalgamation of the two companies. On 4th December 1922 "... reject the scheme as not attractive enough to proceed further in the matter".*

16.1.1923   *Isherwood, Foster and Stacey (later acquired by Fremlins) express an interest in purchasing the share capital of the company. They subsequently made an offer of £207,000 for the tied houses, but this was declined.*

26.4.1923   *Solicitors were instructed to formulate an offer of £145,000 for the purchase of Ash's East Kent Brewery. At the same board meeting the directors were advised that Isherwood, Foster and Stacey had made an offer of £108,000 for the houses in Chatham and District. Again this was declined. Truman, Hanbury and Buxton then made an offer of £115,000 for these houses. They were told the company would accept £125,000.*

5.6.1923   *Truman paid the higher figure and the transfers were made on 25th June 1923. At the same time Jude increased their offer for Ash's East Kent Brewery to £165,000, which was accepted.*

20.9.1923   *Following a feasibility study it was decided to move the brewery operations to the Dane John Brewery in Canterbury (the former Ash brewery). It would be necessary to upgrade plant and machinery at a cost of £8,000 to have sufficient capacity for present tied houses and future growth. If put in hand now work should be finished by the year end.*

25.10.1923   *Chatham houses sold. Managing director to receive a pay rise to £2,500 free of tax in lieu of a bonus.*

6.11.1923   *Proposed purchase of the Tenterden Brewery Company Limited.*

23.11.1923   *The whole of the share capital of the Tenterden Brewery Company Limited, 16,250 £1 shares fully paid, transferred to Jude Hanbury.*

10.12.1923   *Leney purchase from the company four West Kent houses, including the "Rose and Crown", Stone Street, for £8,000.*

3.3.1924   *Agreement to hire of steam waggons, trailers and petrol lorries from Wingham Engineering Co. Limited. This company was controlled by the O'Brien family – Mrs. O'Brien was a member of the Rigden family.*

30.4.1924   *Conveyance of certain freehold houses from A. Leney and others.*

20.6.1924   *Conveyance of the Kent Brewery, Wateringbury, to Abol Limited.*

2.9.1924	Messrs. Bushell, Watkins and Smith Limited of Westerham proposed that they swap six of their houses in East Kent for a similar six houses in the Tunbridge Wells area – one to be the "Black Lion", Mereworth. On 26th November 1925 five houses were exchanged, not including the "Black Lion", and Jude Hanbury acquired the "General Wolfe"; "Eight Bells" at Wingham Well; "Basketmakers"; "Woodman's Arms", Barham; and "Carpenter's Arms", South Alkham.
7.10.1924	S. Holden was willing to sell his mineral water business for £5,500. This offer was not pursued.
20.1.1925	Conveyance of half-share in the Wickham brewery building to Frederick Leney & Sons Limited. This, with the cottage adjoining, was then sold for £650 to W.J. Hawes.
3.6.1925	Isherwood, Foster and Stacey wished to exchange the "Maidstone Arms", Ramsgate, for the "Red Lion", Offham. This was not pursued.
24.7.1925	The high cost of transport from Canterbury to the East Sussex houses was causing concern. A feasibility study would be prepared.
7.10.1925	Donation of £10 to Holy Trinity Church, Larkfield, towards a new organ.
4.11.1925	In view of the advances made in the coal fields in East Kent by Messrs. Pearson and Dorman Long Limited, steps should be taken to obtain the grant of new licences in the new villages which were in the course of formation at Snowdown and Betteshanger.
13.1.1927	Would bid up to £4,000 for a site at Aylesham. This was acquired for £3,500 and became the "Greyhound".
1929	The company was acquired by Whitbread.
25.3.1929	Made an offer to Messrs. H. & G. Simonds Limited of Reading to purchase all of the preference and ordinary shares in Mackeson Limited for £370,000. The offer was accepted on 3rd April 1929. Completion took place at 2p.m. Monday 27th May 1929 at the Brewery, Bridge Street, Reading. To finance the purchase £270,000 was provided by Whitbread and 27 debentures of £10,000 were issued to Whitbread and the share capital of the company was increased by the creation of £160,000 additional ordinary shares of £1 each fully paid – the total share capital following the issue was £450,000. Brewing was to remain at Hythe and Dane John was to be used as a depot and distributing base for the time being.
21.3.1930	Heads of agreement whereby Frederick Leney would take over the management of about 50 houses in the mid-Kent and Hastings area.
27.4.1931	The company's seven houses in East Sussex were sold to Frederick Leney on the basis of £15 per barrel sold. This amounted to £20,055. The "Royal Oak" at Wrotham Heath was also sold for £5,795 and all unlicensed premises, including the Dane John Brewery, were transferred to the Tenterden Brewery in exchange for two hotels.
6.1933	The company sold the East Kent brewery buildings in Strand Street, Sandwich, which were then converted into an animal-feed mill.
16.2.1934	The last board meeting was held at Chiswell Street, EC1. Present:- J.E. Martineau, M.E. Ratcliff, and N.C.M. Findlay.
5.3.1934	The last A.G.M. was held at Chiswell Street.
3.5.1934	An extraordinary general meeting was held at the brewery, Chiswell Street, London EC1. with S.O. Nevile in the chair. It was resolved to sell the majority of the company's tied houses to Mackeson for £197,900 and the remainder to Frederick Leney for £84,600.

When the company was purchased by Whitbread it became their "nominated" company in Kent and Jude Hanbury made all acquisitions.

MACKESON & CO. LIMITED

James Pashley established a brewery in Hythe in 1669. Little is known about its very early history but probably in about 1750 the business had been acquired by John Friend who came from Ashford. Under his stewardship the business prospered and he also had farming and hop-growing interests, supplying malt, hops etc.

During 1776 he had carted to Barming near Maidstone 81 loads of dung. At the time he was supplying ale to a group of about ten beer houses but unfortunately his records only provide the landlords' names not those of their houses. A note in his ledger dated 3rd March 1778 states: "John Hurst at Richmond borough in London to Robert Heathorne, Maltster, wants a publick house". John was obviously an approachable fellow much interested in the well being of his tenants. He received the following letter dated 11th August 1792. "I hope you will excuse my taking the liberty to solicit your patronage to the Kentish Herald a Free and Independent Newspaper on Genuine, but moderate Whig principles … and favour me with what advertisements you may have occasion to insert. W. Epps".

Possibly due to age John sold the Hythe Brewery plus nine houses on Monday 19th October 1801 to William and Henry Mackeson, late of Deal. It is probable that through their business dealings they were already well acquainted. The purchase price for each pub was 28 times the annual rental. This was a very high multiplier indeed but one has to bear in mind the value of the beer trade being acquired and the possible elimination of competition. The most expensive pub was the "White Hart" at Hythe at £1,200. The brothers agreed to pay £3,130 on 1st November 1801 and a further £1,820 on 1st April 1802. John Friend died the following year. During the 19th century the Mackeson brothers established the business and acquired additional houses either by private treaty or at auction. In December 1875 the brothers leased for a period of 19 years at a rent of £48 p.a. the Sandgate Brewery but we do not know for what purpose they acquired these premises. Eleven years later, in 1886, they purchased the Tontine Brewery, Tontine Street, Folkestone, which traded as A. Langton & Co., plus 16 public houses.

The partnership was incorporated in 1900 following which we witness rapid expansion.

26.10.1900	*Date of first board meeting. Governing directors – Henry and George Laurie Mackeson. Secretary – Stephen Godden. Solicitor – G.S. Wilks.*
31.12.1900	*Assets – freehold and leasehold estate £209,080/17/2. The title to almost all of the public houses was vested in the names of Annie Adair Mackeson, Henry and George Laurie Mackeson. On 15th February 1901 title was transferred to the limited company. The houses were mortgaged to debenture trustees who were mainly family members or professional advisors.*
27.4.1903	*With a view to keeping the public houses properly conducted the directors would endeavour in all cases where possible to see the police once a quarter to ascertain whether they are satisfied with the conduct of the same.*
1907	*An experiment using lactose, or milk sugar, went on to produce the brew famous all over the world, namely Mackeson Milk Stout.*
27.11.1907	*Henry Mackeson reported that he had purchased the freehold of the Sun Brewery, (De Trafford & Co.) Littlebourne together with five public houses.*
28.3.1919	*Purchased the Moor Brewery, Hawkhurst, for £1,150. It supplied beer to the trade, owning no public houses.*
5.1920	*Company acquired by H. & G. Simonds Limited of Reading.*
1921	*Death of William Mackeson.*
27.5.1929	*Jude Hanbury purchased the share capital of the company from H. & G. Simonds Limited for £370,000.*

3.5.1934	Purchased properties to the value of £197,900 from Jude Hanbury when that company ceased to trade.
24.8.1934	Resolved to sell eight houses (six in East Sussex plus the "Chequers" at both Biddenden and High Halden) to Frederick Leney for £21,476 with Leney taking over the mortgage of £3,533 on the "Warriors Gate" Hotel.
22.3.1945	The board decided that every reasonable step must be taken to develop the supply of refreshments and food in the houses belonging to the company.
1950	Death of George Laurie Mackeson.
28.10.1958	John Marchant retired from the board of directors with effect from 1st October 1958.
1961	Last board meeting held.
3.5.1968	Brewing ceased.

The acquisition by Whitbread of these three major brewers led to that company's strong presence in the county. These three had developed by acquiring smaller competitors mentioned below.

ALFRED LENEY & CO. LIMITED

Alfred Charles Leney, the younger son of Charles Leney of Wateringbury brewers Frederick Leney & Sons Limited, married Catherine Fremlin in 1860. The following year he purchased, with his father-in-law James Evenden, a brewery in Dolphin Lane, Dover. Probably to feel at home he renamed it the Phoenix Brewery. The building was an impressive sight with its 122-foot-high chimney.

The original brewery had been established in about 1740 and had several owners before coming into the hands of James and Thomas Walker. Alfred purchased the brewery in 1861 from the Walker Brothers' trustees. As he was only 23 years old it is possible that, in part, the purchase was financed by James Evenden who remained a partner until his death in 1868. Alfred then became a sole trader assisted by his two sons.

The business was incorporated in 1895 and that year acquired the Castle Brewery, 4/8 Russell Street, Dover, operated by D.P. Poulter. The following year it acquired the Eagle Brewery at Rye, and in 1898 the Army & Navy Co-operative Breweries Limited. This company was established in 1895 as a result of the merger of the business of George Belgrave, established in 1846, operating at the Gun Brewery, Folkestone and the Friary Brewery Co. of Aldershot. As a result, by 1900 the company owned about 100 houses situated mainly in East Kent and East Sussex. A further acquisition in 1923 was the business of Flint & Co. Limited of Canterbury, which in turn had swallowed up the Stourmouth Brewery, plus eleven tied houses, operated by F.A. White.

On 15th March 1897 Alfred Leney conveyed about seven houses into the name of the limited company. In 1910 the company established a successful mineral water business using the "Pharos" trade mark and this continued to trade long after brewing had ceased. In March 1927 it was registered as Leney's Table Waters Limited. In about 1897 the Diamond Brewery in Dover owned by Edwin Dawes & Sons was taken over by Thomas Phillips of West Malling, but by 1912 it was under the control of this company. Brewing ceased in 1916.

On 30th April 1924 certain freehold licensed houses owned by the company were conveyed to Jude Hanbury along with the company's leasehold interest in the "Ypres Castle". Two years later the brewery and tied houses were leased to Fremlins for a term of 36 years with the freeholds bought outright in 1959. Brewing ceased in 1927 and ultimately the brewery was demolished in 1965. A car park now occupies the site.

Alfred, an immensely popular man, died in 1900 and over 400 mourners attended his funeral service held at St. Andrew's Church, Buckland, plus an estimated 1,000 people crammed into the churchyard.

THE ASH GROUP

Ash & Co.

This concern was founded in 1772 and by 1832 George Ash was brewing at the Dane John Brewery, St. John's Lane, Canterbury. In 1862 his two sons Thomas and George joined him in the business. George Ash died on 16th August 1867 and in his will, dated 31st March 1866, left his estate equally to his two sons. Thomas Ash died on 12th March 1875 and his son, Thomas Junior, died on 11th May 1895.

On 28th October 1878 Richard Moxon, (son-in-law of Thomas Ash) George Collard and Henry Cooper Ash were trading as a partnership and in the early 1890's they traded as Ash & Co. The business prospered and in 1920 amalgamated with the East Kent Brewery Co. Limited of Sandwich and traded as Ash's East Kent Brewery Co. Limited.

East Kent Brewery Co. Limited

In 1823 John Hoile was brewing in Strand Street, Sandwich, and the business remained within his family until about 1869 when it was acquired by Gillow and Wareham. In 1878 the firm was trading as Gillow and Co. and by March 1887 George Stapleton and Co. were trading from the brewery. At this time Baxter & Co. of the Export Brewery, Sandwich, was acquired. The following year the business was purchased by Mr. Barnett Joyce and Colonel William Henry Pitt Draffen, Colonel Commanding 4th Battalion Border Regiment. Later, in 1895, they also took over Woodhams & Levi of Bulwark Hill Brewery, Dover. It is not known when this firm was established but prior to 1823 it traded as E. Kingsford; in 1865 as Cliffe's Brewery; in 1888 as H. Cliffe & Co., in which year it changed again to J.A. Rolls. The final name change occurred in 1890.

The memorandum and articles of association were registered on 22nd March 1899 and on 3rd June the Colonel sold to the company twenty public houses, the brewery building and four unlicensed premises. In 1920 the company merged with Ash and Co. to become Ash's East Kent Brewery Co. Limited.

Ash's East Kent Brewery Co. Limited

This company had a short life as on 26th April 1923 the directors of Jude Hanbury instructed their solicitors to formulate an offer of £145,000 for the company. This was rejected, but on 5th June 1923 a higher offer of £165,000 was accepted. Three months later, following a feasibility study, Jude moved all of their brewing operations to the Dane John Brewery in Canterbury. It was necessary to upgrade plant and machinery at a cost of £8,000 in order to have sufficient capability for present tied houses and future growth. It was anticipated that this work would be completed by the year-end. Brewing ceased at the East Kent brewery in June 1933 when the buildings were sold and converted to an animal-feed mill.

BEANEY'S BREWERY

This modest concern operated from the Star Brewery in Wye. The brewery buildings were to the rear and side of the "King's Head".

In about 1800 Allard and Mason started brewing here. Thomas Beaney was the brewer from 1860 until 1877 when John Allard Beaney (surely a relative of the original brewer) took over. It would appear that the company finances became overstretched and the company assets were sold by auction on 24th June 1879. It was at this time that Henry Bean Mackeson paid £1,300 for the leasehold interest in the "Locomotive" at Ashford.

However, records indicate that from 1887 brewing continued under George Kennett but on 26th October 1889 the brewery was subject to an arson attack and burnt out. The "King's Head" also suffered severe damage. Brewing ceased in 1891.

ALFRED BEER & CO.

A Mr. Hill, back in the 1770's, converted parts of the gatehouse of St. Augustine's Monastery, Canterbury, into a brewhouse, public house, and maltings. His son, John, was the brewer in the early 1800's at which time he took into partnership John Saunders Bennett but Hill was quickly replaced by William Beer, a grocer, from Canterbury. This partnership was dissolved on 22nd December 1826 when William Beer became a sole trader operating from the brewery and No. 65 Burgate Street, Canterbury. Bennett continued to trade in his own name from the Longport Brewery in the city until about 1840.

Under Beer's leadership business boomed. About this time there was a strong desire to rededicate the buildings to religious purposes and Beer bowed to this pressure and erected a purpose-built brewery in Broad Street which he named the Original Brewery. The new brewery was operating within a week of the old one closing. About this time Alfred joined his father's business as a partner. William named his new brewery the Original to distinguish it from the business of his eldest son, George, who was brewing from the Star Brewery, also in Broad Street. This firm merged with Rigden's of Faversham in 1922.

William died in 1871 and Alfred inherited the business. Whilst a skilled brewer, the financial side of the business was beyond him, and in 1891 he was declared bankrupt. During all those years he never produced audited accounts. The assets of the company passed to a hop merchant based in Southwark, a Mr. Alfred Walton, and it was he who sold the business in 1894 to B.C. Bushell & Company Limited together with 18 licensed houses. It is quite possible that included within these were the "Eight Bells" at Wingham Well and the "Woodman", Barham.

BENJAMIN BAKER

Based in Tonbridge, the Baker family built up a good regional business. Benjamin Baker senior, who died on 31st August 1870, founded the firm and was later joined by two of his sons, Benjamin Junior and John Taylor Baker. The younger Benjamin built the "South Eastern Hotel" in 1865 and in 1871 acquired the "Old House at Home". John Taylor, in 1865, acquired the land on which the "Star and Garter" stands.

On 1st August 1892 for a 30-year term commencing 24th June 1892, Benjamin Baker Junior leased 36 houses plus the Royal Victoria and Quarry Hill breweries, both in Tonbridge, to Augustus Leney at a rent of £3,100 apportioned amongst the various properties. On 16th November 1905 Frederick Leney & Sons Limited purchased the freehold interest in these houses. The conveyance was between Benjamin Baker Junior to the devisces in trust for sale under the will of the late J.T. Baker, who died on 3rd November 1893.

The Quarry Hill brewery, probably owned by John Taylor Baker, was last listed in 1892 with the Royal Victoria brewery ultimately passing to E. & H. Kelsey.

BUSHELL, WATKINS & SMITH LIMITED

The Black Eagle Brewery, Westerham, was the home for this business, which was registered in July 1894 as B.C. Bushell & Co. Limited although the brewery was established in the 1830's by Robert Day. It grew by acquisition, including the Canterbury business of Alfred Beer and Co. in 1894, and by July 1899 was known by the name in the title. One of the firms purchased, in about 1898, was owned by Rolfe Field whose home brew house called the "Two Brewers" was based in Littlebourne. It had been in the Field family since 1832. The "Two Brewers" was ultimately re-named the "Basketmakers".

This concern is mentioned here as, in September 1924, they proposed to Jude Hanbury that they exchange six of their East Kent houses for a similar six in the Tunbridge Wells area, one of which was to be the "Black Lion" Mereworth. On 26th November 1925 an exchange of five houses took place. There is the distinct possibility that the houses in question, the "Basketmakers"; "Woodman"; "Eight Bells", Wingham Well; "General Wolfe", Ramsgate; and the "Carpenter's Arms" at South Alkham came into their possession when they acquired Field's business, but on the other hand they could have been acquired via Alfred Beer.

The company was taken over in 1948 by Taylor Walker & Co. Limited.

DELMAR & PIERCE

This modest concern operated in Canterbury. In 1875 it was acquired by W.E. & J. Rigden Limited of Court Street, Faversham, which was taken over in 1922 by George Beer & Rigden Limited which in turn was acquired by Fremlins in 1949. Delmar & Pierce supplied beer to the "Brents Tavern".

DE TRAFFORD & CO.

This was a modest concern trading from the Sun Brewery at Littlebourne. On 27th November 1907 Henry Mackeson reported to the directors of Mackeson that he had purchased the freehold of the brewery together with the freeholds of the following public houses:- "Foresters Arms", Littlebourne; "Yew Tree", Deal; "Gate Inn" and land at Rhodes Minnis; "White Horse", Wincheap Street, Canterbury; and the unexpired term of the lease of the "Whitehall", Harbledown.

The firm had traded as Hewitt & Clark from 1877 until 1882, then as Herbert D Phelps until 1894 then Rawdon and Hugh Havens until 1898, then as Humphrey E. De Trafford and finally, from 1903, as De Trafford & Co.

FLINT & CO. LIMITED

This business was founded in 1797 and operated from the St. Dunstan's Brewery in Canterbury. Until the 1860's it traded as Flint & Kingsford and by 1892 as Frederick Flint & Sons, the same year that it incorporated as Flint & Co. Limited. In 1904 it took over the Stourmouth Brewery plus eleven tied houses operated by F.A. White. The share capital was acquired by Alfred Leney & Co. Limited in 1923 but brewing continued until 1929.

FREMLINS LIMITED

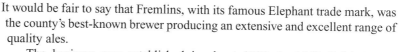

It would be fair to say that Fremlins, with its famous Elephant trade mark, was the county's best-known brewer producing an extensive and excellent range of quality ales.

The business was established in about 1790. In 1851 Ralph James Fremlin was employed by his uncle, John Beal Jude, as an assistant clerk at Jude's brewery. Having gained valuable experience, in 1861, Ralph, whose sister Catherine had married Alfred Leney of the Phoenix Brewery, Dover, the previous year, purchased the almost derelict Pale Ale Brewery in Earl Street, Maidstone, together with ten public houses from the executors of John Heathorn.

Ralph was an unusual fellow to be a brewer. A deeply religious man his principles were averse to the ownership of public houses so one must assume he disposed of the tied houses. He drove his horse and van supplying direct to the family trade.

Despite this handicap the business expanded and he took into partnership his three brothers Richard, Walter and Frank, and a new brewery was built in 1871. Ralph died in 1910 and the second brother, Richard, died in 1915. After the Great War, in 1920, a private company was formed, to be known as Fremlin Brothers. The original board comprised Messrs. Walter and Frank Fremlin, Henry Hills and A.L. Brown both of whom had joined the old firm as boys straight from school. A public company was floated in 1928 with a capital of £700,000. Mr. H. Hills was elected the first chairman and managing director of the new company.

By now the company was expanding rapidly. In 1926 an arrangement was made with Alfred Leney & Co. Limited of Dover and Flint & Co. Limited of Canterbury, whereby Fremlins took a 36-year lease of the whole of the former companies' fully licensed properties. The Dover brewery was closed. 1929 saw the outright purchase of Isherwood, Foster & Stacey Limited of Maidstone. Further expansion continued outside the county with the acquisition in 1938 of Harris Browne Limited of Hadley Brewery, Barnet. 1939 saw the acquisition of T.F. Adams & Son brewery of Halstead, Essex. Both establishments ceased to brew.

In 1949 the share capital of George Beer and Rigden Limited of Faversham was bought and in 1959 the public houses formerly held on lease from Alfred Leney and Flints were bought outright. On the 1st November 1960 the company went on to acquire the capital of Frederick Leney & Sons Limited together with 189 houses.

Sadly all this history came to an end in 1967 when the company was taken over by Whitbread. At the time the business owned about 800 licensed properties, including the acquisitions from Frederick Leney, which thus quickly reverted back to Whitbread. Brewing ceased at Maidstone in 1972 and the brewhouse was demolished in 1976. The large fermenting block suffered a similar fate in 1981 and the town river-side changed for ever.

GARDNER & CO. LIMITED GROUP

This business, based in Ash, was founded in what was the parish workhouse, which had been converted in 1837 into a brewery by George Bushell. William Gardner purchased the brewery in 1840 and, on his death in 1850, it came into the possession of his brother Austen Gardner. By 1852 the firm was trading as Gardner & Godden and in 1857 it took over the nearby Littlebourne brewery, owned by William Gardener. Was it this gentleman, or his son, who attended the first board meeting of the newly formed limited company when the business was registered as a private company in 1898? Godden, Baxter & Co., trading from the White Post Brewery, Ash, was acquired in 1880.

> *30.9.1898*   *The first meeting of the directors of the new company was held at the brewery and afterwards adjourned to Street End House, Ash. Present were Mrs. H. Gardner, Walter V.*

	Lister, W. Gardener and A. Gardner. Walter Lister acted as chairman. Bankers appointed were Hammond & Co. of Canterbury and London & County Bank, Sandwich.
11.10.1899	*Accepted estimate of £673/7/- from Messrs. LeGrand & Sutcliffe for sinking and boring a new well for the brewery.*
2.11.1904	*Mr. Youde be authorised to treat with Messrs. Worsfold & Hayward (who were the architects for the "Newcastle Inn") for the purchase of the Stourmouth Brewery and houses attached for a sum not exceeding £15,000 including everything. This did not proceed. Francis Alexander White, the owner, had offered the brewery together with eleven public houses for sale on 9th July 1904.*
21.12.1904	*In consequence of the falling off in trade:-*
	a) Christmas box list to staff be suspended.
	b) All workers' and draymens' wages be reduced by 1/- a week.
	c) All coopers' wages to average not more than 31/- shillings per week each.
20.12.1905	*The time had now arrived when they could no longer put off bottling their own ales and the requisite plant was to be obtained.*
14.2.1912	*Letter be written to Mr. Frank Vincent Tritton at Staple, offering £1,750 for the brewery property at Barnswell to include the goodwill of the business. The purchase proceeded on 6th April 1912. The brewery is now the "Black Pig" freehouse.*
28.7.1915	*An agreement with the East Kent Breweries as to prices.*
9.1915	*Reviewed the position of the store in Hastings and the "Prince Alfred", Cross Street, St. Leonards. The store closed in April 1916 and in September 1921 the brewers accepted £3,000 for loss of licence of the pub.*
7.3.1917	*In view of further restrictions on brewing proposed by the government, to take steps to close stores at Elham, Ash and Canterbury.*
4.4.1923	*Offer, on behalf of the creditors, to sell to them Ash's East Kent Brewery for £115,000 cash plus £25,000 ordinary shares in Gardner & Co. Limited. The offer was declined.*
4.4.1925	*Took a shareholding in H. & G. Watts Limited, wine merchants of Sandwich.*
18.5.1927	*Authorised to offer Edgar Austin a sum not exceeding £2,500 for the remaining six years of his lease of the Regent Brewery, Ramsgate plus two Ramsgate pubs. This proceeded but at a price of £3,000.*
3.7.1929	*Purchased the freehold of the Regent Brewery plus two houses for £16,000.*
10.6.1936	*Regent Brewery demolished at a cost of £220.*
15.11.1950	*Owing to state of trade today, as soon as practicable, to combine their business with Tomson & Wotton Limited.*
1951	*Amalgamated with Tomson & Wotton Limited to form Combined Breweries (Holding) Limited.*

TOMSON & WOTTON

Founded in 1634 this was Britain's oldest brewery. In 1635 Robert Sampson, a yeoman, sold his messuage and house, malthouse, brewhouse, barns, stables, plus 52 acres of land for £220. Thomas Tomson purchased the Queen Street, Ramsgate, brewery in about 1680. The Wotton connection occurred in 1854 when Thomas Wotton was employed as a brewer, and he was admitted to partnership in 1867. The Ramsgate Cannon brewery, plus twelve houses, was purchased in 1876. Tomson & Wotton was registered as a private company in 1892.

24.3.1892	*A meeting of the new board of directors was held at the company office. Present – Mr. T. Tomson, Mr. Wotton and Mr. J. Wotton. Edward Wotton was to be the company solicitor. The National Provincial Bank of England, Ramsgate, was appointed as banker.*

9.6.1892	First board meeting held at Queens Street Brewery offices to ratify the above.
1892	Acquired Paramor & Son who traded from the Phoenix brewery, Margate.
7.11.1919	That the sum of £500 be invested in shares of a company now being formed in Ramsgate for the purchase of two steam trawlers to be employed in the fishing industry.
1923	Death of Thomas Tomson.
8.3.1926	That the company bid for the "Queen's Head", Canterbury £6,500 at the forthcoming sale. The vendors were George Beer & Rigden. They were outbid by Jude Hanbury who paid £6,600.
15.11.1927	Smiths potato crisps to be sold on the premises.
1951	Amalgamated with Gardner & Co. Limited to form Combined Breweries (Holding) Limited.

COMBINED BREWERIES (HOLDING) LIMITED

In 1951 the group controlled 102 public houses.

1955	Gardner & Co. ceased brewing at Ash.
15.11.1960	Ash brewery to be sold for £7,000 to Graham Puttick & Co. Limited. The brewhouse dominated the village of Ash but has now been demolished.
5.6.1962	Sale of the company's shareholding in H. & G. Watts (1935) Limited.
1.6.1965	That one automatic machine (one-armed bandit) be authorised in each of the company houses – to be supplied by A. Valente of Whitstable and M. Fisher of Stelling Minnis.
20.7.1965	Agreement to lease the company tied public houses (Gardner & Co. Limited) to Tomson & Wotton.
6.1968	Taken over by Whitbread and brewing ceased at the Ramsgate brewery in October 1968 – the brewery was subsequently demolished.
20.8.1969	Last board meeting of Gardner & Co. Limited held at Pale Ale Brewery, Maidstone. Present:- W.A. Wotton and L.P. Mieville.
31.3.1970	It was reported that the company had ceased trading and it was agreed that the company should transfer to Whitbread/Fremlins Limited its fixed assets, at their book values, and the current net assets.

HARTRIDGE BREWERY

The Milton Brewery, based in Milton Regis, was established in about 1850 by Edward Hartridge. On 31st July 1899 he sold the firm to Frederick Leney & Sons Limited for £27,000 with £15,000 left on mortgage at an interest rate of 4%. The brewery came with five local tied freehold houses and other residential property. On 15th May 1913 the brewery building was sold to the guardians of the poor of the Milton beacon. By then brewing had ceased.

HEWETT & CO. and BREEDS & CO. LIMITED

Hewett & Co. traded from the St. Leonard's Brewery, Shepherd Street, St. Leonards-on-Sea and supplied ale to the "British Queen". It was first registered in 1864 and went into voluntary liquidation in 1907, being taken over by Breeds & Co. Limited of the Hastings Brewery, High Street, Hastings. This concern was established in 1828 and was known as Thomas Breeds & Co. by 1897, which was the year it incorporated. The "Hope Inn", Guestling Green, was one of their houses. They in turn fell to George Beer & Rigden in 1931 and thus finished up within the Fremlins stable.

ISAAC KENNETT

Isaac operated from about 1770 until the early 1800's from a brewery in Elham. Although he supplied several local ale houses his beers may have been of indifferent quality. The Mackeson brothers made several complaints and in November 1805 were prompted to complain about the "Poor deliveries of Malt delivered by his Waggoners".

In 1778 he had purchased the "Anchor" at Stowting, then known as the "Four Bells". On 26th May 1802 the Mackeson brothers entered into an agreement for the purchase of the "Anchor" for £300 before 5th July. The pub was in the occupation of Abigail Bradley. The two brothers agreed to buy his stock and in return Isaac undertook, with effect from 1st June 1802, not to supply from his brewhouse in Elham beers or ales to the "Anchor"; the "Red Lion" at Paddlesworth; the "Bowl" in the Alkham valley area; and the "Star" at Newington.

ISHERWOOD, FOSTER, & STACEY LIMITED

This was quite a large concern, thought to have been established in the mid-1600's, and first registered in August 1891. It traded from the Lower Brewery, Lower Stone Street, Maidstone. The brewery, together with 151 tied houses, was acquired by Fremlins in 1929 and closed down. The impressive brewery buildings, which stood on the banks of the River Len, were demolished in 1973 at which time the area was redeveloped.

In 1923 the company made a tentative offer to acquire Jude Hanbury and, when this was declined, offered £108,000 for the Jude Chatham and District houses. Again this offer was rebuffed. Apart from this the link is tenuous but a member of the Stacey family owned the "Fleur-De-Lis".

LANGDON & CO.

Records here are sketchy but the Tontine Street Brewery could date back to the 1700's. It was quite a large concern owned by the Baker family. By 1801 it was owned by Valentine Hoile and was named the Cinque Ports Brewery. Could he have been a relative of John Hoile who was brewing in Strand Street, Sandwich, in 1823? (Please refer to East Kent Brewery Co. Limited.) By 1865, G. & H. Hills, the new owners, had re-named it Atlas Brewery. It then came into the possession of Bryan Tomlinson and Austen Dickenson until they dissolved their partnership in 1873. The following year the firm was sold to the Langdon brothers who in turn sold it to Henry Bean Mackeson, together with 16 tied houses, in 1886 and brewing ceased. In 1866 one of the buildings was converted into a chapel.

H. & V. NICHOLL'S BREWERY CO. LIMITED

In 1887 the firm was trading as Harry and Vincent Nicholl and that year the partnership was registered as a limited company, which was acquired by Whitbread in 1891. Based at the Anchor Brewery, Lewisham the premises were then converted into Whitbread's first bottling and distribution centre. At that time the company held the lease of the "Plough" at Eynsford from the Hart-Dykes family of Lullingstone.

MOOR BREWERY, HAWKHURST

This modest concern was founded by James Wicken in around 1850. Later he was joined by his brother, Edward, and they supplied cask beer to the family trade, owning no public houses. Edward died in about 1895 and his son, Edward Thomas, carried on until his death in 1906 when the brewery passed to his widow, Mrs. C. Wicken. She was assisted by Richard Relf and they continued to trade until 1919.

Perhaps their ales were of a superior quality as on 28th March 1919 Mackeson paid £1,150 for the business. The brewery has been demolished.

OBADIAH EDWARDS & SONS
Later the TENTERDEN BREWERY CO. LIMITED

In 1872 Obadiah was the owner of the Tenterden Brewery, but its history goes back much further – to 1745. The brewery buildings, situated behind the "Vine Inn", have been demolished.

Built in 1745 the brewery was a thriving business carried on by Isaac and Faithfull Cloake until about 1821. On the death of Isaac, circa 1820, it was sold to Mr. Shepherd who extended the building. It then passed to Mr. William Curtess and then to Mr. R.C.M. Young. In 1872 it was purchased by Obadiah Edwards, who at the time was keeping the "Grosvenor Hotel", Tunbridge Wells.

Obadiah died on 18th March 1905 and the brewery passed to his sons Henry, Robert and Frederick who were already involved in the firm. In 1921 the business was incorporated as the Tenterden Brewery Co. Limited. Jude Hanbury & Co. Limited paid £28,700 for the share capital on 1st February 1922 and brewing ceased.

9.3.1922	The first board meeting of the company was held at 73 Basinghall Street, London EC. Those present:- Ernest A. Baker, Percy Terrill, Sholto C.M. Douglas, (Later Lord Chilston whose estate was at Lenham), A.G. Barnes. The company solicitor was W.J. Payne and a bank account was opened with Lloyds Bank in Tenterden. Percy Terrill lived in Caves Road, St. Leonards-on-Sea, close to the "Marina Inn". Subsequent board meetings were held at various venues including the "Vine Inn".
14.12.1922	Tenants of the tied houses to be given £1 each at Christmas and men employed at the brewery 5/- each.
13.7.1923	Challenge cup be given to the Tenterden branch of the British Legion for their annual marathon race.
30.11.1923	15,650 directors shares were issued to Jude Hanbury & Co. Limited plus 200 to Major Philip Hanbury. This gentleman was on the board of Jude Hanbury and effectively ran that business. He lived at Mote Hall, Bearsted. At this meeting it was resolved that John Q. Rowett, John D. Whitehead and Philip Hanbury be elected directors.
10.12.1923	Meeting held at Eastcheap Buildings, 19 Eastcheap, EC3. It was agreed that Jude Hanbury would clear the company overdraft of £4,250 with Lloyds Bank and fresh arrangements were to be made.
3.2.1925	Accepted an offer of £750 for brewery, plant and machinery etc. from T.C. Chapman. Brewing had ceased in 1922.
20.9.1928	Purchased the "Falstaff Hotel", Canterbury, for £10,000, which was then let to Jude

> Hanbury at a rent of £500 p.a. The hotel was leased at the time to C.W. Adams for a term of 14 years from 31st October 1928 at a rent of £200. The company guaranteed his loan of £2,000 with the Midland Bank.

31.3.1931 The company exchanged with Jude Hanbury the "Bell Hotel", Sandwich and the "Falstaff Hotel" for 28 unlicensed properties. Jude Hanbury took over the liability of the "Falstaff" loan.

3.5.1934 Board meeting held at the Brewery, Chiswell Street, EC. In the chair was S.O. Nevile of Whitbread, and the directors present were W.H. Whitbread, J.E. Martineau, and Lieutenant Commander N.C.M. Findlay. It was resolved to sell 22 unlicensed premises adjoining licensed premises to Jude Hanbury for £2,860.

8.4.1937 Resolved that an extraordinary general meeting of the company be held on 6th May 1937 at the Brewery, Chiswell Street to pass the following special resolution namely:- That the company be wound up voluntarily and that Charles Harry Adams of the Brewery, Chiswell Street, be appointed Liquidator for the purpose of such winding-up.

It was always thought that the Tenterden Brewery was quite a modest affair controlling about ten tied outlets at the time it was acquired by Jude Hanbury. It obviously developed into a useful vehicle in the transfer of properties within the group.

SANDGATE BREWERY

This business was established by Robert Hills of Lyminge in 1836. It was sited on Brewers Hill close by the "Clarendon" on the site now occupied by cottages. About 1865, when Mr. Hills was in his 70's, he let the brewery together with a few "tied houses" to Frederick Sladden. In 1871 Frederick was employing six men and a youngster as a clerk. It is likely that in about 1874 Mr. Sladden passed the business on to H.E. Wraight. This gentleman could well be the Herbert Edwards Wright who was brewing around 1875 at the Diamond Brewery in Dover.

The Folkestone Chronicle dated 4th December 1875 gave notice that on 9th December Messrs. Cobay of Hythe were to auction on the premises the plant and machinery of the brewery. We do not know the outcome but shortly afterwards a lease of 19 years at a rental of £48 was granted to the Mackeson brothers. We do not know what they wanted the premises for. A reference in 1882 refers to Louis Faggetter, a mineral water manufacturer, operating from the brewery and in May 1895 part of the site was sold by Mr. Pledge, an auctioneer based in Folkestone. That is the last we hear of this concern.

About 1870 a court case tells us that "the accused went to the house at the brewery and spent two hours drinking there". The brewery tap is almost certainly the "Clarendon".

SHARPE & WINCH

This concern can be dated back to 1832 when it was run by Newnham and Tooth – Robert Tooth was the sole owner by 1840. William Barling Sharpe purchased the "Swan", Wittersham, in September 1842 when he was described as a brewer from Cranbrook. In 1890 he sold the "Swan" to William Francis Winch also of Cranbrook, an auctioneer, and by 1892 they were trading as Sharpe & Winch.

In July 1928 this partnership, plus 13 tied houses situated in the Weald, was purchased for £20,000 by Frederick Leney & Sons Limited. The Cranbrook Brewery stood at Baker's Cross.

SMITH'S OF LAMBERHURST LIMITED

The company was registered in 1899 but was brewing as Smith & Co. T/A Smith and Simpson from the 1830's. It was a reasonable-sized concern with tied houses spread around Kent and East Sussex. Alan Simpson, the managing director, wished to retire and on 9th September 1921 the company was offered for sale by auction. The directors of Jude Hanbury agreed to bid up to £12,000 for various houses but were unsuccessful owing to "the excessive prices ruling". They did, however, purchase the "British Queen". In all 54 houses were sold for £134,610. The brewery buildings remained unsold and were purchased in the following year by the Dartford Brewery, which was later taken over by Style & Winch, the large Maidstone brewers.

FRANK VINCENT TRITTON

The brewery was managed by Mrs. Robert Tritton until 1877 and she was succeeded by John Tritton. He handed the business over, in 1892, to Mrs. Charlotte Tritton who passed it on, in 1898, to Frank Vincent Tritton. In 1912 Frank sold the firm for £1,750 to Gardner & Co. Limited and completion took place on 6th April 1912. The brewery building now houses the "Black Pig" freehouse at Barnswell.

CHARLES FREDERICK WACHER

Charles brewed at the Brewery, Crowhill, Broadstairs, from 1872 until 1895. Up until 1887 he was simply known as Charles Wacher adding his middle name thereafter. There is no record of the firm being taken over so one can only assume he either ceased to trade or went bankrupt. The "Three Kings", Sandwich, advertised his fine ales and porter.

H.T. WICKHAM & CO

This local business operated from the Yalding Brewery, situated to the rear of the "Two Brewers" – part of which still stands today. Until 1884 it was trading as James Rayfield and in that year it became known as Loud & Wickham. Were they the two brewers to whom the pub is dedicated? It took its final name in 1898. In February 1921 the directors of Frederick Leney & Sons Limited noted that this business was being advertised for sale by way of auction. They decided, in conjunction with Jude Hanbury, to bid no higher than £30,000. The auction was held on 22nd March 1921 and they obtained the business for £20,000. The eleven tied houses were split between them – five going to Leney and six to Jude. All were local with one unexplained exception – the "Dripping Spring" at St. Leonards-on-Sea. How on earth did they acquire it and supply it with beer? In January 1925 the brewery building was sold for £650.

SHEPHERD NEAME LIMITED

Finally we come to Shepherd Neame Limited who, as the Whitbread estate was broken up, purchased or leased many of the pubs.

Originally called the Faversham Pale Ale Brewery, established in 1698 by Richard Marsh, its products are well-known throughout the beer-drinking world. It was the daughter of Richard Marsh junior, Si(y)lvester, who in 1741 sold the brewery to Samuel Shepherd, a brewer, of Mongeham, near Deal. Over the years the firm has traded as Shepherd & Hilton, Shepherd & Mares, Shepherd, Mares and Neame which developed into Shepherd Neame & Co. The brewery was rebuilt and re-equipped during 1896 and 1897.

In 1914, following the death of Percy Beale Neame, a private limited company was formed.

For a long while the directors had wished to produce their own hops, and the opportunity arose in 1944 when the company purchased Queen Court farm, Ospringe, from Mrs. Lewis Finn. The soil produced hops of varieties particularly suitable for brewing. Hop production came to an end in 1982 following the sale of most of the land.

The company continued to expand and, following the government's decision to force major brewers to sell off houses, in 1972 32 Whitbread pubs, several in the Canterbury area, were purchased. Regular acquisitions were seen thereafter. On 6th May 1992 a good number of houses were leased from the same source with most of these subsequently purchased.

Justifiably proud of its family traditions and the quality of its products the company looks to the future with confidence. It is now the oldest independent brewer in the country.

"The atmosphere, from the dryness of the summer, and the attendant heat, is laden with innumerable animacula which infect the air. We strongly recommend our readers to abstain from drinking spirit, and to be very abstemious in porter.

Kentish Gazette, 22nd August 1800.

BIBLIOGRAPHY OF REFERENCE SOURCES USED

Kentish Gazette (various)
The Tonbridge Courier – Warwick Notebook – Frank Chapman
The Dover Express – Memories with Bob Hollingsbee
Kelly's Directories (various)
Archives held at the Centre for Kentish Studies, Canterbury, Maidstone and Whitfield
Canterbury Library, Local Studies Room
Cranbrook and Sissinghurst Local History Society
Hawkhurst Parish Magazine, 1980
Headcorn Local History Society
Herne Bay Historical Records Society
Tenterden and District Museum Association
An unknown Wye publication
A New History of Wye, Wye Historical Society
Inns of Canterbury by Edward Wilmot (1988)
Canterbury Pubs Past and Present by Michael G. Heenan
Chatham Inns and Signs Past and Present by Edwin Harris (1914)
Recollections of Rural Life around Godmersham, Crundale and Waltham by Rex Lancefield
"By the Way" Pubs of Dover by Barry Smith (August 1991 edition)
Pubs of Eynesford by W G Duncombe
The Inns and Taverns of Faversham by Frank Haley (1982)
Old Folkestone Pubs by C H Bishop (1979)
Hollingbourne – The History of a Kentish Parish by Helen Allinson
Hunton – A Kentish Village by Desmond Morey
Hythe Haven by Duncan Forbes (Revised paperback edition 1991)
The Taverns and Alehouses of Hythe by Michael David Mirams
Kent Inns and Inn Signs by Michael David Mirams (1987)
Kent Inns, A Distillation by Anne Roper and H.R. Pratt Boorman (1955)
Lydden – A Parish History by Christopher Buckingham
Old Maidstone's Public Houses in Postcards and Photographs
by Irene Hales (1982)
Down Memory Lane – A compilation of stories by village people living in the Platt area
Plaxtol within Living Memory – A collection of memories by village people
Old Ramsgate Pubs by Michael David Mirams
Ramsgate Pubs Past and Present by John Land
Inns of Southborough by A.M. Macfarlane
Village Pubs of Thanet Past and Present by John Land
Old Pubs of Tunbridge Wells and District by Keith Hetherington and Alun Griffiths (1986)
Wateringbury Revisited or Fifty Years Ago by George Newman, Enlarged and Illustrated by Dail Whiting (2001)
A brief History of the Black Eagle Brewery, Westerham by Peter Moynihan and Ken Goodley
Ales and Tales – Pubs in the Story of Whitstable by Geoffrey Pike, Mike Page and John Cann (1993) Published by
	Whitstable Improvement Trust.
Tales from the Tap Room by Martin Easdown and Eamonn Rooney (2000)
More Tales from the Tap Room by Martin Easdown and Eamonn Rooney (2004)
A Saunter through Kent with Pen and Pencil by Charles Igglesden (1914)
A Bridge over the Stream – East Peckham 1894-1994 by Margaret Lawrence
Bygone Breweries by Keith Osborne (1982)
A Century of British Brewers by Norman Barber of the Brewery History Society
Where have all the Breweries Gone? By Norman Barber of the Brewery History Society
The Cockell and Laming Guide to Collecting Whitbread Inn-Signia (1996)
Friedrich's Gazetteer of the Breweries of the British Isles
A Dictionary of Pub Names by Leslie Dunkling and Gordon Wright (1987)
Kent at War by Bob Ogley (1994)
Shepherd Neame Limited, Faversham – Brewers (1948)
Whitbread's Breweries by H.A. Monckton (1984)
Inns of Kent – The Whitbread Library (1948)
The House of Whitbread Magazines (various)
Folders full of Memories supplied by B.M. Parks of Cranbrook 01580 713432

ACKNOWLEDGEMENTS

This book could not have been written without the active encouragement and unstinting assistance of very many people. I am particularly indebted to the following individuals who appear in alphabetical order:-

Robin Cook for his extensive knowledge of the Kentish brewing scene in particular the three main brewers Frederick Leney, Jude Hanbury and Fremlins and the houses they owned throughout the county. Robin must have spent many hours in preparing historical information for me.

Victoria Harper for her technical expertise in resolving many Information Technology problems.

Keith Hetherington who supplied me with a steady flow of information covering the brewer, Benjamin Baker, and pubs in the Tonbridge and Tunbridge Wells area.

John Hodges whose detailed records of those houses situated in East Sussex proved invaluable and for accompanying me, together with his wife Denise, on my frequent visits to the three county archives. Also I must acknowledge John's endless patience in preparing top-quality photographic material for use in this publication.

Roy Murrant who from his vast library covering the Medway towns, was always to hand to provide records and an interesting story.

Ian Newman who spent many hours proof-reading my material.

Chris White many an enjoyable hour was spent with Chris, now in his eighties, driving around his old haunts when he was an abroad cooper with Mackeson. Detailed information and long-forgotten stories relating to these houses were vividly brought to light.

To these individuals I must add the staff at the **Kent Archives Service** offices at Canterbury, Maidstone and Whitfield for their unfailing cheerfulness as they sought out yet another obscure document. **The Kent Messenger** and other local newspaper editors who published my letters and to the readers who responded to my requests for information. To the numerous landlords and members of the public who supplied information either at the pub or in their home. I must thank **George Barnes** at Shepherd Neame Limited for providing me with details of that brewery's acquisitions from Whitbread. **Mike Umbers** of the Hythe Civic Society for so readily giving of his time in ferreting out many unique photographs taken in the 1940's by the late Hythe photographer **Jack Adams**. Other vital sources of background information came from **John Smee**, **Sid Thompsett**, **Tony Gosby**, **Martin Easdown**, **Linda Sage**, **Chris Laming**, **Margaret Iddon**, **Ken Cooper**, **Alan Collins** and **Brian Tucker**. I have talked to numerous individuals and do apologise for any names that I have omitted.

Picture Acknowledgements:
The publisher is grateful to **Whitbread Limited** for granting permission to use any photographic material originally owned by the company, coupled with the willing co-operation of the staff at the **Kent Archives Service** based at both Maidstone and Whitfield in making this material available. **Robin Cook** for use of his extensive photographic collection. **The Hythe Civic Society** for use of the late Jack Adams collection. **The Kent Messenger** collection which have been individually identified. **The John Hodges** collection. **The Chris Lamming** collection. **The Keith Hetherington** collection. **Irene Hales**. *Every effort has been made to obtain permission for the reproduction of the photographs in this book; apologies are offered for any omissions.*

Beer Labels:
The author is grateful to **Keith Osborne** for reproduction of labels from his unique personal collection.

Front cover:
Drawn by **Zoe L. Male**.

Finally it has been great fun over the last nine years, five spent in Sutton Coldfield, researching this book and I do hope the public enjoy reading it. I have taken great pains as to the accuracy of the information and will welcome any corrections or additional information. There still remain many gaps in my photographic collection, and other memorabilia, and I would welcome contact with any readers who have items in their possession and would be prepared to let me copy them.

I intend to write a further book covering other Whitbread houses not included in the Whitbread Inn Sign series and would welcome any factual information, stories or incidents from the past.

David Harper,
2005